Jekka McVicar

seeds

Jekka McVicar

seeds

the ultimate guide to growing successfully from seed

Special photography by Marianne Majerus

Kyle Cathie Limited

In association with the Royal Horticultural Society

contents

This revised edition published in Great Britain in 2008 by
Kyle Cathie Limited, 122 Arlington Road, London NW1 7HP
general.enquiries@kyle-cathie.com
www.kylecathie.com

In association with the Royal Horticultural Society

First published in 2001

ISBN 978 1 85626 832 5

Senior Editor Helen Woodhall
Editorial Assistant Esme West
Copy Editor Helena Attlee
Design Vanessa Courtier
Design Assistant Gina Hochstein
Production Sha Huxtable
Index Helen Snaith

A CIP catalogue record for this title is available from the British Library

Printed and bound in Singapore by Star Standard

For over 200 years, the Royal Horticultural Society, Britain's leading gardening charity, has been promoting horticultural excellence by providing inspiration through its shows, gardens and expertise. Funded mainly from membership subscriptions, the RHS provides advice and information to its members, whatever their level of skill. For more information and to join the RHS, please contact:
RHS Membership Department
PO Box 313, London SW1P 2PE.
www.rhs.org.uk <http://www.rhs.org.uk/>

Page 2: *Cleome hassleriana* seedpods

introduction

As a young child I remember being transfixed by the magic of placing a round pellet of paper into water and watching it develop into a Japanese garden. Today I am as equally enthralled by watching tiny seeds develop into handsome plants, some of which will live for hundreds of years.

If you stop just for a moment and look closely at a single seed, you will find that it is amazing exciting, miraculous, precious and irreplaceable. Seeds come in all shapes and sizes from orchid seeds so fine that they cannot be seen individually with the naked eye to the largest known seed in the world – the Coco de Mer, a species of Indian Ocean palm (coconut) found on Praslin Island which is 35–40cm (14–16in) in length and weighs up to 40kg (88lb).

Each seed is a complete self contained work of art, a unique life capsule containing the blue print for the whole plant with every cell, hair, vein, leaf, petal and root preprogrammed and waiting for germination and growth in order to manifest itself to its full potential. Seeds are a master of ingenuity when it comes to survival. Some are able to lie dormant for many seasons or even years waiting for the right conditions in which to germinate, others evolve slowly adapting to changes in environment. Arctic Lupin seeds have been found to be viable after lying in permafrost conditions for 10,000 years. The means of seed dispersal is equally staggering – some fly, some fall, some float. The Dandelion seed can travel 200km (125 miles) in a storm, and fern spores have been known to travel 20,000km (12,400 miles) from their parent. They use the air, water, animals, birds and humans to arrive at their destination and start their cycle all over again.

The first time I sowed some seed was many years ago when I lived in the city of Bristol. I thought it would be a good idea to be self-sufficient. So I bought lots of different packets of vegetable seed, 10 seed trays, read the backs of the packets, worked out a sowing schedule, and sowed the complete seed packet into each seed tray. We had hundreds of lettuce, spinach and courgette plants all at the same time. Undaunted by my first mistake I ploughed on, thinned the seedlings, pricked out the strongest seedlings and had a wonderful crop which I could share with my neighbours and my neighbours' neighbours.

From that day the excitement of watching young seedlings magically appearing has never left me. Even today, where on my herb nursery I grow hundreds of thousands of plants, I still get enthusiastic when I walk through the glass house in early spring and see the seedlings emerging. Equally, when I find a new variety, the sense of achievement that I experience when the seedling appears and then flourishes into a new plant is very satisfying. It is this satisfaction that makes gardening such a pleasure for me and I hope that you will experience a similar sense of achievement from growing plants from seed with the help of this book

All the plants in this book have been chosen with simple criteria in mind. They are all either common garden plants, whose seeds are simple to collect, or plants whose seeds are easily available through retailers. Turn to the suppliers' list at the back of the book if you have difficulty in tracking any of them down.

This book is to be used as a springboard into the world of growing plants from seed. By following a few simple steps (as simple as baking a cake), and not being too ambitious at the start, you will be rewarded by having a flourishing garden at a minimal financial cost with maximum pleasure and a great sense of achievement.

alpines & rock plants

A true 'alpine plant' is one that flourishes between the limits of eternal snow and the line beyond which even coniferous trees cease to grow. Some of the plants in this section fit these criteria but others, which are also suitable for growing in rock gardens, have already adapted to milder climates. It is worth noting that quite a few of the plants mentioned in the following section do benefit from a period of cold (known as stratification) before germinating. For the best results it is therefore a good idea to start sowing these plants in early autumn. As these plants naturally grow in rocky conditions, it is important to make sure that they are planted in well-drained soil or compost. Adding extra grit and sand to either medium will be of great benefit.

Viola tricolor seedhead, see page 31

Acaena *Rosaceae*

A genus of mainly low growing perennial evergreens, which have small flowers in compact rounded heads in summer. Plant in full sun to partial shade in a well-drained soil.

Acaena microphylla AGM **(Scarlet Bidi Bidi, New Zealand Bur)**
Medium seeds: 1,000 per gram
Hardy perennial
Height 7cm (3in)
Trailing habit
Bright red flowers
Flowers in summer
Grey-green foliage

Sow in autumn to early spring into pots or modules using a standard, loam-based seed compost (substrate) mixed with 5mm (1/4in) sharp grit. Mix to a ratio of 1 part compost + 1 part grit. Cover lightly with compost and place in a cold frame. Germination takes 1–3 months.

Acantholimon *Plumbaginaceae*

A genus of evergreen perennials, which have tight cushions of spiny leaves and star-shaped flowers in summer. Dislikes very wet winters, an ideal alpine house plant. If planting outside, position in full sun and in a very well-drained soil.

Acantholimon glumaceum **(Prickly thrift)**
Medium seeds: 75 per gram
Evergreen perennial
Height 10cm (4in)
Small spikes of star-shaped pink flowers
Flowers from late spring to early summer
Spear-shaped, spiny, dark green leaves

Sow fresh seed (germination of old seed can be erratic) in late summer into pots or modules, using a standard loam-based seed compost (substrate) mixed with 5mm (1/4in) sharp grit. Mix to a ratio of 1 part compost + 1 part grit. Cover lightly with compost and place in a cold frame. Germination takes 1–3 months.

Adonis *Ranunculaceae*

A genus of hardy perennials which have attractive flowers in spring and feathery leaves. Plant in a moist but well-drained soil in semi-shade.

Adonis annua **(Pheasant's eye)**
Medium seeds: 100 per gram
Annual
Height 30cm (12in)
Anemone-shaped, scarlet flowers which bloom singly at the tips of stems
Flowers in early spring
Mid-green feathery leaves

Adonis vernalis **(Bird's eye)**
Medium seeds: 100 per gram
Hardy perennial
Height 23cm (9in)
Buttercup-like, greenish-yellow flowers which bloom singly at the tips of stems
Flowers in early spring
Mid-green leaves delicately dissected

Sow fresh seed (old seed can be erratic) in late summer into pots or modules using a standard, loam-based seed compost (substrate) mixed with 5mm (1/4in) sharp grit. Mix to a ratio of 1 part compost + 1 part grit. Cover lightly with sharp grit and place in a cold frame. Germination takes 1–3 months.

Aethionema *Brassicaceae*

A genus of prolific, summer flowering, hardy, short-lived perennials. Plant in full sun and a well-drained soil. Most species self seed.

Aethionema cordifolium **(Lebanon stone cress)**
Small seeds: 2,000 per gram
Hardy evergreen or semi-evergreen perennial
Height 15cm (6in)
Loose sprays of tiny, rose-pink flowers
Flowers in summer
Narrow, blue-green leaves

Sow in autumn into pots or modules, using a standard loam-based seed compost (substrate). Cover with vermiculite or perlite and place in a cold frame. Germination takes 1–4 months.

Ajuga *Lamiaceae*

A genus of fully-hardy annuals and perennials, the majority of which are excellent ground cover, thriving in moist conditions. Plant in sun or shade.

Ajuga reptans **(Bugle)**
Medium seeds: 720 per gram
Hardy perennial
Height 15cm (6in)
Creeping habit
Whorls of blue flowers
Flowers in summer
Green foliage

Sow in spring into pots or modules, using standard soil-less seed compost (substrate) either a peat free proprietary brand or composted fine propagating bark, mixed with 2–3mm (1/16–1/8in) fine grit. Mix to a ratio of 3 parts compost + 1 part fine grit. Cover with perlite or vermiculite. Place in a cold frame. Germination takes 1–2 months.

Alchemilla *Rosaceae*

A genus of hardy perennials which have greenish-yellow flowers in summer and leaves of interesting shapes. Plant in sun or partial shade in most soils, with the exception of bogs. Most species self-seed.

Ajuga reptans

Alchemilla alpina
Small seeds: 4,600 per gram
Hardy perennial
Height 15cm (6in)
Spreading habit
Upright spikes of greenish-yellow flowers
Flowers in summer
Rounded, lobed, green leaves covered in silky hairs

Sow fresh seed in autumn into pots or modules using a standard loam-based seed compost (substrate). Cover lightly with compost and place in a cold frame. Germination takes 4–6 weeks and can be a bit erratic. May flower in its first year.

Alyssoides *Brassicaceae*

A genus of one species, details below. Plant in full sun in a well-drained soil. Ideal for dry banks and walls.

Alyssoides utriculata (Bladderpod)
Medium seeds: 154 per gram
Hardy, evergreen perennial
Height 30cm (12in)
Loose sprays of small, bright yellow flowers followed by attractive balloon-like seed pods
Flowers in spring
Oval, glossy, dark green leaves

Sow in spring into pots or modules using standard, soil-less seed compost (substrate), either a peat free proprietary brand or composted fine propagating bark, mixed with extra-silver or fine sand for extra aeration. Mix to a ratio of 3 parts compost + 1 part sand. Cover with perlite or vermiculite and place in a cold frame. Germination takes 2–3 weeks. Flowers in its second year.

Alyssum *Brassicaceae*

A genus of fully-hardy perennials, evergreens and annuals. Attractive racemes of scented flowers in spring. Plant in full sun in a well-drained soil.

Alyssum montanum 'Berggold' (Mountain Gold)
Small seeds: 1,000 per gram
Hardy evergreen perennial
Height 15cm (6in)
Small, spherical racemes of fragrant, lemon-yellow flowers
Flowers in spring
Small, oval, hairy, grey leaves

Sow in spring into pots or modules, using standard soil-less seed compost (substrate), either a peat free proprietary brand or composted fine propagating bark, mixed with 2–3mm (1/16–1/8in) fine grit. Mix to a ratio of 3 parts compost + 1 part fine grit. Cover with perlite or vermiculite and place in a cold frame or with protection at 18°C (65°F). Germination 2–3 weeks cold or 4–5 days with heat.

Anacyclus *Asteraceae*

A genus of hardy perennials which have a prostrate, spreading habit and flower in the summer. Plant in full sun in a well-drained soil.

Anacyclus pyrethrum var. *depressus* 'Garden Gnome' **(Mount Atlas daisy)**
Small seeds: 1,750 per gram
Hardy perennial (short-lived)
Height 5cm (2in) spreading habit
Large, white, daisy-like flowers with deep red backs to petals; flowers close in dull light
Flowers in summer
Grey-green, fern-like leaves

Sow in early spring into pots or modules using a standard, loam-based seed compost (substrate) mixed with coarse horticultural sand. Mix to a ratio of 1 part compost + 1 part sand. Do not cover seeds. Refrigerate first for 4 weeks, then place under protection at 18°C (65°F). Germination 1–2 weeks once in the warmth.

***Recipe for sowing, planting and growing* Anacyclus *var.* depressus**

This plant makes a very attractive cushion of finely-cut foliage which is covered with small, daisy-like flowers all summer. As it dislikes being wet in winter, it is a good idea to grow this plant with a collar of sharp grit to protect it from excessive moisture.

Ingredients
10 seeds per module or 15 seeds per pot (or as near as you can manage)
I plastic bag, plus tie and label
1 waterproof felt tip pen
1 handful of fine horticultural sand, which has been dampened
1 piece white card 14 x 8.5cm (5½ x 3½in) folded in half
1 module tray
OR
1 x 8cm (4in) pot
Standard loam-based seed compost (substrate) mixed with coarse horticultural sand to a ratio of 1 part compost + 1 part sand
White plastic plant label

Method First mix a small amount of seed (enough for your sowing) with a handful of damp, fine horticultural sand. Place this mixture in a plastic bag, seal and label with the plant's name and the date, using a waterproof felt tip pen. Place the bag in the refrigerator – not the freezer – for 4 weeks. This is called stratification (see page 233).

After 4 weeks remove the seed from the refrigerator. Fill the tray or pot with compost, smooth over, tap down and water well. Put the seed and sand mix into the crease of a folded card. Gently tap the card to sow the seed thinly on to the surface of the compost. There is no need to add an extra covering of compost. Label with the plant name and date. Place the tray or pot in a warm, light place out of direct sunlight, at an optimum temperature of 18°C (65°F). Keep watering to a minimum until germination has taken place. Germination takes 7–14 days with warmth. Shortly after germination has taken place, and when the seedlings are fully emerged, put the containers in a cooler environment, around 15°C (59°F).

Prick out when the seedlings are large enough to handle, or if you are using modules, plant direct into a container or the garden after a period of hardening off and when there is no threat of frost.

Anaphalis *Asteraceae*

A genus of hardy perennials with small, papery flowers. Plant in well-drained soil in semi-shade.

Anaphalis margaritacea 'Neuschnee' (New Snow) **(Pearl Everlasting)**
Tiny seeds: 20,000 per gram
Hardy perennial
Height 25cm (9in)
White, everlasting, flat flowerheads
Flowers in high summer
Lance-shaped, grey-green or silvery-grey leaves
Good for dried flower arrangements

Sow in spring into pots using standard soil-less seed compost (substrate), either a peat free proprietary brand or composted fine propagating bark. As these are very fine seeds, mix them with the finest sand or talcum powder for an even sowing. Do not cover. Water from the bottom or with a fine spray. Place in a cold frame. Germination takes 2–3 weeks.

Androsace *Primulaceae*

A genus of annuals and evergreen perennials which have a compact habit. Plant in a sunny situation in a free-draining soil. They will rot if over wet in winter. Some species prefer an acid soil.

Androsace sarmentosa (Rock Jasmine)
Small seeds: 1,500 per gram
Hardy perennial evergreen
Height 4–10cm (1 1/2–4in)
Clusters of flattish, bright pink flowers with a tiny yellow centre
Flowers from spring to early summer
Open rosettes of small, narrow, hairy, green-grey leaves

Sow seed in autumn using pots or modules. Always use fresh seed, as the germination of old seed can be erratic. Use a standard, loam-based seed compost (substrate) mixed with 5mm (1/4in) sharp grit to a ratio of 1 part compost + 1 part grit. Cover lightly with sharp grit. Place in a cold frame. Germination takes 1–3 months but can be as long as one year. Flowers in its second or third season.

Anemone *Ranunculaceae*

A genus of fully-hardy perennials, which have mainly shallow, cup-shaped flowers. Plant most species in full sun to dappled shade in a well-drained soil which is rich in humus.

Anemone sylvestris (Windflower)
Small seeds: 2,000 per gram
Perennial
Height 30cm (12in)
Carpeting habit, can be invasive
Fragrant white flowers with yellow centres
Flowers in late spring early summer
Mid-green divided leaves

Use fresh seed. Sow in spring into pots or modules using standard, soil-less seed compost (substrate), either a peat free proprietary brand or composted fine propagating bark, mixed with 2–3mm (1/16–1/8in) fine grit. Mix to a ratio of 3 parts compost + 1 part fine grit. Cover with perlite or vermiculite and place under protection at 15°C (60°F). Germination takes 3 weeks. Flowers in its second or third season.

Antennaria *Asteracea*

A genus of fully-hardy, evergreen or semi-evergreen perennials. Plant in a sunny situation and a well-drained soil.

Antennaria dioica (Cat's ears, Pussy-toes, Ladies' tobacco)
Tiny seeds: 17,000 per gram
Hardy semi-evergreen perennial
Height 5–10cm (2–4in)
White flowers with pale pink tips
Flowers from late spring to early summer
Tiny, oval green leaves that are usually woolly

Sow in autumn with fresh, ripe seed or in the following spring. Use pots or modules and fill with standard, loam-based seed compost (substrate) mixed with 5mm (1/4in) sharp grit. Mix to a ratio of 1 part compost + 1 part grit. As these are very fine seeds, mix them with the finest sand or talcum powder for an even sowing. Cover lightly with sharp grit and place in a cold frame. Germination takes 1–2 months. Do not over water. Flowers in its second season.

***Recipe for sowing, planting and growing* Antennaria dioica**
This is a neat, mat-forming plant which is ideal for the edge of a path or grown in gravel. Alternatively, it looks lovely nestling in a rock garden.

Ingredients
10 fresh, ripe seeds per module or 15 fresh ripe seeds per pot (or as near as you can manage)
Talcum powder, or fine plain white flour
1 piece white card 14 x 8.5cm (5 1/2 x 3 1/2in) folded in half
1 module tray
OR
1 x 8cm (4in) pot
Standard loam-based seed compost (substrate)
White plastic plant label

Method In autumn fill the tray or pot with compost, smooth over, tap down and water in well. As the seeds are very fine it is a good idea to mix them with talcum powder or extra fine white flour. This will show the seeds up and enable you to sow them evenly. Put a very small amount of the seed mix into the crease of the folded card. Tap it gently and sow the seed thinly on to the surface of the compost. Cover lightly with sharp grit. Label with the plant name and date. Place the tray or pot in a cold frame. Keep watering to the minimum and only water either with a fine spray or from below, so as not to disturb the fine seed. Germination takes 4–8 weeks. Over-winter seedlings in the cold frame.

Prick out when the seedlings are large enough to handle, harden the seedlings off before planting out. If you are using modules, you can plant directly into the garden after hardening off and when there is no threat of frost.

Anthyllis *Papilionaceae*

A genus of frost-hardy, bushy perennials. Plant in a sunny situation and a well-drained soil.

Anthyllis hermanniae
Medium seeds: 200 per gram
Hardy perennial
Height 60cm (24in)
Small yellow pea-like flowers
Flowers in summer
Small, bright green leaves

Sow fresh seed in autumn in pots or modules using standard, loam-based seed compost (substrate). Cover lightly with compost and place in a cold frame. Germination takes 5–6 months.
OR
Sow in spring in pots or modules using standard, soil-less seed compost (substrate), either a peat free proprietary brand or composted fine propagating bark. Place under protection at 20°C (68°F). Germination takes 2–3 weeks. Flowers in its second year.

Aquilegia *Ranunculaceae*

A genus of fully- to frost-hardy, short-lived perennials. Attractive bell-shaped, spurred flowers in spring and summer. Plant in a sunny situation and a well-drained soil. Germination of both species can be erratic, but it's worth persevering.

Aquilegia alpina **(Columbine)**
Medium seeds: 600 per gram
Hardy perennial
Height 45cm (18in)
Clear blue or violet-blue spurred flowers
Flowers in spring and early summer
Basal rosettes of rounded, finely divided mid-green leaves

Aquilegia flabellata 'Ministar'
Medium seeds: 800 per gram
Hardy perennial
Height 25cm (10in)
Bright blue flowers with a white corolla
Flowers in summer
Rounded, finely divided mid-green leaves

Old *Aquilegia* seed is viable for 5 years. Sow in autumn in pots or modules using a standard, loam-based seed compost (substrate) mixed with 5mm (1/4in) sharp grit. Mix to a ratio of 1 part compost + 1 part grit. Cover lightly with compost, place in a cold frame. Germination takes 5–6 months.
OR
Sow fresh seed in summer in pots or modules, using a standard loam-based seed compost (substrate) mixed with 5mm (1/4in) sharp grit. Mix to a ratio of 1 part compost + 1 part grit. Cover with perlite or vermiculite and place in a cold frame. Germination takes 3–4 weeks.

Arabis *Brassicaceae*

A genus of fully- to frost-hardy evergreen perennials. Excellent mat-forming ground cover. Plant in a sunny situation and a well-drained soil.

Arabis alpina subsp. *caucasica* 'Schneehaube' AGM **(Arabis snowcap, Rock cress, Wall cress)**
Small seeds: 3,000 per gram
Hardy evergreen perennial
Height 13–15cm (5–6 in)
A profusion of single, fragrant 4-petalled flowers
Flowers in spring
Oval, toothed, mid-green leaves
Excellent for a dry bank

Arabis blepharophylla 'Frühlingszauber' AGM **(Spring Charm)**
Small seeds: 2,000 seeds per gram
Hardy evergreen perennial
Height 13–15cm (5–6in)
Fragrant carmine, single, 4-petalled flowers
Flowers in spring
Oval, mid-green leaves with hairy edges
Makes excellent ground cover, but dislikes wet winters

Sow fresh seed into pots or modules in early summer using standard soil-less seed compost (substrate), either a peat free proprietary brand or composted fine propagating bark. Cover with perlite or vermiculite, place in a cold frame. Germination takes 2–3 weeks.
OR
Sow old seed into pots or modules in autumn using standard soil-less seed compost (substrate), either a peat free proprietary brand or composted fine propagating bark, mixed with extra silver or fine sand for extra aeration. Use a ratio of 3 parts compost + 1 part sand. Cover lightly with compost and place in a cold frame. Germination takes 3–4 months.

Arenaria *Caryophyllaceae*

A genus of fully- to frost-hardy annuals and perennials which flower in the spring and summer. Plant in a sunny situation in a well-drained, preferably sandy soil.

Arenaria montana AGM **(Sandwort, Mountain sandwort)**
Medium seeds: 850 per gram
Hardy perennial
Height 5cm (2in)
Large white, round flowers
Flowers in summer
Loose mats of small, narrow, oval, mid-green leaves

Sow in spring in pots or modules using standard, soil-less seed compost (substrate), either a peat free proprietary brand or composted fine propagating bark. Cover with perlite or vermiculite and place under protection at 20°C (68°F). Germination takes 4–6 weeks. Flowers in its second year.

Armeria *Plumbaginaceae*

A genus of fully- to frost-hardy evergreen perennials which grow in tufty clumps and flower in the spring and summer. Plant in a sunny situation in a well-drained soil.

Armeria maritima **(Sea pink, Thrift)**
Medium seeds: 400–700 per gram
Hardy evergreen perennial
Height 10cm (4in)

Armeria maritima

Small pink or white, globe-shaped flowers
Flowers in early summer
Leaves are dark green and grass like, growing in little mounds
Good as an edging plant

Sow in autumn into pots or modules using a standard, loam-based seed compost (substrate). Home-collected seed will need to be scarified (see page 233). Seed is viable for 3 years. Cover lightly with compost. Place in a cold frame. Germination takes 2–3 months, but is erratic.

Aubrieta *Brassicaceae*

A genus of fully- to frost-hardy evergreen perennials which grow in mounds or are trailing. Flowers in the spring or summer. Plant in a sunny situation and a well-drained soil.

Aubrieta 'Red Cascade' (Cascade series) AGM
Small seeds: 2,500 per gram
Hardy evergreen perennial
Height 10cm (4in)
A profusion of carmine-red flowers
Flowers in early summer
Rounded, toothed, soft mid-green leaves

Sow in spring into pots or modules using standard, soil-less seed compost (substrate), either a peat free proprietary brand or composted fine propagating bark. Cover with perlite or vermiculite and place in a cold frame or under protection at 15°C (60°F). Germination takes 2–3 weeks cold or 7–14 days with protection. Flowers during the following year.

Aurinia *Brassicaceae*

A genus of fully- to frost-hardy evergreen perennials which either grow in mounds or are trailing. Flowers in the spring or summer. Plant in a sunny situation in a well-drained soil

Aurinia saxatilis 'Gold Dust'
Medium seeds: 1,000 per gram
Hardy evergreen perennial
Height 15cm (6in)
Small racemes of 4-petalled yellow flowers
Flowers in late spring
Small, oval, hairy, grey-green leaves

Sow in spring into pots or modules using standard, soil-less seed compost (substrate), either a peat free proprietary brand or composted fine propagating bark. Cover with perlite or vermiculite and place in a cold frame or under protection at 20°C (68°F). Germination takes 2–3 weeks cold or 3–8 days with protection. Flowers during the following year. Excellent for growing over a wall.

Ballota *Lamiaceae*

A genus of frost-hardy perennials and evergreens. Flowers in the summer. Plant in a sunny situation and a well-drained soil.

Ballota pseudodictamnus AGM
Medium seeds: 700 per gram
Hardy, evergreen perennial
Height 60cm (24in)
Whorls of pink flowers with pale green calyces
Flowers in summer
Hairy/woolly, grey-green, rounded leaves
Good, large rock garden plant with all year interest

Sow in autumn into pots or modules using a standard loam-based seed compost (substrate). Cover lightly with compost and place in a cold frame. Germination, which is erratic, takes 2–4 months.

Bellis *Asteraceae*

A genus of perennials, cultivars often grown as biennials. Plant in sun to semi-shade in a fertile soil that is well-drained.

Bellis perennis **(Daisy, English daisy, Double daisy)**
Small seeds: 4,900 per gram
Hardy perennial
Height 15cm (6in)
Small, flat, double-petalled, white flowers with a touch of pink
Flowers in summer
Oval, mid-green leaves

Sow in summer into pots or modules using standard, soil-less seed compost (substrate), either a peat free proprietary brand or composted fine propagating bark. Cover with perlite or vermiculite and place in a cold frame. Germination takes 2–3 weeks. Flowers the following season.

Calandrinia *Portulacaceae*

A genus of perennial and annual plants which have a spreading or trailing habit and fleshy leaves. The flowers close in dull weather and at night. Plant in a sunny situation and well-drained soil.

Calandrinia umbellata **(Rock purslane)**
Small seeds: 9,000 per gram
Hardy perennial, sometimes grown as a biennial
Height 10–15cm (4–6in)
Vivid crimson, cup-shaped flowers
Flowers in summer
Grey-green, slightly hairy leaves

Sow in spring into pots or modules, using standard soil-less seed compost (substrate), either a peat free proprietary brand or composted fine propagating bark. As these are very fine seeds, mix them with the finest sand or talcum powder for an even sowing. Cover with perlite or vermiculite, place in a cold frame. Germination takes 3–4 weeks. May flower in its first season.

Campanula *Campanulaceae*

A genus of half-hardy to hardy perennials, biennials and annuals which flower in the spring and summer. Plant in sun or shade in a moist but well-drained soil.

Campanula carpatica AGM **(Harebell, Carpathian harebell)**
Small seeds: 7,000 per gram
Hardy perennial
Height 10cm (4in)
Broadly bell-shaped, blue or white flowers
Flowers in summer
Rounded to oval toothed green leaves

Sow in spring into pots or modules using standard, soil-less seed compost (substrate), either a peat free proprietary brand or composted fine propagating bark. Cover with perlite or vermiculite. Place in a cold frame, or under protection at 20°C (68°F). Germination takes 3–4 weeks or 1–2 weeks with heat. Can flower in first season in mid-summer.

Carlina *Asteraceae*

A genus of hardy annuals, biennials and perennials. All have attractive flowers. Plant in a sunny situation in a well-drained soil.

Carlina acaulis subsp. *simplex* (Carlina, Silver thistle)
Medium seeds: 250 per gram
Hardy perennial
Height 15cm (6in)
Stemless, single, off-white or pale brown flowers with papery bracts
Flowers in summer
Long, deeply cut leaves with a spiny margin, forming rosettes

Sow in autumn into pots or modules, using a standard loam-based seed compost (substrate). Cover lightly with compost and place in a cold frame. Germination takes 4–6 months. Flowers the following season.

Cerastium *Caryophyllaceae*

A genus of fully-hardy annuals and perennials with star-shaped flowers. Plant in a sunny situation in a free draining soil.

Cerastium tomentosum (Snow in summer)
Small seeds: 2,500 per gram
Hardy perennial
Height 8cm (3in) creeping habit
Star-shaped, pure white flowers
Flowers in summer
Small, silvery-grey, serrated leaves

Sow in autumn into pots or modules using a standard, soil-less seed compost (substrate), either a peat free proprietary brand or composted fine propagating bark, mixed with silver or fine sand for extra aeration. Mix to a ratio of 3 parts compost + 1 part sand. Cover with perlite or vermiculite and place in a cold frame. Alternatively, sow in spring and place under protection at 18°C (65°F). Germination takes 2–4 months cold or 1–2 weeks with warmth. Can flower in its first season. Makes a vigorous ground-cover plant.

Chaenorhinum *Scrophulariaceae*

A genus of fully- to frost-hardy annuals, biennials and perennials. Plant in sun or light shade in a well- drained soil.

Chaenorhinum origanifolium 'Blue Dream'
Small seeds: 1,250 per gram
Hardy perennial, commercially grown as a biennial for pot production
Height 12cm (5in)
Cushion habit
Lots of small, pale blue or mauve flowers
Flowers in summer
Small, oval mid-green leaves

Sow in spring into pots or modules using standard soil-less seed compost (substrate), either a peat free proprietary brand or composted fine propagating bark. Cover with perlite or vermiculite and place under protection at 18–20°C (65–68°F). Germination takes 1–2 weeks.

Codonopsis *Campanulaceae*

A genus of fully- to frost-hardy perennials and herbaceous, twining climbers. Plant in partial shade in light, well-drained soil.

Codonopsis clematidea
Small seeds: 1,600 per gram
Hardy perennial
Height 50cm (20in)
Light blue, bell-shaped flowers with a white tinge
Flowers in summer
Ideal for banks and dry walls

Sow in spring into pots or modules using standard, soil-less seed compost (substrate), either a peat free proprietary brand or composted fine propagating bark. Cover with perlite or vermiculite and place in a cold frame or under protection at 18–20°C (65–68°F). Germination takes 1–6 weeks or 1–3 weeks with warmth.

Corydalis *Papaveraceae*

A genus of fully- to frost-hardy annuals, perennials and evergreens some with tuberous or fibrous roots. Plant in full sun or partial shade in a well-drained soil.

Corydalis lutea (Golden bleeding heart)
Medium seeds: 750 per gram
Hardy evergreen perennial
Height 30cm (12in)
Yellow flowers with short spurs, which grow in dense racemes
Flowers from spring and through the summer
Basal, divided, grey-green leaves

Sow in autumn or early spring into pots or modules, using a standard loam-based seed compost (substrate) mixed with coarse horticultural sand. Mix to a ratio of 1 part compost + 1 part sand. Cover lightly with compost and place in a cold frame. Germination takes 3–12 months (do not give up). Flowers during the following year.

Cyclamen *Primulaceae*

A genus of hardy to frost-tender tuberous perennials, some evergreen, all with attractive pendent flowers. Plant in a humus-rich, well-drained soil in sun to partial shade.

Cyclamen hederifolium AGM
Medium seeds: 100 per gram
Hardy perennial
Height 15cm (6in)
Lovely, small, pink, pendent flowers
Flowers from late summer to early autumn
Deep green, ivy-shaped leaves with attractive silver markings

Soak fresh seeds in warm water with a little washing up liquid for 12 hours prior to sowing. Sow in autumn into pots using standard, loam-based seed compost (substrate) mixed with coarse horticultural grit. Mix to a ratio of 1 part compost + 1 part 5mm (1/4in) grit. Cover with sharp grit. Place the container under protection at a minimum temperature of 15°C (60°F). Germination takes 3–4 weeks. Flowers during its second season.

***Recipe for sowing, planting and growing* Cyclamen hederifolium**

This is a charming plant, it looks lovely grown in clusters or drifts on a rocky bank or under deciduous trees. The seeds of *Cyclamen hederifolium* take a season to ripen on the plant. In nature, the seed capsules coil down to the ground. They are covered in a sticky coating which is attractive to ants – Nature's seed sowers of this species.

Ingredients

2 seeds per module or 4 seeds per pot
Small china bowl
Warm water with a minute dash of washing up liquid
1 x 8cm (4in) pot
Standard loam-based seed compost (substrate)
Coarse horticultural grit
Additional coarse grit for covering
White plastic plant label

Method Collect fresh seeds in autumn. Fill a china bowl with warm water. Add a minute dash of washing up liquid. Soak the fresh seeds in the liquid for 12 hours. Fill the pot with a mixture of compost and grit, mixed to a ratio of 1 part compost + 1 part grit. Smooth over, tap down and water in well. Put 4 seeds in each pot, spaced equally and placed on the surface of the compost. Cover the seeds with sharp grit and label with the plant name and date. Place the pot into a warm spot out of direct sunlight at an optimum temperature of 15°C (60°F).

Keep watering to a minimum until germination has occured, which takes 3–4 weeks with warmth. Shortly after germination, when the seedlings have emerged fully, put the container into a cold frame for the winter. If you have not overcrowded the pot with seedlings it is a good idea to leave them in this pot undisturbed for the season. Split the tubers when they are dormant, re-pot in the same compost mix and put the young plants in the cold frame for the remains of the winter. Plant out into a prepared site in the garden in spring.

Dianthus *Caryophllaceae*

A genus of hardy to semi-hardy annuals, biennials, perennials evergreens or semi-evergreen plants grown for their flowers. They are often scented and some are excellent for cutting. Flowering is mainly from late spring to late summer. The majority prefer to be planted in full sun and in a well-drained, slightly alkaline soil.

Dianthus deltoides AGM (Maiden pinks)
Small seeds: 1,700 per gram
Hardy, evergreen perennial
Height 15cm (6in)
Mat forming
Small white, pink or cerise flowers
Flowers from early summer until early autumn
Narrow, lance-shaped, dark green leaves

Dianthus gratianopolitanus (caesius) AGM (Cheddar pink)
Medium seeds: 700 per gram
Hardy, evergreen perennial
Height 20cm (8in); creeping habit
Pale pink, very fragrant flowers
Flowers in summer
Narrow, grey-green leaves

Sow in spring into pots or modules using standard, soil-less seed compost (substrate), either a peat free proprietary brand or composted fine propagating bark. Cover with perlite or vermiculite and place in a cold frame or under protection at 20–22°C (68–72°F). Germination takes 2–3 weeks or 7–10 days with warmth.

Draba *Brassicaceae*

A genus of hardy to frost hardy annuals and evergreen or semi-evergreen perennials. Plant in a gritty, well-drained soil in a sunny situation. Hates wet winters.

Draba aizoides (Yellow whitlow grass)
Small seeds: 3,500 per gram
Hardy, semi-evergreen perennial
Height 2 1/2cm (1in)
Bright yellow, 4-petalled flowers
Flowers in spring
Lanced-shaped, bristle-like, grey-green leaves

Sow in spring into pots or modules using standard, soil-less seed compost (substrate), either a peat free proprietary brand or composted fine propagating bark. Cover with perlite or vermiculite, place in a cold frame. Germination takes 2–3 weeks.

Dryas *Rosaceae*

A genus of fully-hardy, evergreen, prostrate perennials. Plant in a gritty, peaty, well-drained soil in a sunny situation.

Dryas octopetala AGM (Mountain avens)
Medium seeds: 1,000 per gram
Hardy, evergreen perennial
Height 6cm (2in); prostrate,mat-forming habit
Cup-shaped, creamy-white flowers
Flowers in spring and early summer
Leathery, oval, dark green leaves

Sow with fresh seed in autumn into pots or modules using standard, soil-less seed compost (substrate), either a peat free proprietary brand or composted fine propagating bark, mixed with 2–3mm (1/16–1/8in) fine grit. Mix in a ratio of 3 parts compost + 1 part fine grit. Cover lightly with compost and place in a cold frame. Germination takes 2–3 months.

Erinus *Scrophulariaceae*

A genus of fully-hardy, semi-evergreen, short-lived perennials. Plant in a well-drained soil in a sunny situation.

Erinus alpinus AGM (Lever balsam, Fairy foxglove)
Tiny seeds: 16,000 per gram
Hardy perennial
Height 8cm (3in)

Dryas octopetala

Small pink, purple or white flowers
Flowers in late spring and summer
Rosettes of small, soft, mid-green leaves

Sow in spring into pots or modules using a standard, loam-based seed compost (substrate) mixed with coarse horticultural sand. Mix to a ratio of 1 part compost + 1 part sand. As these are very fine seeds, mix them with the finest sand or talcum powder for an even sowing. Cover with perlite or vermiculite. Place in a cold frame. Germination takes 3–4 weeks. This plant self seeds freely.

Eriophyllum *Asteraceae*

A genus of hardy perennials and evergreen sub-shrubs with attractive, daisy-like flowers. Plant in a well-drained soil and a sunny situation.

Eriophyllum lanatum
Small seeds: 2,000 per gram
Hardy perennial
Height 30cm (12in)
Daisy-like, yellow flowers
Flowers in summer
Cushions of divided, silvery leaves

Sow in spring into pots or modules using standard, soil-less seed compost (substrate), either a peat free proprietary brand or composted fine propagating bark. Cover with perlite or vermiculite and place in a cold frame. Germination takes 2–8 weeks.

Euphorbia *Euphorbiaceae*

A genus of fully-hardy to frost-tender shrubs, succulents, perennials and annuals. Plant in a moist but well-drained soil in sun or partial shade.

Euphorbia myrsinites AGM **(Milkweed, Spurge, Myrtle euphorbia)**
Medium seeds: 80 per gram
Hardy evergreen perennial
Height 5–8cm (2–3in)
Clusters of bright yellow-green flowers
Flowers in spring
Pointed, fleshy, grey leaves
Good for planting in walls

Sow in autumn into pots or modules using a standard, loam-based seed compost (substrate) mixed with coarse horticultural sand. Mix to a ratio of 1 part compost + 1 part sand. Cover with perlite or vermiculite and place in a cold frame or under protection in spring at 18–21°C (65–70°F). Germination takes 2–6 months cold or 7–14 days with warmth. Germination can be erratic. Flowers during its second season.

Gentiana *Gentianaceae*

A genus of fully-hardy annuals, biennials and perennials, some of which are evergreen or semi-evergreen. Grown for their stunning flowers. Plant in a humus-rich, well-drained, neutral to acid soil in sun or semi-shade.

Gentiana acaulis AGM **(Stemless gentian)**
Small seeds: 3,000 per gram
Hardy, evergreen perennial
Height 3cm (1in)
Clump forming
Attractive, dark blue, trumpet-shaped flowers with green spotted throats
Flowers in spring and often autumn
Narrow, oval, glossy leaves

Gentiana lutea **(Great yellow gentian)**
Medium seeds: 875 per gram
Hardy perennial
Height 1–1.2m (3–4ft)
Whorls of yellow tubular flowers
Flowers in summer
Oval, stalkless, mid-green leaves

Sow with fresh seed (seed loses viability quite quickly) in autumn into pots or modules. Use standard, loam-based seed compost (substrate) mixed with coarse horticultural sand. Mix to a ratio of 2 parts compost + 1 part sand. Cover lightly with coarse sand and place in a cold frame. Germination takes 1–12 months. Flowers the following season.

Geum *Rosaceae*

A genus of hardy, summer flowering perennials. Plant in a moist, well-drained soil in a sunny situation.

Geum montanum AGM **(Alpine avens)**
Medium seeds: 290 per gram
Hardy perennial
Height 10cm (4in)
Shallow, cup-shaped, golden-yellow flowers
Flowers in spring
Pinnate green leaves with a rounded terminal lobe

Sow in autumn into pots or modules, using a standard loam-based seed compost (substrate) mixed with coarse horticultural sand. Mix to a ratio of 2 parts compost + 1 part sand. Cover with perlite or vermiculite and place in a cold frame, or in spring under protection at 10°C (55°F). Germination takes 3–4 months cold or 2–4 weeks with warmth.

***Recipe for sowing, planting and growing* Geum montanum**
This is a most attractive spring-flowering alpine plant, which looks a picture nestling in the rock garden.

Ingredients
3 seeds per module or 5 seeds per pot
1 module tray
OR
1 x 8cm (4 in) pot
Standard loam-based seed compost (substrate) mixed with coarse horticultural sand at a ratio of 2 part compost + 1 part sand
Perlite fine-grade (wetted) or vermiculite
White plastic plant label

Method In autumn, fill the tray or pot with compost, smooth over, tap down and water in well. Sow the fresh seed spaced out on the surface of the compost. Press gently into the compost with the flat of the hand. Cover with the wetted, fine-grade perlite or vermiculite. Label with the plant name and date. Place the tray or pot in a cold frame. Keep watering to the absolute minimum until germination has taken place. Germination will take 3–4 months. Winter the young seedlings undisturbed in the cold frame. Pot up or plant out in the spring when the seedlings are large enough, after a period of hardening off, when there is no threat of frost.

OR

Sow the seeds in spring following the instructions as above, but this time place the container in a warm, light place out of direct sunlight. Keep watering to a minimum until germination has taken place. Germination takes 14–28 days. Prick out when the seedlings are large enough to handle or, if you are using modules, plant directly into a container or the garden after a period of hardening off and when there is no threat of frost. Whichever method you choose, flowering will take place in the following season.

Globularia *Globulariaceae*

A genus of hardy, mainly evergreen shrubs and sub-shrubs which grow in dome-shaped hummocks. Plant in a well-drained soil and a sunny situation.

Globularia cordifolia AGM
Small seeds: 2,600 per gram
Hardy evergreen shrub
Height 10cm (4in)
Creeping habit
Round, fluffy, stemless, blue/mauve/lavender flowers
Flowers in summer
Tiny, oval, green leaves

Sow in autumn into pots or modules using a standard loam-based seed compost (substrate) mixed with coarse horticultural sand. Mix to a ratio of 1 part compost + 1 part sand. Cover lightly with compost and place in a cold frame. Germination takes 6–10 weeks.

Gypsophila *Caryophyllaceae*

A genus of hardy annuals, perennials and semi-evergreen plants. Plant in a well-drained soil. Alpines prefer sandy, stony soils and a sunny situation.

Gypsophila cerastioides
Small seeds: 1,200 per gram
Hardy perennial
Height 3cm (1in)
Attractive, purple veined, white saucer-shaped flowers
Flowers in late spring and early summer
Rounded, soft, velvety, mid-green leaves

Sow in spring into modules using standard, soil-less seed compost (substrate), either a peat free proprietary brand or composted fine propagating bark. Cover with perlite or vermiculite and place under protection at 15°C (60°F). Germination takes 15–20 days.

Haberlea *Gesneriaceae*

A genus of hardy evergreen perennials. Plant in a moist soil in partial shade.

Haberlea rhodopensis AGM
Minute seeds: 25,000 per gram
Hardy evergreen perennial
Height 10cm (4in)
Funnel-shaped, dark blue/violet flowers with white throats
Flowers from late spring to early summer
Oblong, toothed, hairy, dark green leaves

Sow in autumn into pots or modules using a standard, loam-based seed compost (substrate) mixed with coarse horticultural sand. Mix to a ratio of 2 parts compost + 1 part sand. As these are very fine seeds, mix them with the finest sand or talcum powder for an even sowing. Cover lightly with coarse sand, place in a cold frame. Germination takes 6–10 weeks. Do not prick out seedlings until spring. Flowers in its second season.

Helianthemum *Cistaceae*

A genus of fully- to frost-hardy evergreen shrubs and subshrubs. Plant in a well-drained soil and a sunny situation.

Helianthemum nummularium (Rock rose, Sun rose)
Medium seeds: 490 per gram
Hardy evergreen perennial
Height 10cm (4in)
Smallish, yellow, saucer-shaped flowers
Flowers throughout the summer
Small, oblong leaves, green with grey underneath

Sow in spring into pots or modules using standard soil-less seed compost (substrate), either a peat free proprietary brand or composted fine propagating bark. Cover with perlite or vermiculite, place in a cold frame or under protection at 21–24 °C (70–75°F). Germination takes 2–4 weeks cold or 5–15 days with warmth. Flowers during its second season.

Hepatica *Ranunculaceae*

A genus of fully-hardy perennials. Flower before the leaves are properly formed. Plant in a rich, moist, alkaline soil in partial shade.

Hepatica nobilis AGM (syn. *Anemone hepatica*) (American liverwort, Kidneywort)
Small seeds: 2,000 per gram
Hardy semi-evergreen perennial
Height 10cm (4in)
Intense blue, shallow, cup-shaped flowers
Flowers in early spring
Soft, green, 3-lobed leaves

Sow fresh seed in summer or in winter into pots or modules, using a standard loam-based seed compost (substrate) mixed with coarse horticultural sand to a ratio of 2 parts compost + 1 part sand. Cover lightly with coarse sand and place in a cold frame. Germination takes 1–5 months, being quicker with fresh seed. The following spring, prick out and pot up seedlings. Flowers in its third season.

Herniaria *Caryophyllaceae*

A genus of hardy, short-lived, evergreen perennials. Plant in well-drained soil in sun or semi-shade.

Herniaria glabra **(Rupture wort)**
Small seeds: 5,000 per gram
Hardy, evergreen perennial
Height 10cm (4in)
Creeping habit
Small, green flowers
Flowers in summer
Small, oblong, deep green, grass-like leaves

Sow in spring into pots or modules using standard, soil-less seed compost (substrate), either a peat free proprietary brand or composted fine propagating bark. Cover with perlite or vermiculite, place in a cold frame, or under protection at 18–21°C (65–70°F). Germination takes 2–3 weeks cold or 5–15 days with warmth. Flowers during its second season. Good for growing in walls.

Heuchera *Saxifragaceae*

A genus of fully- to frost-hardy evergreen perennials. Excellent for ground cover. Plant in moist but well-drained soil in semi-shade.

Heuchera villosa 'Palace Purple'
Tiny seeds: 20,000 per gram
Hardy perennial
Height 45cm (18in)
Sprays of small white flowers
Flowers in summer
Heart-shaped, deep purple leaves

Sow in spring into pots or modules using standard, soil-less seed compost (substrate), either a peat free proprietary brand or composted fine propagating bark. As these are very fine seeds, mix them with the finest sand or talcum powder for an even sowing. Do not cover. Water from the bottom or with a fine spray and place in a cold frame or under protection at 21°C (70°F). Germination takes 3 weeks cold or 5–15 days with warmth. Flowers during its second season.

Hieracium *Asteraceae*

A genus of fully-hardy perennials. Plant in a well-drained soil in a sunny situation.

Hieracium villosum
Medium seeds: 600 per gram
Hardy perennial
Height 15cm (6in)
Bright yellow, dandelion-like flowers
Flowers in summer
Silvery-grey, woolly leaves

Sow in spring into pots or modules using standard, soil-less seed compost (substrate), either a peat free proprietary brand or composted fine propagating bark. Cover with perlite or vermiculite and place in a cold frame or under protection at 20°C (69°F). Germination takes 2–3 weeks cold or 5–15 days with warmth. Flowers during its second season.

Hypericum *Clusiaceae*

A genus of fully- to half-hardy, yellow flowering perennials, semi-evergreens, evergreens, shrubs and sub-shrubs.

Hypericum calycinum **(Rose of Sharon, Aaron's beard)**
Small seeds: 2,400 per gram
Hardy, evergreen or semi-evergreen dwarf shrub
Height 30cm (12in)
Bright yellow flowers
Flowers from mid-summer to mid-autumn
Dark green, oval leaves

Hypericum polyphyllum
Small seeds: 3,400 per gram
Hardy, evergreen perennial
Height 20cm (8in)
Bright yellow flowers all summer
Small, finely-textured, mid-green leaves

Sow from early to mid-spring into pots or modules using standard, soil-less seed compost (substrate), either a peat free proprietary brand or composted fine propagating bark. Cover with perlite or vermiculite and place in a cold frame or under protection at 18°C (65°F). Germination takes 1–3 months cold or 10–21 days with warmth.

Iberis *Brassicaceae*

A genus of fully- to half-hardy annuals perennials, evergreens and shrubs. All are very good rock garden plants. Plant in a well-drained soil and a sunny position.

Iberis sempervirens **(Candytuft)**
Medium seeds: 330 per gram
Hardy, evergreen subshrub
Height up to 30cm (12in)
Dense clusters of round heads of white flowers
Flowers from spring to early summer
Narrow, oblong, dark green leaves

Sow in spring into pots or modules using standard, soil-less seed compost (substrate), either a peat free proprietary brand or composted fine propagating bark. Cover with perlite or vermiculite and place in a cold frame or under protection at 18 °C (65°F). Germination takes 3 weeks cold or 14–21 days with warmth. Flowers during its second season.

Leontopodium *Asteraceae*

A genus of short-lived hardy perennials grown for their attractive flowers. Plant in a well-drained soil in a sunny position. These plants hate being overly wet at any time of year, so plant with a good collar of sharp grit.

Leontopodium alpinum AGM **(Edelweiss)**
Small seeds: 7,500 per gram
Hardy perennial (short-lived)
Height 15–20cm (6–8in)
Lovely, silvery-white flowers surrounded by star-shaped bracts
Flowers in spring
Lance-shaped, slightly woolly, silvery-green leaves

Iberis sempervirens

Sow in spring into pots or modules using a standard, loam-based seed compost (substrate) mixed with 5mm (1/4in) sharp grit. Mix to a ratio of 1 part compost + 1 part grit. As these are very fine seeds, mix them with the finest sand or talcum powder for an even sowing. Do not cover. Water from the bottom or with a fine spray, place in a cold frame, or under protection at 18°C (65°F). Germination takes 3 weeks cold or 14–21 days with warmth. Flowers in its second season.

Lewisia *Portulacaceae*

A genus of hardy perennials and evergreens. Plant in a rich, moist or well-drained, neutral to acid soil in semi-shade. Herbaceous species should be planted in full sun.

Lewisia cotyledon AGM
Small seeds: 1,500 per gram
Hardy evergreen perennial
Height up to 30cm (12in)
Clusters of small flowers in shades of pink
Flowers all summer
Large, thick, mid-green leaves
Hates being wet in winter, so put a collar of fine grit around it
Ideal for rock gardens and alpine houses

Lewisia nevadensis
Small seeds: 1,500 per gram
Hardy perennial
Height 4–6cm (1–2in)
Pretty, cup-shaped, white flowers
Flowers all summer
Narrow, dark green leaves

Sow in spring into pots or modules using standard soil-less seed compost (substrate), either a peat free proprietary brand or composted fine propagating bark. Cover with perlite or vermiculite and place in a cold frame or under protection at 18°C (65°F). Germination takes 1–2 months cold, 14–21 days warm. Flowers in second season.

Linaria *Scrophulariaceae*

A genus of hardy annuals, biennials and perennials. Plant in any well-drained soil in sun or partial shade.

Linaria alpina (Alpine toadflax)
Small seeds: 4,500 per gram
Hardy perennial (short lived)
Height 15cm (6in)
Purple and violet flowers with yellow centres which grow in loose racemes
Flowers all summer
Linear to lance-shaped, fleshy, grey-green leaves

Linaria cymbalaria (Cymbalaria muralis) (Ivy-leaved toadflax)
Small seeds: 5,000 per gram
Hardy perennial
Height 5cm (2in)
Creeping habit
Small, snapdragon-like flowers in purple, mauve and white
Flowers all summer
Bright green, round lobed leaves
Lovely growing in walls

Sow in spring into pots or modules using standard, soil-less seed compost (substrate), either a peat free proprietary brand or composted fine propagating bark. Cover with perlite or vermiculite and place in a cold frame. Germination takes 2–3 weeks. Flowers in the first year.

Linum *Linaceae*

A genus of fully- to half-hardy annuals, biennials, perennials and evergreens grown for their attractive flowers. Plant in a rich but well-drained, peaty soil in a sunny situation.

Linum perenne

Linum flavum (Golden flax, Yellow flax)
Medium seeds: 800 per gram
Hardy perennial
Height 30cm (12in)
Clusters of yellow, funnel-shaped flowers
Flowers all summer
Narrow, oval, green leaves

Linum perenne
Medium seeds: 300 per gram
Hardy perennial
Height 30cm (12in)
Clusters of open, funnel-shaped, lovely, clear blue flowers
Flowers in succession all summer
Grass-like, slender leaves

Sow in spring into pots or modules using standard, soil-less seed compost (substrate), either a peat free proprietary brand or composted fine propagating bark. Cover with perlite or vermiculite and place in a cold frame. Germination takes 3–4 weeks. Flowers in the first year.

Lychnis *Caryophyllaceae*

A genus of hardy annuals, biennials and perennials. Plant in a well-drained soil in a sunny position.

Lychnis alpina
Tiny seeds: 10,000 per gram
Hardy perennial
Height 5–15cm (2–6in)
Pale to deep pink flowers with frilled petals
Flowers all summer
Dark green, linear leaves

Sow in spring or autumn into pots or modules using standard soil-less seed compost (substrate), either a peat free proprietary brand or composted fine propagating bark. As these are very fine seeds, mix them with the finest sand or talcum powder for an even sowing. Do not cover. Water from the bottom or with a fine spray, place in a cold frame. Germination takes 2–3 weeks. If sowing in autumn, overwinter young plants in the cold frame.

Moltkia *Boraginaceae*

A genus of fully-hardy perennials, evergreens and deciduous shrubs. Plant in a well-drained, neutral to acid soil, in a sunny situation.

Moltkia petraea
Medium seeds: 550 per gram
Hardy semi-evergreen
Height 30cm (12in)
Clusters of violet-blue, funnel-shaped flowers
Flowers in summer
Narrow, hairy, long, mid-green leaves

Sow in autumn into pots or modules using a standard loam-based seed compost (substrate) mixed with coarse horticultural sand (2 parts compost + 1 part sand). Cover lightly with coarse sand and place in a cold frame. Germination takes 1–2 months. Overwinter young plants in a cold frame.

Nepeta *Lamiaceae*

A genus of hardy, summer flowering perennials. Plant in a well-drained soil in a sunny position.

Nepeta x *faassenii (mussinii)* (Catmint)
Small seeds: 1,300 per gram
Hardy perennial
Height 45cm (18in)
Small, tubular, lavender-blue flowers in loose spikes
Flowers all summer
Aromatic, greyish-green, small, oval leaves with slightly serrated edges

Sow in spring into pots or modules using standard, soil-less seed compost (substrate), either a peat free proprietary brand or composted fine propagating bark. Cover with perlite or vermiculite and place under protection at 18°C (65°F). Germination takes 14–21 days.

***Recipe for sowing, planting and growing* Nepeta *x* faassenii**

The common name of *Nepeta* x *faassenii* is catmint. This is because cats are passionate about it, especially when it is young or a piece of it has been broken. To prevent your cat demolishing the plant and to give it a chance to get established, it is a good idea to place an upturned metal/wire mesh hanging basket over the crown. The plant can then grow through the mesh and give you a wonderful display. You will even have enough to give your cat some as a reward.

Ingredients
6 seeds per module or 10 seeds per pot (approximately)
1 piece white card 14 x 8.5cm ($5^{1}/_{2}$ x $3^{1}/_{2}$in) folded in half
1 module tray
OR
1 x 8cm (4in) diameter pot
Standard soil-less seed compost (substrate), either a peat free proprietary brand or composted fine propagating bark
Fine-grade perlite (wetted) or vermiculite
White plastic plant label

Method Fill the tray or pot with compost, smooth over, tap down and water in well. Put a small amount of seed into the crease of the folded card and tap gently in order to sow thinly on to the surface of the compost. Press the seed gently into the compost with the flat of the hand. Cover with fine-grade perlite (wetted) or vermiculite. Label with the plant name and date. Place the tray or pot into a warm, light place out of direct sunlight at an optimum temperature of 18°C (65°F). Keep watering to a minimum until germination has taken place, after 14–21 days in spring with warmth. Shortly after germination, when the seedlings have fully emerged, put the containers into a cooler environment at 15°C (59°F). Pot up or prick out approximately 4 weeks later. If you are using modules, you can plant directly into containers. Wait to plant out into the garden until the young plants have had a period of hardening off and there is no threat of frost.

Oenothera *Onagraceae*

A genus of hardy annuals, biennials and perennials grown for their short-lived, wonderful flowers. Plant in a well-drained soil (can be sandy) in full sun.

Oenothera macrocarpa AGM **(Ozark sundrop, Missouri evening primrose)**
Medium seeds: 200 per gram
Hardy perennial
Height 10cm (4in)
Lovely, bell-shaped, yellow flowers
Flowers throughout the summer
Lance-shaped, mid-green leaves

Sow in spring into pots or modules using standard soil-less seed compost (substrate), either a peat free proprietary brand or composted fine propagating bark. Cover with perlite or vermiculite and place in a cold frame or under protection at 21°C (70°F). Germination takes 3 weeks cold or 8–15 days warm. Flowers in second season.

Ononis *Papilionaceae*

A genus of hardy, summer flowering perennials and evergreens and deciduous shrubs grown for their pea-like flowers. Plant in a well-drained soil in a sunny position.

Ononis spinosa
Medium seeds: 170 per gram
Hardy perennial
Height 25cm (10in)
Rose/purple pea-like flowers
Flowers from summer until early autumn
Small, mid-green, round or oval, 3-part, leaves

Sow in spring into pots or modules using a standard loam-based seed compost (substrate). Cover with perlite or vermiculite, place in a cold frame. If using seed more than a year old, you should soak the seed for 12 hours, removing any floating seeds prior to sowing. Germination takes 1–3 months. Flowers during its second season.

Petrorhagia *Caryophyllaceae*

A genus of hardy annuals and perennials suited to a well-drained, sandy soil and a sunny position. These plants self seed readily.

Petrorhagia saxifraga AGM **(Tunic flower)**
Small seeds: 1,500 per gram
Hardy perennial
Height 10cm (4in)
A profusion of cup-shaped, double, white or pale pink flowers, occasionally with deeper pink veins
Flowers in summer
Narrow, grass-like leaves
Looks lovely growing in walls or in dry rockeries

Sow seeds in autumn into pots or modules using a standard, loam-based seed compost (substrate). Cover lightly with coarse sand and place in a cold frame. Germination takes 2–4 months. Overwinter young plants in the cold frame. Flowers during its second season.

Phuopsis *Rubiaceae*

A single species genus, hardy, summer flowering perennial. Plant in a well-drained soil and a sunny situation.

Phuopsis stylosa (Crucianella stylosa)
Medium seeds: 500 per gram
Hardy perennial
Height 30cm (12in)
Sweetly scented clusters of small, tubular, pink/mauve flowers
Flowers all summer
Small, pale green, linear leaves

Sow fresh seeds in autumn into pots or modules using a standard, loam-based seed compost (substrate). Cover lightly with coarse sand and place in a cold frame. Germination takes 2–4 months. Overwinter young plants in the cold frame. Flowers during its second season.

Platycodon *Campanulaceae*

A genus of fully-hardy perennials grown for their balloon-shaped flower buds. Plant in a light, sandy soil in full sun.

Platycodon grandiflorus AGM **(Balloon flower, Chinese bellflower)**
Medium seeds: 850 per gram
Hardy perennial
Height up to 60cm (24in)
Clusters of large, balloon-like buds opening to bell-shaped, blue/purple flowers
Flowers in summer
Oval, lance-shaped, blue/green leaves

Sow fresh seeds in autumn into pots or modules using a standard loam-based seed compost (substrate). Cover lightly with coarse sand, and place in a cold frame. Germination takes 2–4 months. Overwinter young plants in the cold frame. Flowers during its second season.

Primula *Primulaceae*

A genus of hardy to tender annuals, biennials, perennials and some evergreens. All have primrose-shaped flowers. There are primulas suitable for almost every type of site, wet, dry, sunny and shady. Some species dislike wet winters and others dislike full summer heat.

Primula auricula **(Alpine auricula)**
Small seeds: 3,000 per gram
Hardy perennial
Height 15–25cm (6–10in)
Umbels of fragrant, flat, yellow flowers
Flowers in spring
Oval, soft, pale green or grey-green leaves which are densely covered with white farina

Sow in spring into pots or modules using standard soil-less seed compost (substrate), either a peat free proprietary brand or composted fine propagating bark. Cover with perlite or vermiculite, place in a cold frame, or under protection at 15 °C (60°F). Germination takes 3–4 weeks cold or 14–21 days with warmth. Plant in a well-drained, alkaline soil in full sun or partial shade.

Primula vulgaris AGM **(Primrose)**
Medium seeds: 800 per gram

Hardy perennial
Height up to 20cm (8in)
Wonderful, scented, open, pale yellow flowers, with a darker eye
Flowers in early spring
Oval, lance-shaped, bright green leaves

Sow fresh seed in late summer into pots or modules using standard, soil-less seed compost (substrate), either a peat free proprietary brand or composted fine propagating bark. Cover with perlite or vermiculite, place in a cold frame. Germination takes 2–3 weeks. Can flower in first season, however there is a better show in the second. Primroses prefer soil that does not dry out and a site in sun or partial shade. It is essential to use fresh seed for easier germination.

Pulsatilla *Ranunculaceae*

A genus of hardy perennials and some evergreens grown for their feathery leaves and bell- or cup-shaped flowers. Plant in a humus-rich, well-drained soil in a sunny situation.

Pulsatilla alpina subsp. *apiifolia* AGM (Pasque flower)
Medium seeds: 200 per gram
Hardy perennial
Height up to 30cm (12in)
Bell-shaped pale yellow flowers
Flowers in spring
Soft, hairy, feathery green leaves

Pulsatilla vulgaris AGM
Medium seeds: 400 per gram
Hardy perennial
Height 15–30cm (6–12in)
Nodding, cup-shaped, flowers in white, blue, pink or purple
Flowers in spring and early summer
Soft, hairy, feathery leaves

Sow fresh seeds in autumn into pots or modules using a standard, loam-based seed compost (substrate) mixed with coarse horticultural sand. Mix to a ratio of 2 parts compost + 1 part sand. Cover lightly with coarse sand and place in a cold frame. Germination takes 14–28 days, however can be as long as one year so do not give up. Overwinter young plants in the cold frame. Flowers during its second season.

Roscoea *Zingiberaceae*

A genus of fully-hardy tuberous perennials. Plant in a humus-rich soil, which should not dry out in summer, in sun or partial shade.

Roscoea alpina
Medium seeds: 300 per gram
Hardy perennial
Height 15– 20cm (6–8in)
Dark purple, hooded, orchid-like flowers
Flowers in summer
Lance-shaped, erect leaves

Sow fresh seed in autumn into pots or modules using a standard, loam-based seed compost (substrate) mixed with coarse horticultural sand. Mix to a ratio of 1 part compost + 1 part sand. Cover lightly with compost and place outside to get all weathers. (see 'Breaking Seed Dormancy', page 233, for more information). Germination takes 1–12 months, so do not give up. Flowers in its second year. This plant originates in the Himalayas where it grows happily at 6–11,000 feet.

***Recipe for sowing, planting and growing* Roscoea alpina**
This plant is a member of the ginger family. It has truly orchid-like flowers that are stunning in any rock garden.

Ingredients
5 seeds per module or 8 seeds per pot
1 module tray
OR
1 x 8cm (4 in) pot
Standard loam-based seed compost (substrate) mixed with coarse horticultural sand. Mix to a ratio of 1 part compost + 1 part sand
Extra coarse horticultural sand to cover the pot
White plastic plant label

Method In autumn fill the tray or pot with compost, smooth over, tap down and water in well. Sow the seeds thinly on to the surface of the compost. Press gently into the compost with the flat of the hand. Cover the seed with coarse horticultural sand. Label with the plant name and date. Place the tray or pot outside, on a level surface, so it is exposed to all weathers, including frosts.

Do not worry if you live in a snowy area and the containers get immersed in snow, the melting snow will aid germination. If you do not live in an area which will get a winter frost, it is a good idea to put the seed plus a handful of damp sand into a clearly marked plastic bag. Seal the bag and place it in the refrigerator for 3 weeks. Remove and sow as mentioned in the first paragraph, then place outside.

Whichever method you use, germination is a bit erratic, taking anything from 1–12 months. Do not give up and discard your compost, it might germinate next week! Whichever method you follow, prick out when the seedlings are large enough to handle. If you are using modules, you can plant directly into the garden as soon as the soil is warm enough to dig over prior to planting out.

Sagina *Caryophyllaceae*

A genus of fully-hardy annuals, perennials and evergreens. Plant in gritty, moist soil in a sunny situation.

Sagina subulata (Heath pearlwort)
Minute seeds: 40,000 per gram
Hardy perennial
Height 4cm ($1\frac{1}{2}$in)
A myriad tiny, star-shaped, white flowers
Flowers in summer
Bright green mat of foliage

Sow in late summer into pots or modules using standard soil-less seed compost (substrate), either a peat free proprietary brand or composted fine propagating bark. As these are very fine seeds, mix them with the finest sand or talcum powder for an even sowing. Do not cover. Water from the bottom or with a fine spray and place in a cold frame. Germination takes 2–3 weeks. Flowers in the following season. Good for planting in between paving stones or as an edging to paths.

Saponaria *Caryophyllaceae*

A genus of hardy annuals and perennials, ideal for rock gardens, screes and banks. Plant into a well-drained soil and a sunny position.

Saponaria ocymoides AGM (Tumbling Ted)
Medium seeds: 500 per gram
Hardy perennial
Height up to 8cm (3in)
Creeping habit
Masses of flat, tiny, pale pink to crimson flowers
Flowers all summer
Compact, oval leaves which form a sprawling, hairy mat

Sow in spring into pots or modules using standard, soil-less seed compost (substrate), either a peat free proprietary brand or composted fine propagating bark. Cover with perlite or vermiculite and place in a cold frame. Germination takes 3–4 weeks. Flowers in the following season.

Saxifraga *Saxifragaceae*

A large genus of hardy to half-hardy perennials and evergreens. Excellent for rock gardens. There are saxifrages suitable for many conditions, from moist to dry soil and from shade to full sun. Check which species you have so that you can plant it in the ideal situation.

Saxifraga umbrosa (London pride, St. Patrick's cabbage)
Tiny seeds: 18,000 per gram
Hardy perennial
Height 45cm (18in)
Loose panicles of pink, starry flowers
Flowers all summer
Rosettes of spatula-shaped, leathery leaves

Sow fresh seed in autumn into pots or modules, using a standard, loam-based seed compost (substrate) mixed with coarse horticultural sand. Mix to a ratio of 1 part compost + 1 part sand. As these are very fine seeds, mix them with the finest sand or talcum powder for an even sowing. Cover lightly with compost and place outside exposed to all the weathers. (See 'Breaking Seed Dormancy', page 233, for more information). Germination takes 1–12 months, do not give up. Flowers in its second year.

Recipe for sowing, planting and growing **Saxifraga umbrosa**

This plant is a very useful for ground cover. It likes being planted in soil that is moist and does not dry out in high summer, but does not get water logged in winter. It prefers partial shade.

Ingredients

20 seeds per module or 30 seeds per pot (or as near as you can manage)
Talcum powder, or fine plain white flour
1 piece white card 14 x 8.5cm ($5\frac{1}{2}$ x $3\frac{1}{2}$in) folded in half
1 module tray

OR

1 x 8cm (4in) pot
Standard, loam-based seed compost (substrate) mixed with coarse horticultural sand. Mix to a ratio of 1 part compost + 1 part sand
Extra coarse horticultural sand to cover the pot
White plastic plant label

Method In autumn fill the tray or pot with compost, smooth over, tap down and water in well. As the seeds are very fine, it is a good idea to mix them with talcum powder or extra fine white flour, in which the seeds will show up. Put a very small amount of the seed mix into the crease of folded card. Gently tap the card to sow the seed thinly. Cover the seed with coarse horticultural sand. Label with the plant name and date. Place the tray or pot outside on a level surface, so it is exposed to all the weathers, including frosts. Do not worry if you live in a cold area and the containers get immersed in snow, as the melting snow will aid germination.

If you do not live in an area which will get a winter frost, it is a good idea to put the seed and flour mix plus a handful of damp sand into a clearly marked plastic bag. Seal the bag and place in the refrigerator for 3 weeks. Remove and sow as mentioned in the first paragraph, then place outside.

Whichever method you use, germination is a bit erratic, taking anything from 1 to 12 months. Do not give up and discard your compost, it might germinate next week!

Prick out the seedlings when they are large enough to handle. If you are using modules, you can plant the seedlings directly into the garden as soon as the soil is warm enough to dig over, prior to planting out.

Scutellaria *Lamiaceae*

A genus of hardy to frost-tender perennials. Plant it in a well-drained soil in a sunny situation.

Scutellaria alpina (Alpine skullcap)
Medium seeds: 900 per gram
Hardy perennial.
Height up to 30cm (12in)
Compact clusters of slender, tubular, hooded flowers, bright blue/violet, shading to almost white just above the calyx
Flowers in summer
Small mat-forming downy leaves

Sow in spring into pots or modules using standard, soil-less seed compost (substrate), either a peat free proprietary brand or composted fine propagating bark. Cover with perlite or vermiculite and place in a cold frame. Germination takes 4–8 weeks. Occasionally flowers in its first season.

Sedum *Crassulaceae*

A genus of frost-hardy to frost-tender annuals, biennials and evergreens. Plant in any soil but prefers a fertile, well-drained soil. In sun or partial shade.

Sedum acre (Wall pepper, Stonecrop)
Small seeds: 8,000 per gram
Hardy evergreen perennial
Height up to 10cm (4in)
Creeping habit
Star-shaped, bright yellow flowers
Flowers all summer
Mat-forming, succulent, bright green leaves

Sedum rupestre L. (*reflexum* L.) (Stone orpine, Rock stonecrop, Recurved yellow stonecrop)
Tiny seeds: 15,000 per gram
Hardy, evergreen perennial
Height up to 20cm (8in)
Creeping habit
Clusters of yellow, star-shaped flowers
Flowers all summer
Narrow, fleshy, grey-green leaves

Sow fresh seed in autumn into pots or modules using a standard, loam-based seed compost (substrate) mixed with coarse horticultural sand. Mix to a ratio of 2 parts compost + 1 part sand. As these are very fine seeds, mix them with the finest sand or talcum powder for an even sowing. Do not cover. Water from the bottom or with a fine spray and place under protection at 15°C (60°F). Germination takes 1–4 months. Overwinter young plants in a frost-free place. May take up to 3 years to flower.

Silene *Caryophyllaceae*

A genus of hardy annuals, perennials and some evergreens. Plant in a well-drained soil in a sunny position.

Silene pendula 'Compacta' (Nodding catchfly)
Small seeds: 1,200 per gram
Hardy annual
Height 20cm (8in)
Clusters of double flowers of pink, red and white
Flowers from summer until early autumn
Mid-green, oval, hairy leaves

Sow in spring into pots or modules using standard, soil-less seed compost (substrate), either a peat free proprietary brand or composted fine propagating bark. Cover with perlite or vermiculite and place in a cold frame. Germination takes 1–2 weeks.

Sisyrinchium *Iridaceae*

A genus of hardy to half-hardy annuals, perennials and some semi-evergreens. This plant will adapt to most conditions apart from full shade and very wet soils.

Sisyrinchium idahoense var. *bellum*
Medium seeds: 600 per gram
Hardy, semi-evergreen perennial
Height up to 12cm (5in)
Pretty, purple/mauve, star-shaped flowers with yellow eyes
Flowers over a long period from summer until early autumn
Bluish-green, tuft- or grass-like foliage

Sow fresh seed in autumn into pots or modules using a standard, loam-based seed compost (substrate) mixed with coarse horticultural sand. Mix to a ratio of 1 part compost + 1 part sand. Cover lightly with compost and place in a cold frame. Germination takes 2–4 weeks. Overwinter young plants in a cold frame. Flowers in its second year. Ideal for rockeries and self seeds readily.

Symphyandra *Campanulaceae*

A genus of short-lived, hardy perennials. Plant in a well-drained soil and a sunny situation.

Symphyandra hofmannii (Bell flower)
Small seeds: 1,400 per gram
Short lived, hardy perennial, sometimes grown as a biennial
Height 60cm (24in)
Dense spikes of creamy white, nodding, bell-shaped flowers
Flowers all summer
Slightly soft, hairy plant with dense, spiky foliage

Sow in spring into pots or modules using standard, soil-less seed compost (substrate), either a peat free proprietary brand or composted fine propagating bark. Cover with perlite or vermiculite and place under protection 20°C (68°F). Germination takes 1–2 weeks.

Tellima *Saxifragaceae*

A genus of one species, hardy, semi-evergreen plants that prefer a well-drained soil and a sunny position. Will also thrive in partial shade beneath shrubs.

Tellima grandiflora (Fringe cups)
Small seeds: 1,600 per gram
Hardy, semi-evergreen perennial
Height 60cm (24in)
Racemes of lime-green flowers that turn copperish with age
Flowers in summer
Heart-shaped, slightly hairy leaves with a purple tint

Sow fresh seed in autumn into pots or modules using a standard, loam-based seed compost (substrate) mixed with coarse horticultural sand. Mix to a ratio of 1 part compost + 1 part sand. Cover lightly with compost and place outside exposed to all weathers (see 'Breaking Seed Dormancy', page 233, for more information). Germination takes 1–12 months, do not give up. Flowers in its second year.

Thymus *Lamiaceae*

A genus of hardy evergreen perennials all of which have aromatic leaves. Plant in a well-drained soil in a sunny position.

Thymus serpyllum
Small seeds: 6,000 per gram
Hardy, evergreen perennial
Height 1cm (1/2in)
Small, clustered, 2-lipped flowers in purple, mauve or white
Flowers all summer
Very small, oval, aromatic, green leaves

Tiarella wherryi

Sow in spring into pots or modules using standard, soil-less seed compost (substrate), either a peat free proprietary brand or composted fine propagating bark. Cover with perlite or vermiculite and place under protection 20°C (68°F). Germination takes 1–2 weeks. Do not over water after germination has taken place, as this causes damping off.

Tiarella *Saxifragaceae*

A genus of hardy perennials some of which are evergreen. Plant in a well-drained soil in partial shade.

Tiarella wherryi AGM
Small seeds: 1,800 per gram
Hardy perennial
Height 10cm (4in)
Racemes of tiny, star-shaped, soft pink or white flowers
Flowers from late spring to early summer
Small, hairy, mid-green leaves

Sow fresh seed in autumn into pots or modules using a standard, loam-based seed compost (substrate) mixed with coarse horticultural sand. Mix to a ratio of 1 part compost + 1 part sand. As these are very fine seeds, mix them with the finest sand or talcum powder for an even sowing. Cover lightly with compost, place outside exposed to all weathers (see 'Breaking Seed Dormancy', page 233, for more information). Germination takes 1–12 months, so do not give up. Flowers in its second year.

Veronica *Scrophulariaceae*

A genus of hardy perennials some of which are evergreen, grown for their blue flowers. Plant in a well-drained soil in a sunny position.

Veronica repens (Creeping speedwell)
Small seeds: 7,000 per gram
Hardy perennial
Height 5cm (2in)
Creeping habit
Numerous, bluish-white flowers
Flowers in late summer
Vivid green, mat-forming leaves

Sow in spring into pots or modules using standard, soil-less seed compost (substrate), either a peat free proprietary brand or composted fine propagating bark. As these are very fine seeds, mix them with the finest sand or talcum powder for an even sowing. Do not cover. Water from the bottom or with a fine spray, place under protection at 20°C (68°F). Germination takes 1–2 weeks.

Viola *Violaceae*

A genus of hardy annuals, perennials and some semi-evergreens, all grown for their attractive flowers. Plant in a well-drained but moisture retentive soil in sun or partial shade.

Viola 'Königin Charlotte' (Vt)
Medium seeds: 1,000 per gram
Hardy perennial
Height 15cm (6in)
Dark blue, traditional, violet-shaped flowers which are richly scented
Flowering from early spring
Heart-shaped, mid-green leaves

Sow fresh seed in autumn into pots or modules using a standard, loam-based seed compost (substrate) mixed with coarse horticultural sand. Mix to a ratio of 1 part compost + 1 part sand. As the shells of these seeds are hard, it is a good idea to scarify with fine sandpaper before sowing (see page 233). Then place outside, exposed to all weathers (see 'Breaking Seed Dormancy', page 233, for more information). Germination takes 1–4 months. Flowers in its second year.

Recipe for sowing, planting and growing* Viola *'Queen Charlotte'

The wonderful scent of the sweet violet makes it worth growing in the garden, and the attractive spring flowers are another bonus. If you do not have space in the garden, it looks lovely in a container, which can be abandoned outside for the whole season.

Ingredients

6 seeds per module or 10 seeds per pot (or as near as you can manage)
1 Sheet of fine sandpaper cut in half
1 piece white card 14 x 8.5cm ($5^{1}/_{2}$ x $3^{1}/_{2}$in) folded in half
1 module tray
OR
1 x 8cm (4 in) pot
Standard loam-based seed compost (substrate) mixed with coarse horticultural sand. Mix to a ratio of 1 part compost + 1 part sand
White plastic plant label

Method In autumn fill the tray or pot with compost, smooth over, tap down and water in well. Select a small amount of seed, place it on a half sheet of fine sandpaper and cover it with the other half. Hold between both hands and slide the sheets of sandpaper back and forth, gently scratching the surface of the seed. Alternatively, you can simply put the other half of the sandpaper on top of the seed and gently push the paper up and down, this will have the same effect. Put a small amount of this scarified seed into the crease of the folded card. This will allow you to sow the seed thinly on to the surface of the compost. Cover with coarse horticultural sand. Label with the plant name and date. Place the tray or pot outside, on a level surface, so it is exposed to all weathers, including frosts. Do not worry if you live in a cold area and the containers get immersed in snow. The melting snow will aid germination.

If you do not live in an area which will get a winter frost, it is a good idea to put the scarified seed plus a handful of damp sand into a plastic bag which is clearly marked. Seal the bag and place in a refrigerator for 3 weeks. Remove and sow as described above. Then place outside. Germination will occur in the following spring and flowering the year after that.

Prick out when the seedlings are large enough to handle. If you are using modules, you can plant directly into the garden as soon as the soil is warm enough to dig over, prior to planting out.

annuals & biennials

It is natural for annuals to reproduce from seed, making your task easier. The crucial thing is to care for the seedlings properly once they have germinated. Planting seedlings out too late or in unsuitable growing conditions will trigger a panic reaction. Programmed to survive at all costs, the plant will rapidly go into flower, producing seeds to ensure its survival the following year. Also, bear in mind what will happen to the plant when it dies back. If it is a self-seeder, ask yourself whether allowing the plant to seed freely will cause problems the following year. Once you have taken these points on board, you will be free to enjoy your annuals, revelling in their magnificent displays of colour and texture and their glorious scents.

Papaver somniferum, see page 54

Ageratum *Asteraceae*

A genus of half-hardy annuals and biennials, which attract bees and butterflies. Plant in fertile, well-drained soil in a sunny situation. Do not allow the plants to dry out as this will inhibit flowering.

Ageratum houstonianum 'Blue Danube' **(Floss Flower)**
Small seeds: 6,700 per gram
Half-hardy annual
Height 15cm (6in)
Clusters of feathery, mid-blue flowers
Flowers from early summer to early autumn
Oval, mid-green leaves

As these are very fine seeds, mix them with the finest sand or talcum powder for an even sowing. Sow in spring in pots or modules using a soil-less seed compost (substrate), either a peat free proprietary brand or composted fine propagating bark. Do not cover. Water from the bottom of the pot or use a fine spray. Place under protection at 15°C (60°F). Germination takes 8–10 days.
OR
Sow in prepared, open ground in late spring when air temperature does not go below 9°C (48°F) at night. Germination will take 14–20 days.

Alcea *Malvaceae*

A genus of hardy biennials (sometimes grown as annuals) and short-lived perennials. All have attractive spikes of flowers. Plant in free draining soil in a sunny situation.

Alcea rosea Chater's Double Group **(Hollyhocks)**
Medium seeds: 45 per gram
Hardy biennial
Height 1.8m (6ft)
Attractive spikes of rosette-like double flowers in varying colours from white to yellow, pink and maroon
Flowers from summer to early autumn
Lobed, mid-green leaves

Alcea rosea 'Nigra'
Medium seeds: 45 per gram
Hardy biennial
Height 1.5m (5ft)
Attractive spikes of rosette-like, double flowers in varying colours from white to deep maroon
Flowers from summer to early autumn
Lobed, mid-green leaves

Sow in spring or late summer in pots or modules using a soil-less seed compost (substrate), either a peat free proprietary brand or composted fine propagating bark. Cover with perlite or vermiculite and place under protection at 18°C (65°F). Germination takes 6–10 days.

By sowing seed in late summer, you may be able to trigger flowering in the first year. Over-winter young plants in a cold frame.

Amaranthus *Amaranthaceae*

A genus of half-hardy annuals grown for their colourful foliage and dense clusters of tiny flowers. Plant in a fertile, well-drained soil in a sunny situation.

Amaranthus caudatus **(Love-lies-bleeding, Tassel flower)**
Small seeds: 1,500 per gram
Half-hardy annual
Height 1.2m (4ft)
Red flowers clustered in attractive, hanging tassels
Flowers from summer to early autumn
Pale green, oval leaves with pointed tips

Sow in spring in pots or modules using a soil-less seed compost (substrate), either a peat free proprietary brand or composted fine propagating bark. Cover with perlite or vermiculite and place under protection at 15°C (60°F). Germination takes 8-14 days.

Ammi *Apiaceae*

A genus of hardy annuals and perennials which have attractive white flowers. These plants will adapt to most gardens, but they prefer a well-drained soil and a sunny situation.

Ammi majus **(Bishop's flower)**
Small seeds: 1,300 per gram
Hardy annual
Height 1m (3½ft)
Large clusters of lacy white flowers
Flowers in summer
Small oblong mid green leaves

Sow fresh seed in late spring into prepared, open ground when the air temperature does not fall below 10°C (50°F) at night. Germination takes 14–21 days.

Ammobium *Asteraceae*

A genus of Australian annuals with 'everlasting' flowers. Plant in a well-drained, sunny situation.

Ammobium alatum
Medium seeds: 1,000 per gram
Half-hardy annual
Height 90cm (3ft)
Silvery-white, 'everlasting' flowers with yellow centres
Flowers in the summer
Oblong, mid-green leaves

Sow in spring or late summer in pots or modules using a soil-less seed compost (substrate), either a peat free proprietary brand or composted fine propagating bark. Cover with perlite or vermiculite and place under protection at 18°C (65°F). Germination takes 5–7 days. Sowing in late summer can trigger flowering in the first year. Overwinter the young plants in a cold frame.

Anagallis *Primulaceae*

A genus of hardy annuals and creeping perennials. Plant in a fertile, moist soil in an open, sunny situation.

Anagallis arvenis var. *caerulea* **(Pimpernel, Scarlet pimpernel)**
Small seeds: 1,400 per gram
Hardy annual
Height 20cm (8in)

The lacy white flowers of *Ammi majus* with the pink flowers of *Lavatera* 'Bredon Springs'.

Blue flowers that close in the evening
Flowers all summer
Small, bright green, oval leaves

Sow in spring in pots or modules using a soil-less seed compost (substrate), either a peat free proprietary brand or composted fine propagating bark. Cover with perlite or vermiculite and place under protection at 18°C (65°F). Germination takes10–14 days.

Antirrhinum *Scrophulariaceae*

A genus of hardy annuals, perennials and semi-evergreen subshrubs which flower from spring until autumn. Regular dead-heading will prolong flowering. Plant in a rich, well-drained soil in a sunny situation.

Antirrhinum majus (Snapdragon)
Small seeds: 5,500 per gram
Perennial grown as half-hardy annual
Height 20–45cm (8–18in)
Attractive spikes of 2-lipped, sometimes double flowers in white, pink, red, purple or yellow
Flowers from summer until early autumn
Lance-shaped, mid-green leaves

Sow in spring in pots or modules using a soil-less seed compost (substrate) either a peat free proprietary brand or composted fine propagating bark. Cover with perlite or vermiculite and place under protection at 18°C (65°F). Germination takes 7–14 days.
OR
Sow in late spring into prepared, open ground when the air temperature does not drop below 10°C (50°F) at night. Germination takes 14–21 days.

Arctotis *Asteraceae*

A genus of tender annuals and perennials. Grow at a minimum temperature of 1–5°C (35–40°F). Plant in a well-drained soil and full sun.

Arctotis x *hybrida* hort. 'Harlequin'
Medium seeds: 130 per gram
Half-hardy annual
Height 50cm (20in)
Daisy-like, multi-coloured flowers, ranging from red to cream with lovely blue centres
Flowers from summer until early autumn
Chrysanthemum-shaped, dark green leaves with grey undersides

Arctotis stoechadifolia (African daisy)
Medium seeds: 150 per gram
Half-hardy perennial often grown as an annual
Height 50cm (20in)
Daisy-like, creamy-white flowers with lovely blue centres
Flowers from summer until early autumn
Chrysanthemum-shaped, dark green leaves with grey undersides

Sow in spring in pots or modules using a soil-less seed compost (substrate), either a peat free proprietary brand or composted fine propagating bark. Cover with perlite or vermiculite and place under protection at 21°C (70°F). Germination takes 4–8 days.

Bassia *Chenopodiaceae*

A genus of annuals and perennials with striking foliage. Plant in fertile, well-drained soil in a sunny situation. Stake on windy sites.

Bassia scoparia f. *trichophylla* (*Kochia scoparia* f. *trichophylla*)
(Burning bush, Mock cypress, Belvedere)
Medium seeds: 1,000 per gram
Half-hardy annual
Height 90cm (3ft)
Insignificant, small flowers
Flowers in summer
Light green foliage that turns deep red in autumn

Sow in spring in pots or modules using a soil-less seed compost (substrate), either a peat free proprietary brand or composted fine propagating bark. Cover with perlite or vermiculite and place under protection at 20°C (68°F). Germination takes 4–10 days.

Begonia *Begoniaceae*

A large genus which includes annuals, perennials, evergreens, deciduous shrubs and small trees. Grown for their attractive flowers or foliage. Plant in a slightly acid soil in semi-shade to full sun.

Begonia semperflorens Cultorum Group (Wax begonia)
Seeds so small they appear as dust: 70,000 per gram
Half-hardy evergreen
Height 25–30cm (10–12in)
Small, pink flowers, sometimes with a white centre
Flowers from spring until early autumn – when grown as an annual flowers in the summer
Dark green, round, fleshy leaves with a light green underside

There are many named hybrids available from seed companies, all with different attributes. For example, *Begonia semperflorens* 'Cocktail' has pink, red or white flowers with waxy bronze leaves.

Begonia sutherlandii AGM
Seeds so small they appear as dust: 60,000 per gram
Height trailing to 1m (3½ft)
Clusters of small orange flowers
Flowers in summer
Lance-shaped, bright green leaves with red veins
Good for hanging baskets or cascading over tubs

Sow in spring in pots or modules using a soil-less seed compost (substrate), either a peat free proprietary brand or composted fine propagating bark. As these are very fine seeds, mix them with the finest sand or talcum powder for an even sowing. Do not cover. Water from the bottom or with a fine spray, place under protection at 21°C (70°F). Germination takes 14–28 days.

Bellis *Asteraceae*

A genus of hardy perennials, some cultivars are grown as biennials, all are grown for their daisy-like flowers. Plant in fertile, well draining soil in sun to partial shade.

Bellis perennis 'Monstrosa'
Small seeds: 5,500 per gram

Hardy perennial grown as a biennial
Height 15cm (6in)
Attractive white or pink double flowers
Flowers from spring to mid-summer
Oval, mid-green leaves

Sow in summer into modules using a soil-less seed compost (substrate), either a peat free proprietary brand or composted fine propagating bark. Cover with perlite or vermiculite and place in a cold frame. Germination takes 2–3 weeks. Over-winter the young plants in the cold frame. They will flower in their second year.
OR
Sow in spring or autumn in pots or modules using a soil-less seed compost (substrate), either a peat free proprietary brand or composted fine propagating bark. Cover with perlite or vermiculite, place under protection at 21°C (70°F). Germination takes 7–14 days in spring and 14–28 days in autumn. The plants grown from spring-sown seeds will flower the following year and those from autumn-sown seeds will flower the following spring.

***Recipe for sowing, planting and growing* Bellis perennis**
Daisies are cheerful plants to have in the garden. This cultivated variety looks great in containers or at the front of a border. It is worth dead-heading after the first flush of flowers to prolong the plants' flowering season.

Bellis perennis seeds can be sown at 3 different times of year. If you start your seeds off in spring, you will grow a hardy plant that can be planted out and over-wintered in the garden, to flower the following spring. Seeds sown in the summer can be germinated and over-wintered in the cold frame. Alternatively, you can sow in the autumn. Plants will have to be over-wintered in a frost-free place. Watch out for rot. There is a bonus to autumn planting – your plants will flower in their first season. Whenever you start your sowing, the method is basically the same.

Ingredients
10 seeds per module or 15 seeds per pot
1 piece white card 14 x 8.5cm ($5^{1}/_{2}$ x $3^{1}/_{2}$in) folded in half
1 module tray
OR
1 x 8cm (4in) pot
Soil-less seed compost (substrate), either a peat free proprietary brand or composted fine propagating bark
Fine-grade perlite (wetted) or vermiculite
White plastic plant label

Method Fill the tray or pot with compost, smooth over, tap down and water thoroughly. As the seeds are so fine, it is worth putting a very small quantity of seed into the crease of a folded card. You can then sow the seed by gently tapping the card. This will let you to see what you are sowing and allow you to sow thinly on to the surface of the compost. Cover the seed with perlite or vermiculite and then label clearly with the plant name and the date.

For spring sowings, place the tray or pot in a warm, light place out of direct sunlight at an optimum temperature of 21°C (70°F). Summer-sown seed should be placed in a cold frame or a cool greenhouse. Keep the compost damp, but not wet, until the seed germinates. This takes 7–14 days in spring if the seed is put in a warm place. Summer germination in a cold frame takes 14–21 days and seed given some warmth in autumn will germinate after 14–28 days.

Put pots of spring and summer sown seeds in a cooler environment of about 15°C (59°F) shortly after germination has taken place and the seedlings have fully emerged. You can prick out and pot up approximately 2–3 weeks after germination. The spring seedlings will be ready to plant out approximately 4 weeks after that. If you are using modules you can plant out directly into the garden after a period of hardening off and when there is no threat of frost. The summer seedlings should be left in pots to over-winter in the cold frame. Autumn-sown plants can be pricked out at 4–8 weeks, depending on light levels after germination, potted up and over-wintered with frost protection. Alternatively, if you have sown thinly and the seedlings are not overcrowded, you can wait until early spring for potting up or planting out. Whichever way you choose, you can plant out in the garden as soon as all threat of frost is passed.

Bidens *Asteraceae*
A genus of hardy annuals and perennials. Plant in a well-drained soil in a sunny position.

Bidens ferulifolia 'Goldie' (Spanish needles)
Small seeds: 1,200 per gram
Hardy annual
Height 45cm (18in) trailing habit
Attractive golden flowers
Flowers throughout the summer
Mid-green, serrated leaves
This variety is good for hanging baskets or tubs

Sow in early spring in pots or modules using a soil-less seed compost (substrate), either a peat free proprietary brand or composted fine propagating bark. Cover with perlite or vermiculite, place under protection at 20°C (68°F). Germination takes 14–21 days.

Brachyscome *Asteraceae*
A genus of hardy annuals and perennials with daisy-like flowers. Plant in a fertile, well-drained soil in a sunny, sheltered position.

Brachyscome iberdifolia (Swan River daisy)
Small seeds: 5,000 per gram
Hardy annual
Height 45cm (18in)
Small blue (sometimes pink, mauve, purple or white) fragrant, daisy-like flowers
Flowers in summer to early autumn
Deeply cut, mid-green leaves

Sow in early spring in pots or modules using a soil-less seed compost (substrate), either a peat free proprietary brand or composted fine propagating bark. Cover with perlite or vermiculite, place under protection at 18°C (65°F). Germination takes 10–14 days.

Browallia *Solanaceae*
A genus of tender perennials usually grown as annuals in northern climates. Plant in a fertile, well-drained soil in sun or partial shade.

Browallia speciosa 'Starlight' **(Bush violet)**
Small seeds: 4,000 per gram
Half-hardy perennial, grown as an annual
Height 15cm (6in)
Attractive, violet-blue flowers with white eyes
Flowers in the summer
Oval, mid-green leaves

Sow in early spring in pots or modules using a soil-less seed compost (substrate), either a peat free proprietary brand or composted fine propagating bark. Cover with perlite or vermiculite and place under protection at 22°C (72°F). Germination takes 14–21 days. In controlled conditions this plant will flower from seed in about 90 days. It looks lovely in hanging baskets or patio containers.

Bupleurum *Apiaceae*

A genus of hardy annuals, perennials and evergreen shrubs. Plant in a well-drained soil in full sun. These plants thrive in coastal gardens.

Bupleurum griffithii **(Thoroughwax)**
Medium seeds: 300 per gram
Hardy annual
Height 80cm (30in)
Umbels of green/yellow flowers
Flowers in summer
Eucalyptus-shaped leaves
The foliage is lovely as a filler in flower arrangements. May need staking in exposed sites.

Sow in late spring into a prepared, open ground when air temperature does not go below 10°C (50°F) at night. This plant is best grown where it is to flower. Germination takes 14–21 days.

Calandrinia *Portulacaceae*

A genus of fleshy, hardy to tender, annual or perennial, spreading or trailing plants.

Calandrinia umbellata
Small seeds: 5,000 per gram
Tender perennial grown as an annual
Height 15cm (6in)
Bright crimson-magenta, cup-shaped flowers
Flowers in summer
Linear, hairy, mid-green leaves

Sow in early spring in pots or modules using a soil-less seed compost (substrate), either a peat free proprietary brand or composted fine propagating bark. Cover with perlite or vermiculite, place under protection at 18°C (65°F). Germination takes 7–14 days. Flowers close at night and when the weather is cloudy.

Calceolaria *Scrophulariaceae*

A genus of hardy to frost-tender annuals, biennials and evergreen perennials. Plant in well-drained soil, in a sunny site with a bit of protection from the midday sun. Dislikes cold and wet, especially intolerant of wet winters.

Calceolaria integrifolia AGM **(Slipper flower)**
Medium seeds: 850 per gram
Evergreen sub-shrub often grown as an annual
Height 23cm (9in)
Pouch-shaped, yellow/reddish-brown flowers
Flowers in summer
Elliptic, mid-green leaves

Sow in early spring or late summer in pots or modules using a soil-less seed compost (substrate), either a peat free proprietary brand or composted fine propagating bark. Cover with perlite or vermiculite and place under protection at 18°C (68°F). Germination takes 7–10 days. Sowing in late spring will produce flowering plants in early autumn, so protect from early frosts. Sowing in late summer may trigger flowering in the first year. Over-winter young plants in a cold frame.

Callistephus *Asteraceae*

A one-species genus, half-hardy annual. Plant in a fertile, well-drained soil in a sunny and sheltered site. There are many named forms of this flower, available in a full range of colours.

Callistephus chinensis **(China aster)**
Medium seeds: 410 per gram
Half-hardy annual
Height 15–90cm (6–36in)
The flowers vary from daisy to chrysanthemum, double to single in shades of white, pink and blue
Flowers from spring until early autumn
Oval toothed, mid-green leaves

Callistephus chinensis **'Matador mix'**
Medium seeds: 500 per gram
Half-hardy annual
Height 90cm (3ft)
Large chrysanthemum-like flower heads, slightly in-curved, in shades of pink, white and purple
Flowers from summer until early autumn
Oval, mid-green toothed leaves
This variety is good for cut flowers

Sow in spring in pots or modules using a soil-less seed compost (substrate), either a peat free proprietary brand or composted fine propagating bark. Cover with perlite or vermiculite, place under protection at 21°C (70°F). Germination takes 8–10 days.
OR
Sow in late spring into prepared, open ground when air temperature is at least 10°C (50°F) at night. Germination takes 14–21 days.

Carthamus *Asteraceae*

A genus of hardy annuals. Plant in well-drained soil in a sunny situation.

Carthamus tinctorius **(Safflower, False Saffron, Saffron Thistle)**
Medium seeds: 20 per gram
Annual
Height 90cm (3ft)
Lovely, orange, thistle-like flowers in summer
Oval, spine-toothed leaves

Dries well for flower arrangements
Also used as a dye plant

Sow in late spring into prepared, open ground, when air temperature does not go below 10°C (50°F) at night. Germination takes 14–21 days.

Celosia *Amaranthaceae*

A genus of half-hardy perennials often grown as annuals. Plant in fertile, well-drained soil in a sunny, sheltered situation.

Celosia argentea var. *cristata* (Cockscomb, Crested celosia)
Medium seeds: 1,000 per gram
Tender perennial, often grown as an annual
Height 1–2ft (20–60cm)
Unusual, pyramid-shaped, feathery flower heads in red, yellow, pink or apricot
Oval, mid-green leaves

Sow in spring in pots or modules using a soil-less seed compost (substrate), either a peat free proprietary brand or composted fine propagating bark. Cover with perlite or vermiculite and place under protection at 18°C (65°F). Germination takes 8–10 days.
OR
Sow in late spring into prepared, open ground when the air temperature does not drop below 10°C (50°F) at night. Germination takes 14–21 days.

Centaurea *Asteraceae*

A genus of hardy annuals and perennials all grown for their attractive flowers. Plant in well-drained soil and a sunny situation.

Centaurea cyanus (Cornflower, Bluebottle)
Medium seeds: 200 per gram
Hardy annual
Height 60cm (24in)
Lovely, daisy-like flowers in shades of blue, pink, white or purple
Lance-shaped, grey green leaves
Excellent for cutting

Centaurea cyanus

Cerinthe major 'Purpurascens'

Sow in spring into prepared, open ground when the air temperature does not go below 10°C (50°F) at night. Germination takes 14–21 days.

Cerinthe *Boraginaceae*

A genus of hardy annuals and perennials grown for their interesting foliage. Plant in fertile soil that retains a certain amount of moisture, will grow happily in a clay soil in a sunny situation.

Cerinthe major 'Purpurascens' (Blue Honeywort)
Medium seeds: 60 per gram
Hardy annual
Height 60cm (24in)
Attractive, deep blue bracts around rich purple-blue, bell-shaped flowers tinged with cream
Flowers from late spring and through the summer
Handsome, glaucous, green-blue leaves
Attractive to bees

Sow in spring in pots or modules using a soil-less seed compost (substrate), either a peat free proprietary brand or composted fine propagating bark. Cover with perlite or vermiculite, place under protection at 18°C (65°F). Germination takes 8–10 days.
OR
Sow in late spring into prepared, open ground when air temperature does not go below 10°C (50°F) at night. Germination takes 14–21 days.

Chenopodium *Chenopodiaceae*

A very interesting genus of annuals, perennials and sub-shrubs, widely distributed throughout the world. These plants will adapt to most situations. The species mentioned below should be planted in a free draining soil and a sunny situation.

Chenopodium botrys (Jerusalem Oak, Ambrosia Jerusalem Oak)
Small seeds: 6,000 per gram
Half-hardy annual
Height 30–90cm (1–3ft)
Spikes of feathery, aromatic, small flowers
Flowers in summer until early autumn
Hairy, aromatic, pinnate, pale green leaves

Sow in late spring into prepared, open ground, when air temperature is at least 9°C (48°F) at night. Germination takes 14–21 days. Flowers are long lasting which makes them good for dried flower arrangements.

Clarkia *Onagraceae*

A genus of fully-hardy annuals which are grown for their flowers. Plant in a fertile, well-drained soil in a sunny situation.

Clarkia amoena (Satin flower, Farewell to spring)
Medium seeds: 1,000 per gram
Hardy annual
Height 60cm (2ft)
Attractive spikes of single or double flowers in shades of pink
Flowers all summer
Lance-shaped, mid-green leaves
These plants look lovely if grown in large clumps

Clarkia 'Brilliant'
Small seeds: 2,000 per gram
Hardy annual
Height 60cm (2ft)
Attractive, double rosettes of bright pink or red flowers in long spikes
Flowers all summer
Oval, mid-green leaves

Sow in late spring into prepared, open ground when air temperature does not go below 9°C (48°F) at night. Germination takes 14–21 days.

Cleome *Capparaceae*

A genus of half-hardy annuals and evergreen shrubs, all grown for their unusual, spidery flowers. Plant in a fertile, well-drained soil in a sunny position.

Cleome hassleriana 'Cherry Queen' (Spider flower)
Medium seeds: 400 per gram
Half-hardy annual
Height 90cm (3ft)
Large, open, airy, bright rose-coloured, narrow petalled flowers with strong scent
Flowers all summer until the first frosts
Mid-green, divided, lance-shaped leaves

Sow in spring in pots or modules using a soil-less seed compost (substrate), either a peat free proprietary brand or composted fine propagating bark. Cover with perlite or vermiculite and place under protection at 21°C (70°F). Germination takes 8–14 days, however germination can be very erratic and very seasonal.

Coreopsis *Asteraceae*

A genus of hardy annuals and perennials which have daisy-like flowers. Plant in a fertile, well-drained soil in a sunny situation.

Coreopsis tinctoria (Tick-seed)
Medium seeds: 300 per gram
Hardy annual
Height 60–90cm (2–3ft)
Large, daisy-like, bright yellow flowers with red veins
Flowers throughout the summer until early autumn
Lance-shaped, mid-green leaves

Sow in spring in pots or modules using a soil-less seed compost (substrate), either a peat free proprietary brand or composted fine propagating bark. Cover with perlite or vermiculite, place under protection at 18°C (65°F). Germination takes 8–10 days.
OR
Sow in late spring into prepared, open ground when air temperature is at least 10°C (50°F) at night. Germination takes 14–21 days.

Cosmos *Asteraceae*

A genus of hardy and half-hardy annuals and perennials which are grown for their attractive flowers. Plant in moist but not wet soil in a sunny position. Never let the plants dry out completely.

Cosmos bipinnatus 'Sonata'
Medium seeds: 180 per gram
Half-hardy annual
Height 60cm (2ft)
Attractive, showy, single, daisy-like flowers in a variety of colours, from pink and red to white
Flowers from late summer to early autumn
Feathery, compact, mid-green leaves
Looks lovely in the garden or grown in containers

Sow in spring in pots or modules using a soil-less seed compost (substrate), either a peat free proprietary brand or composted fine propagating bark. Cover with perlite or vermiculite and place under protection at 21°C (70°F). Germination takes 5–8 days.

Craspedia *Asteraceae*

A genus of half-hardy perennials which are often grown as annuals in cooler climates. Plant in a well-drained soil and a sunny situation.

Craspedia globosa (Billy Buttons, Drumsticks)
Small seeds: 2,000 per gram
Half-hardy perennial grown as an annual in wet winter climates
Height 75cm (30in)
Bright yellow, ping-pong ball shaped flowers
Flowers in summer
Flowers dry well and can be used in arrangements
Narrow, oval, mid-green leaves

Sow fresh seed in late summer or early autumn in pots or modules, using a soil-less seed compost (substrate), either a peat free proprietary brand or composted fine propagating bark. Cover with perlite or vermiculite and place under protection at 20°C (68°F). Germination takes 7–14 days.

Over-winter young plants under protection and plant out in the garden when the frosts have passed.

Datura *Solanaceae*

A genus of hardy to tender annuals, perennials, evergreen or semi-evergreen shrubs and trees. They all have lovely flowers. Plant in a light, well-drained soil in a sunny situation.

Datura stramonium (Thorn apple, Devil's apple) POISONOUS PLANT
Medium seeds: 90 per gram
Half-hardy annual
Height 2m (6ft)
White, funnel-shaped flowers followed by oval, prickly seed capsules
Flowers in summer
Oval leaves with an unpleasant smell

Sow in spring in pots or modules using a soil-less seed compost (substrate), either a peat free proprietary brand or composted fine propagating bark. Cover with perlite or vermiculite and place under protection at 18°C (65°F). Germination takes 14–21 days. Do not allow the compost to dry out and keep potting on as the plant makes rapid growth. Despite all the adverse press, this makes a striking container plant.

Dianthus *Caryophyllaceae*

A genus of hardy to semi-hardy annual, biennial, perennial, evergreen or semi-evergreen plants grown for their flowers, many of which are scented and excellent for cutting. The majority prefer well-drained, slightly alkaline soil in a sunny situation.

Dianthus 'Telstar'
Medium seeds: 800 per gram
Hardy annual
Height 25cm (10in)
Very attractive flowers ranging from purple to scarlet, which can be bi-coloured
Flowers perpetually throughout the summer
Lance-shaped leaves

Sow in spring in pots or modules using a soil-less seed compost (substrate), either a peat free proprietary brand or composted fine propagating bark. Cover with perlite or vermiculite. Place under protection at 18°C (65°F). Germination takes 10–14 days.

Diascia *Scrophulariaceae*

A genus of hardy and tender annuals and perennials. Need humus-rich, well-drained soil that does not dry out in a sunny situation.

Diascia 'Pink Queen'
Small seeds: 4,000 per gram
Half-hardy perennial grown as an annual
Height 30cm (12in)
Small, rose-pink, tubular flowers with yellow centres
Flowers throughout the summer
Small, pale green leaves
Good for pots, tubs and hanging baskets

Sow in spring in pots or modules using a soil-less seed compost (substrate), either a peat free proprietary brand or composted fine propagating bark. Cover with perlite or vermiculite and place under protection at 18°C (65°F). Germination takes 14–21 days. In ideal conditions it takes about 12 weeks from seed to flower.

Digitalis *Scrophulariaceae*

A genus of about 20 species of biennial or perennial plants with very attractive, showy flowers. Plant in semi-shade in most garden soils, dislikes very light soils.

Digitalis purpurea (Foxglove) POISONOUS PLANT AND SEED
Small seeds: 10,000 per gram
Hardy biennial
Height up to 1.8m (up to 6ft)
Purple or white, tubular flowers with purple spots in throat
Flowers in second spring to early summer
Large, green leaves

Digitalis purpurea 'Apricot' POISONOUS PLANT AND SEED
Small seeds: 10,000 per gram
Hardy biennial
Height up to 1.5m (up to 5ft)
Creamy-orange, tubular flowers with apricot spots in throat
Flowers in second spring to early summer
Large, green leaves

Sow fresh seeds into pots in autumn using a standard loam-based seed compost mixed with silver or fine sand (3 parts compost to 1 part sand) for extra aeration. Mix seeds with fine sand or talcum powder for even sowing. Do not cover. Water from the bottom or with a fine spray, place in a cold frame. Germination takes 5–7 weeks. Sometimes, germination is delayed until the following year. Plants flower in their second year.
OR
Sow treated seeds in spring. Use pots or modules with a soil-less seed compost (substrate), either a peat free proprietary brand or composted fine propagating bark. Prepare and water the seeds. Place under protection at 18°C (65°F). Germination takes 14–21 days. Flowers during second year.

***Recipe for sowing, planting and growing* Digitalis purpurea**
These lovely, graceful woodland plants look good in dappled shade, flowering from late spring to early summer. The *Digitalis purpurea* is famous for digoxin and digitoxin, used in medicine as heart stimulants.

There are 2 methods of growing foxgloves, one using seed that you have collected yourself and the other using seed brought from commercial producers. Both methods flower in the second season.

Ingredients
Approximately 10 seeds per module or 15 seeds per pot
Talcum powder or fine, plain white flour
1 piece white card 14 x 8.5cm (5½ x 3½in) folded in half
1 module tray or 1 x 8cm (4in) pot
Standard loam-based seed compost mixed with extra silver or fine sand (3 parts compost to 1 part sand) for extra aeration
White plastic plant label

Method In autumn, fill the tray or pot with compost, smooth over, tap down and water well. As the seeds are very fine, it is a good idea to mix them with talcum powder or extra fine white flour to make them more visible. Put a very small amount of this seed mix into the crease of the folded card. Gently tap the card, sowing the seed thinly on to the surface of the compost. Do not cover. Label with the plant name and date. Place the tray or pot outside on a level surface, so that it is exposed to all weathers, including frosts. Do not worry if the containers get covered in snow, the melting snow will aid germination.

If you live in a mild area which does not get frost in winter, it is a good idea to put the seed and flour with a handful of damp sand into a clearly marked plastic bag. Seal the bag and place it in a refrigerator for 3 weeks. Remove and sow as mentioned in the first paragraph, then place outside. Germination will occur in the following spring and flowering the year after that. In spring, if you are using seed merchant's seed, follow the instructions in the first paragraph. However, it is a good idea to use a standard, soil-less seed compost (substrate), either a peat free proprietary brand or composted fine propagating bark. Do not cover the seeds. Place the tray or pot in a warm, light place out of direct sunlight at an optimum temperature of 18°C (65°F). Keep watering to a minimum until germination has taken place and then only water from the bottom or with a fine spray so as not to disturb the tiny seeds. Germination takes 14–21 days in spring if warmth is provided. When the seedlings have fully emerged, reduce the temperature of their environment to 15°C (59°F).

With both methods, prick out when the seedlings are large enough to handle and harden them off before planting out. If you are using modules, you can plant direct into the garden after hardening off, when there is no threat of frost.

Dimorphotheca *Asteraceae*

A genus of half-hardy annuals, perennials and evergreen sub-shrubs which originate in Africa and are grown for their attractive flowers. Plant in a well-drained soil in a sunny situation.

Dimorphotheca pluvialis 'Sinuata' (Cape marigold, Rain daisy)
Medium seeds: 400 per gram
Half-hardy annual
Height 30cm (12in)
Lovely, small daisy-like flowers in orange, yellow, apricot and white
Flowers in summer
Oval, hairy, deep green leaves

Sow in spring in pots or modules using a soil-less seed compost (substrate), either a peat free proprietary brand or composted fine propagating bark. Cover with perlite or vermiculite and place under protection at 18°C (65°F). Germination takes 14–21 days.

Dorotheanthus *Aizoaceae*

A genus of half-hardy succulent annuals. Plant in a poor, well-drained soil in a sunny position.

Dorotheanthus bellidiformis (*Mesembryanthemum criniflorum*) (Livingstone daisy, Ice plant)
Small seeds: 3,500 per gram
Half-hardy annual
Height 10cm (4in)
Lovely, daisy-like flowers, which close on cloudy days
Flowers in shades of red, pink, white or cream
Flowers all summer
Pale green, lance-shaped, succulent leaves

Sow in early spring in pots or modules using a soil-less seed compost (substrate) either a peat free proprietary brand or composted fine propagating bark. Cover with perlite or vermiculite, place under protection at 18°C (65°F). Germination takes 14–21 days.

Erysimum *Brassicaceae*

A genus of hardy annuals, biennials, evergreen and short-lived perennials. Plant in well-drained soil in a sunny situation

Erysimum hieraciifolium (Siberian wallflower, English wallflower)
Medium seeds: 650 per gram
Evergreen, short-lived, perennial grown as a hardy biennial
Height 45cm (18in)
Heads of scented, orange flowers
Flowers in spring
Lanced-shaped, mid-green leaves

Sow in spring or late summer into prepared, open ground when air temperature does not go below 9°C (48°F) at night. If sown in late summer these plants can over-winter outside in situ, with temperatures no lower than -4°C (25°F), and they will flower in late spring the following year. Germination takes 14–21 days.

Eschscholzia *Papaveraceae*

A genus of hardy annuals grown for their poppy-like flowers. Plant in a well draining soil in a sunny situation. Dead-head regularly to prolong flowering.

Eschscholzia californica AGM (Mission bells, California poppy)
Medium seeds: 700 per gram
Hardy annual
Height 30cm (12in)
Lovely, cup-shaped, orangey-yellow flowers
Flowers all summer until the first frosts
Feathery, blue-green leaves

Sow in spring in prepared open ground when air temperature does not go below 9°C (48°F) at night. Germination takes 14–21 days.

Eustoma *Gentianaceae*

A genus of half-hardy annuals and perennials with attractive flowers, a mixture of a rose and a poppy. Plant in a well-drained soil in a sunny situation. In cooler climates they make very good pot plants.

Eustoma grandiflorum (russellianum) (syn. *Lisianthus*)
Minute seeds: 21,000 per gram
Half-hardy annual
Height 45cm (18in)
Poppy or rose-like flowers in pink, blue or white
Flowers all summer
Lance-shaped, green leaves
Good for cut-flower arrangements

Sow in spring in pots or modules using a soil-less seed compost (substrate), either a peat free proprietary brand or composted fine propagating bark. Do not cover the seed. Place under protection at 21°C (70°F). Germination takes14–21 days.

Exacum *Gentianaceae*

A genus of tender annuals, biennials and perennials with a minimum growing temperature of 7°C (45°F), grown for their mass of flowers. These plants make lovely pot plants. For the garden, plant in a well-drained soil in a sunny situation.

Exacum affine AGM (Persian violet, German violet, Tiddly winks)
Minute seeds: 35,000 per gram
Tender, evergreen biennial
Height 20cm (8in)
Tiny, scented, saucer-shaped purple flowers with a yellow eye
Flowers in summer and early autumn
Oval, glossy leaves

Sow in early spring or late summer in pots or modules using a soil-less seed compost (substrate), either a peat free proprietary brand or composted fine propagating bark. As these are very fine seeds, mix them with the finest sand or talcum powder for an even sowing. Do not cover. Water from the bottom or with a fine spray and place under protection at 21°C (70°F). Germination takes 14–21 days. Spring-sown plants will flower the following summer. Summer-sown plants flower the following spring. In cool climates this plant will need protection at all times of the year.

Felicia *Asteraceae*

A genus of hardy to frost-tender annuals, perennials, evergreens and sub-shrubs. Grown for their blue daisy-like flowers. Plant in well-drained soil in a sunny situation. These plants do not like being over wet, nor do they tolerate cold, wet winters.

Felicia bergeriana (Kingfisher daisy)
Medium seeds: 800 per gram
Hardy annual
Height 15cm (6in)
Small, blue, daisy-like flowers with yellow centres, which close at night and on cloudy days
Flowers in summer and early autumn
Lance-shaped, hairy, green-grey leaves

Sow in early spring in pots or modules using a soil-less seed compost (substrate), either a peat free proprietary brand or composted fine propagating bark. Cover with perlite or vermiculite and place under protection at 20°C (68°F). Germination takes 7–14 days.

Gomphrena *Amaranthaceae*

A genus of half-hardy annuals, biennials and perennials. Plant in well-drained, fertile soil in a sunny situation.

Gomphrena globosa (Globe amaranth)
Medium seeds: 400 per gram
Half-hardy annual
Height 25cm (10in)
Small, clover-like flower heads in pink, purple, white, yellow and orange
Flowers in late summer and early autumn
Good for dried flower arrangements
Hairy, light green, oblong leaves

Sow in early spring in pots or modules using a soil-less seed compost (substrate), either a peat free proprietary brand or composted fine propagating bark. Cover with perlite or vermiculite and place under protection at 18°C (65°F). Germination takes 12–14 days.

Helianthus *Asteraceae*

A genus of annuals and perennials which are grown for their large, daisy-like flowers that follow the sun with their flower heads. Plant in well-drained soil in a sunny position. The tall varieties will need staking in exposed, windy sites.

There are many cultivars of sunflower now available – tall, short, multi-coloured, or even double flowered. The seed count varies according to cultivar, so I have taken an average count and given a general description.

Helianthus annus (Sunflower)
Medium seeds: 30 per gram
Hardy annual
Height 30cm–3m (1ft–10ft)
Lovely, large, yellow flowers with a brown or purplish centre
Flowers in summer
Large, oval, serrated, mid-green leaves

Helianthus annus

Sow in spring into prepared open ground when air temperature does not go below 10°C (50°F) at night. Germination takes 14–21 days.
OR
Sow dwarf varieties, using 2 seeds per 15cm (6in) pot. Use a soil-less seed compost (substrate), either a peat free proprietary brand or composted fine propagating bark. Cover lightly with compost, place under protection at 12°C (55°F). Germination takes 6–12 days.

***Recipe for sowing, planting and growing* Helianthus annus**
Sunflowers are as good as their name, it is wonderful to watch their heads turn to follow the sun. There are many stunning varieties now available, short ones and tall ones, in colours ranging from yellow to orange, red, and brown. All of them can be grown from seed, which is easy to handle. Sunflowers are a great way to introduce children to gardening. Even when the flower is over, the seed head is spectacular and a great favourite with wild birds such as finches and bluetits.

When planting in the garden, choose a sunny site with well-drained soil. If your site is exposed make sure you give the plants some shelter from the prevailing wind, it is also a good idea to stake the tall plants because the flower heads do become very heavy and are liable to snap the stem. They look stunning when planted around the base of a tree or in large clumps against a dark fence.

Ingredients
2 seeds per pot
1 x 15cm (6in) diameter pot
Soil-less seed compost (substrate), either a peat free proprietary brand or composted fine propagating bark
White plastic plant label
OR
Prepare a site in the garden

Method Fill the pot with compost, smooth over, tap down and water well. Sow the seeds by placing them in the pot well apart and not too close to the edge. Press gently into the compost with the flat of the hand. Cover lightly with compost and label with the plant name and date. Place the pot in a warm, light place, out of direct sunlight at an optimum temperature of 12°C (55°F). Keep watering to a minimum until germination has taken place, which takes 6–12 days in spring with warmth. The seedling will be ready to plant out or pot up approximately 2–3 weeks after germination.
OR
Sow directly into a prepared site in the garden when the night time temperature does not fall below 10°C (50°F). Space the seeds 30–45cm (12–18in) apart, gently press into the soil, lightly cover and water in well. Germination takes 14–21 days.

Helichrysum *Asteraceae*

A genus of fully-hardy to frost-tender annuals, perennials and evergreens. Plant in a well-drained soil in a sunny situation.

Helichrysum bracteatum Monstrosum Series (Strawflower, Everlasting daisy)
Small seeds: 1,500 per gram
Half-hardy annual
Height 90cm (3ft)
Papery, double flowers in white, pink, red, orange and yellow which dry very well
Flowers throughout summer until early autumn

Sow in early spring in pots or modules using a soil-less seed compost (substrate), either a peat free proprietary brand or composted fine propagating bark. Cover with perlite or vermiculite and place under protection at 18°C (65°F). Germination takes 14–18 days.
OR
Sow in spring into prepared, open ground when air temperature does not go below 10°C (50°F) at night. Germination takes 21–28 days.

Heliotropium *Boraginaceae*

A genus of hardy to frost-tender annuals and evergreen plants. Plant in well-drained, fertile soil and a sunny position.

Heliotropium arborescens 'Marine' (Heliotrope, Cherry pie)
Small seeds: 1,600 per gram
Half-hardy, evergreen perennial often grown as an annual in cool climates
Height 45cm (18in)
Small, sweet scented, deep violet-blue flowers in dense clusters
Flowers in the summer
Dark green, lance-shaped, slightly wrinkled leaves

Sow in early spring in pots or modules using a soil-less seed compost (substrate), either a peat free proprietary brand or composted fine propagating bark. Cover with perlite or vermiculite and place under protection at 16°C (60°F). Germination takes 14–21 days.

Helipterum *Asteraceae* (now known as **Rhodanthe**)

A genus of half-hardy annuals and perennials. Plant in poor, very well-drained soil in a sunny situation.

Rhodanthe manglesii
Medium seeds: 600 per gram
Half-hardy annual
Height 30cm (12in)
Papery, daisy-like flowers in a variety of colours, red, pink or white
Flowers from late spring until the first frosts
Pointed, oval, grey-green leaves

Rhodanthe chlorocephala subsp. *rosea* (Strawflower)
Medium seeds: 300 per gram
Half-hardy annual
Height 30cm (12in)
Small, pink, papery, daisy-like flowers
Flowers from late spring until the first frosts
Lance-shaped, grey-green leaves
Flowers dry wonderfully for winter arrangements.

Sow in late spring into prepared, open ground when air temperature does not go below 10°C (50°F) at night. Germination takes 14–21 days.
OR
Sow in early spring in pots or modules using a soil-less seed compost (substrate), either a peat free proprietary brand or composted fine propagating bark. Cover with perlite or vermiculite and place under protection at 20°C (68°F). Germination takes 7–14 days.

Hypoestes *Acanthaceae*

A genus of tender, mainly evergreen perennials and shrubs with a minimum growing temperature of 10°C (50°F). In cooler climates they make good pot plants because of their attractive foliage. Plant out in the garden in a well-drained soil and a sunny situation.

Hypoestes phyllostachya 'Pink splash' **(Freckle face, Polka-dot plant)**
Medium seeds: 600 per gram
Height 75cm (30in)
Small tubular, lavender flowers
Flowers in summer
Tender evergreen perennial often grown as an annual in cool climates
Attractive dark green leaves covered with irregular pink blotches

Sow in spring in pots or modules using a soil-less seed compost (substrate) either a peat free proprietary brand or composted fine propagating bark. Cover with perlite or vermiculite, place under protection at 20°C (68°F). Germination takes 7–14 days. With good light conditions this plant can be sown at any time.

Impatiens *Balsaminaceae*

A genus of hardy to tender annuals and evergreen perennials. Plant in soil that is moist but not waterlogged, in sun to partial shade.

Impatiens balsamina **(Balsam)**
Medium seeds: 100 per gram
Half-hardy annual
Height 75cm (30in)
Small, cup-shaped, pink or white flowers
Flowers all summer until the first frosts
Lance-shaped, mid-green leaves

Impatiens Novette Series **(Busy Lizzie, Patience plant)**
Small seeds: 1,000 per gram
Half-hardy evergreen perennial grown as a half-hardy annual
Height 15cm (6in)
Attractive 5-petalled, spurred flowers in red, pink or variegated – white and pink etc
Flowers from summer until the first frosts
Reddish stems with oval, toothed, mid-green leaves

Sow in early spring in pots or modules using a soil-less seed compost (substrate), either a peat free proprietary brand or composted fine propagating bark. Cover with perlite or vermiculite and place under protection at 21°C (70°F). Try to keep the temperature as even as possible. Water with tepid water, not cold water straight from the tap, which would inhibit germination or cause the seedling to wilt. Germination takes 14–21 days.

Isotoma *Campanulaceae*

A genus of tender annuals and perennials. Nearly all of them make lovely pot plants. Plant in a fertile, moisture-retaining soil, not clay or water logged, in a sunny situation. This plant has been classified as *Laurentia* and *Soleonopsis*, but is currently known as *Isotoma*.

Isotoma axillaris 'White' **(Flying angels)**
Small seeds: 6,000 per gram
Half-hardy annual
Height 25cm (10in)
Five-petalled, star-shaped, pure white flowers
Flowers all summer
Small, linear, serrated, mid-green leaves
Looks stunning in tubs, pots and baskets

Sow in early spring or autumn in pots or modules using a soil-less seed compost (substrate), either a peat free proprietary brand or composted fine propagating bark. Cover with perlite or vermiculite and protect at 20°C (68°F). Germination takes 8–14 days. Over-winter young plants sown in autumn in a frost-free environment other than the house.

***Recipe for sowing, planting and growing* Isotoma axillaris**

This plant is a stunner in a container or hanging basket, flowering profusely all summer. The star-shaped flowers come in lovely shades of pink, white, blue and pale mauve. I have seen an old wooden wheelbarrow planted with 3 different shades of flowers which gently cascaded over the edge, it looked wonderful.

Ingredients
10 seeds per module or 15 seeds per pot
1 piece white card 14 x 8.5cm ($5^{1}/_{2}$ x $3^{1}/_{2}$in) folded in half
1 module tray
OR
1 x 8 cm (4 in) pot
Soil-less seed compost (substrate), either a peat free proprietary brand or composted fine propagating bark
Fine-grade perlite (wetted) or vermiculite
White plastic plant label

Method Fill the tray or pot with compost, smooth over, tap down and water in well. As the seeds are very fine, it is worth putting a very small amount of seed into the crease of the folded card. Gently tap the card in order to sow the seed thinly on to the surface of the compost. Cover with perlite or vermiculite and label with the plant name and date. Place the tray or pot in a warm, light place out of direct sunlight at an optimum temperature of 20°C (68°F). Keep watering to a minimum until germination has taken place, which takes 8–14 days. Shortly after germination, and when the seedlings have fully emerged, put the containers in a cooler environment 15°C (59°F). Spring-sown plants can be pricked out and potted up 2–3 weeks after germination. They will be ready to plant out approximately 4 weeks after that. If you are using modules you can plant out direct into a container or hanging basket as soon as they have rooted right down the module. Keep the container or hanging basket protected until all threat of frost has passed, then harden off before leaving out all night. If you wish to plant in the garden, make sure the seedling has a period of hardening off, then plant out when there is no threat of frost. The autumn-sown seedlings should be left in pots or modules to overwinter in a frost-free environment, not centrally heated, somewhere cool and light. Make sure they are not overcrowded or they will wilt. Modules can be potted up, but keep watering to a minimum as over watering will lead to damping off. In the spring these seedlings can be treated in the same way as the spring-sown ones. The advantage of autumn-sown plants is that they will flower earlier and therefore longer, however they do need a little more care.

Lavatera *Malvaceae*

A genus of hardy annuals, biennials and perennials. Plant in well-drained soil and a sunny situation.

Lavatera trimestris Beauty Series (Tree mallow)
Medium seeds: 150 per gram
Hardy annual
Height 60cm (24in)
Shallow, trumpet-shaped flowers in pink, rose, salmon and white
Flowers from early summer until early autumn
Oval, lobed leaves

Sow in late spring into prepared, open ground when air temperature does not go below 10°C (50°F) at night. Germination takes 14–21 days.

Limnanthes *Limnanthaceae*

A genus of fully-hardy annuals. Plant in a fertile, well-drained soil in a sunny position.

Limnanthes douglasii AGM (Meadow foam, Poached-egg flower)
Medium seeds: 130 per gram
Hardy annual
Height 15cm (6in)
Cup-shaped, lightly scented flowers with yellow centres
Flowers from summer until early autumn
Light green, feathery leaves

Sow in late spring into prepared, open ground when air temperature does not go below 10°C (50°F) at night. Germination takes 14–21 days.

Limonium *Plumbaginaceae*

A genus of fully-hardy to frost-tender perennials sometimes grown as annuals. Plant in well draining soil in a sunny situation.

Limonium sinuatum (*Statice sinuata*) (Annual statice)
Medium seeds: 400 per gram
Half-hardy perennial grown as an annual in cool climates
Height 45cm (18in)
Clusters of tiny, papery flowers in blue, pink or white
Flowers from summer to early autumn
Lance-shaped, lobed, deep green leaves
Flowers are good for drying

Limonium platyphyllum (*latifolium*) (Sea lavender)
Medium seeds: 1,000 per gram
Hardy perennial, often grown as an annual
Height 30cm (12in)
Masses of small, blue-mauve clusters of flowers
Flowers throughout the summer
Good for dried flower arrangements
Large, leathery, dark green leaves

Sow in late spring into prepared open ground when air temperature does not go below 10°C (50°F) at night. Germination takes 14–21 days.

Lobelia *Campanulaceae*

A large genus of half-hardy annuals, perennials and sub-shrubs. Plant in a light, free-draining soil with added leaf mould to retain moisture through the summer. Bedding lobelias do not like to dry out or be waterlogged. All lobelias hate being wet in winter in cold climates. As *Lobelia erinus* seeds are minute, pelleted seeds are easier to use. At the time of publication there are no organic pelleted seeds available.

Lobelia erinus compacta
Minute seeds: 25,000 per gram
Half-hardy annual
Height 10cm (4in)
Small, 2-lipped flowers in a range of colours – white, purple pink, blue – often with a white eye
Flowers throughout the summer until the first frosts
Small, mid-green oval or lance-shaped leaves
Ideal for containers, tubs and hanging baskets

Sow in early spring in pots or modules using soil-less seed compost (substrate), either a peat free proprietary brand or composted fine propagating bark. As these are very fine seeds, mix them with the finest sand or talcum powder for an even sowing. Do not cover. Water from the bottom or with a fine spray and place under protection at 20°C (68°F). Germination takes 8–14 days.

Lobelia cardinalis AGM (Cardinal flower)
Tiny seeds: 20,000 per gram
Hardy perennial often grown as a hardy annual
Height 1m (3½ft)
Attractive, 2-lipped scarlet flowers
Flowers from mid- to late summer
Lance-shaped, mid-green or red-bronze leaves
Good for containers and as a summer-flowering border plant

Sow in early spring in pots or modules using soil-less seed compost (substrate), either a peat free proprietary brand or composted fine propagating bark. As the seeds are very fine, mix them with the finest sand or talcum powder for an even sowing. Do not cover. Water from the bottom or with a fine spray, place in a cold frame under protection at 9°C (48°F) at night for 10 days. Then give the seeds heat at 20°C (68°F). Germination takes 8–14 days after heat is applied.

Recipe for sowing, planting and growing **Lobelia cardinalis**

If you want a 'Wow!' factor in the garden, then the Cardinal flower is a must. The flowers are vibrant crimson. It is a great plant for the garden because it likes moist, cool, shady places. It does not mind dry cold in winter, but it hates wet cold. It is happier in Canada than in the UK, where it is grown as an annual. It also makes a stunning feature plant in a container collection. Remember that it likes being moist, so make sure the container does not dry out and position it well out of the midday sun or in partial shade.

Ingredients

10 seeds per module or 15 seeds per pot (as accurately as you can manage)
Talcum powder or fine plain white flour
1 piece white card 14 x 8.5 cm (5½ x 3½in) folded in half
1 module tray

Limnanthes douglasii (planted with geraniums)

Lunaria annua

OR

1 x 8 cm (4in) diameter pot

Soil-less seed compost (substrate), either a peat free proprietary brand or composted fine propagating bark

White plastic plant label

Method Fill the tray or pot with compost, smooth over, tap down and water in well. As the seeds are very fine, it is a good idea to mix them with talcum powder or extra fine white flour, which will show the seeds up. Putting a very small amount of this seed mix into the crease of folded card, you can then gently tap the card, sowing the seed thinly on to the surface of the compost. Do not cover, label with the plant name and date. Place the tray or pot in a cold frame for 10 days, when the temperature does not fall below 9°C (48°F) at night in the frame. Then bring the tray or pot inside and place in a warm light place out of direct sunlight at an optimum temperature of 20°C (68°F). Keep watering to a minimum until germination has taken place and then only water from the bottom or with a fine spray so as not to disturb the fine seeds. Germination takes 8–14 days with warmth. Shortly after germination has taken place, and when the seedlings are fully emerged, put the containers in a cooler environment 15°C (59°F). Prick out when the seedlings are large enough to handle or, if you are using modules, plant directly into a container or the garden after a period of hardening off and when there is no threat of frost.

Lunaria *Brassicaceae*

A genus of hardy biennials and perennials which produce lovely, silvery seed pods. Plant in well-drained soil in partial shade.

Lunaria annua (Honesty)

Medium seeds: 50 per gram

Biennial

Height 75cm (30in)

Scented, 4-petalled, white or purple flowers

Flowers from spring to mid-summer usually in second year

Rounded, silvery seed pods which are lovely for dried flower arrangements

Oval, pointed, serrated, mid-green leaves

Sow the seeds fresh in late summer into prepared, open ground. Do not protect the seed from winter weather as this allows natural stratification to occur (see page 233). The seeds will germinate the following spring and occasionally flower the same year.

OR

Sow fresh seed in autumn in pots using a standard, soil-less seed compost (substrate). Cover lightly with the compost and place in a cold frame. Germination will take place the following spring.

Matthiola *Brassicaceae*

A genus of hardy to frost-tender annuals, biennials, perennials and evergreen sub-shrubs. Plant in fertile well-drained soil, (prefers lime) in a sun or partial shade.

Matthiola incana (Stock, Brompton stock)

Medium seeds: 600 per gram

Biennial or short-lived perennial

Height 30–60cm (1–2ft)

Highly scented 4-petalled spikes of pink, apricot, cream or lilac flowers

Flowers throughout the summer

Lance-shaped, grey-green leaves

Sow in late spring into a prepared open ground when air temperature does not go below 10°C (50°F) at night. Germination takes 14–21 days.

OR

Sow in early spring in pots or modules using soil-less seed compost (substrate), either a peat free proprietary brand or composted fine propagating bark. Cover with perlite or vermiculite and place under protection at 18°C (65°F). Germination takes 8–14 days.

Mimulus *Scrophulariaceae*

A genus of fully- to half-hardy annuals, perennials and evergreen shrubs. Plant in a moist to wet soil in a sunny situation.

Mimulus luteus (Monkey flower, Monkey musk)

Tiny seeds: 20,000 per gram

Half-hardy perennial often grown as an annual

Height 30cm (12in)

Yellow, snapdragon-shaped flowers

Flowers throughout the summer

Oval, toothed, hairy, mid-green leaves

Mimulus 'Tigrinus'

Minute seeds: 23,000 per gram

Half-hardy annual

Height 20cm (8in)

Lovely, yellow flowers splashed with red

Flowers throughout the summer

Oval, toothed, mid-green leaves

Sow in early spring in pots or modules using soil-less seed compost (substrate), either a peat free proprietary brand or composted fine propagating bark. Cover with perlite or vermiculite, place under protection at 18°C (65°F). Germination takes 14–21 days.

Mirabilis *Nyctaginaceae*

A genus of half-hardy annuals and perennials. Plant in a well-drained soil and a sheltered position in full sun.

Mirabilis jalapa (Four o'clock flower, Marvel of Peru)

Large seeds: 10 per gram

Tender perennial often grown as an annual in cooler climates

Height 60cm–1.2m (2–4 ft)

Fragrant trumpets of crimson, pink, white or yellow flowers which open in the evening (after 4 o'clock)

Flowers in summer

Mid-green, oval, tipped leaves

Sow in early spring in pots or modules using soil-less seed compost (substrate), either a peat free proprietary brand or composted fine propagating bark. Cover with perlite or vermiculite, place under protection at 18°C (65°F). Germination takes 14–21 days.

Moluccella *Lamiaceae*

A genus of half-hardy annuals and perennials. Plant in a rich, very well-drained soil in a sunny situation.

Moluccella laevis (Bells of Ireland, Shell flower)
Medium seeds: 150 per gram
Height 60cm (2ft)
Spikes of small, tubular, white flowers surrounded by pale green calyces
Flowers all summer
Round, pale green leaves

Sow the seeds fresh in late summer into prepared, open ground. Do not protect the seed from winter weathers, as this will allow natural stratification to occur (see page 233). Germination will take place the following spring. It occasionally flowers in the same year.
OR
Sow fresh seed in autumn in pots or modules using a standard soil-less seed compost (substrate), either a peat free proprietary brand or composted fine propagating bark. Cover lightly with compost and place in a cold frame. Germination will take place the following spring.

Myosotis *Boraginaceae*

A genus of hardy annuals, biennials and perennials all grown for their pretty flowers. Plant in fertile, well-drained soil in sun or semi-shade.

Myosotis arvensis (Field forget-me-not)
Medium seeds: 1,000 per gram
Hardy annual
Height 15–40cm (6–20in)
Small, bright blue flowers with creamy yellow eyes
Flowers in summer
Lance-shaped, hairy, mid-green leaves

Myosotis alpestris (Alpine forget-me-not)
Small seeds: 1,500 per gram
Hardy biennial
Height 10–15cm (4–6in)
Clusters of bright blue flowers with creamy yellow eyes
Will flower in the first year, but a better show will appear in the second
Flowers from late spring until early summer
Lance-shaped, hairy, mid-green leaves

Sow fresh seed in autumn in pots or modules using a standard, soil-less seed compost (substrate), either a peat free proprietary brand or composted fine propagating bark. Cover lightly with the compost and place in a cold frame. Germination will take place the following spring. Prefers a gritty soil when planted out.

Nemesia *Scrophulariaceae*

A genus of half-hardy annuals, perennials and evergreen sub-shrubs often grown in cooler climates as greenhouse or conservatory plants. Plant in a well-drained, fertile soil in a sunny situation.

Nemesia strumosa
Small seeds: 5,000 per gram
Half-hardy annual
Height 20–45cm (8–18in)
Trumpet-shaped flowers in yellow, red, orange, white or purple
Flowers in summer
New hybrids can have bi-coloured flowers
Pale green, serrated leaves

Sow in early to late spring in pots or modules using a standard, soil-less seed compost (substrate), either a peat free proprietary brand or composted fine propagating bark. Cover with perlite or vermiculite. Place under protection at 15°C (59°F). Germination takes 14–21 days. Do not be tempted to sow at high temperatures as this can inhibit germination, as do fluctuating temperatures.
OR
Sow in late spring into a prepared, moisture-retentive soil when air temperature does not go below 10°C (50°F) at night. Germination takes 21–28 days. Cut back to 4–5cm (1 1/2–2in) after first flowering to get a second flush.

Nemophila *Hydrophyllaceae*

A genus of fully-hardy annuals. Plant in a fertile, well-drained soil in sun or semi-shade.

Nemophila maculata (Five-spot baby)
Small seeds: 3,000 per gram
Hardy annual
Height 15cm (6in)
Small, bowl-shaped, white flowers with purple-tipped petals
Flowers in summer
Mid-green, lobed leaves

Nemophila menziesii (Baby blue-eyes)
Medium seeds: 550 per gram
Hardy annual
Height 20cm (8in)
Sky blue, bowl-shaped flowers with white centres
Flowers throughout summer
Feathery, mid-green leaves

Sow in late spring into a prepared site when air temperature does not go below 10°C (50°F) at night. Germination takes 14–21 days.

Nicotiana *Solanaceae*

A genus of hardy to frost-tender annuals and perennials. Plant in a fertile, well-drained soil in a sunny situation.

Nicotiana sylvestris AGM (Tobacco plant)
Minute seeds: 29,000 per gram
Half-hardy perennial often grown as an annual
Height 1.5m (5ft)
Evening-scented, tubular, white flowers
Flowers in late summer
Oval, long, rough, mid-green leaves

Sow in late spring into a prepared site, when air temperature does not go below 10°C (50°F) at night. Germination takes 14–21 days.
OR
Sow in early spring in pots or modules using a standard, soil-less seed compost (substrate), either a peat free proprietary brand or composted fine propagating bark. Cover with perlite or vermiculite and place under protection at 21°C (70°F). Germination takes 7–14 days, but can be erratic – the seedlings can start germinating on day 5 and trickle on to day 28 or even longer. Prick plants out as soon as they are large enough to handle, leaving the pot/tray to see if other seedlings appear.

Nierembergia *Solanaceae*

A genus of frost to half-hardy perennials, often grown as annuals in cooler climates, and semi-evergreen sub-shrubs. Plant in a moist but well draining soil in a sunny situation.

Nierembergia linariifolia AGM **(Cup flower)**
Small seeds: 6,000 per gram
Half-hardy perennial, grown as an annual in cooler climates
Height 15–30cm (6–12in)
Gorgeous, blue, funnel-shaped flowers
Flowers all summer
Narrow, lance-shaped, mid-green leaves

Sow in spring in pots or modules using a standard, soil-less seed compost (substrate), either a peat free proprietary brand or composted fine propagating bark. Cover with perlite or vermiculite. Place under protection, no extra heat needed. Germination takes 14–21 days.

Nigella *Ranunculaceae*

A genus of hardy and half-hardy annuals grown for their attractive flowers and seed heads. Plant in a well draining soil in a sunny situation.

Nigella damascena **(Persian Jewels, Love-in-a-mist)**
Hardy annual
Medium seeds: 400 per gram
Height 60cm (2ft)
Many petalled, spurred, blue or white flowers
Flowers all summer
Feathery, bright green leaves.

Sow the seeds fresh in late summer into a prepared, open ground. Do not cover the seed or protect it from winter weather as this will allow natural stratification to occur (see page 233). Germination takes place the following spring. This plant does not transplant well, so sow where you want it to flower. Flowers are followed by inflated, rounded, attractive seed pods. Seed heads are good for drying and using in autumn flower arrangements

Nolana *Nolanaceae*

A genus of frost-hardy annuals. Plant in well-drained, poor or gritty soil in full sun.

Nolana paradoxa (atriplicifolia, grandiflora)
Medium seeds: 170 per gram
Hardy annual
Height 8cm (3in)
Funnel-shaped, purple-blue flowers with a white ring above a yellow throat
Flowers all summer
Small, oval, mid-green leaves

Sow in early spring in pots or modules using a standard, soil-less seed compost (substrate), either a peat free proprietary brand or composted fine propagating bark. Cover with perlite or vermiculite, place under protection at 20°C (68°F). Germination takes 7–10 days. Good for hanging baskets, tubs or window boxes that sit in the blazing sun.

Onopordum *Asteraceae*

A genus of hardy annuals, biennials and perennials. Plant in a rich, well-drained soil in sun or semi-shade.

Onopordum acanthium **(Cotton thistle, Scotch thistle)**
Medium seeds: 70 per gram
Hardy biennial
Height 1.8m (6ft)
Pink-purple flower heads
Flowers in summer
Large, spiny, lobed, silver-grey leaves

Sow the seeds fresh in late summer into a prepared, open ground. Do not cover the seed or protect it from winter weathers as this allows natural stratification to take place (see page 233). Germination takes place the following spring. After flowering, remove seed heads if you do not want a garden full of thistles. Collect some seed for sowing the following year.

Osteospermum *Asteraceae*

A genus of hardy to tender annuals, perennials and evergreens. Thrives best in warm climates. Plant in a fertile soil and a sunny, sheltered position.

Osteospermum hyoseroides 'Passion' **(African daisy)**
Medium seeds: 100 per gram
Half-hardy annual
Height 30cm (12in)
Highly decorative, daisy-shaped flowers of pink, rose, purple and white with blue centres
Flowers all summer
Lance-shaped, grey-green leaves
Excellent for borders and containers

Sow in early spring in pots or modules using a standard, soil-less seed compost (substrate), either a peat free proprietary brand or composted fine propagating bark. Cover with perlite or vermiculite and place under protection at 18°C (65°F). Germination takes 14–21 days.

Papaver somniferum

Papaver *Papaveraceae*

A genus of hardy annuals, biennials and perennials. A stunning variety is *Papaver somniferum* 'Peony-flowered mixed'. Double varieties are available in single and mixed colours. Plant in a moist but well-drained soil in sun or partial shade.

Papaver somniferum (Opium poppy)
Small seeds: 3,000 per gram
Hardy annual
Height 75cm (30in)
Large, single flowers in shades of red, pink or purple with darker centres
Flowers in summer
Oblong, grey-green, lobed leaves

Papaver nudicaule 'Meadow Pastels' (Iceland poppy, Arctic poppy)
Small seeds: 4,000 per gram
Hardy perennial, often grown as an annual, especially in warmer climates
Fragrant flowers in white, yellow or orange
Flowers in summer
Soft, green, oval, toothed leaves

Sow fresh seeds in late summer into prepared, open ground. Do not cover. Germination will take place the following spring.

OR

Sow the seeds in spring into prepared, open ground when the air temperature does not go below 9°C (48°F) at night. Do not cover the seed. Germination takes 2–4 weeks.

Petunia *Solanaceae*

Half-hardy perennials usually grown as annuals. Plant in a fertile well-drained soil in a sunny sheltered position.

Petunia x *hybrida* 'Grandiflora'
Small seeds: 9,000 per gram
Half-hardy perennial
Height 15–30cm (6–12in)
Flared, trumpet-shaped flowers in many colours
Rose, crimson, blue, cream or white coloured flowers, which can be mixed or striped
Flowers throughout summer until the first frosts
Oval, mid-green leaves

Petunia x *hybrida* 'Multiflora'
Small seeds: 8,000 per gram
Half-hardy perennial grown as an annual
Height 15–30cm (6–12in)
Flared, trumpet-shaped flowers, smaller than 'Grandiflora'
Flowers are often double frilled
Available in many colours
Flowers throughout the summer until the first frosts
Oval, mid-green leaves

Sow in early spring in pots or modules using a standard, soil-less seed compost (substrate), either a peat free proprietary brand or composted fine propagating bark. Cover with perlite or vermiculite and place under protection at 21°C (70°F). Germination takes 7–10 days.

Phacelia *Hydrophyllaceae*

A genus of hardy annuals, biennials and perennials, good for the front of borders or in containers. Plant in a fertile, well-drained soil in a sunny situation.

Phacelia campanularia (California bluebell)
Medium seeds: 1,000 per gram
Hardy annual
Height 20cm (8in)
Bell-shaped, gentian-blue flowers
Flowers throughout the summer until the first frosts
Oval, serrated, mid-green leaves

Sow fresh seeds in autumn into a prepared open ground. Do not cover the seed. Germination will take place the following spring.
OR
Sow the seeds in spring into a prepared open ground, when air temperature does not go below 9°C (48°F) at night. Do not cover the seed. Germination takes 2–4 weeks.

Phlox *Polemoniaceae*

A genus of fully- to half-hardy annuals, perennials and evergreens. Plant in a fertile, moist, not waterlogged soil in sun or semi-shade.

Phlox drummondii Twinkle Series
Medium seeds: 500 per gram
Half-hardy annual
Height 15cm (6in)
Star-shaped flowers in many shades of bright colours some with contrasting centres
Flowers all summer
Pale green, lance-shaped leaves

Sow the seeds in spring into a prepared, open ground when air temperature does not go below 9°C (48°F) at night. Do not cover the seed. Germination takes 2–4 weeks.
OR
Sow in early spring in pots or modules using a standard soil-less seed compost (substrate), either a peat free proprietary brand or composted fine propagating bark. Do not cover. Place under protection at 16°C (60°F). Germination takes 10–20 days. Phlox does not perform well if transplanted from a seed tray so use modules and pots.

Recipe for sowing, planting and growing* Phlox drummondii *Twinkle Series

This is a very popular dwarf bedding annual which produces a profusion of lovely starry flowers in a mixture of colours – pinks, purples, reds – with contrasting centres. For example, pale pink can have a darker pink centre or purple can have white edges and white centres. You could describe these flowers as paint splodges from on high. They look great in the front of the border or in containers and hanging baskets.

Ingredients

4 seeds per module or 8 seeds per pot
1 module tray
OR
1 x 8cm (4in) pot
Soil-less seed compost (substrate), either a peat free proprietary brand or composted fine propagating bark
White plastic plant label

Method Fill the tray or pot with compost, smooth over, tap down and water in well. Sow thinly into the container, spacing the seeds well. Press gently into the compost with the flat of the hand. Do not cover, label with the plant name and date. Place the tray or pot into a warm, light place out of direct sunlight at an optimum temperature of 16°C (60°F). Keep watering to a minimum until germination has taken place, which takes 10–20 days in spring with warmth. Pot up or prick out approximately 4 weeks later. If you are using modules, you can plant directly into containers. Wait to plant out in the garden until the young plants have had a period of hardening off and there is no threat of frost.
OR
Sow directly into a prepared site in the garden when the night time temperature does not fall below 9°C (48°F) at night. Space the seeds 10cm (4in) apart, gently press into the soil, do not cover, water in well. If you are plagued by birds or mice it may be worth covering with agricultural fleece to stop your seeds being stolen. Germination takes 14–28 days. Remove the cover as soon as you see that they have germinated.

Portulaca *Portulacaceae*

A genus of half-hardy annuals and perennials with succulent leaves and flowers that open in the sun and close in the shade.

Portulaca grandiflora (Moss rose, Sun plant)
Small seeds: 9,000 per gram
Half-hardy annual
Height 15–20cm (6–8in)
Bowl-shaped flowers in shades of yellow, pink, red and white with conspicuous stamens
Flowers in summer and early autumn
Bright green, lance-shaped, succulent leaves

Sow in early spring in pots or modules using a standard, soil-less seed compost (substrate), either a peat free proprietary brand or composted fine propagating bark. Cover with perlite or vermiculite, place under protection at 20°C (68°F). Germination takes 10–14 days.

Ricinus *Euphorbiaceae*

A genus of a single species, a half-hardy perennial grown as an annual in cooler climates. Plant in a humus-rich, well-drained soil in a sheltered sunny position.

Ricinus communis 'Gibsonii' (Castor oil plant, Palma-christi, Castor bean)
ALL PARTS OF THIS PLANT ARE POISONOUS
Large seeds: 2 per gram
Half-hardy perennial
Height 120cm (4ft)
Green, petal-free, female flowers are followed by red capsules each containing 3 seeds
Flowers in summer
Dark green stems with large, lobed, toothed, bronze leaves

Sow in early spring in pots or modules using a standard, soil-less seed compost (substrate), either a peat free proprietary brand or composted fine propagating bark. Cover with perlite or vermiculite, place under protection at 21°C (70°F). Germination takes 14–21 days.

Rudbeckia *Asteraceae*

A genus of hardy annuals, biennials and perennials. Plant in a moist but well-drained soil in sun or partial shade.

Rudbeckia hirta 'Rustic Dwarfs' (Coneflower)
Small seeds: 2000 per gram
Short-lived perennial grown as a hardy annual
Height 30cm–1m (1–3½ft)
Large, daisy-like flowers, yellow, mahogany or bronze with dark centres
Flowers all summer until the first frosts
Mid-green, lance-shaped leaves

Sow in early spring in pots or modules using a standard, soil-less seed compost (substrate), either a peat free proprietary brand or composted fine propagating bark. Cover with perlite or vermiculite and place under protection at 18°C (65°F). Germination takes 10–14 days.

Salpiglossis *Solanaceae*

Half-hardy annuals and biennials. Plant in a rich, well-drained soil in a sunny situation. Flower stems may need support in exposed sites.

Salpiglossis sinuata Bolero Series 'Painted tongue'
Small seeds: 4,000 per gram
Half-hardy annual
Height 60cm (2ft)
Trumpet shaped, veined flowers in a mixture of colours, yellow, orange, red, blue
Flowers all summer until the first frosts
Pale green, lance-shaped leaves

Sow in early spring in pots or modules using a standard, soil-less seed compost (substrate), either a peat free proprietary brand or composted fine propagating bark. Cover the seed with black plastic, check regularly, remove as soon as germination starts. Place under protection at 18°C (65°F). Germination takes 10–14 days.

Salvia *Lamiaceae*

see also PERENNIALS and HERBS. A large genus of hardy to half-hardy annuals, biennials, perennials and evergreen shrubs. Plant in well-drained, fertile soil in a sunny situation.

Salvia splendens 'Blaze of Fire'
Medium seeds: 300 per gram
Half-hardy perennials often grown as an annual
Height 30cm (12in)
Dense spikes of brilliant, scarlet, 2-lipped flowers
Flowers all summer until the first frosts
Bright green, oval, serrated leaves

Sow in early spring in pots or modules using a standard, soil-less seed compost (substrate), either a peat free proprietary brand or composted fine propagating bark. Cover with perlite or vermiculite, place under protection at 18°C (65°F). Germination takes 14–21 days.

Sanvitalia *Asteraceae*

A genus of hardy perennials and annuals. Plant in a fertile, well-drained soil in a sunny situation.

Sanvitalia procumbens 'Gold Braid' (Creeping zinnia)
Small seeds: 1,600 per gram
Hardy annual
Height 15cm (6in)
Daisy-like yellow flowers with black centres
Flowers all summer
Mid-green, oval, pointed leaves

Sow in early spring in pots or modules using a standard, soil-less seed compost (substrate), either a peat free proprietary brand or composted fine propagating bark. Cover with perlite or vermiculite and place under protection at 15°C (59°F). Germination takes 14–21 days.

Ricinus communis

Schizanthus *Solanaceae*

A genus of half-hardy to frost-tender annuals, all of which have showy flowers. Plant in a fertile, well-drained soil in a sunny, sheltered position.

Schizanthus Pansy-flowered Series **(Butterfly plant, Poor man's orchid)**
Small seeds: 1,600 per gram
Half-hardy annuals
Height 60cm–1m (2–3½ft)
Large, pansy-like, bi-coloured flowers with attractive throat markings
Flowers all summer until the first frosts
Feathery, bright green leaves

Sow in early spring in pots or modules using a standard, soil-less seed compost (substrate), either a peat free proprietary brand or composted fine propagating bark. Cover with perlite or vermiculite and place under protection at 18°C (65°F). Germination takes 14–21 days.

Senecio *Asteraceae*

A genus of fully- to frost-tender annuals, succulents and non-succulent perennials and evergreens. Plant in a well-drained soil in a sunny situation.

Senecio cineraria 'Silver Dust' AGM *(Cineraria maritima)*
Small seeds: 2,000 per gram
Half-hardy evergreen often grown as a half-hardy annual
Height 30cm (12in)
Small daisy-like yellow flowers
Flowers in summer
Very attractive deeply lobed, serrated silver leaves

Sow in early spring in pots or modules, using a standard soil-less seed compost (substrate), either a peat free proprietary brand or composted fine propagating bark. Cover with perlite or vermiculite and place under protection at 18°C (65°F). Germination takes 14–21 days.

Spraguea *Portulacaceae*

An American, single species genus, half-hardy perennial which is often grown as a half-hardy annual. Plant in well draining soil in a sunny situation. This plant suits containers and pots. Put a collar of sharp grit around the plants to protect from rain splashings.

Spragueaz 'Powder Puff'
Medium seeds: 1,000 per gram
Half-hardy perennial often grown as a half-hardy annual
Height 10cm (8in)
Pretty, small, powder-pink, fluffy flowers
Flowers from summer until autumn
Lance-shaped, silver foliage

Sow in early spring in pots or modules using a standard, soil-less seed compost (substrate), either a peat free proprietary brand or composted fine propagating bark. Cover with perlite or vermiculite and place under protection at 20°C (68°F). Germination takes 14–21 days.

Tagetes *Asteraceae*

A genus of half-hardy annuals. Plant in a well-drained, fertile soil and a sunny situation. This is an excellent companion plant.

Tagetes minuta **(Mexican Marigold)**
Small seeds: 1,900 per gram
Half-hardy annual
Height up to 1.2m (4ft)
Clusters of single, yellow flowers
Flowers all summer
Deeply divided, aromatic, mid-green leaves

Tagetes patula **(French marigold)**
Medium seeds: 300 per gram
Height 30cm (12in)
Single or double flowers in yellow, orange red or mahogany
Flowers all summer
Deeply divided, aromatic, dark green leaves

Sow in early spring in pots or modules using a standard, soil-less seed compost (substrate), either a peat free proprietary brand or composted fine propagating bark. Cover with perlite or vermiculite. Place under protection at 20°C (68°F). Germination takes 14–21 days.

Tithonia *Asteraceae*

A genus of hardy to tender annuals. Plant in a fertile, well-drained soil in a sunny situation.

Tithonia rotundifolia 'Torch' **(Mexican sunflower)**
Medium seeds: 50 per gram
Half-hardy annual
Height 90cm (3ft)
Brilliant, scarlet-orange, daisy-shaped flowers
Flowers all summer
Oval, lobed, mid-green leaves

Sow in early spring in pots or modules using a standard, soil-less seed compost (substrate), either a peat free proprietary brand or composted fine propagating bark. Cover with perlite or vermiculite and place under protection at 20°C (68°F). Germination takes 10–14 days. Flowers may need support in exposed sites.

Tropaeolum *Tropaeolaceae*

A genus of hardy to frost-tender annuals, perennials and climbers with lovely flowers. Plant in a well-drained soil and a sunny position.

Tropaeolum majus 'Empress of India' **(Nasturtium)**
Large seeds: 8 per gram
Annual
Height 20cm (8in)
Dark red, trumpet-shaped flowers
Flowers from early summer until early autumn
Dark green, rounded leaves

Sow in pots in early spring using a standard, soil-less seed compost (substrate), either a peat free proprietary brand or composted fine propagating bark. Press seeds into the compost, cover gently and place under protection, no added heat needed. Germination takes 10–20 days.

OR

Sow the seeds in spring into prepared, open ground when air temperature does not go below 9°C (48°F) at night. Germination takes 14–21 days.

Verbascum *Scrophulariaceae*

A genus of hardy biennials, perennials, evergreens and shrubs. Plant in a well-drained soil in sun to partial shade.

Verbascum bombyciferum 'Arctic summer'
Small seeds: 7,000 per gram
Hardy biennial
Height 1.2–2m (4–6 ft)
Thick, upright clusters of yellow flowers displayed in upright racemes
Flowers in summer
Silver hairs cover the stems and oval leaves

Verbascum thapsus (Great mullein)
Tiny seeds: 13,500 per gram
Hardy biennial
Height 30cm–2m (1–6ft)
Tall spikes of densely packed, yellow flowers in second year
Flowers in second summer
Large, downy, grey-green leaves

Sow fresh seeds in autumn into a prepared open ground. As these are very fine seeds, mix them with the finest sand for an even sowing. Do not cover. Water with a fine spray. Germination will take place the following spring, but can be erratic.

OR

Sow in early spring in pots or modules using a standard soil-less seed compost (substrate), either a peat free proprietary brand or composted fine propagating bark. As these are very fine seeds, mix them with the finest sand or talcum powder for an even sowing. Do not cover. Water from the bottom or with a fine spray. Place under protection with no added heat. Germination takes 14–21 days. This method suits *Verbascum bombyciferum*.

Verbena *Verbenaceae*

A genus of hardy to frost-tender biennials and perennials. Plant in a well-drained soil and a sunny situation.

Verbena x *hybrida* 'Peaches and Cream'
Medium seeds: 400 per gram
Half-hardy perennial grown as an annual
Height 30cm (12in)
Clusters of small, tubular flowers in pastel shades from apricot to orange
Flowers all summer
Mid-green, lobed leaves

Sow in early spring in pots or modules using a standard soil-less seed compost (substrate) either a peat free proprietary brand or composted fine propagating bark. Place under protection at 20°C (68°F). Cover the pots or modules with black plastic, check from day 8 to see if germination has started. Remove plastic as soon as it has and proceed as normal. Germination takes 10–14 days.

Recipe for sowing, planting and growing Verbena x hybrida 'Peaches and Cream'

This verbena is renowned, it has an abundance of lovely flowers throughout summer and autumn. The flowers start off as a shade of coral, then turn from peachy to creamy, then orange and yellow, resulting in an ever-changing palette of pastel shades. A lovely bedding plant or an even more stunning container plant. The best place of all is a hanging basket planted up simply with this one plant. A stunner.

Ingredients
4 seeds per module or 8 seeds per pot
1 module tray
OR
1 x 8 cm (4 in) pot
Soil-less seed compost (substrate), either a peat free proprietary brand or composted fine propagating bark
Black plastic large enough to cover tray or pot and not let the light in
White plastic plant label

Method Fill the tray or pot with compost, smooth over, tap down and water in well. Sow thinly into the container, spacing the seeds apart. Press gently into the compost with the flat of the hand. Cover with black plastic and label with the plant name and date. Place the tray or pot in a warm, light place out of direct sunlight at an optimum temperature of 20°C (68°F). Lift the black plastic from day 8 and check for germination. If the seeds are starting to chit, (break their shells) return cover, check again the next day, repeat this process until you see the first speck of green. When you see this, remove the black cover and keep the tray or pot warm. Keep watering to a minimum until germination has taken place, which takes 10–14 days in spring with warmth. Shortly after germination, when the seedlings are fully emerged, put the containers in a cooler environment 15°C (59°F). Pot up or prick out approximately 4 weeks later. If you are using modules, you can plant direct into containers. Wait to plant out into the garden until the young plants have had a period of hardening off and there is no threat of frost.

Zinnia *Asteraceae*

A genus of hardy and half-hardy annuals which have dahlia-like flowers. Plant in a well-drained fertile soil in a sunny position.

Zinnia elegans 'Giant Dahlia Series' (Traditional garden zinnia)
Medium seeds: 100 per gram
Hardy annual
Height 60–75cm (24–30in)
Large purple flower heads very like dahlias
Flowers all summer
Pale green oval or lance-shaped leaves

Sow in early spring in pots or modules using a standard soil-less seed compost (substrate) either a peat free proprietary brand or composted fine propagating bark. Cover with perlite or vermiculite, place under protection at 18°C (65°F). Germination 7–14 days.

aquatic plants

Water is wonderful in a garden. There is nothing more beautiful than the sun dancing over the water, and the plants growing in or beside it reflected in the shimmering mirror. Even a small pond will give you great pleasure and will attract lots of wildlife to your garden. Unlike any other plants in this book, water plants must be kept moist at all times during germination. Approximate seed sizes only are given in this chapter as more specific information is not easily available. Refer to page 242 for more information on seed sizes.

Gunnera manicata, see page 62

Alisma *Alismataceae*

A genus of hardy deciduous perennial marginal water plants. Plant in muddy, wet soil or in water up to 20cm (8in) deep in a sunny position.

Alisma plantago aquatica (Water plantain)
Small seeds
Hardy deciduous perennial
Height up to 50cm (30in)
Loose clusters of small pale pink/white flowers
Flowers in summer
Oval bright green leaves

Sow seeds in autumn into pots using standard loam-based seed compost (substrate) mixed with coarse grit to a ratio of 1 part compost + 1 part grit. Cover with coarse horticultural sand and stand in water so that the compost remains wet. Place outside, exposed to all weathers (See 'Breaking Seed Dormancy', page 233, for more information.) Germination takes 4–6 months. Overwinter young plants in a cold frame and keep damp.

Caltha *Ranunculaceae*

A genus of hardy, deciduous, perennial, marginal water plants, bog plants or alpine plants, grown for their attractive flowers. Plant in a moist soil in a sunny position.

Caltha palustris AGM (Kingcup, Marsh marigold)
Small seeds
Hardy deciduous perennial
Height 60cm (24in)
Clusters of cup-shaped bright golden-yellow flowers
Flowers in spring
Rounded dark green leaves

Sow seeds in late summer into pots or modules, using standard soil-less seed compost (substrate), either a peat free proprietary brand or composted fine propagating bark. Cover with coarse horticultural sand. Place under protection at 10°C (50°F). During germination use a hand spray to keep the compost moist. Germination takes 4–6 weeks. Overwinter young plants in a cold frame, keep damp.

Gunnera *Gunneraceae*

A genus of hardy perennials which generally have very large leaves. Plant in poor, moist soil in a sheltered, sunny position.

Gunnera manicata AGM
Medium seeds
Hardy perennial
Height 2m (6ft)
Light green flower spikes followed by orange brown seed pods
Flowers in early summer
Very large, rounded serrated green leaves

Sow fresh seeds in late summer, as soon as they are ripe, into pots or modules using standard soil-less seed compost (substrate), either a peat free proprietary brand or composted fine propagating bark. Cover with coarse horticultural sand. Place under protection at 21°C (70°F), using a hand spray to keep the compost moist but not wet. Germination takes 4–6 weeks. Overwinter young plants in a cold frame; keep damp.

Hottonia *Primulaceae*

A genus of hardy, deciduous, perennial submerged water plants. Plant in still or running water in a sunny situation.

Hottonia palustris (Water violet)
Medium seeds
Hardy perennial
Height 30cm (12in)
Delicate pale mauve flowers with a yellow throat
Flowers in summer
Finely-divided mid-green leaves

Sow fresh seeds in late summer using standard soil-less seed compost (substrate), either a peat free proprietary brand or composted fine propagating bark. Cover with coarse horticultural sand. When you have sown the seed, stand the pots in water so the compost remains wet at all times. Place under protection at 15°C (60°F). Germination takes 4–6 weeks. Overwinter young plants in a cold frame and keep damp.

Recipe for sowing, planting and growing **Hottonia palustris**
This is a lovely and elegant flower that should have a place in every pond. It is not a violet, as its common name suggests, it is a member of the primrose family, and as such is the only one to grow in water.

Ingredients
10 seeds per pot
1 x 8cm (4in) pot
Standard soil-less seed compost (substrate), either a peat free proprietary brand or composted fine propagating bark
White plastic plant label
Container without drainage holes, large enough to hold the pot

Method In spring fill the pot with compost, smooth over, tap down and water in well. Sow the fresh seeds thinly on to the surface of the compost. Press gently in with the flat of the hand. Cover thinly with compost, and label with the name and date. Place pot into the container, fill the container with water to just below the rim of the pot and place in a warm light place out of direct sunlight, at an optimum temperature of 15°C (60°F). Germination will take anything from 2–6 weeks. Once germinated, remove from the heat, keep the two containers together and place in a warm light place to allow the seedlings to grow on. When large enough to handle, pot up into soil-less potting compost (substrate). Place the new pots into containers holding water. Grow on in a cold frame for the first winter, and plant into the pond the following spring.

Hydrocharis *Hydrocharitaceae*

A genus with a single, hardy species. Plant in still water in a sunny position.

Hydrocharis morsus-ranae (Frogbit)
Small seeds
Hardy deciduous perennial
Height 10cm (4in)
Small white flowers with a yellow eye
Flowers in summer
Rosettes of kidney-shaped olive green leaves

Caltha palustris

Gunnera manicata

Sow seeds in late summer into pots, using standard soil-less seed compost (substrate), either a peat free proprietary brand or composted fine propagating bark. Cover with coarse horticultural sand. When you have sown the seed, stand the pots in water so that the compost remains wet at all times. Place under protection at 10°C (50°F). Germination takes 4–6 weeks. Overwinter young plants in a cold frame.

Menyanthes *Menyanthaceae*

A genus of hardy perennial deciduous marginal water plants. Plant in a moist soil in a sunny position.

Menyanthes trifoliata (Bog Bean)
Small seeds
Height up to 30cm (12in)
Hardy perennial
Lovely pink buds which, when open, are attractive white stars
Flowers in spring
Oval green leaves

Sow seeds in spring into pots using standard soil-less seed compost (substrate), either a peat free proprietary brand or composted fine propagating bark. Press the seeds well into wet compost, do not cover. Stand the pots in water so the compost remains wet at all times. Place the container in a cold frame or cold greenhouse. Germination takes 4–6 weeks. Grow on in a cold frame for the first winter, plant into the pond the following spring.

Nymphaea *Nymphaeaceae*

A genus of tender 10°C (50°F) to fully hardy perennial water plants grown for their lovely flowers. Plant in still water in a sunny position.

Nymphaea alba (Waterlily)
Small seeds
Hardy deciduous perennial
Height 10cm (4in)
Lovely, star-shaped, semi-double, white flowers with golden centres
Flowers in summer
Round dark green floating leaves

Waterlily seeds germinate under water. In summer, get into the pond and select some fading flowers. Wrap muslin around the flower head. When the flower has gone and the seed pod has sunk below the surface of the water it is time to pick it. Remember, the pods explode when they are ripe.

Sow seeds in spring into pots using standard soil-less seed compost (substrate), either a peat free proprietary brand or composted fine propagating bark. Push the seeds well into the compost and submerge in water. Place the container in a cold frame or a cold greenhouse. Germination takes 4–6 weeks. When large enough, plant back in the pond.

Ranunculus *Ranunculaceae*

A genus of half-hardy to hardy annuals, perennials and aquatics, some of which are evergreen. Plant in any soil that does not dry out in summer, in sun or partial shade.

Ranunculus aquatilis (Water buttercup, Water-crowfoot)
Small seeds
Hardy perennial
Height 30cm (12in)
Lovely small white cupped flowers
Flowers in summer
Small mid-green wedge-shaped leaves that can be very divided

Sow seeds in autumn into pots using standard soil-less seed compost (substrate), either a peat free proprietary brand or composted fine propagating bark. Press the seeds well into wet compost, do not cover. Stand the pots in water so the compost remains wet at all times. Place the container in a cold frame or cold greenhouse. Germination takes 4–6 weeks. Overwinter in the cold frame, keep moist at all times, plant out in the spring.

Rodgersia *Saxifragaceae*

A genus of hardy rhizomatous perennials. Plant in a moist soil in sun or partial shade.

Rodgersia aesculifolia AGM
Small seeds
Hardy perennial
Height 1m (3½ft)
Clusters of fragrant pinky white flowers
Flowers in summer
Bronze crinkled lobed foliage, rather like the horse chestnut
Ideal for growing around ponds or in a bog garden

Sow seeds in spring into pots using standard loam-based seed compost (substrate) mixed with coarse grit. Mix in a ratio of 1 part compost + 1 part grit. Put a layer of moss on the surface of the compost and sow the seeds directly on to the moss. Water in, do not cover. When you have sown the seeds, stand the pots in water so the compost remains wet at all times. Place under protection at 15°C (60°F). Germination takes 2–3 weeks. Grow on in a cold frame for the first winter, plant into the pond the following spring.

Sagittaria *Alismataceae*

A genus of tender to fully hardy perennial deciduous marginal and submerged water plants. Plant in water in a sunny position.

Sagittaria sagittifolia (Common arrow-head)
Small seeds
Hardy deciduous perennial
Height 45cm (18in)
White flowers with dark purple centres
Flowers in summer
Mid-green arrow-shaped leaves

Sow seeds in late summer into pots using standard loam-based seed compost (substrate) mixed with coarse grit. Mix to a ratio of 1 part compost + 1 part grit. Cover with coarse horticultural sand then stand the pots in water so the compost remains wet at all times. Place under protection at 10°C (50°F). Germination takes 2–3 weeks. Grow on in a cold frame for the first winter, plant into the pond the following spring.

cacti & succulents

Cacti and succulent plants are immensely collectable and are, in the majority of cases, very straightforward to grow from seed. As I only grow a few cacti and a couple of succulents on the farm, I consulted Bryan Goodey, one of the UK's foremost cacti growers, before writing this chapter. I am very grateful for his help. Seed is usually sold by amount rather than weight, so in this section I give an indication of seed size only. For the best results seed should be sown fresh, and so seed collected at home can prove more reliable than purchased seed. All cacti need as much light as possible when germinating, so do not cover. If you have 'grow lights' use them for the first 12 weeks, as this will be of great benefit. Even a household light bulb in an angle-poise lamp will help.

Astrophytum myriostigma, see page 69

Aeonium *Crassulaceae*

A genus of tender perennials and evergreen succulents. Plant in a very well-drained soil in partial shade.

Aeonium tabuliforme AGM

Seeds so small they appear as dust
Tender perennial (short lived), minimum temperature 5°C (40°F)
Height 5cm (2in)
Star-shaped, yellow flowers
Flowers in spring (plant dies after flowering)
Succulent, bright green leaves form a basal rosette on a short stem
Seed must be sown fresh, as it quickly loses its viability

Sow seeds in spring or autumn in small pots or modules using standard, soil-less seed compost (substrate), either a peat free proprietary brand or composted fine propagating bark, mixed with fine, 3mm (1/8in) sharp grit to a ratio of 1 part compost + 1 part grit. Mix seeds with the finest sand or talcum powder for an even sowing. Water from the bottom or with a fine spray and cover the container with glass or cling film. Place under protection at 21°C (70°F). Germination takes 2–3 weeks. Once the seed starts to germinate, remove the glass or cling film and cover gently with silver sand. This seed can prove a challenge for the inexperienced grower.

Aporocactus *Cactaceae*

A genus of tender, perennial cacti. Plant in an extremely free-draining soil in partial shade.

Aporocactus flagelliformis (Rat's-tail cactus)

Tiny seed

Aeonium tabuliforme (top right) with *Echeveria* 'Strawberry Fayre', *Aloe arborescens* and *Aeonium canariense*.

Tender perennial, minimum temperature 5°C (40°F)
Height up to 1m (3$^{1}/_{2}$ft)
Stunning, double, cerise pink flowers along the stems
Flowers in spring
Pencil thick, green stems with short, golden spines

Sow fresh seeds in spring into small pots or modules using standard, soil-less seed compost (substrate), either a peat free proprietary brand or composted fine propagating bark, mixed with fine 3mm ($^{1}/_{8}$in) sharp grit. Mix to a ratio of 3 parts compost + 1 part grit. Sow thinly on the surface of the compost. As these are tiny seeds, you may find it easier to use a piece of white folded card (see page 240). Water from the bottom or with a fine spray and cover the container with glass or cling film. Place under protection at 21°C (70°F). Germination takes 14–21 days. Once the seed starts to germinate, remove the glass or cling film and cover gently with silver sand. The germination can be staggered between 2 and 6 weeks, so it is a good idea to prick seedlings out soon after germination, so that you can continue to provide the correct conditions for late-germinating seed while giving the early germinators air.

Astrophytum *Cactaceae*

A genus of tender, perennial cacti. Plant in a very free-draining soil with minimum organic matter and in full sun. If growing under glass, plants will need shading in summer. Dry out completely in winter, this cacti is prone to rot if over wet and cold.

Astrophytum myriostigma (Bishop's cap, Bishop's mitre)
Small seed
Tender perennial, minimum temperature 5°C (40°F)
Height 30cm (12in)
Yellow flowers
Flowers in summer
4–6 pronounced ribs on a fleshy stem that is flecked with tiny white spines

Sow fresh seeds in spring into small pots or modules using standard, loam-based seed compost (substrate) mixed with coarse horticultural grit. Mix in a ratio of 1 part compost + 1 part 5mm ($^{1}/_{4}$in) grit. Sow thinly on to the surface of the compost. Water from the bottom or with a fine spray and cover the container with glass or cling film. Place under protection at 21°C (70°F). Germination 4–7 days. Once the seed starts to germinate, remove the glass or cling film and cover gently with silver sand.

Cereus *Cactaceae*

A genus of tender perennial cacti. Plant in a well-drained soil in a sunny position.

Cereus peruvianus
Tiny seed
Tender perennial, minimum temperature 7°C (45°F)
Height up to 5m (15ft)
Cup-shaped, beautiful, white flowers followed by pear-shaped red fruits
Flowers at night in summer,
Spiny, silvery-blue stem with 4–8 sharply indented ribs

Sow fresh seeds in spring into small pots or modules using standard, soil-less seed compost (substrate), either a peat free proprietary brand or composted fine propagating bark, mixed with 3mm ($^{1}/_{8}$in) sharp grit to a ratio of 3 parts compost + 1 part grit. Sow thinly on to the surface of the compost. As these are tiny seed, you may find using a piece of white folded card helpful (see page 240). Water from the bottom or with a fine spray, cover the container with glass or cling film and place under protection at 21°C (70°F). Germination takes 4–7 days. Once the seed starts to germinate, remove the glass or cling film and cover gently with silver sand.

Conophytum *Aizoaceae*

A genus of tender perennial succulents. Plant in a well-drained soil in a sunny position.

Conophytum bilobum
Seed so small it appears as dust
Tender perennial, minimum temperature 4°C (39°F)
Height 4cm (1$^{1}/_{2}$in)
Attractive, yellow flowers
Flowers in late summer
Lobed, fleshy, green leaves

Sow fresh seeds in spring into small pots or modules using standard, soil-less seed compost (substrate), either a peat free proprietary brand or composted fine propagating bark, mixed with 3mm ($^{1}/_{8}$in) sharp grit. Mix to a ratio of 3 parts compost + 1 part fine grit. As these are very fine seeds, mix with the finest sand or talcum powder for an even sowing. Do not cover the seeds. Water from the bottom or with a fine spray. Place under protection at 12°C (70°F). Germination takes 7–14 days.

Echeveria *Crassulaceae*

A genus of tender, perennial succulents with long-lasting flowers. Plant in well-drained soil in a sunny position with good air flow.

Echeveria elegans AGM
Seed so small it appears as dust
Tender perennial, minimum temperature 5°C (40°F)
Height 5cm (2in)
Pink flowers in summer
Fleshy, pale, broad, silvery-blue leaves edged with a hint of red which grow in basal rosettes

The seed of this plant has a short viability. Sow fresh seeds in spring into small pots or modules using standard, soil-less seed compost (substrate), either a peat free proprietary brand or composted fine propagating bark, mixed with 3mm ($^{1}/_{8}$in) sharp grit. Mix in a ratio of 3 parts compost + 1 part fine grit. As these are very fine seeds, mix them with the finest sand or talcum powder for an even sowing. Water from the bottom or with a fine spray and cover the container with glass or cling film. Place under protection at 18°C (65°F). Germination takes 14–21 days. Once the seed starts to germinate, remove the glass or cling film and cover gently with silver sand. This seed can prove a challenge to the inexperienced grower.

Echinocereus *Cactaceae*

A genus of tender cacti, plant in a very well-drained soil in full sun.

Echinocereus reichenbachii **(Hedgehog cactus)**
Tiny seeds
Tender perennial, minimum temperature 7°C (45°F)
Height 35cm (14in)
Trumpet-shaped purple, pink flowers
Flowers in spring and summer
Comb-like spines on multicoloured stems with up to 23 ribs

Sow fresh seeds in spring into small pots or modules, using standard, soil-less seed compost (substrate), either a peat free proprietary brand or composted fine propagating bark, mixed with 3mm (1/8in) sharp grit . Mix in a ratio of 3 parts compost + 1 part fine grit. Sow thinly on to the surface of the compost. As these are very small seeds, you may find it helpful to use a piece of folded white card (see page 240). Water from the bottom or with a fine spray and cover the container with glass or cling film. Place under protection at 21°C (70°F). Germination takes 7–14 days. Once the seed starts to germinate, remove the glass or cling film and cover gently with silver sand.

Echinopsis *Cactaceae*

A genus of tender cacti which are easy to grow. Plant in a very well-drained soil in full sun.

Echinopsis multiplex
Tiny seeds
Tender perennial, minimum temperature 5°C (40°F)
Height 30cm (12in)
Lovely tubular, white flowers with a hint of lavender
Flowers in spring and summer
Green stem with 13–15 ribs and long spines

Sow fresh seeds in spring or summer into small pots or modules using standard, soil-less seed compost (substrate), either a peat free proprietary brand or composted fine propagating bark, mixed with 3mm (1/8in) sharp grit. Mix in a ratio of 3 parts compost + 1 part fine grit. Sow thinly on the surface of the compost. As these are very small seeds, you may find using a piece of white folded card helpful (see page 240). Water from the bottom or with a fine spray and cover the container with glass or cling film. Place under protection at 21°C (70°F). Germination takes 7–14 days. Once the seed starts to germinate, remove the glass or cling film and cover gently with fine vermiculite.

Epiphyllum *Cactaceae*

A genus of tender orchid cactus. Plant in a fertile, free-draining soil in dappled shade.

Epiphyllum crenatum
Tiny seeds
Tender perennial, minimum temperature 11°C (52°F)
Height up to 3m (10ft)
Funnel-shaped, scented, white flowers
Flowers in spring
Flattened stems

Sow fresh seeds in spring or summer into small pots or modules using standard, soil-less seed compost (substrate), either a peat free proprietary brand or composted fine propagating bark, mixed with 3mm (1/8in) sharp grit. Mix in a ratio of 3 parts compost + 1 part fine grit. Sow thinly on to the surface of the compost. As these are very small seeds, you may find using a piece of white folded card helpful (see page 240). Water from the bottom or with a fine spray and cover the container with glass or cling film. Place under protection at 21°C (70°F). Germination takes 7–14 days. Once the seed starts to germinate, remove the glass or cling film and cover gently with fine vermiculite.

Germination can be staggered between 2–6 weeks, so it is a good idea to prick out soon after germination to allow later seeds the correct conditions and give the early germinators air. Plants will flower in 4–7 years from seed.

Haworthia *Alliaceae*

A genus of tender perennial succulents. Plant in very well-drained soil. If grown in partial shade it stays green, if grown in sun it turns red and growth will be slow.

Haworthia attenuata
Tiny seeds
Tender perennial, minimum temperature 5°C (40°F)
Height 7cm (3in)
Tubular, bell-shaped, white flowers on long, slender stems
Flowers from spring until early autumn
Dark green, triangular leaves which grow in basal rosettes

Sow fresh seeds, as seed loses its viability after 6 months. Sow in autumn or early spring into small pots or modules using standard, soil-less seed compost (substrate), either a peat free proprietary brand or composted fine propagating bark, mixed with 3mm (1/8in) sharp grit. Mix in a ratio of 3 parts compost + 1 part fine grit. Sow thinly on the surface of the compost. As the seeds are small, you may find using a piece of white folded card helpful, see below. Water from the bottom or with a fine spray and cover the container with glass or cling film. Place under protection at 21°C (70°F). Germination takes 7–14 days. Once the seed starts to germinate, remove the glass or cling film and cover gently with silver sand.

Recipe for sowing, planting and growing **Haworthia attenuata**
An attractive, undemanding South-African cactus.

Ingredients
20 seeds per module or 30 seeds per pot (do not sow thickly)
1 piece white card 14 x 8.5cm (5 1/2 x 3 1/2in) folded in half
1 module tray
OR
1 x 8cm (4in) pot
Standard, soil-less seed compost (substrate), either a peat free proprietary brand or composted fine propagating bark, mixed with 3mm (1/8in) sharp grit. Mix in a ratio of 3 parts compost + 1 part fine grit
Piece of glass or plastic, or cling film large enough to cover the container
White plastic plant label
Angle-poise lamp or horticultural light
Silver sand

Method In autumn or early spring, fill the tray or pot with compost, smooth over, tap down and water in well. As the seeds are fine, it is worth putting a very small amount of seed into the crease of a folded

Haworthia attenuata

card so you can gently tap the card, which will not only allow you to see what you are sowing but also enable you to sow thinly on to the surface of the compost. Cover with a piece of glass, clear plastic or cling film. Label with plant name and date. Place the container in a warm, light place, with extra light if possible in the form of an angle-poise lamp or horticultural lights, but out of direct sunlight and at an optimum temperature of 21°C (70°F). Germination takes 7–14 days.

Once the seed starts to germinate, remove the glass or cling film and cover gently with silver sand. Remove the container from the very warm area and allow the seedlings to continue growing under protection at 15°C (60°F). Keep using the extra light for a further 2 weeks.

When the seedlings are large enough to handle, prick out and pot up into small containers using a loam-based compost mixed in equal parts with sharp grit.

Keep the plant warm but well ventilated and do not over water.

Parodia *Cactaceae*

A genus of tender perennial cacti. Plant in a very well-drained soil in sun or partial shade.

Parodia novisa
Small seeds
Tender perennial, minimum temperature 7°C (45°F)
Height up to 15cm (6in)
Bright red flowers
Flowers in summer
Ribbed, green stem covered with white spines with a white, woolly crown

Sow fresh seeds in spring into small pots or modules using standard, soil-less seed compost (substrate), either a peat free proprietary brand or composted fine propagating bark, mixed with 3mm (1/8in) sharp grit. Mix in a ratio of 3 parts compost + 1 part fine grit. Sow thinly on to the surface of the compost. As these are small seed, you may find it helpful to use a piece of white folded card, see recipe above. Water from the bottom or with a fine spray, cover the container with glass or cling film and place under protection at 20°C (68°F). Germination takes 14 –21 days. Once the seed starts to germinate, remove the glass or cling film and cover gently with silver sand.

This seed can prove a challenge for the inexperienced grower. If you would like an easier one, try *Parodia maranana* which has smaller seeds and is grown at the same temperature.

Schlumbergera truncata

Rebutia *Cactaceae*

A genus of tender perennial cacti. Plant in a well-drained soil in sun or partial shade.

Rebutia spegazziniana
Minute seeds
Tender perennial, minimum temperature 5°C (40°F)
Height 10cm (4in)
Masses of slender, tubed orange-red flowers
Flowers in late spring
Spherical, spined green stem

Sow fresh seeds in spring into small pots or modules using standard, soil-less seed compost (substrate), either a peat free proprietary brand or composted fine propagating bark, mixed with 3mm (1/8in) sharp grit. Mix in a ratio of 3 parts compost + 1 part fine grit. As these are very fine seeds, mix with the finest sand or talcum powder for an even sowing. Water from the bottom or with a fine spray, cover the container with glass or cling film and place under protection at 21°C (70°F). Germination takes 7–14 days. Once the seed starts to germinate, remove the glass or cling film and cover gently with silver sand.

Schlumbergera *Cactaceae*

A genus of tender perennial cacti. Plant in a rich, well-drained soil in partial shade.

Schlumbergera truncata (Lobster cactus, Crab cactus)
Tiny seeds
Tender perennial, minimum temperature 10°C (50°F)
Height 15cm (6in)
Red/purple flowers
Flowers in early autumn and winter
Oblong stem segments with toothed margins

Sow fresh seeds in spring into small pots or modules using standard, soil-less seed compost (substrate), either a peat free proprietary brand or composted fine propagating bark, mixed with 3mm (1/8in) sharp grit. Mix in a ratio of 3 parts compost + 1 part fine grit. Sow thinly on to the surface of the compost. As these are very small seeds, you may find using a piece of white folded card helpful (see page 240). Water from the bottom or with a fine spray and cover the container with glass or cling film. Place under protection at 20°C (68°F). Germination takes 7–14 days. Once the seed starts to germinate, remove the glass or cling film and cover gently with fine vermiculite.

Germination can be staggered between 2–6 weeks, so it is a good idea to prick out soon after germination, allowing later seeds the correct conditions and giving the early germinators air.

Sedum *Crassulaceae*

A genus of frost-hardy to frost-tender annuals, biennials and evergreens. Plant in any soil, but prefers a fertile well-drained soil in sun or partial shade.

Sedum acre (Wall pepper, Stonecrop)
Tiny seeds
Hardy, evergreen perennial
Height up to 10cm (4in)
Creeping habit
Star-shaped, bright yellow flowers
Flowers all summer
Mat-forming, succulent, bright green leaves

Sedum rupestre L. (*reflexum* L.) (Stone orpine, Rock stonecrop, Recurved yellow stonecrop)
Minute seeds
Hardy, evergreen perennial
Height up to 20cm (8in)
Creeping habit
Clusters of yellow, star-shaped flowers
Flowers all summer
Narrow, fleshy, grey-green leaves

Sow fresh seeds in spring or summer into small pots or modules, using standard, soil-less seed compost (substrate), either peat or a peat substitute, mixed with 3mm (1/8in) sharp grit. Mix in a ratio of 3 parts compost + 1 part fine grit. As these are very fine seeds, mix with the finest sand or talcum powder for an even sowing. Water from the bottom or with a fine spray and cover the container with glass or cling film. Place under protection at 15°C (60°F). Germination takes 7–14 days. Once the seed starts to germinate, remove the glass or cling film and cover gently with fine vermiculite. Flowers in 1–3 years.

Sempervivum *Crassulaceae*

A genus of hardy, evergreen perennials. Plant in a well-drained, gritty soil in a sunny position.

Sempervivum tectorum AGM (Common houseleek, Roof houseleek)
Minute seeds
Hardy evergreen perennial
Height up to 15cm (6in)
Clusters of star-shaped, red/purple flowers
Purple-tipped, succulent leaves which grow in rosettes

Sow fresh seeds in spring or summer into small pots or modules using standard, soil-less seed compost (substrate), either a peat free proprietary brand or composted fine propagating bark, mixed with 3mm (1/8in) sharp grit. Mix in a ratio of 3 parts compost + 1 part fine grit. As these are very fine seeds, mix with the finest sand or talcum powder for an even sowing. Water from the bottom or with a fine spray and cover the container with glass or cling film. Place in a frost-free environment, such as a cold frame or the cold window of a garage. Germination takes 1–6 months. Once the seed starts to germinate, remove the glass or cling film and cover gently with fine sand.

climbers

Climbing plants are very useful in the garden. They can transform a tree stump into a living feature, cascade over a wall, climb up and cover a boring fence or even camouflage a garage. Some have the most attractive foliage, others have stunning flowers and some varieties combine the two. Whichever climber you choose, it is sure to be a bonus, whatever the size of your garden.

Wisteria seed pods, see page 85

Actinidia *Actinidiaceae*

A genus of hardy to half-hardy climbers. Plant in any well-drained soil that does not dry out in summer, and in partial shade. To obtain fruits, both male and female plants must be grown.

Actinidia deliciosa (Chinese gooseberry, Kiwi fruit)
Medium seeds: 500 per gram
Hardy deciduous perennial
Height up to 10m (30ft)
Clusters of cup-shaped, white flowers that turn cream coloured as they age, followed by edible, hairy, brown fruits
Flowers in summer
Large, heart-shaped leaves

Sow fresh seeds extracted from the fruit in autumn into pots or modules using a standard, soil-less seed compost (substrate). Cover with perlite or vermiculite, place under protection at 20°C (68°F). Germination takes 2–3 weeks. Overwinter young plants in a frost-free environment.
OR
Sow old seed in autumn into pots or modules, using standard, loam-based seed compost (substrate) mixed with coarse horticultural sand. Mix in a ratio of 1 part compost + 1 part sand. Cover with coarse horticultural sand. Place outside, exposed to all weathers (see 'Breaking Seed Dormancy', page 233, for more information). Germination takes 4–6 months but can be erratic. Be patient and do not discard the container.

Cardiospermum *Sapindaceae*

A genus of half-hardy herbaceous or deciduous climbers grown for their fruits. Plant in a light, well-drained soil in a sunny position.

Cardiospermum halicacabum (Heart seed, Winter cherry, Balloon vine)
Medium seeds: 14 per gram
Tender perennial grown as an annual or sometimes a biennial in cool climates. Minimum temperature 5°C (40°F)
Height up to 3m (10ft)
Whitish flowers followed by straw-coloured, heart-shaped seed pods
Flowers in summer
Leaves divided into leaflets which are heavily toothed

Sow seeds in early spring into pots or modules using a standard, soil-less seed compost (substrate). Cover with perlite or vermiculite, place under protection at 20°C (68°F). Germination takes 3–4 weeks. If growing as a container plant, use a soil-less compost (substrate), either a peat free proprietary brand or composted fine propagating bark.

Clematis *Ranunculaceae*

A genus of fully- to half-hardy deciduous and evergreen climbers and herbaceous perennials. Plant in a rich, well-drained soil in a sunny position, however will tolerate some shade.

Clematis tangutica (Virgin's bower)
Medium seeds: 600 per gram
Hardy perennial
Height up to 6m (20ft)
Lantern-shaped, single, bright yellow flowers followed by feathery seed heads
Flowers in summer and early autumn
Pointed, oval, green leaves

Sow seeds in early spring into pots or modules using a standard, soil-less seed compost (substrate). Cover with perlite or vermiculite. Place under protection at 20°C (68°F) for 2 weeks, then put in a cold frame at 2–4°C (36–40°F) for a month. Move container to a warm situation, increasing the warmth slowly until the seed germinates, about 1 week after being introduced to the warmth.

Clematis viticella AGM
Medium seeds: 40 per gram
Hardy perennial
Height up to 3m (10ft)
Open, bell-shaped, single, purple-mauve flowers
Flowers in late summer
Oval leaves divided into lance-shaped leaflets

Sow seeds in early spring into pots or modules using a standard, soil-less seed compost (substrate). Cover with perlite or vermiculite, place under protection at 20°C (68°F). Germination takes 7–14 days.

Cobaea *Cobaeaceae*

A genus of a single species, half-hardy evergreen climber. Plant in any well-drained soil in a sunny position.

Cobaea scandens AGM (Cathedral bells, Cup and saucer vine)
Medium seeds: 15 per gram
Tender perennial, often grown as an annual in cool climates, with a minimum temperature of 4°C (39°F)
Height 4–5m (12–15ft)
Bell-shaped, green/white flowers which turn deep purple with age
Flowers from late summer until the first frosts
Leaves divided into oval leaflets

Sow seeds in early spring into pots or modules using a standard, soil-less seed compost (substrate). Cover with perlite or vermiculite. Place under protection at 21°C (70°F). Germination takes 4–10 days.

Convolvulus *Convolvulaceae*

A genus of hardy and half-hardy climbing annuals, perennials and evergreen shrubs. Plant in any well-drained soil in a sunny position.

Convolvulus tricolor (*Convolvulus minor*)
Medium seeds: 50 per gram
Tender annual, with a minimum temperature 2°C (36°F)
Height up to 3m (10ft)
Saucer-shaped, blue or white flowers with yellowish-white throats
Flowers in summer
Oval, lance-shaped, mid-green leaves

Sow seeds in early spring into pots or modules using a standard, soil-less seed compost (substrate). Cover with perlite or vermiculite. Place under protection at 18°C (65°F). Germination takes 3–4 weeks.

Actinidia chinensis

Dolichos *Papilionaceae*

A genus of a single species. Half-hardy perennial climber grown for its attractive pea-like flowers. Plant in any well-drained soil in a sunny position.

Dolichos lablab (*Lablab purpureus*) (Lablab bean, Hyacinth bean, Dolichos, Australian pea)
Large seeds: 5–10 per gram
Tender perennial, often grown as an annual in cool climates, with a minimum temperature of 5°C (40°F)
Height up to 9m (30ft)
Purple, pink or white flowers followed by long pods with edible seeds
Flowers in summer
Purple-hued stems, leaves and seed pods

Sow seeds in early spring into pots or modules using a standard, soil-less seed compost (substrate). Cover with perlite or vermiculite, place under protection at 21°C (70°F). Germination takes 5–8 days.

Eccremocarpus *Bignoniaceae*

A genus of half-hardy, evergreen climbers. Plant in any well-drained soil in a sunny position.

Eccremacarpus scaber (Glory vine, Chilean glory flower)
Large seeds: 10 per gram
Tender perennial, often grown as an annual in cool climates, with a minimum temperature of 5°C (40°F)
Height up to 3m (10ft)
Clusters of small, orange flowers which are followed by inflated fruit pods
Flowers in summer
Small, mid-green leaves

Sow seeds in early spring into pots or modules using a standard, soil-less seed compost (substrate). Cover with perlite or vermiculite and place under protection at 18°C (65°F). Germination takes 3–4 weeks.

Hardenbergia *Papilionaceae*

A genus of half-hardy evergreen climbers and subshrubs. Plant in a well-drained soil that does not dry out in summer, prefers a sunny position.

Hardenbergia comptoniana AGM
Medium seeds: 80 per gram
Evergreen tender perennial. Minimum temperature 7°C (45°F)
Height up to 2.5m (8ft)
Racemes of pea-like deep purple-blue flowers
Flowers in early summer
Narrow oval leaves

Soak the seeds in warm water for 24 hours before sowing. Sow seeds in early spring into pots or modules using a standard, soil-less seed compost (substrate). Cover with perlite or vermiculite, place under protection at 20°C (68°F). Germination takes 6–10 days.

Hedera *Araliaceae*

A genus of hardy and half-hardy, evergreen, perennial climbers and trailing plants. Plant in a well-drained soil in semi- to full shade.

Hedera helix (Ivy, Common English ivy) TOXIC PLANT
Medium seeds: 20 per gram
Hardy evergreen perennial
Height up to 30m (100ft)
Yellowish-green flowers followed by round black berries
Flowers in late summer
Five-lobed, dark green, glossy leaves

Sow seeds extracted from berries in autumn into pots or modules using standard, loam-based seed compost (substrate) mixed with coarse horticultural sand. Mix in a ratio of 1 part compost + 1 part sand. Cover with coarse horticultural sand. Place outside, exposed to all weathers (see 'Breaking Seed Dormancy', page 233, for more information). Germination takes 4–6 months but can be erratic, so be patient and do not discard container.

***Recipe for sowing, planting and growing* Hedera helix**

Ivies are lovely plants. As evergreens, they give year-round interest and are very important for wild life. The late flowers are full of nectar and the berries are eaten by the birds well into the winter.

Ingredients
Rubber gloves
Kitchen towel
3 seeds per module or 7 seeds per pot
1 module tray
OR
1 x 8cm (4in) pot
Standard, loam-based seed compost (substrate) mixed with coarse horticultural sand. Mix in a ratio of 1 part compost + 1 part sand for autumn sowing
Extra coarse sand
White plastic plant labels

Method Collect ivy seeds in winter. They are ripe when soft to touch. Wear rubber gloves because ivy is a toxic plant. To extract the seed from the berry, which is a pithy variety, gently squeeze the fruit between your fingers and the seed will pop out. Do not allow the seeds to dry out. Either sow immediately or store in damp sand. Fill the tray or pot with compost, smooth over, tap down and water in well. Sow thinly on to the surface of the compost press the seeds gently into the compost and cover with coarse sand. Label with the plant name and date. Place the pot outside, on a level surface, so it is exposed to all weathers, including frosts. Do not worry if you live in a snowy area and the containers get immersed in snow, for melting snow will aid germination. If you do not live in an area which will get a winter frost, it is a good idea to put the seed mixed with a handful of damp sand into a clearly labelled, sealed plastic bag. As a precaution, because the seed is toxic, place the sealed bag in another bag, seal and mark clearly. Place in a refrigerator for 3 weeks. Remove and sow as mentioned above, then place outside. Whichever method you use, germination is a bit erratic, taking anything from 1–12 months. Do not give up and discard your compost, it might just germinate next week!

Humulus *Cannabaceae*

A genus of hardy and half-hardy herbaceous climbers. Plant in any well-drained soil in sun or semi-shade.

Humulus lupulus (Hops)
Medium seeds: 40 per gram
Hardy perennial
Height up to 6m (10ft)
Clusters of female, greenish pendent flowers
Flowers in summer
Green leaves divided into 3 or 5 lobes

Sow seeds in autumn into pots or modules using standard, loam-based seed compost (substrate) mixed with coarse horticultural sand. Mix in a ratio of 1 part compost + 1 part sand. Cover with coarse horticultural sand. Place outside exposed to all weathers (see 'Breaking Seed Dormancy', page 233, for more information). Germination takes 4–6 months but can be erratic. Be patient and do not discard container, as the seeds can germinate in the following year.

Ipomoea *Convolvulaceae*

A genus of half-hardy perennials, biennials and evergreen shrubs or climbers. Plant in humus-rich, well-drained soil in a sunny position.

Ipomoea purpurea 'Grandpa Otts'
Medium seeds: 25 per gram
Semi-evergreen, tender perennial, often grown as an annual in cool climates, with a minimum temperature of 5°C (40°F)
Height up to 3m (10ft)
Profusion of intense violet-blue flowers which have pink throats
Flowers in summer
Green heart-shaped leaves

Soak the seeds overnight. Sow in early spring into pots or modules using a standard, soil-less seed compost (substrate). Cover with perlite or vermiculite and place under protection at 20°C (68°F). Germination takes 6–10 days.

Ipomoea lobata (*Mina lobata*) (Spanish flag)
Medium seeds: 30 per gram
Semi-evergreen, tender perennial, often grown as an annual in cool climates. Minimum temperature 7°C (45°F)
Height up to 5m (15ft)
One-sided clusters of pretty, small, tubular, 2-toned flowers of red and cream
Flowers in summer
Three-lobed green leaves

Humulus lupulus

Lathyrus latifolius

Sow seeds in early spring into pots or modules using a standard, soil-less seed compost (substrate). Cover with perlite or vermiculite and place under protection at 21°C (70°F). Germination takes 3–6 days.

Jasminium *Oleaceae*

A genus of hardy and half-hardy, deciduous or evergreen shrubs and climbers. Plant in a fertile, well-drained soil in a sunny position.

Jasminum officinale AGM (Common jasmine)
Medium seeds: 20 per gram
Semi-evergreen, hardy perennial
Height up to 12m (40ft)
Clusters of pink buds which develop into scented, small, white flowers followed by black berries
Flowers in summer
Green leaves divided into small pointed leaflets

Sow seeds extracted from berries in autumn into pots or modules using standard, loam-based seed compost (substrate) mixed with coarse horticultural sand. Mix in a ratio of 1 part compost + 1 part sand. Cover with coarse horticultural sand, then place outside, exposed to all weathers (see 'Breaking Seed Dormancy', page 233, for more information). Germination takes 4–6 months but can be erratic, so be patient and do not discard the container.

Lathyrus *Papilionaceae*

A genus of hardy, tendril climbers which all have attractive, and in the case of *Lathyrus odoratus*, sweet-smelling flowers. Plant in a rich, fertile well-draining soil in full light. To maintain flowering, dead head regularly.

Lathyrus latifolius AGM (Everlasting pea)
Medium seeds: 20 per gram
Hardy herbaceous perennial
Small racemes of pink/purple flowers
Flowers in summer until early autumn
Broad, lance-shaped leaves with a pair of leaflets

Lathyrus odoratus (Sweet pea)
Medium seeds: 12 per gram
Hardy annual
Height up to 3m (10ft)
Scented flowers in shades of pink, white, blue, purple, apricot
Flowers in summer
Oval, mid-green leaves with tendrils

Lathyrus sylvestris (Everlasting pea, Perennial pea)
Medium seeds: 20 per gram
Hardy herbaceous perennial
Height up to 2m (6ft)
Lovely racemes can be as many as 10 flowers which are rose/pink and marked with green and purple
The oval, mid-green leaves have a pair of leaflets attached

Soak seeds in water for 24 hours before sowing or pre-germinate on kitchen paper, see recipe. Sow seeds from autumn until early spring into pots using a standard, soil-less seed compost (substrate). Cover with perlite or vermiculite, place under protection at 10–15°C (50–60°F). Germination takes 1–2 weeks. Plant out as soon as all threat of frost has passed, after a period of hardening off.
OR
Sow in spring, any time after the hard frosts 5°C (41°F) have gone, into prepared drills 4cm (2in) deep. Germination takes 7–14 days. Late spring sowings (May onwards) will produce plants with little flower.

***Recipe for sowing, planting and growing* Lathyrus odoratus**
The scent of sweet peas is very evocative, personally they remind me of both my childhood and of flower shows.

Ingredients
3 seeds per pot
Sandpaper
Small china bowl or kitchen paper
Warm water
1 x 13cm (12in) pot
Standard, soil-less seed compost (substrate)
Fine-grade perlite (wetted) or vermiculite
White plastic plant label

Method Whether you sow into pots or directly into the soil, you will get a better rate of germination if you soak the seeds in water prior to sowing. Before soaking the seeds, scarify them by rubbing gently on sandpaper. This will allow the water to penetrate more easily. Then, either soak the seeds overnight in warm water prior to sowing, or soak 2 or 3 layers of kitchen paper on a plate, space the seeds evenly on the paper and cover with 2 or 3 further layers of pre-soaked kitchen paper. Keep moist and check daily by lifting the corner of the paper. When the seeds begin to sprout they can be gently transplanted to pots of compost.

Between autumn and early spring, fill the pots with compost, smooth over, tap down and water in well. Plant 3 pre-soaked and scarified seeds per pot, equally spaced on the surface of the compost. Gently press the seeds into the compost. Cover the seeds with fine-grade perlite (wetted) or vermiculite and label with the plant name and date. Place the pot in a cool, light place out of direct sunlight at an optimum temperature of 10–15°C (50–60°F). Germination of seeds that have not sprouted prior to planting will take 7–14 days. Place the pots in a cold frame or unheated glasshouse. It is important to grow sweet peas in as cool an environmet as possible, only giving protection if the weather is very cold. If grown in warm conditions, the young plant will become soft and leggy. It is also necessary to pinch out the growing tips of seedlings sown in winter or spring, although autumn-sown plants should not need it.

Plant the seedlings out in spring when the temperature does not fall below 5°C (40°F) after a period of hardening off in a site that has been prepared the previous autumn with well-rotted manure. The plants will rapidly cover the supports given to them, so do not skimp on the height, allow a minimum of 2m (6ft).

Alternatively, you can sow the pre-soaked and scarified seeds directly into a prepared site (see above) in the garden when the night-time temperature does not fall below 5°C (40°F). The site must be well prepared in early autumn. Space the seeds 45cm (18in) apart, next to some support, either canes or a frame, minimum height 2m (6ft). Gently press into the soil and lightly cover, water in well. Germination takes 7–14 days.

Lonicera *Caprifoliaceae*

A genus of half-hardy to hardy, deciduous or evergreen shrubs and climbers. Plant in any fertile, well-drained soil in sun or semi-shade.

Lonicera periclymenum (Honeysuckle, Woodbine)
Medium seeds: 175 per gram
Hardy perennial
Height up to 7m (22ft)
Cream combined with dark yellow and pink flowers, very fragrant
Flowers in summer
Mid-green, oval leaves

Sow seeds extracted from berries in autumn into pots or modules using standard, loam-based seed compost (substrate) mixed with coarse horticultural sand. Mix in a ratio of 1 part compost + 1 part sand. Cover seeds with coarse horticultural sand, then place outside exposed to all weathers (see 'Breaking Seed Dormancy', page 233, for more information). Germination takes 4–6 months but can be erratic, so be patient and do not discard container. Plants will flower in 3 years.

Lophospermum *Scrophulariaceae*

A genus of half-hardy perennials and evergreen climbers which are herbaceous in cold climates. Plant in any well-drained soil in a sunny situation.

Lophospermum scandens (Twining snapdragon)
Minute seeds: 40,000 per gram
Evergreen, tender perennial. Minimum temperature 5°C (40°F)
Height up to 3m (10ft)
Deep purple, small, snapdragon-like flowers
Heart-shaped leaves with toothed edges

Sow the seeds in early spring into pots or modules using a standard, soil-less seed compost (substrate). As these are very fine seeds, mix with the finest sand or talcum powder for an even sowing. Do not cover. Water from the bottom or with a fine spray. Place under protection at 21°C (70°F). Germination takes 5–8 days.

Maurandya *Scrophulariaceae*

A genus of half-hardy perennials and evergreen climbers which are herbaceous in cold climates. Plant in any well-drained soil in a sunny situation.

Maurandya barclayana (*Asarina barclayana*)
Small seeds: 1,500 per gram
Evergreen, tender perennial. Minimum temperature 5°C (40°F)
Height up to 2m (6ft)
Trumpet-shaped, purplish-blue flowers with white throats
Flowers from summer to autumn
Heart-shaped, mid-green leaves

Sow seeds in early spring into pots or modules using a standard, soil-less seed compost (substrate). Cover with perlite or vermiculite. Place under protection at 18°C (65°F). Germination takes 3–4 weeks. If growing as a container plant, use a peat free proprietary brand or composted fine propagating bark.

Pandorea *Bignoniaceae*

A genus of half-hardy, evergreen climbers grown for their lovely flowers. Plant in any well-drained soil in a sunny position.

Pandorea jasminoides (Bower vine)
Small seeds: 1,500 per gram
Evergreen tender perennial. Minimum temperature 5°C (40°F)
Height up to 5m (15ft)
Clusters of white, funnel-shaped flowers with pink flushed throats
Flowers from late winter to summer
Leaves divided into small, oval, pointed leaflets

Sow seeds in early spring into pots or modules using a standard, soil-less seed compost (substrate). Cover with perlite or vermiculite and place under protection at 21°C (70°F). Germination takes 3–6 days.

Parthenocissus *Vitaceae*

A genus of hardy and half-hardy deciduous climbers grown for their leaves' lovely autumn colours. Plant in a well-drained soil in semi-shade or full shade.

Parthenocissus tricuspidata 'Veitchii' (*Ampelopsis*) (Virginia creeper)
Medium seeds: 25 per gram
Hardy perennial
Height up to 20m (70ft)
Insignificant, green flowers, followed by attractive, dull-blue berries
Flowers in summer
Spectacular, red-purple leaves in autumn

Sow fresh seed extracted from the berry in autumn into pots or modules using standard, loam-based seed compost (substrate). Cover lightly with compost, place in a cold frame. Germination takes 3–4 weeks. If no germination occurs during this period, place container outside exposed to all weathers (see 'Breaking Seed Dormancy', page 233, for more information). Germination can take a further 5–7 months on average, or even as long as 2 years. When germination has taken place, overwinter young plants in the cold frame.

Passiflora *Passifloraceae*

A genus of half-hardy, evergreen and semi-evergreen climbers. Many species have edible fruits.

Passiflora caerulea AGM (Common passion-flower, Blue passion-flower)
Medium seeds: 120 per gram
Tender perennial. Minimum temperature 5°C (40°F)
Height up to 10m (30ft)
White flowers with a pink flush and bands of blue and purple
Flowers in summer
Hand-shaped, dark green leaves

Sow seeds in early spring into pots or modules using a standard, soil-less seed compost (substrate). Cover with perlite or vermiculite, place under protection at 20°C (68°F). Germination takes 3–4 weeks.

Passiflora edulis (Passion-flower, Passion-fruit, Wild passion-flower)
Medium seeds: 60 per gram
Tender perennial. Minimum temperature 5°C (40°F)
Height up to 5m (15ft)
Beautiful, intricate, purple and white flowers
Flowers in summer
Large, 3-lobed, serrated leaves

Sow seeds in early spring into pots or modules using a standard, soil-less seed compost (substrate). Cover with perlite or vermiculite, place under protection at 21°C (70°F). Germination takes 2–4 weeks.

Plumbago *Plumbaginaceae*

A genus of half-hardy annuals, perennials, evergreen shrubs and climbers, grown for their attractive flowers. Plant in a fertile, well-drained soil in sun or partial shade.

Plumbago auriculata AGM (*Capensis*) (Plumbago, Leadwort)
Medium seeds: 60 per gram
Tender perennial. Minimum temperature 5°C (40°F)
Height up to 6m (20ft)
Pale blue flowers
Flowers from late spring until early autumn

Sow fresh seeds in early spring into pots or modules using a standard, soil-less seed compost (substrate). Cover with perlite or vermiculite and place under protection at 21°C (70°F). Germination takes 7–14 days and can be erratic.

Rhodochiton *Scrophulariaceae*

A single species genus, grown for its unusual flowers. Plant in any well-drained soil in a sunny position.

Passiflora caerulea

Tropaeolum peregrinum

Rhodochiton atrosanguineus AGM (Purple bell vine, Rhodochiton)
Small seeds: 3,500 per gram
Evergreen, tender perennial, grown as an annual in cool climates, with a minimum temperature of 5°C (40°F)
Height up to 3m (10ft)
Tubular, dark maroon/purple flowers surrounded by bell-shaped, red/purple calyces
Flowers all summer
Oval, toothed, mid-green leaves

Sow fresh seeds in early spring into pots or modules using a standard, soil-less seed compost (substrate). Cover with perlite or vermiculite, and place under protection at 21°C (70°F). Germination takes 6–10 days.

Solanum *Solanaceae*

A large genus of annuals, perennials, evergreens, shrubs and climbers. Plant in a rich, moist, neutral soil in sun or partial shade.

Solanum dulcamara (Bittersweet, Woody nightshade – not Deadly nightshade) POISONOUS PLANT
Medium seeds: 100 per gram
Hardy perennial
Height up to 2m (6ft)
Small, exotic looking purple and yellow flowers, followed by green berries that turn scarlet in winter
Flowers in summer
Large, green, oval, pointed leaves

Sow seeds extracted from berries in autumn into pots or modules using standard loam-based seed compost (substrate) mixed with coarse horticultural sand. Mix in a ratio of 1 part compost + 1 part sand. Cover with coarse horticultural sand, then place outside exposed to all weathers (see 'Breaking Seed Dormancy', page 233, for more information). Germination takes 4–6 months but can be erratic, so be patient and do not discard container.

Thunbergia *Acanthaceae*

A genus of half-hardy annual and perennial evergreen climbers. Plant in any fertile, well-drained soil in sun or partial shade.

Thunbergia alata (Black-eyed Susan vine)
Medium seeds: 40 per gram
Tender annual. Minimum temperature 10°C (50°F)
Height up to 3m (10ft)
Pretty orange-yellow flowers with very dark brown centres
Heart-shaped, mid-green leaves with toothed edges

Sow fresh seeds in early spring into pots or modules using a standard, soil-less seed compost (substrate). Cover with perlite or vermiculite and place under protection at 21°C (70°F). Germination takes 7–14 days.

Tropaeolum *Tropaeolaceae*

A genus of hardy to frost-tender annuals, perennials and climbers, all have lovely flowers. Plant in a well-drained soil in a sunny position.

Tropaeolum peregrinum (Canary creeper)
Large seeds: 8 per gram
Tender perennial, often grown as an annual in cool climates, with a minimum temperature of 5°C (40°F)
Height up to 2m (6ft)
Single, small, bright yellow flowers in summer until the first frosts
Grey-green, lobed leaves

Sow fresh seeds in early spring into pots or modules using a standard, soil-less seed compost (substrate). Cover with perlite or vermiculite, place under protection at 18°C (65°F). Germination takes 5–12 days.

Tropaeolum speciosum AGM (Flame creeper, Flame nasturtium)
Medium seeds: 20 per gram
Hardy perennial
Height up to 3m (10ft)
Scarlet flowers which are followed by bright blue fruits
Flowers in summer
Blue-green lobed leaves
The roots of this plant like to be kept in the shade so they do not dry out in hot summers

Sow fresh seed in autumn into pots or modules using standard, loam-based seed compost (substrate). Cover lightly with compost and place in a cold frame. Germination takes 3–4 weeks. If germination does not occur during this time, place container outside exposed to all weathers (see 'Breaking Seed Dormancy', page 233) for more information). Germination takes 5–7 months on average, but can take as long as 2 years. When germination has occurred, overwinter young plants in a cold frame. If you are using old seeds, soak them for 24 hours before sowing. Flowers after 3 years, or occasionally as long as five.

Wisteria *Papilionaceae*

A genus of hardy, deciduous climbers grown for their lovely flowers. Plant in a fertile, well-drained soil in a sunny position.

Wisteria sinensis AGM (Wisteria)
Large seeds: 3 per gram
Hardy deciduous perennial
Height up to 9m (24ft)
Sweetly scented, mauve/purple, pea-like flowers which hang in clusters
Flowers in early summer
Divided, mid-green leaves with oval leaflets

Soak seeds for 24 hours before sowing. Sow in spring into pots or modules using standard, soil-less seed compost (substrate), either a peat free proprietary brand or composted fine propagating bark. Cover with perlite or vermiculite. Place in a cold frame. Germination takes 1–6 months. Wisteria grown from seed will take up to 7 years before flowering. Plants raised in this way are often used as root stock for grafting.

ferns

Ferns are beautiful plants that come in a wide variety of forms and textures. They are excellent for the shady garden. They are primitive plants that do not flower but reproduce sexually from spores rather than seeds. There are two distinct stages in the life cycle of a fern. During the first stage, the mature plants produce spores on the underside of their leaves. During the second stage, the spores are dispersed from the fern and they germinate. After germination they grow into small, heart-shaped plants known as prothalli. Male and female cells are produced on these plants and, after fertilisation, the adult fern begins to develop.

Dicksonia antartica shoots, see page 89

Adiantum *Adiantaceae*

A genus of tender to hardy, semi-evergreen, evergreen or deciduous ferns. Plant in a moist, acid soil in semi-shade.

Adiantum capillus-veneris (Maidenhair fern)
Propagated by spores
Half-hardy, semi-evergreen or evergreen fern
Height 30cm (12in)
Very dainty, triangular, light green fronds on black stems

Sow fresh spores at 21°C (70°F) following the instructions on page 91 and using a standard, ericaceous seed compost (substrate) for sowing and potting on.

Asplenium *Aspleniaceae*

A genus of tender to hardy, semi- evergreen or evergreen ferns. Plant in any moist soil in semi-shade.

Asplenium nidus AGM (Bird's nest fern)
Propagated by spores
Half-hardy evergreen fern
Height up to 1.2m (4ft)
Broad, lance-shaped, glossy, green fronds that grow in the shape of a shuttlecock

Sow fresh spores at 21°C (70°F) following the sowing instructions on page 91.

Asplenium nidus

Dicksonia *Dicksoniaeae*

A genus of tender to half-hardy evergreen or semi-evergreen tree ferns. Plant in a humus-rich, moist soil in semi-shade.

Dicksonia antarctica AGM (Australian tree fern)
Propagated by spores
Half-hardy evergreen tree fern
Height up to 10m (30ft)
Stout trunk covered in brown fibres
Lovely, long, palm-like fronds which are lance-shaped and very divided

Sow fresh spores at 21°C (70°F) following the sowing instructions on page 91.

Dryopteris *Dryopteridaceae*

A genus of half-hardy to hardy semi-evergreen or deciduous ferns. Plant in any moist soil in shade.

Dryopteris dilatata AGM (Broad buckler fern)
Propagated by spores
Hardy, semi-evergreen or deciduous fern
Height 1m (3½ft)
Lance-shaped, very divided, arching, mid-green fronds on stout, dark brown stems

Sow fresh spores at 15°C (60°F) following the sowing instructions on page 91.

Dicksonia antartica

Matteuccia struthiopteris

Collecting spores, sowing method and potting on

To collect spores
In mid to late summer, place a portion of mature fern frond on a piece of paper in a dry place. If spores are ripe they will be shed on to the paper and will appear as black, brown or yellow 'powder' which is a mixture of spores and fragments of the spore cases (sporangia).

Sowing method
It is important to sterilise the germination mixture before sowing the fern spores. Do this by pouring boiling water over it. This kills the spores of fungi and other plants that may germinate and crowd out the developing fern prothalli.

Spores should be sparsely sprinkled on a suitable medium, such as finely chopped tree fern fibre, peat moss or sphagnum moss. Two parts peat moss mixed with one part coarse grit also forms an excellent germination base.

Once sown, the containers should be covered with cling film, plastic or glass (allowing some airspace) and kept in indirect light at around 20°C (68°F) for cool-temperate ferns and 26°C (80°F) for tropical ferns. Spores take from 2 to 6 weeks to germinate.

Potting on
After a few weeks the germinating spores appear as a velvety green haze on the surface of the compost (substrate). If it is slimy there may be algae contamination. In this case I recommend that you discard it, because contaminated spores are difficult to rescue. Next time, make sure everything is spotlessly clean, taking the extra precaution of sterilising the compost with boiling water prior to sowing.

When the prothalli are formed and well developed, the spring following sowing, fill some spotlessly clean pots with the sterile, soil-free seed compost. With a clean knife lift small pieces of prothalli and gently place them on the surface of the compost. Spray with sterilised water, cover with cling, film, plastic or glass and place back under protection. The container should be covered with glass or plastic until the fern fronds appear. When the young fronds are growing well, harden off gradually by admitting more light and air. When they are 8cm (3in) tall divide and pot up individually, using a compost mix of two parts peat moss with one part coarse grit, then grow on in partial shade. The hardy varieties of fern will be large enough to plant out in 2–3 years.

Matteuccia *Woodsiaceae*

A genus of hardy, rhizomatous deciduous ferns. Plant in wet soil in semi-shade.

Matteuccia struthiopteris AGM (Ostrich fern)
Propagated by spores
Hardy deciduous fern
Height 1m (3½ft)
Lance-shaped green divided fronds which look rather like ostrich feathers and grow in a shuttlecock habit

Sow fresh spores at 15°C (60°F) following the instructions left.

Platycerium *Polypodiaceae*

A genus of tender evergreen ferns. In cool climates these are best grown in hanging baskets.

Platycerium bifurcatum AGM (Stag's-horn fern)
Propagated by spores
Tender evergreen fern
Minimum temperature 5°C (40°F)
Height 1m (3½ft)
Broad sterile fronds and long arching forked grey-green fertile fronds

Sow fresh spores at 21°C (70°F) following the instructions left.

Polypodium *Polypodiaceae*

A genus of tender to hardy semi-evergreen or evergreen ferns. Plant in moist but not wet soil in semi-shade.

Polypodium vulgare (Common polypody)
Propagated by spores
Hardy evergreen fern
Height 30cm (12in)
Narrow lance-shaped divided mid-green fronds

Sow fresh spores at 15°C (60°F) following the instructions left.

Thelypteris *Thelypteridaceae*

A genus of hardy deciduous ferns. Plant in moist soil in semi-shade.

Thelypteris palustris (Marsh fern)
Propagated by spores
Hardy deciduous fern
Height 75cm (30in)
Long lance-shaped pale green fronds which are very divided

Sow fresh spores at 15°C (60°F) following the instructions left.

grasses

There is a huge range of plants in the grass family, from the common lawn to fashionable bamboos and ornamental grasses. They are great in the garden, giving colour, texture, sound and graceful movement. Another benefit of growing ornamental grasses is that they dry wonderfully for winter flower arrangements.

Grasses are very rewarding plants to grow from seed, and the seeds are easy to collect. In the late summer and early autumn pick the grass stem with the flower, allowing the bracts, which hold the seed, to fluff up or fully dry out. This will take a few days. Strip the seeds from each stem. As most grasses do not need a period of stratification, either sow immediately or store until spring.

Cortaderia selloana, see page 96

Bouteloua *Poaceae*

A genus of hardy to frost-tender annuals, perennials and semi-evergreens. Plant in any well-drained soil in sun to partial shade.

Bouteloua gracilis (Blue grama, Mosquito grass)
Medium seeds: 750 per gram
Hardy perennial, semi-evergreen
Height 37cm (15in)
Comb- or mosquito-shaped flowering spikes which hang at right angles to the stem
Flowers in summer
Decorative, narrow, nodding brown-green leaves which grow in tufts
Good for flower arrangements, fresh or dried

Sow in late summer/early autumn into prepared open ground when air temperature does not go below 10°C (50°F) at night. Germination takes 14–21 days.
OR
Sow in spring in pots or modules using standard, soil-less seed compost (substrate), either a peat free proprietary brand or composted fine propagating bark. Place under protection at 15°C (59°F). Cover with perlite or vermiculite. Germination takes 7–14 days.

Briza *Poaceae*

A genus of hardy to frost-tender annuals, perennials and semi-evergreens. Plant in any well-drained soil in sun to partial shade. This genera self seeds readily.

Briza maxima (Greater quaking grass)
Medium seeds: 400 per gram
Hardy annual
Height up to 50cm (20in)
Loose panicles of pendent, oval-shaped, purplish-green spikes
Panicles borne in summer, up to 10 panicles on a single stem
Mid-green narrow leaves

Briza media (Common quaking grass, Doddering dillies)
Small seeds: 3,300 per gram
Hardy perennial
Height up to 60cm (24in)
Open panicles of pendent, heart-shaped, purplish-brown spikes
Panicles borne in summer, up to 30 panicles on a stem
Mid-green narrow leaves at the base of the plant
Lovely in dry flower arrangements

Sow in late summer to early autumn into prepared open ground, when air temperature does not go below 9°C (48°F) at night. Germination takes 10–15 days.
OR
Sow in spring in pots or modules using standard, soil-less seed compost (substrate). Place under protection at 10°C (50°F), cover with perlite or vermiculite. Germination takes 7–14 days. Will flower within 14 weeks of sowing.

Bromus *Poaceae*

A genus of hardy to frost-tender mainly annuals and some perennials. Plant in any well-drained soil in sun to partial shade.

Bromus macrostachys
Medium seeds: 250 per gram
Hardy annual
Height up to 60cm (24in)
Large spikes with spreading awns
Awns borne in early summer
Narrow compact leaves

Sow in late summer to early autumn into prepared open ground, when air temperature does not go below 9°C (48°F) at night. Germination takes 10–15 days.
OR
Sow in spring in pots or modules using standard, soil-less seed compost (substrate). Place under protection at 10°C (50°F), cover with perlite or vermiculite. Germination takes 7–14 days.

Carex *Cyperaceae*

A genus of fully-hardy to frost-tender evergreen, rhizomatous perennials from the sedge family. Grows naturally by water, but will adapt to any soil, in sun or partial shade.

Carex buchananii AGM (Leatherleaf sedge)
Medium seeds: 700 per gram
Hardy evergreen
Height up to 60cm
Rather insignificant, brown spikelet flowers
Flowers in summer
Very narrow copper-coloured leaves which turn red towards the base, making an attractive mound

Carex pendula (Pendulous sedge)
Medium seeds: 700 per gram
Hardy evergreen
Height up to 1m (3½ft)
Pendent green/brown flower spikes, which look rather like a drooping cat's tail
Flowers in summer
Narrow mid-green leaves

Sow in late summer/early autumn into a prepared open ground when air temperature does not fall below 9°C (48°F) at night. Germination takes 10–15 days.
OR
Sow in spring in pots or modules using standard, soil-less seed compost (substrate). Place under protection at 10°C (50°F), cover with perlite or vermiculite. Germination takes 7–14 days.

Briza maxima

Chasmanthium *Poaceae*

A genus of hardy to frost-tender annuals, perennials and semi-evergreens. Plant in any well-drained soil in sun to partial shade.

Chasmanthium latifolium (*Uniola latifolia*) (Wood oats, Spangle grass)
Medium seeds: 120 per gram
Hardy perennial
Height 80cm ($2^{1}/_{2}$ft)
Attractive drooping panicles of flat brown heads
Panicles borne in summer the first year after sowing
Tufted mid-green flat leaves

Sow in late summer/early autumn into prepared, open ground, when air temperature does not fall below 10°C (50°F) at night. Germination takes 14–21 days.
OR
Sow in spring in pots or modules using standard, soil-less seed compost (substrate). Place under protection at 15°C (59°F), cover with perlite or vermiculite. Germination takes 7–14 days.

Cordyline *Agavaceae*

A genus of half-hardy shrubs and trees. Plant in a fertile well-drained soil in sun or partial shade. Makes an impresssive pot plant, cut watering down in the winter.

Cordyline australis AGM (New Zealand cabbage palm)
Medium seeds: 250 per gram
Half-hardy perennial
Height 3m (10ft). In the correct conditions it will grow up to 10m (33ft)
Fragrant creamy-white flowers followed by small black berries
Mature plants flower in summer
Dense clusters of narrow, sword-like, grey-green leaves
Makes a great feature as a large pot plant

Cordyline indivisa (Cabbage Palm, Dracaena)
Medium seeds: 200 per gram
Half-hardy perennial, often grown as an annual bedding plant
Height 3m (10ft)
Clusters of tiny star-shaped white flowers
Flowers in summer on mature plants only
Long, 60cm–2m (2–6ft) tapering mid-green leaves with a midrib of red or yellow
Makes a good feature as a pot plant

In their countries of origin, both of the above are small trees. Away from their native conditions, they make lovely container plants which display their distinctive leaves to great advantage.

Sow in spring in pots or modules using standard, soil-less seed compost (substrate). Place under protection at 21°C (70°F), cover with perlite or vermiculite. Germination takes 30–40 days.

***Recipe for sowing, planting and growing* Cordyline**

Cordylines are not grasses or palms. As their common name suggests, they are evergreen trees or shrubs. They are grown in many countries, however, as a foliage plant and for this reason they have been grouped with the grasses. They look tremendous planted out during the growing season, their leaves give a texture and structure to the garden. In containers they can form a lovely, striking centre piece.

Ingredients
4 seeds per module or 6 seeds per pot
1 module tray
OR
1 x 8cm (4in) pot
Standard soil-less seed compost (substrate)
Fine-grade perlite (wetted) or vermiculite
White plastic plant label

Method Fill the tray or pot with compost, smooth over, tap down and water in well. Sow the seeds thinly on the top of the compost and press in gently with the flat of the hand. Cover with perlite or vermiculite, and label with the plant name and date. Place the tray or pot into a warm light place out of direct sunlight at an optimum temperature of 21° (70°F). Keep watering to a minimum until germination has taken place, which takes 30–40 days in spring with warmth. Shortly after germination has taken place, and when the seedling are fully emerged, put the containers in a cooler environment at 18° (65°F). You can prick out and pot up approximately 4–6 weeks after germination. These young plants will need a full season's growth with winter protection at not less than 10°C (50°F) before planting out as a summer bedding display. If you are growing the plants on in containers, you will need to split the seedlings as soon as they are large enough to handle. Replant in 8cm (4in) pots, using a soil-less potting compost.

Cortaderia *Poaceae*

A genus of hardy to frost-tender annuals, perennials and semi-evergreens. Plant in any well-drained soil in sun to partial shade.

Cortaderia selloana (Pampas grass)
Small seeds: 5,000 per gram
Hardy evergreen perennial
Height up to 2.5m (8ft)
Very attractive plumes of silver panicles
Panicles borne in summer
Narrow sharp-edged mid-green leaves which can grow to 1.5m (5ft) long

Sow in spring in pots or modules using standard, soil-less seed compost (substrate). Place under protection at 18°C (65°F), cover with perlite or vermiculite. Germination takes 14–21 days.

Eragrostis *Poaceae*

A genus of hardy to frost-tender annuals, perennials and semi-evergreens. Plant in any well-drained soil in sun to partial shade.

Eragrostis curvula (Weeping love grass)
Small seeds: 1,200 per gram
Hardy annual
Height up to 1.2m (4ft)
Drooping panicles of dark olive-grey flowers
Flowers all summer
Impressive mounds of fine dark green arching leaves

Sow in spring in pots or modules, using standard soil-less seed compost (substrate). Cover with perlite or vermiculite and place under protection at 21°C (70°F). Germination takes 4–10 days.

Festuca *Poaceae*

A genus of hardy to frost-tender annuals, perennials and semi-evergreens. Plant in any well-drained, poor soil in a sunny situation.

Festuca glauca (Blue fescue)
Small seeds: 1,300 per gram
Hardy evergreen perennial
Height up to 25cm (10in)
The flowers are inconspicuous spikelets
Flowers in summer
Narrow leaves in shades of blue-green
This plant is very good for edging.

Sow in late summer/early autumn into prepared open ground, when air temperature does not go below 10°C (50°F) at night. Germination takes 14–21 days.
OR
Sow in spring in pots or modules using standard, soil-less seed compost (substrate) and cover with perlite or vermiculite. Place under protection at 15°C (59°F). Germination takes 7–14 days.

Festuca glauca

Hordeum *Poaceae*

A genus of hardy to frost-tender annuals, perennials and semi-evergreens. Plant in any well-drained soil in sun to partial shade.

Hordeum jubatum (Fox-tail barley, Squirrel's-tail grass)
Medium seeds: 550 per gram
Perennial often grown as an annual
Height up to 60cm (24in)
Lovely feathery, plume-like, arching flower spikes with a silky beard at the end of the grain sheath
Flowers in summer
Branching stems with narrow, dark green leaves
This plant looks lovely in gentle winds

Sow in late summer/early autumn into a prepared open ground, when air temperature does not go below 10°C (50°F) at night. Germination takes 14–21 days.
OR
Sow in spring in pots or modules, using standard soil-less seed compost (substrate). Place under protection at 15°C (59°F), cover with perlite or vermiculite. Germination takes 7–14 days.

Koeleria *Poaceae*

A genus of hardy to frost-tender annuals, perennials and semi-evergreens. Plant in any well-drained soil in sun to partial shade.

Koeleria glauca (Glaucous hair grass)
Small seeds: 2,500 per gram
Hardy perennial
Height up to 30cm (12in)
Attractive upright grey-blue flower heads
Flowers in summer
Dense tussocks of narrow blue-grey leaves

Sow in late summer/early autumn into prepared open ground, when air temperature does not go below 9°C (48°F) at night. Germination takes 10–15 days.
OR
Sow in spring in pots or modules, using standard soil-less seed compost (substrate). Place under protection at 21°C (70°F), cover with perlite or vermiculite. Germination takes 3–7 days.

Lagurus *Poaceae*

A genus of hardy to frost-tender annuals, perennials and semi-evergreens. Plant on any well-drained site in a sunny situation, although prefers a sandy soil.

Lagurus ovatus AGM (Hare's-tail grass)
Small seeds: 2,400 per gram
Hardy annual
Height 45cm (18in)
Very attractive egg-shaped, soft panicles of white flower spikes with gold stamens
Flowers in summer
Flat, long, narrow mid-green leaves

Sow in late summer/early autumn into prepared open ground, when air temperature does not go below 10°C (50°F) at night. Germination takes 14–21 days.
OR
Sow in spring in pots or modules, using standard soil-less seed compost (substrate). Place under protection at 20°C (68°F), cover with perlite or vermiculite. Germination takes 7–14 days.

***Recipe for sowing, planting and growing* Lagurus ovatus**
This attractive annual grass looks lovely in the garden grown in clumps or drifts. It is equally happy grown as a container plant.

Ingredients
6 seeds per module or 18 seeds per pot
1 piece white card 14 x 8.5cm ($5^{1}/_{2}$ x $3^{1}/_{2}$in) folded in half
1 module tray
OR
1 x 8cm (4in) pot
Standard soil-less seed compost (substrate)
Fine-grade perlite (wetted) or vermiculite
White plastic plant label

Method Fill the tray or pot with compost, smooth over, tap down and water in well. As the seeds are very fine, use the folded card to help you to sow them thinly (see page 240). Cover with perlite or vermiculite and label with the plant name and date. Place the tray or pot in a warm, light place out of direct sunlight at an optimum temperature of 20°C (68°F). Keep watering to a minimum until germination has taken place, which takes 7–10 days with warmth. Shortly after germination, when the seedlings have fully emerged, put the containers in a cooler environment at 14°C (58°F). Spring-sown plants can be pricked out and potted up approximately 4 weeks after germination. The spring-sown seedlings will be ready to plant out approximately 4 weeks after that. If you are using modules you can plant out directly into a container or the garden as soon as they have rooted right down the module. If you are growing this grass as a container plant, you will need to pot it up in a 1-litre pot which is13cm (5in) in diameter. Otherwise, you can divide the seedlings up and re-pot using a soil-less potting compost (substrate). Keep the container protected until all threat of frost has gone, then harden off before leaving out all night. If you wish to plant in the garden, make sure the seedlings have a period of hardening off, then plant out when there is no threat of frost. Plants grown with heat can bloom within 16 weeks of sowing.

Alternatively, you can sow directly into a prepared site in the garden when the night-time temperature does not fall below 10°C (50°F). Sow the fine seeds thinly, either in a short row, or in a round clump, gently press into the soil with the flat of the hand, and cover lightly. Water in well using a fine rose on the watering can so you will not disturb the fine seeds. Germination takes 14–21 days. If you have sown too thickly it is a good idea to thin the seedlings. Alternatively you can wait until the seedlings have established, then divide them and replant in the garden.

Luzula *Juncaceae*

A genus of hardy annuals, perennials and evergreens from the rush family. Plant in a moist but free-draining soil in sun or partial shade.

Luzula nivea (Snowy woodrush)
Small seeds: 1,600 per gram
Hardy evergreen perennial
Height up to 60cm (24in)
Dense clusters of white flower spikes
Flowers in early summer
Mid-green leaves with white hairy edges

Luzula sylvatica (Greater woodrush)
Small seeds: 2,700 per gram
Hardy evergreen perennial
Height up to 30cm (12in)
Brown flower spikes
Flowers in summer
Mid-green leaves with hairy edges that grow in thick tufts

Sow in spring in pots or modules, using standard soil-less seed compost (substrate). Place under protection at 21°C (70°F), cover with perlite or vermiculite. Germination takes 3–7 days.

These two decorative rushes are very useful in the garden as both like being planted in partial shade.

Pennisetum *Poaceae*

A genus of hardy to frost-tender annuals, perennials and semi-evergreens. Plant in any well-drained soil in sun to partial shade.

Pennisetum setaceum AGM(African fountain grass, Crimson fountain grass)
Small seeds: 1,600 per gram
Half-hardy perennial grown as an annual in cooler or wetter climates
Height up to 1m ($3^{1}/_{2}$ft)
Dense cylindrical panicles of copper-red spikes with attractive bearded bristles
Panicles borne from mid-summer until early winter
Tall fine tufted mid-green leaves

Pennisetum villosum AGM (Feather-top)
Medium seeds: 500 per gram
Half-hardy perennial
Height up to 1m ($3^{1}/_{2}$ft)
Panicles of soft creamy-pink spikes which fade to pale brown with attractive long-bearded bristles
Panicles borne in autumn
Tufted mid-green leaves

Both of these species need winter protection in cold wet climates. Place in a cold frame or cold greenhouse at a minimum temperature of 5°C (40°F) at night.

Sow in late summer/early autumn into prepared open ground, when air temperature does not go below 9°C (48°F) at night. Germination takes 10–15 days.

OR

Sow in spring in pots or modules, using standard soil-less seed compost (substrate). Place under protection at 21°C (70°F), cover with perlite or vermiculite. Germination takes 4–8 days.

Phalaris *Poaceae*

A genus of hardy to frost-tender annuals, perennials and semi-evergreens. Plant in any well-drained soil in sun to partial shade.

Phalaris canariensis (Canary grass)
Medium seeds: 130 per gram
Hardy annual
Height 30cm–1.2m (1–4ft)
The flower heads are white with green veins which are often tinged bright violet
Flowers in summer
Broad mid-green leaves
Canary grass was introduced from the Canary Islands to feed canaries

Sow in late summer/early autumn into a prepared open ground, when air temperature does not go below 10°C (50°F) at night. Germination takes 14–21 days.

OR

Sow in spring in pots or modules, using standard soil-less seed compost (substrate). Place under protection at 15°C (59°F). Cover with perlite or vermiculite. Germination takes 7–14 days.

Polypogon *Poaceae*

A genus of hardy to frost-tender annuals, perennials and semi-evergreens. Plant in a moist/damp soil in sun to partial shade.

Polypogon monspeliensis (Rabbit's-foot grass, Annual beard grass)
Small seeds: 7,000 per gram
Hardy annual
Height up to 60cm (24in)
Dense tawny panicles which resemble a rabbit's foot, soft and bristly
Panicles borne in summer
Flat mid-green leaf, fine and rough to the touch
Grows happily at water margins and along ditches

Sow in late summer/early autumn into a prepared open ground, when air temperature does not go below 9°C (48°F) at night. Germination takes 10–15 days.

OR

Sow in spring in pots or modules, using standard soil-less seed compost (substrate). Place under protection at 10°C (50°F). Cover with perlite or vermiculite. Germination takes 7–14 days.

Setaria *Poaceae*

A genus of hardy to frost-tender annuals, perennials and semi-evergreens. Plant in any well-drained soil in sun to partial shade.

Stipa gigantea

Setaria macrochaeta (Fox-tail grass)
Medium seeds: 500 per gram
Hardy annual
Height up to 90cm (3ft)
Long flower panicles adorned with long, pendulous bristles
Panicles borne in summer
Lance-shaped mid-green leaves

Sow in late summer/early autumn into prepared open ground, when air temperature does not go below 10°C (50°F) at night. Germination takes 14–21 days.
OR
Sow in spring in pots or modules, using standard soil-less seed compost (substrate). Place under protection at 15°C (59°F). Cover with perlite or vermiculite. Germination takes 7–14 days.

Stipa *Poaceae*

A genus of hardy to frost-tender annuals, perennials and semi-evergreens. Plant in any well-drained soil in sun to partial shade.

Stipa gigantea AGM (Golden oats, Giant feather grass)
Medium seeds: 35 per gram
Hardy evergreen perennial
Height up to 2.5m (8ft)
A very elegant grass with open panicles of golden spikes, long awns and dangling golden anthers
Panicles borne from summer until late autumn
Narrow mid-green tufted grass.

Stipa tenuissima (Spear feather, Needle grass, Pony tails)
Medium seeds: 750 per gram
Hardy evergreen perennial
Height up to 40cm (20in)
Arching flower heads, which start greenish white then change to a buff colour
Flowers in summer
Erect, light clumps of thin pale yellow-green leaves

Sow in late summer/early autumn into prepared open ground when air temperature does not go below 10°C (50°F) at night. Germination takes 14–21 days.
OR
Sow in spring in pots or modules using standard soil-less seed compost (substrate). Place under protection at 15°C (59°F). Cover with perlite or vermiculite. Germination takes 7–14 days.

Thamnocalamus *Poaceae*

A genus of hardy to half-hardy perennials, some of which are evergreens. Plant in a well-drained soil, which can be poor. A good mulch of organic matter in spring will feed the plant and retain some moisture. Prefers a sheltered sunny or semi-shaded position.

Thamnocalamus spathaceus (*Sinarundinaria murieiae*) (Muriel bamboo, Umbrella bamboo)
Medium seeds: 100 per gram
Hardy evergreen perennial
Height up to 4m (12ft)
Rather boring flower spikes
Flowers in summer
Attractive young stems with loose, light brown sheathes
Broad lance-shaped apple-green leaves

Sow in spring or early autumn in pots or modules using standard, soil-less seed compost (substrate). Place under protection at 5°C (41°F). Cover with perlite or vermiculite. Germination can be very irregular and periodic over a long period, so do not give up. Do not allow the compost to dry out.

***Recipe for sowing, planting and growing* Thamnocalamus spathaceus**

Bamboos are very attractive and graceful plants which look lovely growing in borders. This species is no exception, with its broad, apple-green leaves.

Ingredients
3 seeds per module or 5 seeds per pot
1 module tray
OR
1 x 8cm (4in) pot
Standard soil-less seed compost (substrate)
Fine-grade perlite (wetted) or vermiculite
White plastic plant label

Method Fill the tray or pot with compost, smooth over, tap down and water in well. Sow the seed thinly on the surface of the compost, cover with perlite or vermiculite, and label with the plant name and date. Place the tray or pot into a warm, light place out of direct sunlight at an optimum temperature of 5°C (41°F). Do not allow the compost to dry out but on the other hand, do not allow it to become soggy. Germination can take anything from 2 weeks to 2 years, so do not discard the container, be patient.

Once the seeds have germinated and are large enough to handle, either pot up from modules into pots or, if seeds have been sown in a pot, divide the seedlings and repot into pots using a soil-based potting compost. Keep the container protected until all threat of frost has gone, then harden off before leaving out all night. If you wish to plant in the garden, make sure the seedlings have a period of hardening off, then plant out when there is no further threat of frost.

herbs

Herbs are some of the most rewarding plants you can grow in any garden, they look good, taste good and do you good. They will adapt to most growing conditions and many are happy growing in containers. What more can you ask from a plant? Most culinary herbs originate from either the Mediterranean or the Tropics, so for those living in cool or cold climates, do not be in too much of a hurry to sow the seed in spring, wait until the weather has warmed up and the light levels increase.

Myrrhis odorata, see page 121

Agrimonia *Rosaceae*

A genus of herbaceous, rhizomatous perennials with long spikes of yellow flowers. Mainly medicinal herbs and also dye plants. Plant in a sunny situation in a well-drained alkaline soil.

Agrimonia eupatoria (Agrimony, Sticklewort)
Medicinal herb
Medium seeds: 115 per gram
Hardy perennial
Height 30–60cm (1–2ft)
Small yellow lightly-scented flowers
Flowers in summer
Elliptic to oval, toothed and hairy green leaves

Sow fresh seed in autumn into pots or modules, using standard loam-based compost (substrate). Cover lightly with compost, place in a cold frame. Germination takes 3–4 weeks. If no germination occurs during this time, place the container outside, exposed to all the weathers (see 'Breaking Seed Dormancy', page 233, for more information). When germination has taken place, overwinter young plants in the cold frame. Can flower in the first year.

Allium *Alliaceae*

This large genus of perennials, some of which are edible, can come in different forms, bulbs, rhizomes or fibrous rootstock, but nearly all have onion-smelling leaves, and most have small flowers which are clustered together into spherical or similar shapes. They are all hardy and in the majority of cases require a sunny site with a well-drained, rich soil.

Allium fistulosum (Welsh onion, Japanese leek)
Culinary and medicinal herb
Medium seeds: 500 per gram
Hardy perennial
Height 50cm (20in)
Large creamy-white global flowers
Flowers in spring to summer of the second year
Long green hollow cylindrical leaves

Allium schoenoprasum (Chives)
Culinary herb
Medium seeds: 800 per gram
Hardy perennial
Height 20cm (8in)
Purple globular flowers
Flowers all summer
Leaves green, hollow and cylindrical

Allium tuberosum (Chinese chives, Garlic chives)
Culinary herb
Medium seeds: 200 per gram
Hardy perennial
Height 30cm (12in)
White star-shaped flowers
Flowers in summer
Flat, solid, thin, lance-shaped, bristly mid-green leaves

Sow in spring in pots or modules, using standard soil-less seed compost (substrate), either a peat free proprietary brand or composted fine propagating bark. Cover with perlite or vermiculite, place under protection at 20°C (68°F). Germination takes 10–20 days.
OR
Sow in late spring into prepared open ground, when the air temperature does not go below 7°C (45°F) at night. Germination takes 14–20 days.

Allium ursinum (Ramsons, Wild garlic)
Culinary and medicinal herb
Medium seeds: 200 per gram
Perennial
Height 30–45cm (12–18in)
Clusters of white star-shaped flowers
Flowers in late spring
Elliptic mid-green leaves

Sow seeds in autumn into pots or modules using a standard loam-based seed compost (substrate) mixed with coarse horticultural sand. Mix to a ratio of 1 part compost + 1 part sand. Cover with coarse horticultural sand and then place outside exposed to all weathers (see 'Breaking Seed Dormancy', page 233, for more information). Germination takes 4-6 months, but it can be erratic, so be patient and do not discard the container.
OR
Sow in early autumn into prepared open ground. Mark the row or area clearly. Germination takes place the following spring, but can be erratic.

Anchusa *Boraginaceae*

A genus of annuals, biennials, or perennials usually with attractive flowers. Plant in a sunny position in a well-drained soil. Dislikes wet winters.

Anchusa officinalis (Alkanet)
Medicinal herb
Medium seeds: 230 per gram
Hardy perennial, sometimes grown as a biennial
Height 1m (3$^{1}/_{2}$ft)
Bright blue flowers, similar to forget-me-nots
Flowers in summer
Rough lance-shaped evergreen leaves.

Anchusa capensis 'Blue Angel'
Medicinal herb
Medium seeds: 500 per gram
Hardy biennial
Height 20cm (8in)
Small clusters of brilliant blue flowers
Flowers in summer
Lance-shaped bristly leaves

Sow fresh perennial seeds in autumn into pots or modules, using standard soil-less seed compost (substrate), either a peat free proprietary brand or composted fine propagating bark. Cover with compost, place in a cold frame. Germination takes 2–16 weeks.

Allium schoenoprasum

Overwinter young plants in a cold frame.
OR
Sow biennial seeds in spring into pots or modules, using standard soil-less seed compost (substrate), either a peat free proprietary brand or composted fine propagating bark. Cover with compost, place in a cold frame. Germination takes 2-3 weeks.
OR
Sow biennial seeds in late spring into prepared open ground, when the air temperature does not go below 7°C (45°F) at night. Germination takes 2-3 weeks

Anethum *Apiaceae*

There is only a single species in this genus, mentioned below. Plant in a sunny site in a well-drained soil. Do not plant by fennel as they can hybridise. The seed is viable for 3–5 years.

Anethum graveolens (Dill)
Culinary and medicinal herb
Medium seeds: 600 per gram
Hardy annual
Height 90cm (3ft)
Umbels of small yellow flowers followed by oval, flat, aromatic seeds
Flowers in summer
Fine thread-like mid-green aromatic leaves

Sow seeds in early spring into pots, using standard soil-less seed compost (substrate), either a peat free proprietary brand or composted fine propagating bark. Cover with perlite or vermiculite, place under protection at 15°C (60°F). Germination takes 5–10 days.
OR
Sow seeds in late spring into prepared open ground, when the air temperature does not go below 7°C (45°F) at night. Germination takes 2–3 weeks.

In my opinion sowing direct into open ground gives the best crop because dill hates being transplanted.

Angelica *Apiaceae*

A genus of short-lived perennials and biennials which have many umbels of small white to purple flowers in summer. The ideal planting situation would be with the roots in the shade and the flowers in the sun. Angelica prefers a damp soil.

Angelica archangelica (Angelica)
Culinary and medicinal herb
Medium seeds: 200 per gram
Biennial
Height 2m (6ft)
Umbels of small green-white flowers
Flowers in late spring of the second year
Large deeply-divided mid-green leaves

It is vital to sow fresh seeds, as seeds are viable for only 3 months. Sow seed in autumn into pots or modules, using a standard loam-based seed compost (substrate) mixed with coarse horticultural sand to a ratio of 1 part compost + 1 part sand. Cover with coarse horticultural sand, then place outside exposed to all the weathers (see 'Breaking Seed Dormancy', page 233, for more information). Germination takes between 10 days and 6 months, but can be erratic, so be patient and do not discard the container. When the seeds have germinated, move young plants to a cold frame. Can flower in its first year.
OR
Sow in early autumn into prepared open ground. Mark the row or area clearly. Germination can take from 10 days to the following spring.

***Recipe for sowing, planting and growing* Angelica archangelica**
Ingredients
5 seeds per module or 8 seeds per pot
1 module tray
OR
1 x 8cm (4in) pot
Standard loam-based seed compost (substrate) mixed with coarse horticultural sand to a ratio of 1 part compost + 1 part sand
White plastic plant label
OR
Prepared site in the garden
2 white plastic plant labels

Method In early autumn fill the module tray or pot with compost, smooth over, tap down and water in well. Use fresh seed, sow 8 seeds per pot or 5 seeds per module. Having sown the seeds into the pots cover lightly with compost. Label with the plant name and date. Place the pot or module outside, on a level surface, so it is exposed to all weathers, including frosts. Do not worry if you live in a snowy area and the containers get immersed in snow, for melting snow will aid germination. If you do not live in an area which will get a winter frost, it is a good idea to put the seed plus a handful of damp sand into a plastic bag which is clearly marked. Seal the bag. Place in the refrigerator for 3 weeks. Remove and sow as described above, then place outside.

Whichever method you use, germination is a bit erratic, taking anything from 10 days to 6 months. Do not give up and discard your compost, it might germinate next week. When the seeds have germinated move young plants to a cold frame. Angelica can flower in its first year.

Alternatively, you can sow directly into a prepared site in the garden in early autumn. Space the seeds 30–45cm (12–18in) apart, gently press into the soil and lightly cover, water in well. Mark the area clearly with 2 labels. Germination can take from 10 days or not until the following spring.

Anthriscus *Apiaceae*

A genus of annual, biennial and perennial herbs. Clusters of a small, white umbels of flowers in summer. Plant in a light soil with a degree of moisture retention and in semi-shade.

Anthriscus cerefolium (Chervil)
Culinary herb
Medium seeds: 425 per gram
Hardy annual (occasional biennial)
Height 30–60cm (1–2ft)
Clusters of tiny white flowers
Flowers in summer
Light green aromatic fern-like leaves
One of the traditional *fines herbes* in French cuisine

Sow fresh seeds in early spring into pots using standard soil-less seed compost (substrate), either a peat free proprietary brand or composted fine propagating bark. Cover with perlite or vermiculite, place under protection at 15°C (60°F). Germination takes 5–10 days.
OR
Sow seeds in late spring into prepared open ground when the air temperature does not go below 7°C (45°F) at night. Germination takes 2–3 weeks.

Apium *Apiaceae*

A genus of annual, biennial or perennial herbs. They all have white flowers. Plant in semi-shade with a damp soil for best results.

Apium graveolens (Celery leaf)
Culinary herb
Small seeds: 3,200 per gram
Hardy biennial
Height 30cm–1m (1–3ft)
Tiny green-white flowers
Flowers in its second summer
Cut mid-green leaves

Sow fresh seeds in early spring into pots using standard soil-less seed compost (substrate), either a peat free proprietary brand or composted fine propagating bark. Cover with perlite or vermiculite, place under protection at 15°C (60°F). Germination takes 5–10 days.
OR
Sow seeds in late spring into prepared open ground, when the air temperature does not go below 7°C (45°F) at night. Germination takes 2–3 weeks.

Arnica *Asteraceae*

A genus of perennial rhizomatous herbs. They are all hardy and have yellow daisy-like flowers throughout the summer. Plant in free-draining, humus-rich soil in a sunny situation. Both the species mentioned are good in rockeries.

Arnica chamissonis (North American arnica)
Medicinal herb
Small seeds: 1,800 per gram
Hardy perennial,
Height 50cm (20in)
Clusters of yellow daisy-like flowers

Apium graveolens

Flowers throughout the summer
Oval light green slightly hairy leaves

Arnica montana (Leopard's bane)
Medicinal herb
Medium seeds: 900 per gram
Hardy perennial
Height 30cm (1ft)
Large single scented yellow flowers
Flowers throughout the summer
Oval, light green, hairy leaves

Sow fresh seed in autumn into pots or modules using standard loam-based compost (substrate). Cover lightly with compost, place in a cold frame. Germination takes 3–4 weeks. If no germination occurs during this time, place the container outside exposed to all the weathers (see 'Breaking Seed Dormancy', page 233, for more information). Germination can take a further 5–7 months on average or even as long as 2 years. When germination has taken place, overwinter young plants in the cold frame. Can flower in its first year.

Artemisia *Asteraceae*

A very large genus of perennials, annuals, shrubs some of which are evergreen or semi-evergreen, nearly all have aromatic foliage. Usually the flowers are small and insignificant, this is made up for by the foliage which in many cases is a very attractive silver. Plant in a sunny situation in a well-drained soil.

Artemisia absinthium (Wormwood)
Medicinal herb
Tiny seeds: 15,000 per gram
Hardy perennial,
Height 1m (3ft)
Tiny insignificant yellow flower heads borne in sprays
Flowers in summer
Abundant, divided, aromatic grey-green leaves

Artemisia annua (Sweet Annie, Sweet wormwood)
Medicinal herb
Minute seeds: 30,000 per gram
Hardy annual
Height 1.5m (5ft)
Tiny yellow flowers in loose panicles
Flowers in summer
Highly aromatic, pinnate, divided, saw-toothed leaves

Artemisia dracunculoides (Russian tarragon)
Culinary herb
Small seeds: 6,000 per gram
Hardy perennial
Height 90cm (3ft)
Tiny insignificant, yellow flower heads borne in sprays
Flowers in summer
Aromatic, long, narrow, slightly coarse green leaves

Artemisia vulgaris (Mugwort, Chinese moxa)
Medicinal herb
Small seeds: 9,000 per gram
Hardy perennial,
Height 120cm (4ft)
Panicles of insignificant red-brown flowers
Flowers in late summer
Pinnate, aromatic, dark green leaves with white undersides

Sow fresh seeds in spring into pots or modules using standard soil-less seed compost (substrate), either a peat free proprietary brand or composted fine propagating bark. As these are very fine seeds, mix with the finest sand or talcum powder for an even sowing. Do not cover. Water from the bottom or with a fine spray. Place under protection at 20°C (68°F). Germination takes 10–20 days.

Borago *Boraginaceae*

A genus of annual and perennial herbs native to the Mediterranean region. They all have attractive flowers. Plant in a sunny situation and a well-drained fertile soil. These plants can self-seed and can be invasive.

Borago officinalis (Borage)
Culinary and medicinal herb
Medium seeds: 60 per gram
Hardy annual
Height 60cm (2ft)
Loose racemes of blue-purple star-shaped flowers
Flowers in summer
Oval to oblong bristly, light green leaves

Borago officinalis 'Alba' (White borage)
Culinary herb
Medium seeds: 60 per gram
Hardy annual
Height 50cm (20in)
Loose racemes of white star-shaped flowers
Flowers in summer
Oval to oblong, bristly, light grey-green leaves

Sow seeds in early spring into pots using standard soil-less seed compost (substrate), either a peat free proprietary brand or composted fine propagating bark. Cover with perlite or vermiculite, place under protection at 20°C (68°F). Germination takes 5–14 days.
OR
Sow seeds in late spring into prepared open ground, when the air temperature does not go below 7°C (45°F) at night. Germination takes 2–3 weeks.

Calendula *Asteraceae*

A genus of shrubs and annuals. The shrubs require a minimum night temperature of 5°C (41°F). The annuals are hardy. Both should be planted in a sunny situation in a free-draining soil.

Calendula officinalis (Pot marigold)
Culinary and medicinal herb
Medium seeds: 150 per gram
Hardy annual
Height 45cm (18in)

Calendula officinalis

Daisy-like single yellow or orange flowers
Flowers from spring to autumn
Light green, slightly aromatic lance-shaped leaves

Calendula officinalis 'Fiesta Gitana' **(Marigold 'Fiesta Gitana')**
Culinary and medicinal herb
Medium seeds: 140 per gram
Hardy annual
Height 20cm (8in)
Daisy-like double yellow or orange flowers
Flowers from spring to autumn
Light green, slightly aromatic, lance-shaped leaves

Sow seeds in early spring into pots using standard soil-less seed compost (substrate), either a peat free proprietary brand or composted fine propagating bark. Cover with perlite or vermiculite, place under protection at 20°C (68°F). Germination takes 5–14 days.
OR
Sow seeds in late spring into prepared open ground, when the air temperature does not go below 5°C (41°F) at night. Germination takes 2–3 weeks.

Calomeria *Asteraceae*

There is only one species in the genus Calomeria which is native to Australia. Plant in well-drained soil in sun or partial shade. In cooler climates it makes a spectacular container plant.

Calomeria amaranthoides (Humea elegans) **(Incense plant, Plume humea, Plume bush) DANGEROUS IRRITANT**
Aromatic herb
Medium seeds: 450 per gram
Half-hardy annual in cool climates. (Biennial or short-lived perennial in warmer climates)
Height 3m (9ft)
Tiny delicate coral bracts with minute cream daisy-like flowers
Flowers from summer until early autumn
Highly aromatic, mid-green, large, oblong-shaped leaves

Sow seeds in autumn into pots or modules, using standard soil-less seed compost (substrate), either a peat free proprietary brand or composted fine propagating bark, mixed with extra perlite or vermiculite for aeration. Mix to a ratio of 3 parts compost + 1 part perlite or vermiculite. Do not cover the seeds, place in a cold frame or unheated greenhouse. Germination takes 7–9 months, but can be erratic.

Carum *Apiaceae*

A genus of annual, biennial or perennial plants which have white or pink flowers displayed in compound umbels. Plant in a sunny situation and a well-drained, fertile soil.

Carum carvi **(Caraway)**
Culinary and medicinal herb
Medium seeds: 300 per gram
Hardy biennial
Height 20cm (8in) in the first year, 60cm (2ft) in the second year
Clusters of small umbels of pinkish-white flowers
Flowers in its second summer
Flowers followed by oblong aromatic seeds
Leaves feathery, light green, similar to carrot leaves

Sow fresh seeds in early spring into pots using standard soil-less seed compost (substrate), either a peat free proprietary brand or composted fine propagating bark. Cover with perlite or vermiculite, place under protection at 15°C (60°F). Germination takes 5–10 days.
OR
Sow fresh seeds in late spring into prepared open ground, when the air temperature does not go below 7°C (45°F) at night. Germination takes 2–3 weeks.
Sowing directly into open ground gives the best crop, because caraway hates being transplanted.

Cedronella *Lamiaceae*

This genus contains the single species *Cedronella canariensis* described below. Plant in a sunny position in a well-drained sandy loam.

Cedronella canariensis **(Balm of Gilead)**
Medicinal herb
Medium seed: 900 per gram
Half-hardy perennial, partial evergreen
Height 1m (3ft)
Aromatic pale mauve/pink 2-lipped flowers
Flowers throughout the summer
Strongly eucalyptus-scented mid-green trifoliate leaves

Sow seeds in spring into pots using standard soil-less seed compost (substrate), either a peat free proprietary brand or composted fine propagating bark. Cover with perlite or vermiculite, place under protection at 20°C (68°F). Germination takes 14–20 days but can be spasmodic, so be patient.

Chamaemelum *Asteraceae*

A genus of annuals and evergreen perennials which have daisy-like flowers in summer. Plant in a sunny position in a fairly dry, light rich soil.

Chamaemelum nobile **(Roman chamomile)**
Medicinal herb
Small seeds: 6,500 per gram
Hardy perennial
Height 30cm (1½ft)
White daisy-like flowers with yellow centres
Flowers all summer
Sweet-smelling finely divided mid-green foliage

Sow seeds in early spring into pots using standard soil-less seed compost (substrate), either a peat free proprietary brand or composted fine propagating bark. Cover with perlite or vermiculite, place under protection at 18°C (65°F). Germination takes 14–20 days.

Chenopodium *Chenopodiaceae*

A genus of about 150 species of herbaceous sub-shrubs and annuals. The flowers are small and insignificant. The leaves and the seeds are both important as vegetable crops. Plant in sun or semi-shade in any alkaline soil. These plants are tolerant of salt.

Chenopodium ambrosioides (Epazote, Mexican wormseed)
Culinary and medicinal herb
Small seeds: 6,750 per gram
Half-hardy annual
Height 1.2m (4ft)
Tiny greenish-brown flowers
Flowers in early summer
Arrow-shaped green leaves with a tinge of red

Chenopodium bonus-henricus (Good King Henry)
Culinary herb
Medium seeds: 420 per gram
Hardy perennial
Height 60cm (2ft)
Tiny greenish-yellow flowers
Flowers in early summer
Green arrow-shaped leaves

Sow seeds in early spring into pots using standard soil-less seed compost (substrate), either a peat free proprietary brand or composted fine propagating bark. Cover with perlite or vermiculite, place under protection at 18°C (65°F). Germination takes 14–20 days.
OR
Sow seeds in late spring into prepared open ground, when the air temperature does not go below 5°C (41°F) at night. Germination takes 2–3 weeks.

Coriandrum *Apiaceae*

A genus of annuals. Plant in a sunny position in a well-drained soil.

Coriandrum sativum (Coriander, Cilantro)
Culinary and medicinal herb
Medium seeds: 140 per gram
Tender annual
Height 60cm (2ft)
Flowers white with a hint of pink
Flowers in summer
Lobed and pinnate aromatic green leaves

Sow seeds in early spring into pots using standard soil-less seed compost (substrate), either a peat free proprietary brand or composted fine propagating bark. Cover with perlite or vermiculite, place under protection at 18°C (65°F). Germination takes 5–10 days.
OR
Sow seeds in late spring into prepared open ground, when the air temperature does not go below 7°C (45°F) at night. Germination takes 2–3 weeks.

***Recipe for sowing, planting and growing* Coriandrum sativum**

Coriander is a very useful herb for the kitchen, combining well with many dishes from curries to salads. It is one plant that hates being transplanted and when it is, it feels threatened and bolts before going to seed. The following methods should give a good crop of leaves before the plant runs to flower.

Ingredients
10–15 seeds
1 x 13cm (5in) pot
Standard soil-less seed compost (substrate), either a peat free proprietary brand or composted fine propagating bark
Fine-grade perlite (wetted) or vermiculite
White plastic label
OR
Prepared site in the garden
2 white plastic labels

Method Fill the pot with the compost, firm and water in well. Sow the seeds thinly on the top of the compost, press gently in with a flat hand, cover with perlite, label with plant name and date. Place the pot in a warm light place 18°C (65°F), not full sun. Keep watering to a minimum until germination has taken place, which takes 5–10 days in late spring. Once the seedlings start germinating, make sure the container gets as much light as possible. If you live in a mild climate, where air temperature does not go below 7°C (45°F), place the container outside during the day, bringing in at night. Continue until the third leaf starts to appear, then the container can be left out all night. If you are keeping the pot on the window sill, rotate daily so the plant does not start growing towards the light. Start picking the leaves once they are large enough, this will encourage the new growth to develop. Start a second pot 4 weeks later to ensure a continuous crop.

Alternatively, you can sow directly into a prepared site in the garden when the night-time temperature does not fall below 10°C (50°F). Space the seeds 2.5cm (1in) apart in a drill 2.5cm (1in) deep. Lightly cover with soil and water in well. Label either end of the seed row. Germination takes 10–20 days. Start picking as soon as the leaves are large enough. Start a second row 4 weeks later to ensure continuous crop.

Cuminum *Apiaceae*

A genus of half-hardy annuals. Plant in a sunny situation in a free-draining soil. The plant needs a minimum of 16°C (60°F) to grow.

Cuminum cyminum (Cumin)
Culinary and medicinal herb
Medium seeds: 300 per gram
Half-hardy annual
Height 15–30cm (6–12in)
Umbels of white or pinkish flowers
Flowers in summer
Dark green finely-divided leaves

Sow seeds in spring into pots using standard soil-less seed compost (substrate), either a peat free proprietary brand or composted fine propagating bark. Cover with perlite or vermiculite, place under protection at 18°C (65°F). Germination takes 5–10 days.

Cymbopogon *Poaceae*

A genus of half-hardy perennial aromatic grasses, mostly tropical. These plants can be grown in pots in a temperature no lower than 7°C (45°F). Keep watering to a minimum in winter.

Cymbopogon citratus
Culinary and medicinal herb
Small seeds: 7,000 per gram
Half-hardy perennial
Height 1m (3ft)
Flowers rarely in cultivation and only in the tropics
Lemon-scented linear leaves

Sow seeds in early spring into pots using standard soil-less seed compost (substrate), either a peat free proprietary brand or composted fine propagating bark. Cover with perlite or vermiculite, place under protection at 20°C (68°F). Germination takes 15–25 days.

Cynara *Asteraceae*

A genus of large thistle-like perennials. Lovely large blue, violet or white flower heads. Plant in a sunny situation in a well-drained fertile soil.

Cynara cardunculus AGM **(Cardoon)**
Culinary herb
Medium seeds: 24 per gram
Hardy perennial
Height 1–2.5m (3–8ft)
Dramatic multi-branched thistle heads and lovely purple flowers
Flowers in mid summer
Handsome grey-blue leaves

Sow seeds in early spring into pots using standard soil-less seed compost (substrate), either a peat free proprietary brand or composted

Cynara cardunculus

fine propagating bark. Cover with perlite or vermiculite, place under protection at 18°C (65°F). Germination takes 5–10 days.
OR
Sow seeds in late spring into prepared open ground, when the air temperature does not go below 7°C (45°F) at night. Germination takes 2–3 weeks.

Diplotaxis *Brassicaceae*

A genus of annuals and perennials native to the Mediterranean area. For the best crop sow directly into the garden in a lightly shaded position in a rich moist soil.

Diplotaxis muralis (Rocket, Wild rocket)
Culinary herb
Small seeds: 4,500 per gram
Perennial
Height 30cm (1ft)
Yellow flowers
Flowers in summer
Green serrated and toothed leaves, very strongly flavoured

Sow seeds in early spring into pots using standard soil-less seed compost (substrate), either a peat free proprietary brand or composted fine propagating bark. Cover with perlite or vermiculite, place under protection at 18°C (65°F). Germination takes 5–10 days.
OR
Sow seeds in late spring into prepared open ground, when the air temperature does not go below 7°C (45°F) at night. Germination takes 2–3 weeks.

Dipsacus *Dipsacaceae*

A genus of hardy erect hairy or prickly biennial plants. Plant in semi-shade in a damp soil (clay).

Dipsacus fullonum subsp. *fullonum* (Teasel fullers)
Medicinal herb
Medium seed: 350 per gram
Hardy biennial
Height up to 2m (6ft)
Small mauve flowers which appear in successive circles around the cone-shaped spiny flower head
Flowers in summer
Bristly green leaves

Sow fresh seeds in autumn into pots or modules using standard soil-less seed compost (substrate), either a peat free proprietary brand or composted fine propagating bark. Cover with compost, place in a cold frame. Germination takes 3 weeks to 4 months and can be erratic. Overwinter young plants in the cold frame. Flowers in second year.

Echinacea *Asteraceae*

A genus of perennial plants native to the United States. All have lovely lightly-scented, daisy-like flowers with conical centres. Plant in a sunny situation in a rich, free-draining soil.

Echinacea pallida (Cone Flower)
Medicinal herb
Medium seeds: 180 per gram
Hardy perennial
Height 1.2m (4 ft)
Purple honey-scented, daisy-like flowers with conical orange-brown centres
Flowers in summer to early autumn
Lance-shaped, mid-green leaves

Sow seeds in early spring into pots using standard soil-less seed compost (substrate), either a peat free proprietary brand or composted fine propagating bark. Cover with perlite or vermiculite, place under protection at 18°C (65°F). Germination takes 15–24 days. If no germination has occurred after 28 days put the container outside on a hardstanding for 21 days then back into the heat for a further 14 days. It can flower in the first year, but is more likely to flower in the second.

***Recipe for sowing, planting and growing* Echinacea pallida**
Echinacea has become a very important medicinal herb. The part used in medicine is the root, so you will need a few plants if you are growing it for this purpose. However, the flower alone makes echinacea worth growing, it looks lovely in any border.

Ingredients
5 seeds per module or 9 seeds per pot
1 module tray,
OR
1 x 8cm (4in) pot
Standard soil-less seed compost (substrate), either a peat free proprietary brand or composted fine propagating bark
Fine-grade perlite (wetted) or vermiculite
White plastic plant label

Method In early spring fill the tray or pot with compost, smooth over, tap down and water in well. Sow the seeds thinly on to the surface of the compost. Cover with perlite or vermiculite and label with the plant name and date. Place the tray or pot in a warm light place out of direct sunlight at an optimum temperature of 18°C (65°F). Keep watering to a minimum until germination has taken place, which takes 15–24 days. If no germination has occurred after 28 days it is worth putting the container outside on a hardstanding for 21 days, then back in a warm light place out of direct sunlight at an optimum temperature of 18°C (65°F) until germination starts. As soon as you see the seedlings emerge, remove the container from the heat, place in a cooler, warm light place and grow on until the seedlings are large enough to handle approximately 3–4 weeks after germination. Either prick out and pot up, or if you are using modules you can plant out directly into the garden after a period of hardening off and when there is no threat of frost.

Echium *Boraginaceae*

A genus of annuals, biennials, perennials and evergreen shrubs, some of which are tender. All grown for their lovely flowers. Plant in a sunny site in a well-drained fertile soil.

Echium vulgare (Viper's bugloss)
Medicinal herb
Medium seeds: 230 per gram
Hardy biennial
Height 50cm (20in)
Lovely flowers, purple in bud, then blue and pink when in flower
Flowers in early summer
Bristly oval leaves

Sow fresh seeds in autumn into pots or modules using a standard loam-based seed compost (substrate) mixed with coarse horticultural sand. Mix to a ratio of 1 part compost + 1 part sand. Cover with coarse horticultural sand, then place outside exposed to all the weathers. (see 'Breaking Seed Dormancy', page 233, for more information). Germination takes 3 weeks to 4 months, but can be erratic, so be patient, and do not discard the container. Flowers in its second year.

Eruca *Brassicaceae*

A genus of annuals and perennials native to the Mediterranean area. For the best crop sow directly into a lightly-shaded position in a rich moist soil.

Eruca vesicaria subsp. *sativa* (Rocket, Salad rocket, Arugola, Rucola)
Culinary Herb
Medium seeds: 700 per gram
Annual
Height 60cm–1m (2–3ft)
Cream flowers with purple veins
Flowers in summer
Green, toothed leaves, tasting of mustard, pepper and beef

Sow seeds in early spring into pots using standard soil-less seed compost (substrate), either a peat free proprietary brand or composted fine propagating bark. Cover with perlite or vermiculite, place under protection at 18°C (65°F). Germination takes 5–10 days.
OR
Sow seeds in late spring into prepared open ground when the air temperature does not go below 7°C (45°F) at night. Germination takes 2–3 weeks.

Eupatorium *Asteraceae*

A genus of hardy and half-hardy shrubs and perennials, grown mainly for their flowers. Plant in moist, free-draining soil in sun or partial shade.

Eupatorium cannabinum (Hemp Agrimony, Thoroughwort)
Medicinal herb
Small seeds: 2,800 per gram
Perennial
Height 30cm–1.2m (1–4ft)
Clusters of mauve-pink flowers
Flowers from summer to early autumn
Green leaves divided into 3 or 5 segments

Eupatorium purpureum (Joe Pye weed, Gravel root, Queen of the Meadow)
Medicinal herb
Small seeds: 3,800 per gram
Perennial
Height 1.2–3m (4–10ft)
Clusters of pink flowers
Flowers from summer to early autumn
Finely-toothed, oval leaves with a faint vanilla scent when crushed

Sow fresh seeds in autumn into pots or modules, using standard loam-based seed compost (substrate). Cover with fine sand and place in a cold frame. Germination takes 6–10 weeks. If no germination has occurred after 28 days it is worth putting the container outside on a hardstanding for 21 days then back into the cold frame (see 'Breaking Seed Dormancy', page 233, for more details). Overwinter young plants in a cold frame.

Filipendula *Rosaceae*

A genus of hardy perennials, most of which are good marginal water plants, flowering from mid-spring to mid-summer. Plant in moist or boggy soil in sun or partial shade.

Filipendula ulmaria (Meadowsweet)
Medicinal herb
Small seeds: 1,200 per gram
Hardy perennial
Height 90cm (3ft)
Frothy creamy-white scented flowers
Flowers in mid-summer
Darkish green, pinnate, serrated leaves, aromatic when crushed

Sow seeds in early spring into pots or modules using standard soil-less seed compost (substrate), either a peat free proprietary brand or composted fine propagating bark. Cover with perlite or vermiculite and then place in a cold frame. Germination takes 1–3 months.

Foeniculum *Apiaceae*

This genus contains the single species *Foeniculum vulgare* described below. Plant in a sunny position in a well-drained sandy loam, dislikes damp cold winters.

Foeniculum vulgare (Fennel)
Culinary and medicinal herb
Medium seeds: 230 per gram
Perennial sometimes biennial
Height 1.5m ($4^1/_2$ft)
Umbels of small yellow flowers which are followed by grey-brown aromatic seeds
Flowers in summer
Soft green feathery aromatic foliage

Sow in spring in pots or modules, using standard soil-less seed compost (substrate), either a peat free proprietary brand or composted fine propagating bark. Place under protection at 20°C (68°F). Germination takes 7–10 days.
OR
Sow in late spring into prepared open ground, when air temperature does not go below 5°C (41°F) at night. Germination takes 14–20 days.

Filipendula ulmaria

Fragaria *Rosaceae*

A genus of hardy low-growing perennials. Plant in a humus-rich soil in sun or partial shade.

Fragaria vesca (Wild strawberry)
Culinary and medicinal herb
Small seeds: 3,000 per gram
Hardy perennial
Height 25cm (9in)
Small white flowers with a yellow centre followed by small sweet fruit throughout the summer and early autumn
Flowers in early summer
Tri-foliate, mid-green toothed leaves

Sow fresh seed in early autumn in pots or modules using standard soil-less seed compost (substrate), either a peat free proprietary brand or composted fine propagating bark. Do not cover seeds, place in a cold frame. Germination takes 6–10 weeks.
OR
Sow in spring in pots or modules. Do not cover. Place under protection at 20°C (68°F). Remove from heat as soon as germination starts and place the container under protection at 15°C (60°F) to grow on.

Galium *Rubiaceae*

A large genus of annuals and perennials. Will grow in most situations but prefers a moist well-drained neutral soil in a shady site, will adapt to sun.

Galium odoratum (Asperula odorata) (Sweet woodruff)
Medicinal herb
Medium seeds: 180 per gram
Hardy perennial
Height 35cm (15in)
Panicles of insignificant red-brown flowers
Flowers in late summer
Pinnate aromatic dark green leaves with white undersides

Galium verum (Lady's bedstraw, Cheese rennet)
Medicinal herb
Tiny seeds: 1,500 per gram
Hardy perennial,
Height 50cm (20in)
Tiny cream or yellow flowers in dense panicles
Flowers in early summer
Thread-like green leaves

Sow fresh seeds in autumn into pots or modules using standard loam-based seed compost (substrate). Cover with coarse horticultural sand and then place outside exposed to all the weathers (see 'Breaking Seed Dormancy', page 233, for more information). Germination takes 1–6 months, but can take up to a year, so do not give up.

Glycyrrhiza *Papilionaceae*

A genus of summer-flowering hardy to semi-hardy perennials. Plant in a rich, deep sandy loam, with a bias to alkaline, in a sunny situation. Home-collected seed in cool climates has a tendency to be non-viable.

Glycyrrhiza glabra (Liquorice)
Medicinal herb
Medium seeds: 120 per gram
Hardy perennial
Height 1.5m (5ft)
Pea-like purple/blue and white flowers borne in short spikes
Flowers in late summer
Large greenish leaves divided into oval leaflets

Sow seeds in spring into pots or modules using standard soil-less seed compost (substrate), either a peat free proprietary brand or composted fine propagating bark. Place under protection at 20°C (68°F). Germination should take 10–14 days, but can be erratic and slow.

Hesperis *Brassicaceae*

A genus of hardy annuals and perennials which flower from spring until mid-summer. Plant in a free-draining soil in a sunny situation.

Hesperis matronalis (Sweet rocket, Dame's rocket)
Culinary and medicinal herb
Medium seeds: 500 per gram
Hardy biennial
Height 60–90cm (2–3ft)
Sweetly-scented pink, mauve, purple and white flowers
Flowers in summer
Green slightly hairy lance-shaped leaves

Sow seeds in spring into pots or modules using standard soil-less seed compost (substrate), either a peat free proprietary brand or composted fine propagating bark. Place under protection at 20°C (68°F). Germination takes 7–10 days.
OR
Sow in late spring into prepared open ground, when air temperature does not go below 5°C (41°F) at night. Germination takes 14 to 20 days. Flowers in its second year.

Hyoscyamus *Solanaceae*

A genus of annuals, biennials and perennials. Plant in free-draining poor soil in a sunny situation, good for dry slopes or walls.

Hyoscyamus niger (Henbane, Poisoned tobacco, Devil's eye, Hogbean)
POISONOUS PLANT
Medicinal herb
Small seeds: 1,400 per gram
Hardy annual/biennial
Height 65cm (2ft)
Purple veined funnel-shaped yellow/brown or cream flowers
Flowers in summer to early autumn
The leaves are hairy with large teeth, the upper leaves have no stalks

Sow seeds in spring into pots or modules using standard soil-less seed compost (substrate), either a peat free proprietary brand or composted fine propagating bark. Place under protection at 20°C (68°F). Germination takes 10–15 days. If you want it to behave like a biennial, sow seeds in early autumn into pots or modules, using standard soil-less seed compost (substrate), either a peat free proprietary brand or composted fine propagating bark. Place under protection at 20°C (68°F). Do not allow the compost to dry out. Germination takes 14–21 days. Overwinter young plants under protection.

Hypericum *Clusiaceae*

A large genus of fully- to half-hardy perennials, semi-evergreens and evergreen plants, all of which have attractive yellow flowers with prominent stamens. The named species below should be planted in a well-drained soil in a sunny situation, it can be invasive.

Hypericum perforatum (St John's wort)
Medicinal herb
Small seeds: 10,000 per gram
Hardy perennial,
Height 30–90cm (1–3ft)
Lightly-scented yellow flowers with minute black dots
Flowers in summer
The small mid-green oval leaves are stalkless and covered with tiny perforations

Sow fresh seeds in spring into pots or modules using standard soil-less seed compost (substrate), either a peat free proprietary brand or composted fine propagating bark. As these are very fine seeds, mix with the finest sand or flour. Do not cover. Water from the bottom or with a fine spray. Place under protection at 20°C (68°F) or in a cold frame. Germination takes 10–20 days with warmth or 15–30 days in a cold frame.

***Recipe for sowing, planting and growing* Hypericum perforatum**

St John's wort has become a very important medicinal herb. The whole of the plant is used in some way for various ailments. It is a native wild flower of the UK and will self seed in the garden. However, as the seeds are very fine I do recommend sowing them in a controlled method rather than sowing the seed directly on to the garden.

Ingredients

10 fresh seeds per module or 15 fresh ripe seeds per pot (or as near as you can manage)
Fine horticultural sand, or fine plain white flour
1 piece of white card 14 x 8.5cm ($5\frac{1}{2}$ x $3\frac{1}{2}$in) folded in half
1 module tray
OR
1 x 8cm (4in) pot
Standard soil-less seed compost (substrate), either a peat free proprietary brand or composted fine propagating bark
White plastic plant label

Method In spring fill the tray or pot with compost, smooth over, tap down and water in well. As the seeds are very fine, it is a good idea to mix them with extra-fine horticultural sand or white flour, which will show the seeds up. Put a very small amount of this seed mix into the crease of the folded card which you can gently tap, this will allow you to see what you are sowing and allow you to sow thinly. There is no need to cover these seeds with anything further. Label with the plant name and date. Put the tray or pot in a warm light place out of direct sunlight at an optimum temperature of 20°C (68°F) or in late spring place the container in a cold frame. Keep watering to the minimum and only water either with a fine spray or from below, so as not to disturb the fine seed. Germination takes 10–20 days with warmth or 15–30 days in a cold frame. Prick out when the seedlings are large enough to handle, harden the seedlings off before planting out. If you are using modules, you can plant directly into the garden after hardening off and when there is no threat of frost.

Hyssopus *Lamiaceae*

A genus of hardy perennials and semi- evergreen or deciduous shrubs. All are attractive to butterflies and bees. Plant in a well-drained soil in a sunny situation.

Hyssopus officinalis (Hyssop)
Culinary and medicinal herb
Medium seeds: 950 per gram
Hardy perennial
Height 80cm (30in)
Dense spikes of small dark blue flowers
Flowers in summer until early autumn
Small narrow lance-shaped aromatic leaves

Sow seeds in spring into pots or modules using standard soil-less seed compost (substrate), either a peat free proprietary brand or composted fine propagating bark. Place under protection at 20°C (68°F). Germination takes 5–10 days.

Inula *Asteraceae*

A genus of hardy, sometimes rhizomatous, perennials all of which have attractive summer flowers. Plant in a well-drained soil in a sunny situation.

Inula helenium (Elecampane)
Medicinal herb
Medium seeds: 500 per gram
Hardy perennial
Height 1.5m (5ft)
Bright yellow, ragged, daisy-like flowers
Flowers in summer
Mid-green, large oval toothed leaves which are slightly downy on the underside

Sow seeds in spring into pots or modules using standard soil-less seed compost (substrate), either a peat free proprietary brand or composted fine propagating bark. Either place under protection at 20°C (68°F) or in a cold frame. Germination takes 1–3 weeks with heat or 3–4 weeks in a cold frame. The cold method of germination can give better results with home-collected seed.

Isatis *Brassicaceae*

A genus of hardy annuals, biennials and perennials. Plant in a well-drained soil in a sunny position.

Lavandula angustifolia

Isatis tinctoria (Woad)
Medicinal herb and dye plant
Medium seeds: 70 per gram
Hardy biennial
Height up to 1.2m (4ft)
Numerous, sweetly-scented, small, yellow flowers followed by pendent black seeds
Flowers in summer
Lance-shaped, mid-green leaves

Sow seeds in spring into pots or modules using standard soil-less seed compost (substrate), either a peat free proprietary brand or composted fine propagating bark. Cover with perlite or vermiculite and place in a cold frame. Germination takes 3–4 weeks.

Laurus *Lauraceae*

A genus of hardy evergreen trees. In extreme cold, the foliage can be scorched. Plant in well-drained, fertile soil in a sheltered position in sun or partial shade.

Laurus nobilis AGM (Bay)
Culinary herb
Large seeds: 1 per gram
Evergreen tree
Height up to 12m (40ft)
Small pale yellow waxy flowers, which are followed by green oval berries that turn black in autumn
Flowers in spring
Oval pointed, aromatic green leaves

Scarify the fresh seed (see page 233) before sowing in autumn into pots, using a standard loam-based seed compost (substrate) mixed with coarse horticultural sand. Mix to a ratio of 1 part compost + 1 part sand. Cover seed with coarse horticultural sand and place under protection at 20°C (68°F) for one month. Then place in a light airy position, either a cold frame or unheated greenhouse with a minimum night temperature of 13°C (55°F). Germination takes 5–12 months, so do not give up. Protect young plants from frost and harsh winds for 2 years.

Lavandula *Lamiaceae*

A genus of hardy to half-hardy evergreen perennials. Plant in a well-drained soil in a sunny position. Lavenders are promiscuous, so growing plants from seed will produce an interesting display of plants, all unique.

Lavandula angustifolia (Common lavender, English lavender, True lavender)
Culinary and medicinal herb
Medium seeds: 1,000 per gram
Hardy evergreen perennial
Height 75cm ($2^{1}/_{2}$ft)
Strongly scented violet flowers
Flowers in summer
Grey-green linear aromatic leaves

Lavandula stoechas AGM (French lavender)
Culinary and medicinal herb
Medium seeds: 1,000 per gram
Evergreen perennial
Height 45cm (18in)
Dark purple scented flowers topped with short paler purple bracts
Flowers in summer
Narrow aromatic light green leaves

Sow in spring in pots or modules using standard soil-less seed compost (substrate), either a peat free proprietary brand or composted fine propagating bark. Cover with perlite or vermiculite, place under protection at 18°C (65°F). Germination takes 18–28 days, but home-collected seed can be spasmodic, so be patient.

Levisticum *Apiaceae*

A single species genus originating from the Mediterranean region. Plant in fertile moist (not soggy) soil, in sun or light shade.

Levisticum officinale (Lovage)
Culinary and medicinal herb
Medium seeds: 325 per gram
Hardy perennial
Height 2m (6ft)
Tiny yellow/ green flowers
Flowers in early summer
Divided aromatic mid-green leaves

Sow in spring or late summer in pots or modules, using standard soil-less seed compost (substrate), either a peat free proprietary brand or composted fine propagating bark. Cover with perlite or vermiculite, place under protection at 18°C (65°F). Germination takes 6 –10 days.

Linaria *Scrophulariaceae*

A genus of hardy annuals, biennials and perennials. Plant in a well-drained soil in light shade or sunny position.

Linaria vulgaris (Toadflax)
Medicinal herb, UK native wild flower
Small seeds: 7,000 per gram
Hardy perennial
Height up to 30cm (1ft)
Small yellow snapdragon-like flowers
Flowers in summer
Small linear mid-green leaves

Sow fresh seed in autumn into pots or modules using standard loam-based seed compost (substrate). Cover lightly with compost, place in a cold frame. Germination takes 3–4 weeks. If no germination occurs during this time, place the container outside exposed to all the weathers (see 'Breaking Seed Dormancy', page 233, for more information). Germination can take a further 5–7 months on average or even as long as 2 years. When germination has occurred, overwinter young plants in the cold frame.

Lycopus *Lamiaceae*

A genus of hardy perennials. Plant in moist to wet soils in sun or partial shade.

Lycopus europaeus (Gipsywort, Bugleweed)
Medicinal herb
Small seeds: 4,000 per gram
Hardy perennial
Height up to 1m ($3^{1}/_{2}$ft)
Tiny white or pinkish, bell-shaped flowers grown in clusters at the base of each pair of leaves
Flowers in summer
Deeply toothed leaves
Beware, this plant can be invasive

Sow fresh seed in autumn into pots or modules using standard loam-based seed compost (substrate). Cover lightly with compost, place in a cold frame. Germination takes 3–4 weeks. If no germination occurs, place container outside exposed to all the weathers (see 'Breaking Seed Dormancy', page 233, for more information). Germination can take a further 5–7 months on average, or even as long as 2 years. When germination has taken place, overwinter young plants in the cold frame.

Mandragora *Solanaceae*

A genus of hardy short-stemmed perennials. Plant in a well-drained humus-rich soil in a sunny or partly shaded, sheltered site.

Mandragora officinarum (Mandrake)
Medicinal herb
WARNING, TOXIC IF EATEN
Medium seeds: 120 per gram
Hardy perennial
Height 15cm (6in)
Small white to blue bell-shaped flowers, which grow on very short stems, followed by aromatic, yellow fruit
Flowers in early spring
Broadly oval slightly hairy leaves

Sow seeds in autumn into pots using a standard loam-based seed compost (substrate) mixed with coarse horticultural sand. Mix to a ratio of 1 part compost + 1 part sand. Cover with coarse horticultural sand and place in a cold frame. Germination takes anything from 4 months to 2 years, so do not discard too soon.

Marrubium *Lamiaceae*

A genus of half-hardy and hardy annuals and perennials. Plant in well-drained soil in a sunny position.

Marrubium vulgare (Horehound)
Medicinal herb, classified as a weed in Australia
Small seeds: 1,100 per gram
Hardy perennial
Height 45cm (18in)
Small creamy flowers
Flowers in summer
Aromatic downy oval grey-green leaves

Sow seeds in early spring into pots or modules using standard soil-less seed compost (substrate), either a peat free proprietary brand or composted fine propagating bark. Cover with perlite or vermiculite, place under protection at 18°C (65°F). Germination takes 1–2 weeks, however some years it can take 3–4 weeks and be a bit spasmodic.

Melissa *Lamiaceae*

A genus of half-hardy and hardy perennials. Plant in a well-drained soil in a sunny situation.

Melissa officinalis (Lemon balm)
Culinary and medicinal herb
Small seeds: 1,600 per gram
Hardy perennial
Height 75cm ($2^{1}/_{2}$ft)
Clusters of small pale yellow/white flowers
Flowers in summer
Oval, toothed slightly wrinkled green leaves, which smell of lemon when crushed

Sow seeds in early spring into pots or modules, using standard soil-less seed compost (substrate), either a peat free proprietary brand or composted fine propagating bark. Cover with perlite or vermiculite, place under protection at 20°C (68°F). Germination takes 1–2 weeks, however some years it can take 3–4 weeks and be a bit spasmodic. Lemon balm can be invasive. It will adapt to all soils, with the exception of waterlogged sites.

Mentha *Lamiaceae*

A genus of hardy perennials, some of which are semi-evergreen. Plant in well-drained soil, in sun or partial shade. Mentha is renowned for being invasive, so plant with care.

Mentha pulegium 'Upright' (Pennyroyal, Pennyroyal Upright)
Culinary and medicinal herb
Tiny seeds: 12,500 per gram
Hardy perennial, semi-evergreen
Height 30cm (12in)
Small mauve flowers
Flowers in late spring
Small bright green leaves which are very strongly peppermint scented

Sow seeds in spring into pots or modules using standard soil-less seed compost (substrate), either a peat free proprietary brand or composted fine propagating bark. As these are very fine seeds, mix with the finest sand or talcum powder for an even sowing. Do not cover. Water from the bottom or with a fine spray. Place under protection at 20°C (68°F). Germination takes 10–20 days.

Micromeria *Lamiaceae*

A genus of hardy and half-hardy shrubs and perennials some of which are evergreen. Plant in a well-drained soil in a sunny situation.

Micromeria (Emperor's mint)
Culinary and medicinal herb
Small seeds: 3,000 per gram
Hardy perennial
Height 30cm (12in)
Small pale pink/grey flowers
Flowers in summer
Small oval pointed grey leaves which have a strong mint aroma and flavour

Sow seeds in early spring into pots or modules using standard soil-less seed compost (substrate), either a peat free proprietary brand or composted fine propagating bark. Cover with perlite or vermiculite, place under protection at 18°C (65°F). Germination takes 1–2 weeks.

Monarda *Lamiaceae*

A genus of hardy annuals and perennials, all of which have aromatic foliage and attractive flowers. Plant in a light well-drained soil in a sunny position.

Monarda citriodora (Lemon bergamot)
Culinary and medicinal herb
Small seeds: 1,850 per gram
Hardy annual
Height 30cm (12in)
Stunning lavender flowers which come in 2 tiers
Flowers in summer
Oval pointed bright green leaves which have a minty lemon scent when crushed

Monarda fistulosa (Wild bergamot)
Culinary and medicinal herb
Small seeds: 3,200 seeds per gram
Hardy perennial
Height 90cm (36in)
Attractive mauve flowers
Flowers in summer
Oval pointed aromatic mid-green leaves

Sow seeds in early spring into pots or modules using standard soil-less seed compost (substrate), either a peat free proprietary brand or composted fine propagating bark. Cover with perlite or vermiculite, place under protection at 18°C (65°F). Germination takes 1–2 weeks.

Melissa officinalis

Myrrhis *Apiaceae*

This genus contains the single species *Myrrhis odorata* described below. Plant in any soil, other than waterlogged, in sun or partial shade. In light soils this plant can be invasive.

Myrrhis odorata (Sweet cicely)
Culinary herb
Medium seeds: 22 per gram
Hardy perennial
Height 90cm (36in)
Large umbels of small white sweetly-scented flowers
Flowers in spring
Fern-like, very divided, bright green leaves which smell of aniseed when crushed

Sow seeds in autumn into pots or modules using a standard loam-based seed compost (substrate). Cover with coarse horticultural sand and place outside exposed to all the weathers (see 'Breaking Seed Dormancy', page 233, for more information). It is most important that you use a loam-based compost. Germination takes 4–6 months, can be erratic, so be patient, and do not discard container.

Nepeta *Lamiaceae*

A genus of hardy perennials. Plant in a well-drained soil in a sunny position.

Nepeta cataria (Catnip, Dog Mint, Nep-in-a-hedge)
Medicinal herb
Small seeds: 1,700 per gram
Hardy perennial
Height 1m (3ft)
White to pale pink small flowers
Flowers from early summer to early autumn
Pungent, aromatic, oval, toothed leaves which the cats adore

Nigella sativa

Nepeta x *fassenii* AGM **(Catmint)**
Medicinal herb
Small seeds: 1,300 per gram
Hardy perennial
Height 50cm (20in)
Spikes of lavender blue/purple small flowers
Flowers from late spring to autumn
Small mildly fragrant greyish-green leaves

Sow seeds in early spring into pots or modules using standard soil-less seed compost (substrate), either a peat free proprietary brand or composted fine propagating bark. Cover with perlite or vermiculite, place under protection at 18°C (65°F). Germination takes 1–2 weeks.

Nigella *Ranunculaceae*

A genus of hardy and half-hardy annuals with attractive flowers and seed heads. Plant in a free-draining soil in a sunny situation.

Nigella sativa (Black cumin, Nutmeg flower, Fennel flower)
Culinary herb
Medium seeds: 430 per gram
Hardy annual
Height 30cm (12in)
Small very pale blue flowers
Flowers in summer
Finely divided leaves

Sow seeds in early spring into pots or modules using standard soil-less seed compost (substrate), either a peat free proprietary brand or composted fine propagating bark. Cover with perlite or vermiculite, place under protection at 18°C (65°F). Germination usually takes 1–2 weeks, but can take 3–4 weeks and be a bit spasmodic.

Ocimum *Lamiaceae*

This is a genus of half-hardy annuals, perennials and shrubs, native of the tropics and especially Africa. Plant in a sunny well sheltered position in a fertile, free-draining soil. Protect plants where night-time temperatures drop below 8°C (48°F).

Ocimum basilicum (Sweet basil, Genovese basil)
Culinary herb
Medium seeds: 700 per gram
Half-hardy annual
Height 45cm (18in)
Whorls of small white tubular flowers
Flowers in summer
Oval green sweetly-scented and strongly-flavoured leaves

Ocimum tenuiflorum (Holy basil, Sacred basil, Tulsi)
Culinary and medicinal herb
Small seeds: 1,500 per gram
Half-hardy annual
Height up to 30cm (1ft)
Small mauve, violet, white flowers in long slender racemes
Flowers in summer
Slightly hairy, green oval leaves with magenta edges which are spicy and pungent

Sow seeds in early spring into pots or modules using standard soil-less seed compost (substrate), either a peat free proprietary brand or composted fine propagating bark. Cover with perlite or vermiculite, place under protection at 20°C (68°F). Germination takes 1–2 weeks.

***Recipe for sowing, planting and growing* Ocimum**

Basil is the Rolls Royce of the kitchen. There are now many varieties available, all of them with unique flavours. It is a warm climate plant and growing basil in cool climates can be problematic. The important thing is not to be in too much of a hurry and start the seeds off too soon, they hate fluctuating temperatures and cold nights. So, wait until spring has truly sprung.

Ingredients

6–8 seeds per module or 15 seeds per pot
1 module tray
OR
1 x 8cm (4in) pot
Standard soil-less seed compost (substrate), either a peat free proprietary brand or composted fine propagating bark
Fine-grade perlite (wetted) or vermiculite
White plastic plant label

Method In early spring fill the tray or pot with compost, smooth over, tap down and water in well, sow the seeds thinly on to the surface of the compost. Cover with perlite or vermiculite and label with the plant name and date. Place the tray or pot in a warm light place out of direct sunlight at an optimum temperature of 20°C (68°F). Keep watering, but do not overwater, until germination has taken place after 7–14 days. Once the seedlings start germinating, water only in the morning, before midday. Basil seedlings hate to be wet at night. It is also important to remove them from the extra heat as soon as you see the seedlings emerge. Place in a cooler, warm, light place and grow on until the seedlings are large enough to handle, approximately 2–3 weeks after germination. Once the seedlings are large enough to handle, or the module is rooted, remove from the tray and pot into an 8cm (4in) pot. Water in, label, and allow to grow on, in a warm, well lit environment until established. If you have started the seeds off in an 8cm (4in) pot, remove the seedlings from the pot, and gently split them, replanting 2 seedlings per pot, using a soil-less compost. Grow on for a further few weeks until the roots are emerging from the bottom of the pot. Plant out in the garden in a very sheltered position when all threat of frost has passed, or pot up into an attractive pot and keep near the kitchen. One word of warning: slugs love basil.

Oenothera *Onagraceae*

A genus of hardy annuals, biennials and perennials. Plant in a well-drained preferably sandy soil, in a sunny position.

Oenothera biennis (Evening primrose)
Medicinal herb
Small seeds: 2,500 per gram
Hardy biennial
Height up to 1m (3½ft)
Lovely trumpet-shaped night-scented yellow flowers which are followed by oval downy pods containing loads of small seeds
Flowers in summer
Oblong green leaves
This species can self seed freely

Sow seeds either in spring or autumn into pots or modules using standard soil-less seed compost (substrate), either a peat free proprietary brand or composted fine propagating bark. Do not cover. Germination takes 3–4 weeks. If sowing in autumn, overwinter the young plants in the cold frame.

Olea *Oleaceae*

A genus of hardy to half-hardy trees, grown for their foliage and edible fruits. Plant in a very well-drained soil in full sun in winter. It is more important to protect it from excessive wet than cold. It will stand moderately cold temperatures if it is dry.

Olea europaea (Olive tree)
Culinary and medicinal herb
Large seed: 1–2 per gram
Evergreen tree
Height up to 12m (40ft)
Cream, fragrant flowers, followed by black fruits
Flowers in early summer
Oval/lance-shaped green/grey leathery leaves.

Cut a small nick in the end of fresh seed and sow in early autumn into pots using a standard loam-based seed compost (substrate) mixed with coarse horticultural sand. Mix to a ratio of 1 part compost + 1 part sand. Cover with coarse horticultural sand and place under protection at 21°C (70°F) for 3–4 weeks. Then lower the temperature to 15°C (60°F). Germination takes 1–12 months, do not give up.

Origanum *Lamiaceae*

A genus of hardy perennials, annuals and deciduous sub-shrubs, some of which have culinary and medicinal uses. Plant in well-drained alkaline soil in a sunny situation.

Origanum majorana (Sweet marjoram, Knot marjoram)
Culinary and medicinal herb
Small seeds: 5,000 per gram
Half-hardy perennial, often grown as an annual in cool climates
Height 30cm (12in)
Tiny white flowers in a knot
Flowers in summer
Round pale green leaves which are highly aromatic and wonderful in cooking

Origanum vulgare (Oregano)
Culinary and medicinal herb
Tiny seeds: 18,000 per gram
Hardy perennial
Height 45cm (18in)
Clusters of small tubular mauve/purple flowers
Flowers in summer
Dark green hairy aromatic, strong tasting leaves

Sow seeds in spring into pots or modules using standard soil-less seed compost (substrate), either a peat free proprietary brand or composted fine propagating bark. As these are very fine seeds, mix with the finest sand or talcum powder for an even sowing. Do not cover. Water from the bottom or with a fine spray. Place under protection at 20°C (68°F). Germination takes 10–20 days.

Perilla *Lamiaceae*

A genus of hardy and half-hardy annuals. Their aromatic leaves are used in cooking. Plant in a well-drained soil in a sunny situation.

Perilla frutescens var. *purpurascens* (Purple shiso, Beefsteak plant)
Culinary herb
Medium seeds: 700 per gram
Hardy annual
Height up to 60cm (2ft)
Spikes of small pink tubular flowers
Flowers in summer
Dark purple, crinkled leaves with cut edges, aromatic and flavourful

Sow seeds in early spring into pots or modules using standard soil-less seed compost (substrate), either a peat free proprietary brand or composted fine propagating bark. Cover with perlite or vermiculite, place under protection at 20°C (68°F). Germination takes 1–2 weeks.

Petroselinum *Apiaceae*

A genus of hardy biennials grown for their culinary uses. Plant in a fertile, deep soil in partial shade.

Petroselinum crispum (Parsley)
Culinary herb
Medium seeds: 650 per gram
Biennial
Height 30cm (1ft)
Flat umbels of small creamy-white flowers
Flowers in second summer
Bright green, crinkled leaves with toothed edges. Good, mild flavour

There are many superstitions associated with sowing parsley, whichever method you choose the most important thing is to not allow the seeds to dry out during germination.

Sow seeds in early spring into pots or modules using standard soil-less seed compost (substrate), either a peat free proprietary brand or composted fine propagating bark. Cover with perlite or vermiculite, place under protection at 18°C (65°F). Germination takes 2–4 weeks.
OR
Sow seeds in late spring into prepared open ground, when the air temperature does not go below 7°C (45°F) at night. Water the site well prior to sowing. Germination takes 2–4 weeks.

Phytolacca *Phytolaccaceae*

A genus of hardy and half-hardy perennials shrubs and trees. Plant in a fertile moist soil. In sun or partial shade.

Phytolacca americana (Pokeroot, Red Ink Plant, Virginian Pokeweed)
Medicinal herb TOXIC PLANT
Medium seeds: 220 per gram
Hardy perennial
Height up to 1.5m (5ft)
Small shallow cup-shaped flowers with a hint of pink, white and green, followed by black juicy pendulous berries
Flowers in summer
Oval lance-shaped mid-green leaves that turn in autumn to pink and orange around the edges

Sow seeds in spring into pots or modules using standard loam-based seed compost (substrate). Cover with coarse horticultural sand and place in a cold frame. Germination takes 3–4 weeks.

***Recipe for sowing, planting and growing* Phytolacca americana**
Pokeroot is a stunning plant in the garden, it makes a great contrast with strong structure and good autumn colours. It is also most attractive to birds. Apart from that, it is a very important medicinal herb.

Ingredients
3 seeds per module or 5 seeds per pot
1 module tray
OR
1 x 8cm (4in) pot
Standard loam-based seed compost (substrate)
Coarse horticultural sand to cover the pot
White plastic plant label

Method In spring fill the tray or pot with compost, smooth over, tap down and water in well. Sow the seeds thinly on to the surface of the compost. Press gently into the compost with the flat of the hand. Cover the seed with coarse horticultural sand. Label with the plant name and date. Place the tray or pot in a cold frame, germination takes 3–4 weeks. Grow the seedlings on until they are large enough to handle. Either prick out and repot a single seedling in each pot, grow on until established and then plant out, or if you have started the seed in modules you can plant out directly into the garden, when there is no threat of frost and the soil has started to warm.

As all parts of the plant are toxic if eaten, do not plant in the vegetable or herb garden.

Pimpinella *Apiaceae*
A genus of hardy and half-hardy annuals, biennials and perennials. Plant in a well-drained soil in sun or partial shade.

Pimpinella anisum (Anise, Aniseed)
Culinary and medicinal herb
Medium seeds: 300 per gram
Half-hardy annual
Height 50cm (20in)
Umbels of tiny creamy-white flowers followed by ribbed seeds
Flowers in summer
Kidney-shaped oval, toothed, divided leaves with a warm aniseed flavour

Sow seeds in early spring into pots or modules using standard soil-less seed compost (substrate), either a peat free proprietary brand or composted fine propagating bark. Cover with perlite or vermiculite, place under protection at 20°C (68°F). Germination takes 1–2 weeks.

Portulaca *Portulacaceae*
A genus of half-hardy annuals and biennials which naturally grow in the temperate regions. Plant in a well-drained rich soil in a sunny position.

Portulaca oleracea (Purslane)
Culinary herb
Small seeds: 3,000 per gram
Half-hardy annual
Height up to 45cm (18in)
Small yellow flowers which open in the sun and close in the shade
Flowers in summer
Thick fleshy spoon-shaped leaves

Sow seeds in early spring into pots or modules using standard soil-less seed compost (substrate), either a peat free proprietary brand or composted fine propagating bark. Cover with perlite or vermiculite, place under protection at 20°C (68°F). Germination takes 1–2 weeks.

Prunella *Lamiaceae*
A genus of hardy semi-evergreen perennials. Plant in any garden soil with the exception of bog, in sun or shade.

Prunella vulgaris (Self-heal, Heal-all)
Medicinal herb
Small seeds: 1,400 seeds per gram
Hardy perennial
Height up to 150cm (6in)
Clusters of purple-blue flowers
Flowers all summer
Oval bright green leaves

Sow fresh seeds in autumn into pots or modules using a standard loam-based seed compost (substrate). Cover with coarse sand, place in a cold frame. Germination takes 3–4 weeks. Overwinter young plants in a cold frame. Flowers in its second season.

Pycnanthemum *Lamiaceae*
A genus of hardy perennials which all have a mint-like aroma. Plant in a fertile free-draining soil in sun or partial shade.

Pycnanthemum pilosum (Mountain mint, American mountain mint)
Culinary and medicinal herb
Small seeds: 5,000 per gram
Hardy perennial
Height up to 90cm (3ft)
Dense clusters of pinky-white attractive flowers
Flowers in summer
Spear-shaped leaves which smell of mint when crushed

Sow seeds in early spring into pots or modules using standard soil-less seed compost (substrate), either a peat free proprietary brand or composted fine propagating bark. Cover with perlite or vermiculite, place under protection at 18°C (65°F). Germination takes 1–2 weeks.

Rosmarinus *Lamiaceae*
A genus of hardy evergreen perennials which all have aromatic foliage. Plant in a well-drained soil in a sunny situation.

Rosmarinus officinalis (Rosemary)
Culinary and medicinal herb
Medium seeds: 750 per gram
Evergreen hardy perennial
Height 1m (3½ft)
Pale blue flowers
Flowers in early spring until summer
Needle-shaped dark green, highly aromatic leaves

Sow seeds in early spring into pots or modules using standard soil-less seed compost (substrate), either a peat free proprietary brand or composted fine propagating bark. Cover with perlite or vermiculite, place under protection at 21°C (70°F). Germination takes 1–2 weeks. It is critical not to over water after germination as the seedlings are prone to damping off.

Ruta *Rutaceae*

A genus of hardy evergreen sub-shrubs. Plant in a well-drained soil in a sunny situation.

Ruta graveolens (Rue)
DANGEROUS IRRITANT
Medicinal herb
Medium seeds: 600 per gram
Evergreen hardy perennial
Height 60cm (24in)
Yellow waxy flowers with 4 or 5 petals
Flowers in summer
Small rounded lobed leaves of a greeny-blue colour

Sow seeds in early spring into pots or modules using standard soil-less seed compost (substrate), either a peat free proprietary brand or composted fine propagating bark. Cover with perlite or vermiculite, place under protection at 18°C (65°F) Germination takes 1–2 weeks.

Salvia *Lamiaceae*

A genus of hardy and half-hardy annuals, biennials, perennials and evergreen shrubs and sub-shrubs. Plant in a fertile well-drained soil in a sunny position.

Salvia officinalis (Sage)
Culinary and medicinal herb
Medium seeds:140 per gram
Evergreen hardy perennial
Height 60cm (2ft)
Mauve/blue 2-lipped flowers
Flowers in summer
Textured oval aromatic green leaves

Salvia sclarea (Clary sage, Muscatel sage)
Culinary and medicinal herb
Medium seeds: 250 per gram
Hardy biennial
Height up to 90cm (3ft)
Small, pale violet flowers with bracts of blue, mauve and white
Flowers in the second summer
Large soft green slightly wrinkled leaves

Salvia viridis (Painted sage)
Culinary and medicinal herb
Medium seeds: 350 per gram
Hardy annual
Height 45cm (18in)
The most striking part of this flower are the colourful bracts which are in shades of pink, purple, or white
Flowers in summer
Oval mid-green leaves

Sow seeds in early spring into pots or modules using standard soil-less seed compost (substrate), either a peat free proprietary brand or composted fine propagating bark. Cover with perlite or vermiculite, place under protection at 18°C (65°F). Germination takes 1–2 weeks.

Sanguisorba *Rosaceae*

A genus of hardy perennials. Plant in a moist (not waterlogged) soil in a sunny position.

Sanguisorba minor (Salad burnet)
Culinary herb
Medium seeds: 100 per gram
Evergreen hardy perennial
Height 30cm (1ft)
Small spikes of dark crimson flowers
Flowers in early summer
Soft mid-green leaves which are divided into oval leaflets with toothed edges

Sow fresh seeds in autumn into pots or modules using standard soil-less seed compost (substrate), either a peat free proprietary brand or composted fine propagating bark. Cover with perlite or vermiculite, place in a cold frame. Germination takes 2–3 weeks. Overwinter young plants in a cold frame.
OR
Sow seeds in early spring into pots or modules using standard soil-less seed compost (substrate), either a peat free proprietary brand or composted fine propagating bark. Cover with perlite or vermiculite, place under protection at 18°C (65°F). Germination takes 2–4 weeks.

Saponaria *Caryophyllaceae*

A genus of hardy annuals and perennials. Plant in a well-drained soil in a sunny position.

Saponaria officinalis (Soapwort, Bouncing Bet)
Medicinal herb
Medium seeds: 510 per gram
Hardy perennial
Height up to 90cm (3ft)
Compact clusters of small pretty pink or white flowers
Flowers in late summer
Smooth oval mid-green leaves
This plant can be invasive

Sow fresh seed in autumn into pots or modules using standard loam-based compost (substrate). Cover lightly with compost, place in a cold frame. Germination takes 3–4 weeks. If no germination occurs during this time, place the container outside exposed to all the weathers (see 'Breaking Seed Dormancy', page 233, for more information). Germination can take a further 5–7 months on average or even as long as 2 years. When germination has taken place, overwinter young plants in the cold frame.

***Recipe for sowing, planting and growing* Saponaria officinalis**
Soapwort, as its name suggests, is a natural form of soap. The herb is also used medicinally and looks most attractive growing in the garden.

Ingredients
10 seeds per module or 18 seeds per pot
1 module tray
OR
1 x 8cm (4in) pot
Standard loam-based seed compost (substrate) mixed with coarse horticultural sand to a ratio of 2 parts compost + 1 part sand
White plastic plant label

Method In autumn fill the tray or pot with standard, loam-based seed compost (substrate) mixed with coarse horticultural sand. Smooth over, tap down and water in well. Sow the seeds thinly on to the surface of the compost. Press gently into the compost with the flat of the hand. Cover the seed with coarse horticultural sand. Label with the plant name and date. Place the tray or pot in a cold frame.

Germination takes 3–4 weeks. If no germination has occurred after 28 days it is worth putting the container outside on a hardstanding exposed to all weathers, including frosts. Do not worry if you live in a snowy area and the containers get immersed in snow, melting snow will aid germination (see 'Breaking Seed Dormancy', page 233, for more information). Germination can take a further 5–7 months on average, or even as long as 2 years. Don't give up. When germination has taken place, overwinter young plants in the cold frame.

After germination prick out the seedlings when they are large enough to handle. If you are using modules, you can plant directly into the garden as soon as the soil is warm enough to dig over, prior to planting out.

Satureja *Lamiaceae*

A genus of hardy annuals and semi- evergreen perennials. Plant in a well-drained soil in a sunny position.

Satureja hortensis (Summer savory)
Culinary herb
Small seeds:1,500 per gram
Hardy annual
Height 30cm (12in)
Small white/mauve flowers
Flowers in summer
Highly aromatic narrow oblong mid-green leaves

Sow seeds in early spring into pots or modules using standard soil-less seed compost (substrate), either a peat free proprietary brand or composted fine propagating bark. Cover with perlite or vermiculite, place under protection at 20°C (68°F). Germination takes 1–2 weeks.

Scutellaria *Lamiaceae*

A genus of hardy and half-hardy rhizomatous perennials. Plant in a well-drained soil in a sunny position.

Scutellaria galericulata (Skullcap)
Medicinal herb
Small seeds: 1,500 per gram
Hardy perennial
Height up to 50cm (20in)
Small purple/blue flowers
Flowers in summer
Lance-shaped green leaves

Sow fresh seeds in autumn into pots or modules using standard soil-less seed compost (substrate), either a peat free proprietary brand or composted fine propagating bark. Cover with perlite or vermiculite, place in a cold frame. Germination takes 3–4 weeks. If no germination occurs during this time, place the container outside exposed to all the weathers (see 'Breaking Seed Dormancy', page 233, for more information). Germination can take a further 5–7 months. Overwinter young plants in a cold frame. Can flower in its first season.

Solidago *Asteraceae*

A genus of hardy perennials. Can be grown in most soils in sun or partial shade.

Solidago virgaurea (Golden Rod)
Medicinal herb
Small seeds: 1,200 per gram
Hardy perennial
Height 45cm (18in)
Small yellow flowers
Flowers in late summer
Small lance-shaped finely toothed mid-green leaves

Sow seeds in autumn into pots or modules using a standard loam-based seed compost (substrate) mixed with coarse horticultural sand. Mix to a ratio of 1 part compost + 1 part sand. Cover with coarse horticultural sand. Then place outside exposed to all the weathers (see 'Breaking Seed Dormancy', page 233, for more information). Germination takes 4–6 months.

Tanacetum *Asteraceae*

A genus of hardy perennials, some of which are evergreen. Plant in a well-drained soil in a sunny position.

Tanacetum cinerariifolium (Pyrethrum)
Medicinal herb
Medium seeds: 650 per gram
Hardy perennial
Height 75cm (2½ft)
White daisy-like flowers with yellow centres
Flowers in summer
Finely divided grey-green leaves with white down on the underside

Tanacetum parthenium

Tanacetum parthenium (Feverfew)
Culinary and medicinal herb
Small seeds: 9,000 per gram
Hardy perennial
Height up to 45cm (18in)
Small white daisy-like flowers with yellow centres
Typical chrysanthemum-shaped leaves mid-green and divided
This plant self seeds readily so can be invasive

Tanacetum vulgare (Tansy)
Culinary and medicinal herb
Small seeds: 8,500 per gram
Hardy perennial
Height 90cm (3ft)
Yellow button flowers in late summer
Deeply indented toothed mid-green aromatic leaves
The roots of this plant can be invasive

Sow seeds in spring into pots or modules using standard soil-less seed compost (substrate), either a peat free proprietary brand or composted fine propagating bark. The small seeds should be mixed with the finest sand or talcum powder for an even sowing. Do not cover. Water from the bottom or with a fine spray, place in a cold frame. The medium sized seeds should be sown on to the surface of the compost, left uncovered and placed in a cold frame. Germination takes 2–3 weeks.

Teucrium *Lamiaceae*

A genus of hardy to half-hardy perennials, evergreens, shrubs and sub-shrubs. Plant in a well-drained soil in a sunny position.

Teucrium scorodonia (Wood sage)
Medicinal herb
Small seeds: 1,500 per gram
Hardy perennial
Height up to 30cm (1ft)
Pale greenish-white flowers
Flowers in summer
Soft green, heart-shaped leaves with a mild smell of garlic when crushed

Sow seeds in autumn into pots or modules using a standard loam-based seed compost (substrate) mixed with coarse horticultural sand. Mix to a ratio of 1 part compost + 1 part sand. Cover with coarse horticultural sand. Then place outside exposed to all the weathers (see 'Breaking Seed Dormancy', page 233, for more information). Germination takes 4–6 months.

Thymus *Lamiaceae*

A genus of hardy and half-hardy evergreen perennials. Plant in a well-drained soil in a sunny position.

Thymus serpyllum (Creeping thyme)
Culinary and medicinal herb
Small seeds: 7,000 per gram
Evergreen hardy perennial
Creeping habit
Small mauve/purple flowers
Flowers in summer
Small dark green oval aromatic leaves

Thymus vulgaris (Common thyme)
Culinary and medicinal herb
Small seeds: 7,000 per gram
Evergreen hardy perennial
Height 30cm (12in)
Small mauve flowers
Flowers in summer
Small oval green highly aromatic leaves

Sow seeds in spring into pots or modules using standard soil-less seed compost (substrate), either a peat free proprietary brand or composted fine propagating bark. As these are very fine seeds, mix with the finest sand or talcum powder for an even sowing. Do not cover. Water from the bottom or with a fine spray. Place under protection at 20°C (68°F). Germination takes 5–10 days.

Valeriana *Valerianaceae*

A genus of hardy perennials. Plant in any soil, including damp, in a sunny situation.

Valeriana officinalis (Valerian)
Medicinal herb
Small seeds: 1,400 seeds per gram
Hardy perennial
Height 1.2m (4ft)
Pale pink/white flowers
Flowers in summer
Mid-green deeply toothed leaves

Sow seeds in spring into pots or modules using standard soil-less seed compost (substrate), either a peat free proprietary brand or composted fine propagating bark. Cover with perlite or vermiculite and place in a cold frame. Germination takes 3–4 weeks.

Verbena *Verbenaceae*

A genus of hardy and half-hardy biennials and perennials. Plant in well-drained soil in a sunny situation.

Verbena officinalis (Vervain)
Medicinal herb
Small seeds: 3,400 per gram
Hardy perennial
Height 75cm (2½ft)
Very small pale lilac flowers
Flowers in summer
Mid-green hairy leaves that are often deeply divided into lobes with curved teeth

Sow seeds in autumn into pots or modules using a standard loam-based seed compost (substrate) mixed with coarse horticultural sand to a ratio of 1 part compost + 1 part sand. Cover with coarse horticultural sand. Then place outside exposed to all the weathers (see 'Breaking Seed Dormancy', page 233, for more information). Germination takes 4–6 months, but can be erratic, so be patient and do not discard container.

palms & cycads

Palms are lovely evergreen tropical, temperate trees, which look graceful growing outside in warm and tropical climates. In cool climates they make a very good architectural plant for a conservatory or hot house.

Cycads have become very popular plants, they are among the most primitive living seed plants, often called 'living fossils', having changed very little in the last 200 million years. A 220-year-old specimen of *Encephalartos*, a relative of *Cycas revoluta*, is on display at the Royal Botanic Garden, Kew, England; the restoration of the famous Palm House required it to be temporarily transplanted to a holding area for more than a year; the move was successful and is an example of the durability of these ancient 'living fossils'. Cycads in cool climates make wonderful house plants as they are very tolerant, only needing a few hours of good light per day.

Cocus nucifera, see page 132

Borassus *Palmaceae*

A genus of palms with one species described below. Plant in a sandy loam in a sunny position. In cool climates grow as a large container plant.

Borassus flabellifer (Toddy palm, Palmyra palm)
Very large seed
Tropical evergreen tree
Height 24m (80ft)
Pale yellow flowers in winter followed by large fruits each holding three seeds in spring.
The leaves are nearly circular and plated like a fan with about 40 ribs radiating from a common centre

As this is a very large fruit which produces a long tap root, sow direct into a deep container in spring using a standard soil-less seed compost (substrate), either coir or peat, mixed with 2–3mm (1/16–1/8in) fine grit. Mix to a ratio of 1 parts compost + 1 part fine grit. Half bury the seed and place under protection at 25°C (77°F). Germination takes 2–4 months.

Grow on as a container plant for 3 years, before planting out in warm climates. Alternatively, in cool climates grow on as container plant using a standard soil-less seed compost (substrate), either a peat free proprietary brand or composted fine propagating bark, mixed with extra fine potting bark for extra aeration. Mix to a ratio of 3 parts compost + 1 fine bark.

Caryota *Arecaceae*

This genus of palms consists of tropical evergreen trees. Plant in a rich, moist well drained soil in sun or partial shade. In cool climates grow as a large container plant.

Caryota mitis AGM (Fish-Tail Palm)
Large seeds
Tropical evergreen tree
Height up to 8m (25ft)
Clusters of cream flowers, followed by round, red to black fruit
Flowers in winter
The slender stem is topped with several bi-pinnate leaves that can reach 9in in length. The light green leaflets are shaped like a fish's lower fin, hence its common name

In spring carefully remove the flesh from the seed (see warning below), then soak the seed for 24 hours and sow immediately into pots using standard soil-less seed compost (substrate), coir mixed with 2–3mm (1/16–1/8in) fine grit. Mix to a ratio of 3 parts compost + 1 part fine grit. Cover with fine grit, then place under protection at 20°C (68°F). Germination takes 1–3 months

Grow on as a container plant for 3 years, before planting out in warm climates. Alternatively, in cool climates grow on as container plant using a standard soil-less seed compost (substrate), either a peat free proprietary brand or composted fine propagating bark, mixed with extra fine potting bark for extra aeration. Mix to a ratio of 3 parts compost + 1 fine bark.

WARNING – Avoid contact with the red fruit produced by this palm. It contains oxalic acid which is toxic when ingested and contact with skin may result in severe chemical burns.

Cocos *Arecaceae*

A single genus of tropical evergreen palm tree, as described below. Plant in a sandy loam in full sun. In cool climates grow as a container plant.

Cocos nucifera (Coconut)
Very large seed
Tropical evergreen tree
Height up to 33m (100ft)
Loose clusters of cream flowers
Flowers in winter
Large, palm shaped leaves with long, pinnate leaflets

As this is a very large fruit which produces a long tap root, in spring or summer soak the seed in water for 2 days, remove all the fibre (coir) from around the nut, scarify (see page 233) then sow direct into a deep container in spring. Use standard soil-less seed compost (substrate), either coir or peat, mixed with 2–3mm (1/16–1/8in) fine grit to a ratio of 1 part compost + 1 part fine grit. Place the seed on its side and only half bury the seed. Then place under protection at 28°C (80°F). Germination takes 2–4 months

Grow on as a container plant for 2 years, before planting out in warm climates. Alternatively, in cool climates grow on as container plant using a standard soil-less seed compost (substrate), either a peat free proprietary brand or composted fine propagating bark, mixed with extra fine potting bark for extra aeration. Mix to a ratio of 3 parts compost + 1 part fine bark.

Cycas *Cycadaceae*

A genus of cycads which consists of tropical and subtropical evergreen shrubs and perennials. Plant in well drained soil, which is rich in humus, in a sunny position. In cool climates this plant makes a very good house plant or conservatory plant.

Cycas circinalis AGM (Fern Palm, Sago Palm)
Large seeds
Tropical evergreen shrub
Height up to 4m (12ft)
Female cone-like structure, which bears nut-like seeds. A mature male and female cycad are needed to produce viable seeds.
A rugged trunk, topped with whorled, feathery leaves

In spring soak the seed for 48 hours, discarding any floating seeds, then make a small nick in the end of the seed, and sow immediately into deep pots using standard soil-less seed compost (substrate), coir mixed with coarse grit. Mix to a ratio of 3 parts compost + 1 part coarse grit. Position the seed sideways, with only the top edge exposed, then place under protection at 12°C (54°F) in shade. Germination takes 3–9 months.

Grow on as a container plant for 3 years, before planting out in warm climates. Alternatively, in cool climates, grow on as container plant using a standard soil-less seed compost (substrate), either a peat free proprietary brand or composted fine propagating bark, mixed with coarse grit for extra aeration. Mix to a ratio of 3 parts compost + 1 coarse grit.

Caryota mitis

Recipe for sowing, planting and growing Cycas circinnalis

Ingredients

1 seed per pot
Small china bowl
Hot not boiling water
1 sharp knife
1 x 8cm (4in) pot
Standard soil-less seed compost (substrate), either coir or peat, mixed with coarse grit to a ratio of 3 parts compost + 1 part grit
Waterproof pen
White plastic plant label
OR
1 plastic bag
Coir or peat compost (substrate)
Airing cupboard or somewhere constantly warm

Method The seed develops over the summer and are ripe by late winter or early spring. Check to see if the seed is viable by shaking the seed: if you hear a rattle discard the seed. With the remaining seed, remove the skin and drop into a bowl of water; if any seed floats, it is not viable. Prior to sowing in spring, soak in water for several days, then remove the skin and make a small nick, not too deep, with a sharp knife into the end of the seed and sow immediately. If you are using purchased rather than fresh seeds, soak the seeds in warm water in a china bowl for 48 hours prior to sowing.

Fill the pots with compost, smooth over, tap down and water in well. Place 1 seed sideways in a pot and press into the compost, leaving the top edge exposed. Label with the plant name and date. Place the pot into a warm place in partial shade at an optimum temperature of 12°C (54°F) in shade. Do not allow the compost to dry out, but be careful not to over water. Germination takes 3–9 months.

Pot up as soon as the seedlings are large enough to handle. Keep the young plants under protection and in partial shade for two years, then slowly introduce to strong sunlight. When potting up, use a coir or peat-based potting compost mixed with extra coarse sand. Mix to a ratio of 3 parts compost + 1 part sand.

Alternatively, you can pre-germinate cycad seeds. After soaking the seed for 48 hours (see above), put some damp (not wet) compost in a plastic bag and mix in the damp seeds. Seal the bag and write the name of the seed on the outside in waterproof pen. Then place this bag in light shade at an optimum temperature of 25°C (77F). Check regularly after 4 weeks to see if there are any signs of sprouting. Pot up very carefully so as not to break the roots, using the potting mixed described above. Place the pots in a warm humid position in partial shade. Grow on for 4 years minimum before planting out in a tropical climate. For those living in a cool climate, grow on as a conservatory plant using a potting mix made of 3 parts compost plus 1 part coarse grit.

Dioon *Zamiaceae*

A single genus of cycads which consists of subtropical evergreen shrubs. Plant in well drained soil, which is rich in humus, in a sunny position. In cool climates this plant makes a very good house plant, as it is quite happy with a few hours of good light per day. Ideal for a conservatory.

Dioon edule AGM (Mexican cycad)
Very large seed
Tropical evergreen shrub
Height up to 4m (12ft)
Female pale brown, oval, cone-like structure, which bears oval, nut-like seeds. A mature male and female cycad are needed to produce viable seeds.
The leaves are light or bright green, blue or blue-green and semi-glossy. There are 50–150 leaves in a crown.

In spring soak the seed for 48 hours. Discard any floating seeds, then make a small nick in the end of the seed and sow immediately into deep pots using standard soil-less seed compost (substrate), either coir or peat mixed with coarse grit. Mix to a ratio of 3 parts compost + 1 part coarse grit. Position the seed sideways, with only the top edge exposed. Cover with coarse grit, leaving the seed exposed, then place under protection at 21°C (70°F) in shade. Germination takes 6–18 months

Grow on as a container plant for 3 years, before planting out in warm climates. Alternatively, in cool climates grow on as container plant using a standard soil-less seed compost (substrate), either a peat free proprietary brand or composted fine propagating bark, mixed with coarse grit for extra aeration. Mix to a ratio of 3 parts compost + 1 coarse grit.

The seed of this plant is often powdered and used as a kind of arrowroot.

Livistona *Palmaceae*

A genus of, in the majority of cases, tall tropical evergreen palms. Plant in light sandy loam in a sunny position. In cool climates grow as a container plant.

Livistona rountidifolia (Fan Palm)
Large seed
Tropical evergreen tree
Height up to 17m (50ft)
Greenish flowers in autumn, followed by oblong, smooth, blue/brown fruit in spring
Nearly round, dark green, palm-shaped leaves deeply divided into 60–90 leaflets with slender points

In spring carefully remove the flesh from the seed (see warning below), then soak the seed for 24 hours, sow immediately into pots using standard soil-less seed compost (substrate), either coir or peat, mixed with 2–3mm ($^{1}/_{16}$–$^{1}/_{8}$in) fine grit. Mix to a ratio of 3 parts compost + 1 part fine grit. Cover with fine grit, then place under protection at 23°C (73°F). Germination takes 2–3 months.

Grow on as a container plant for 3 years, before planting out in warm climates. Alternatively, in cool climates grow on as container plant using a standard soil-less seed compost (substrate), either a peat free proprietary brand or composted fine propagating bark, mixed with extra fine potting bark for extra aeration. Mix to a ratio of 3 parts compost + 1 fine bark.

WARNING – Avoid contact with the fruit produced by this palm. It contains oxalic acid which is toxic when ingested and contact with skin may result in severe chemical burns.

Dioon edule

Phoenix dactylifera

Phoenix *Arecaceae*

A genus of tropical and sub tropical evergreen palms. Plant in a sandy soil in a sunny position. In cool climates grow as a container plant.

Phoenix dactylifera (Date Palm)
Large seed
Tropical evergreen tree
Height up to 33m (100ft). Rarely grows over 10m (30ft) in cool climates.
The flowers, which are small leathery and yellow, are followed by edible, yellow-orange to red fruit that ripen to dark brown.
Flowers in winter
Greenish or bluish-gray, pinnate leaves form a bushy canopy. The leaves are composed of long leaflets, which are arranged in v-shape ranks and run the length of the leaf stem
Female plants will produce dates if a male tree is nearby

In spring carefully remove the flesh from the seed, then soak the seed for 24 hours and sow immediately into pots, using standard soil-less seed compost (substrate), either coir or peat mixed with coarse sand to a ratio of 3 parts compost + 1 part coarse sand. Cover with coarse sand then place under protection at 20°C (68°F). Germination takes 1–2 months.

In warm climates protect young plants from the sun for at least 2 years before planting out. Alternatively, in cool climates grow on as container plant using a standard soil-less seed compost (substrate), either a peat free proprietary brand or composted fine propagating bark, mixed with extra coarse sand for extra aeration. Mix to a ratio of 3 parts compost + 1 part coarse sand.

***Recipe for sowing, planting and growing* Phoenix dactylifera**

Ingredients
2 seeds per pot
Small china bowl
Hot not boiling water
1 x 8cm (4in) pot
Standard soil-less seed compost (substrate), either coir or peat, mixed with coarse sand to a ratio of 3 parts compost + 1 part coarse sand
Waterproof pen
White plastic plant label
OR
1 plastic bag
Coir or peat compost (substrate)
Airing cupboard or somewhere constantly warm

Method As soon as the fruits ripen and change colour from orange to brown collect the seed, remove any pulp from around the seed and sow immediately. If you are using purchased rather than fresh seed, soak the seed in warm water in a china bowl for 48 hours prior to sowing.

Fill the pots with compost, smooth over, tap down and water in well. Place 2 seeds in each pot, equally spaced on the surface of the compost. Cover the seeds with compost the same depth as the seed and label with the plant name and date. Place the pot into a warm light place out of direct sunlight at an optimum temperature of 20°C (68°F).

Do not allow the compost to dry out, but be careful not to over water. Germination takes 1–2 months

Pot up as soon as the seedlings are large enough to handle, keep the young plants under protection and in partial shade for two years, then slowly introduce to strong sunlight. When potting up use a coir or peat based potting compost mixed with extra coarse sand. Mix to a ratio of 3 parts compost, 1 part sand.

Alternatively you can pre-germinate palm seeds. After removing the pulp or soaking, put the seed with some damp (not wet) compost in a plastic bag, seal the bag and write the name of the seed on the outside in waterproof pen. Then place this bag somewhere where it is constantly warm, an airing cupboard or under a greenhouse bench for example.

Check regularly after 4 weeks to see if there are any signs of sprouting. Pot up, being very careful not to break the roots, using the potting mix described above.

Place the pots in a warm humid position in partial shade, and grow on for 2 years in partial shade.

Roystone *Palmaceae*

A genus of tropical evergreen palms. Plant in a sandy acid soil in a sunny position. These palms are one of world's most beautiful. They grace palaces and government buildings throughout the tropical world.

Roystone rigia (Royal Palm)
Large seed
Tropical evergreen tree
Height up to 24m (80ft)
Creamy white, small flowers, followed by oval blue-brown fruit
Flowers in winter
Terminal crowns of large, green, fan-shaped, pinnate leaves

In spring carefully remove the flesh from the seed, then soak the seed for 24 hours and sow immediately into pots using standard soil-less seed compost (substrate), either coir or peat, mixed with coarse sand to a ratio of 3 parts compost + 1 part sand. Cover with coarse sand, then place under protection at 20°C (68°F). Germination takes 2–3 months.

Grow on as a container plant for 2 years, before planting out in warm climates. Alternatively, in cool climates grow on as container plant using a standard soil-less seed compost (substrate), either a peat free proprietary brand or composted fine propagating bark, mixed with extra fine potting bark for extra aeration. Mix to a ratio of 3 parts compost + 1 part fine bark.

perennials

Perennials are wonderful plants for the majority of gardens as they team up so well with with trees, shrubs and roses. Many species make attractive groundcover, and when grown in grand swathes they look stunning in a border. They provide an economical means of creating a display of colour, texture, form and structure. It is wonderful to see old favourites among the herbaceous perennials return after a hard winter, those first spring shoots are inspiring after the cold, dank, dark nights.

Many perennials will flower in their second season. It is usually worth sowing fresh seed for a more reliable germination rate even though many can be stored for use in later years. It is also worth harvesting a few seeds of your favourite plant just in case you lose it in the winter.

Silene dioica seedheads, see page 168

Acanthus *Acanthaceae*

A genus of hardy perennials and semi-evergreens. Plant in a well-drained soil in a sunny situation, will adapt to partial shade.

Acanthus mollis (Bear's breeches)
Large seeds: 5 per gram
Hardy perennial, semi-evergreen
Height 1.2m (4ft)
Purple and white flowers on tall spikes
Flowers in high summer
Long oval deeply-cut bright green leaves

Sow in spring into pots, using standard soil-less seed compost (substrate), either a peat free proprietary brand or composted fine propagating bark. Cover with perlite or vermiculite, place under protection at 18°C (65°F). Germination takes 10-20 days. Protect young plants for the first winter. Flowers in its second or third year.

Achillea *Asteraceae*

A genus of hardy perennials and semi-evergreens, grown for their attractive flowers which dry well. Plant in a well-drained soil in a sunny situation, although it will adapt to most soils and to partial shade.

Achillea filipendulina 'Cloth of gold' AGM
Small seeds: 6,200 per gram
Hardy perennial
Height 1.5m (5ft)
Clusters of brilliant yellow flowers
Flowers in summer
Serrated, fern-like, green leaves

Achillea millefolium 'Cerise Queen'
Small seeds: 5,000 per gram
Hardy perennial
Height 60cm (24in)
Clusters of dark cherry-red flowers
Flowers in summer
Feathery, dark green leaves

Achillea ptarmica (Sneezewort)
Small seeds: 4,300 per gram
Hardy perennial
Height 60cm (24in)
Clusters of dark cherry-red flowers
Flowers in summer
Feathery, dark green leaves

Sow fresh seed in autumn into pots or modules, using standard soil-less seed compost (substrate), either a peat free proprietary brand or composted fine propagating bark. Cover lightly with compost and place in a cold frame. Germination takes 4-6 weeks. Overwinter young plants in the cold frame. Can flower in its first year.
OR
Sow in spring into pots or modules, using standard soil-less seed compost (substrate), either a peat free proprietary brand or composted fine propagating bark. Cover with perlite or vermiculite, place under protection at 20°C (68°F). Germination takes 10-15 days. Can flower in its first year.

Recipe for sowing, planting and growing Achillea

Achillea is a lovely plant which has pretty flowers which grow in clusters forming attractive flat heads in all shades of colour. As the plants are available in all sizes they will suit most gardens from the alpine to the stately border.

Ingredients
20 seeds per module or 30 seeds per pot (do not sow thickly)
1 piece white card 14 x 8.5cm (5 1/2 x 3 1/2in) folded in half
1 module tray
OR
1 x 8cm (4in) pot
Standard soil-less seed compost (substrate), either a peat free proprietary brand or composted fine propagating bark
Fine-grade perlite (wetted) or vermiculite
White plastic plant label

Method In autumn fill the tray or pot with compost, smooth over, tap down and water in well. As the seeds are fine, put a very small amount of seed into the crease of a folded card and gently tap the card to sow. This will not only allow you to see what you are sowing, it will also enable you to sow thinly on to the surface of the compost. Press the seeds gently into the compost with the flat of the hand. Cover with a very fine layer of compost. Label with the plant name and date. Place the tray or pot in a cold frame. Keep watering to the absolute minimum until germination has taken place. Germination takes 4-6 weeks. Overwinter the young seedlings undisturbed in the cold frame. Pot up or plant out in the spring after a period of hardening off when there is no threat of frost.
OR
Sow the seeds in spring following the instructions above, except this time cover the seeds with the wetted fine-grade perlite or vermiculite and place the container in a warm light place out of direct sunlight and at an optimum temperature of 20°C (68°F). Keep watering to a minimum until germination has taken place. Germination takes 10–15 days with warmth. Prick out when the seedlings are large enough to handle or, if you are using modules, plant directly into a container or the garden after a period of hardening off and when there is no threat of frost. Whichever method you choose, flowering will take place during the following season.

Aconitum *Ranunculaceae*

A genus of hardy perennials with hooded flowers. Plant in fertile, well-drained soil in a sunny situation, will tolerate partial shade.

Aconitum napellus (Monkshood, Wolf's Bane)
ALL PARTS OF THIS PLANT ARE POISONOUS TO HUMANS
Medium seeds: 350 per gram
Hardy perennial
Height 1.5m (5ft)
Tall spires of hooded, indigo blue flowers
Flowers in late summer
Deeply-cut mid-green leaves

Sow in autumn into pots or modules using standard loam-based seed compost (substrate). Cover lightly with compost, place in a cold frame. Germination takes 6 months and can be erratic. Flowers in its second year.

Aconitum napellus

OR
Sow in autumn into pots or modules, using standard soil-less seed compost (substrate), either a peat free proprietary brand or composted fine propagating bark. Cover with perlite or vermiculite. Place in the refrigerator for 8-12 weeks at 2–4 °C (35–39°F). Remove and place under protection at 15°C (60°F). Germination takes 4–6 weeks after removing from the refrigerator. Flowers in its second year.

Agapanthus *Alliaceae*

A genus of hardy to half-hardy perennials, some of which are evergreen, grown for their attractive blue flowers. Plant in a moist, well-draining soil in a sunny situation.

Agapanthus africanus AGM (African lily)
Medium seeds: 140 per gram
Half-hardy evergreen perennial
Height 1m (3ft)
Umbels of deep blue flowers on upright stems
Flowers in summer
Broad dark green leaves

Agapanthus campanulatus
Medium seeds: 140 per gram
Hardy perennial
Height up to 1.2m (4ft)
Rounded umbels of blue flowers on long stems
Flowers in summer
Narrow green leaves

Collected seeds may not come true to type, but they can yield some interesting variations. Sow in spring into pots or modules using standard soil-less seed compost (substrate), either a peat free proprietary brand or composted fine propagating bark. Cover with perlite or vermiculite and place under protection at 16°C (61°F). Germination takes 18–24 days. Overwinter seedlings in cold frame and protect from frost. Flowers in its third year.

Allium giganteum

Agastache *Lamiaceae*

A genus of half-hardy, short-lived, summer-flowering perennials. Plant in a well-drained fertile soil in a sunny situation.

Agastache foeniculum 'Alba' **(White anise hyssop)**
Small seeds: 3,000 per gram
Hardy perennial
Height 60cm (24in)
Spikes of tubular white flowers
Flowers in summer
Oval, mid-green, aromatic, toothed leaves

Agastache urticifolia 'Liquorice' **(Mexican Giant Hyssop)**
Small seeds: 2,500 per gram
Hardy perennial
Height 60cm (24in)
Spikes of attractive blue-mauve, tubular flowers
Flowers in summer
Oval, mid-green, toothed leaves

Sow in spring into pots or modules using standard soil-less seed compost (substrate), either a peat free proprietary brand or composted fine propagating bark. Cover with perlite or vermiculite, place under protection at 20 °C (68°F). Germination takes 7-10 days. Flowers in its first year.

Alchemilla *Rosaceae*

A genus of hardy perennials which have greenish-yellow flowers in summer and interesting leaves. Plant in sun or partial shade in most soils with the exception of bogs. Most species self-seed.

Alchemilla mollis AGM **(Lady's mantle)**
Small seeds: 2,900 per gram
Hardy perennial
Height 50cm (22in)
Greeny yellow flowers in conspicuous outer calyces
Flowers in summer
Rounded, pale green leaves with crinkled edges

Alchemilla xanthoclora
Small seeds: 1,600 per gram
Hardy perennial
Height 30cm (12in)
Greeny yellow flowers in conspicuous, outer calyces
Flowers in summer
Rounded pale green leaves, larger than *A. mollis*

Sow fresh seed in autumn into pots or modules using standard loam-based seed compost. Cover lightly with compost, place in a cold frame. Germination takes 4-6 weeks and can be a bit erratic. May flower in its first year.

Allium *Alliaceae*

This large genus of perennials, some of which are edible, can come in different forms – bulbs, rhizomes or fibrous rootstock. Nearly all have onion-smelling leaves, and most have small flowers which are clustered together into spherical or similar shapes. They are all hardy and the majority require a sunny site with a well-drained, rich soil.

Allium giganteum AGM
Small seeds
Hardy perennial
Height up to 2m (6ft)
A dense, round umbel of 50 or more star-shaped purple flowers
Flowers in second summer
Wide, long, mid-green leaves

Sow fresh seed in autumn into pots or modules using standard loam-based seed compost (substrate) mixed with coarse horticultural sand. Mix to a ratio of 1 part compost + 1 part sand. Cover lightly with compost, and place outside, exposed to all the weathers (see 'Breaking Seed Dormancy', page 233, for more information). Germination takes place following spring. May flower in its first year. In autumn these seed heads dry well and look great in arrangements.

Alstroemeria *Alstroemeriaceae*

A genus of hardy summer-flowering tuberous perennials. Plant in a well-drained soil in a sunny, sheltered situation.

Alstroemeria ligtu hybrids
Medium seeds: 60 per gram
Hardy perennial
Height 75cm (30in)
Pink, rose and salmon lily-like flowers
Flowers from June until September
Mid-green, lance-shaped leaves

Sow in autumn into pots or modules using standard soil-less seed compost (substrate), either a peat free proprietary brand or composted fine propagating bark. Cover with perlite or vermiculite. Place under protection at 20°C (68°F) for 3 weeks, then place containers in a cold frame or cold greenhouse at 5°C (40°F) for a further 3 weeks. After this period of chilling, move back under protection at 20°C (68°F). Germination should occur within a further 4 weeks, however it can be erratic.

Althaea *Malvaceae*

A genus of hardy annuals and perennials. Plant in a moist, fertile soil in a sunny situation.

Althaea officinalis **(Marsh mallow)**
Medium seed: 400 per gram
Hardy perennial
Height 80cm (32in)
Pink or white flowers
Flowers in late summer to early autumn
Grey-green, tear-shaped leaves covered with soft hair

Sow fresh seed in autumn into pots or modules using standard soil-less seed compost (substrate), either a peat free proprietary brand or composted fine propagating bark. Cover lightly with compost, and place in a cold frame. Germination takes 2-4 months and can be erratic.

Anaphalis *Asteraceae*

A genus of hardy perennials with small papery flowers, ideal for dried-flower arrangements. Plant in well-drained soil, which retains some moisture, in a sunny situation. They will adapt to partial shade.

Anaphalis margaritacea **(Pearl Everlasting)**
Tiny seeds: 20,000 per gram
Hardy perennial
Height 60cm (24in)
White, bell-shaped flower heads
Flowers from summer until early autumn
Attractive, lance-shaped, grey-green foliage

Anaphalis margaritacea 'New Snow'
Tiny seeds: 20,000 per gram
Hardy perennial
Height 50cm (20in)
Flowers from summer until early autumn
White, bell-shaped flower heads
Attractive, lance-shaped, grey-green foliage

Sow in spring into pots or modules using standard soil-less seed compost (substrate), either a peat free proprietary brand or composted fine propagating bark. Cover with perlite or vermiculite, place under protection at 20°C (68°F). Germination takes 7–10 days.

Anchusa *Boraginaceae*

A genus of hardy annuals, biennials and perennials with some evergreen. The flowers of all species are attractive to bees. Plant in a well-drained soil in a sunny situation. Dislikes wet winters.

Anchusa azurea 'Dropmore' **(Summer Forget-me-not)**
Medium seeds: 40 per gram
Hardy perennial
Height 120cm (4ft)
Bright blue, funnel-shaped flowers
Flowers in summer
Lance-shaped, bristly, mid-green leaves

Sow in spring into pots or modules using standard soil-less seed compost (substrate), either a peat free proprietary brand or composted fine propagating bark. Cover with a thick layer of perlite or vermiculite, and place under protection at 20°C (68°F). Germination takes 12–18 days.

Anchusa capensis 'Blue Angel' **(Italian bugloss)**
Medium seeds: 45 per gram
Hardy biennial/annual
Height 20cm (8in)
Brilliant blue, small, shallow, funnel-shaped flowers
Flowers in summer
Mid-green, lance-shaped, hairy, bristly leaves

Sow in late spring into prepared open ground, when air temperature does not go below 10°C (50°F) at night. Germination takes 14–36 days. These plants are attractive but be warned that they are invasive and, once established, can be difficult to control or eradicate. Also, note that some people are contact allergic to the Boraginaceae family.

Anemone *Ranunculaceae*

A genus of hardy perennials, some tuberous or rhizomatous. Plant in a humus-rich, fertile soil in sun or dappled shade.

Anemone nemorosa AGM **(Wood anemone)**
Medium seeds: 340 per gram
Hardy perennial
Height 15cm (6in)
Masses of star-shaped, single white flowers with yellow stamens
Flowers from spring to early summer
Deeply cut, mid-green leaves

Anemone sylvestris **(Snowdrop, Windflower)**
Small seeds: 1,600 per gram
Hardy perennial
Height 30cm (12in)
Large, slightly cupped, semi-pendent, white scented flowers
Flowers from spring to early summer
Divided mid-green leaves

Sow seed in autumn into pots or modules using standard loam-based seed compost (substrate) mixed with coarse horticultural sand to a ratio of 1 part compost + 1 part sand. Cover lightly with compost and place in a cold frame. Germination takes 5–6 months. Flowers in its second or third season.
OR
Sow fresh seed in spring into pots or modules using standard soil-less seed compost (substrate), either a peat free proprietary brand or composted fine propagating bark mixed with 3mm (1/8in) grit. Mix to a ratio of 3 parts compost + 1 part grit. Cover with perlite or vermiculite and place under protection at 15°C (60°F). Germination takes 15–21 days. Flowers in its second or third season.

Anthemis *Asteraceae*

A genus of hardy perennials, some of which are evergreen. Plant in a well-drained soil in a sunny situation.

Anthemis sancti-johannis
Small seeds: 1,400 per gram
Hardy evergreen perennial
Height 60cm (24in)
Deep orange, daisy-like flowers
Flowers in summer
Fern-like, shaggy, mid-green leaves

Anthemis tinctoria **(Dyers chamomile)**
Small seeds: 2,100 per gram
Hardy perennial
Height 1m (36in)
Yellow daisy-like flowers
Flowers in summer
Deeply cut, crinkled, mid-green leaves

Sow in spring into pots or modules using standard soil-less seed compost (substrate), either a peat free proprietary brand or composted fine propagating bark. Cover with perlite or vermiculite and place under protection at 18°C (65°F). Germination takes 14-21 days. Flowers approximately 3 months after sowing.

Aquilegia *Ranunculaceae*

A genus of hardy, short-lived perennials grown mainly for their attractive, bell-shaped, spurred flowers. Plant in well-drained soil and a sunny situation.

Aquilegia caerula 'McKana Giant' (McKana Group)
Medium seeds: 800 per gram
Hardy perennial
Height 90cm (36in)
Long, spurred flowers of mixed pastel colours
Flowers in summer
Divided, blue-green leaves

Aquilegia vulgaris (Crow's foot, Granny's bonnet)
Native wildflower in the UK
Medium seeds: 750 per gram
Hardy perennial
Height 75cm (30in)
The flowers are mixed colours – shades of pink, crimson, purple and white
Flowers from early spring until mid-summer
Grey-green leaves that are rounded and divided into leaflets

Aquilegia William Guinness (Magpie)
Medium seeds: 700 per gram
Hardy perennial
Height 75cm (30in)
Flowers have almost black sepals with a contrasting white corolla
Flowers in early summer
Grey-green, fern-like, divided leaves

Sow fresh seed in early summer into pots or modules using standard soil-less seed compost (substrate), either a peat free proprietary brand or composted fine propagating bark. Cover with perlite or vermiculite. Place under protection at 10°C (50°F). Germination takes 14-28 days.
OR
Sow old seed (seed is viable for 5 years) in autumn into pots. Use standard loam-based seed compost (substrate) mixed with coarse horticultural sand. Mix to a ratio of 1 part compost + 1 part sand. Cover lightly with compost and place outside, exposed to all the weathers (see 'Breaking Seed Dormancy', page 233, for more information). Germination takes place the following spring but can be erratic. May flower in its first or second season.

***Recipe for sowing, planting and growing* Aquilegia vulgaris**

Aquilegia is the quintessential flower of the traditional cottage garden. It is most attractive and available in many colours. A word of warning, if you have one species that you cherish, do not plant it near others, for it will cross pollinate and the seed you collect will not necessarily be true.

Ingredients
10 seeds per module or 15 seeds per pot
1 piece white card 14 x 8.5cm ($5^1/_2$ x $3^1/_2$in) folded in half
1 module tray
OR
1 x 8cm (4in) diameter pot
Standard soil-less seed compost (substrate), either a peat free proprietary brand or composted fine propagating bark, for summer sowing
OR
Standard loam-based seed compost (substrate) mixed with coarse horticultural sand to a ratio of 1 part compost + 1 part sand for autumn sowing.
Fine-grade perlite (wetted) or vermiculite
White plastic plant label

Method In late summer fill the tray or pot with compost, smooth over, tap down and water in well. Use fresh seed, and sow by putting a small amount of it into the crease of a folded card. Gently tap the card, sowing the seed thinly on to the surface of the compost. Cover with perlite or vermiculite and label with the plant name and date. Place the tray or pot in a warm light place out of direct sunlight at an optimum temperature of 10°C (50°F). Keep watering to a minimum until germination has occurred, which takes 14–28 days with warmth. Prick out into pots or put single seedlings into modules when they are large enough to handle. Overwinter young plants with a bit of protection in a cold frame or cold greenhouse.

Alternatively, in autumn you can sow old seed (old seed is viable for 5 years) into pots following the directions above using the loam-based seed compost mixed with extra sand. Having sown the seeds into the pots cover lightly with compost. Label with the plant name and date. Place the pot outside on a level surface, so that it is exposed to all the weathers, including frosts. Do not worry if you live in a snowy area and the containers get immersed in snow, for melting snow will aid germination. If you do not live in an area which will get a winter frost, it is a good idea to mix the seed with a handful of damp sand and put it into a plastic bag. Seal the bag, mark it clearly and place in a refrigerator for 3 weeks. Remove and sow as described above, then place outside. Whichever method you use, germination is a bit erratic, taking anything from 1–12 months. Do not give up and discard your compost, it might just germinate next week.

The plants may flower in their first or second season. They can be planted out into the garden when all threat of frost has passed.

Aruncus *Rosaceae*

A genus of hardy perennials grown for their fern-like leaves and attractive flowers. Plant in a well-drained soil in a sunny situation – will adapt to moist, not heavy soil and partial shade.

Aruncus aethusifolius AGM
Small seeds: 7,500 per gram
Hardy perennial
Height 30cm (12in)
Showy, upright panicles of many small flowers on red stems
Flowers in summer
Decorative, fine, feathery leaves

Aruncus dioicus (Goats beard, Spirea aruncus)
Small seeds: 9,000 per gram
Hardy perennial
Height up to 2m (6ft)
Masses of tiny, creamy white flowers which grow in light plumes
Flowers all summer
Large, mid-green leaves divided into lance-shaped leaflets

It is imperative to use fresh seed, so sow as soon as possible after collection. Sow fresh seed in autumn into pots or modules using standard loam-based seed compost (substrate) mixed with coarse horticultural sand. Mix to a ratio of 1 part compost + 1 part sand. Cover lightly with coarse horticultural sand and place outside, exposed to all weathers (see 'Breaking Seed Dormancy', page 233, for more information). Germination takes place the following spring. Flowers in second season.

Asclepias *Asclepiadaceae*

A genus of fully to frost-tender perennials and sub-shrubs, some of which are evergreen. All are grown for their attractive flowers.

Asclepias curassavica **(Blood flower, Silk weed)**
Medium seeds: 180 per gram
Half-hardy evergreen
Height 1m (3ft)
Orange/red flowers with yellow centres clustered in umbels. Sets pointed fruits with silky seeds
Flowers throughout the summer
Narrow oval leaves

Asclepias incarnata **(Ice ballet, Milkweed, Swamp milkweed)**
Medium seeds: 120 per gram
Half-hardy evergreen
Height 1m (3ft)
Clear white flowers clustered in umbels
Flowers throughout the summer
Narrow oval leaves

Sow in spring into pots or modules using standard soil-less seed compost (substrate), either a peat free proprietary brand or composted fine propagating bark. Cover with perlite or vermiculite and place under protection at 20°C (68°F). Germination takes 21–28 days. Will flower in the same year.

Asparagus *Asparagaceae*

A genus of hardy to frost-tender perennials, some of which are evergreen, climbers and shrubs all grown for their attractive foliage. Plant in a well-drained rich soil, in partial shade, not direct sunlight.

Asparagus densiflorus Sprengeri Group AGM **(Foxtail fern)**
Medium seeds: 20 per gram
Half-hardy evergreen perennial
Height up to 1m (3ft), trailing habit
White/pale pink flowers followed by red berries
Flowers in summer
Clusters of bright green, narrow, stem-like leaves

Asparagus setaceus AGM (*plumosus*) **(Asparagus fern)**
Medium seeds: 20 per gram
Half-hardy evergreen perennial
Height up to 60cm (2ft)
Fine, feathery, bright green foliage
A popular house plant, ideal for hanging baskets and containers

Sow fresh seed in autumn into pots using standard soil-less seed compost (substrate), either a peat free proprietary brand or composted fine propagating bark. Cover with vermiculite or perlite and place under protection at 21°C (70°F). Germination takes 21–42 days. When using fresh seed, germination can be fairly quick, however it can occur in flushes over a period of time, so do not be in a hurry to pot up. Overwinter young plants at temperatures no lower than 16°C (60°F).
OR
Sow in spring following the directions above. Germination can take longer, but heating bills will be less.

Asphodeline *Asphodelaceae*

A genus of hardy perennials. Plant in a moist but free-draining soil in a sunny position.

Asphodeline lutea **(Yellow candle, Jacob's rod, King's spear)**
Medium seeds: 55 per gram
Hardy perennial
Height up to 1.2m (4ft)
Dense spikes of fragrant, yellow, star-shaped flowers
Flowers in summer
Narrow, grey-green, lance-shaped leaves
This is a very handsome plant

Sow fresh seed in spring into pots using standard soil-less seed compost (substrate), either a peat free proprietary brand or composted fine propagating bark. Cover with perlite or vermiculite and place under protection at 20°C (68°F). Germination takes 8–15 days. When using fresh seed, germination can be fairly quick, however it can occur in flushes over a period of time, so do not discard the pot or module tray too soon. Flowers in its second season.

Astilbe *Saxifracaceae*

A genus of hardy summer-flowering perennials. Plant in a rich moist soil in partial shade. It is advisable to mulch well in the spring with well rotted compost.

Astilbe x arendsii **(Astilbe, False spirea)**
Tiny seeds: 18,000 per gram
Hardy perennial
Height 75cm (30in)
Plume-shaped feathery panicles of small, star-shaped flowers in shades from white through to deep red
Flowers in summer
Broad mid-green leaves which are divided into toothed leaflets

Sow seeds in early spring into pots or modules, using standard soil-less seed compost (substrate), either a peat free proprietary brand or composted fine propagating bark. As these are very fine seeds, mix with the finest sand or talcum powder for an even sowing. Cover with perlite or vermiculite and place under protection at 18°C (65°F). Water with a spray. Germination takes 6–8 weeks.

Astrantia *Apiaceae*

A genus of hardy perennials. Plant in a well-drained soil in sun or partial shade.

Astrantia major (Masterwort, Mountain sanicle)
Medium seeds: 200 per gram
Hardy perennial
Height 60cm (24in)
Lovely, rounded, greenish-white flowers which are tinged with pink and grow in clusters
Flowers all summer from second season
Palmate, lobed, mid-green leaves
Looks wonderful in pressed flower arrangements

Sow seed in autumn into pots or modules using standard loam-based seed compost (substrate) mixed with coarse horticultural sand. Mix to a ratio of 1 part compost + 1 part sand. Cover lightly with coarse horticultural sand and place in a cold frame. Germination takes 5–6 months. Usually flowers in its second season, but occasionally in its first.

Baptisia *Papillionaceae*

A genus of hardy summer-flowering perennials. Plant in a well-drained soil in a sunny situation.

Baptisia australis AGM (False indigo, Blue indigo)
Medium seeds: 80 per gram
Hardy perennial
Height 75cm (30in)
Spikes of indigo, pea-like flowers that then set dark grey seed pods, which are good for winter decoration
Flowers in summer
Mid-green, notched leaves

In late summer soak fresh seeds in hot (not boiling) water for 12 hours prior to sowing. Remove any floating seeds and sow the remainder in pots, using standard soil-less seed compost (substrate), either a peat free proprietary brand or composted fine propagating bark mixed with 3mm (1/8in) grit to a ratio of 3 parts compost + 1 part fine grit. Cover lightly with fine grit and place in a cold frame. Germination takes 2–5 weeks. Overwinter young plants in a cold frame.

***Recipe for sowing, planting and growing* Baptisia australis**
This attractive plant looks lovely grown in large clumps in a perennial border.

Ingredients
3 seeds per module or 5 seeds per pot
Small china bowl
Hot water
1 module tray
OR
1 x 8cm (4in) pot
Standard soil-less seed compost (substrate), either a peat free proprietary brand or composted fine propagating bark mixed with 3mm (1/8in) grit to a ratio of 3 parts compost +1 part fine grit
Extra fine grit for covering
White plastic plant label

Method In late summer collect enough fresh seeds to fill the required module tray or pots. Fill a china bowl with hot, not boiling, water. Add the fresh seeds to the liquid and soak for 12 hours. Fill the module or pots with compost, smooth over, tap down and water in well. Place 3 seeds per module or 5 seeds per pot, equally spaced on the surface of the compost. Cover the seeds with sharp grit, and label with the plant's name and date.

Place the container in a cold frame. Keep watering to a minimum until germination has taken place, which takes 2–5 weeks.

If you have not overcrowded the pot or module, it is a good idea to leave the seedlings undisturbed until the following spring. Then prick out and pot up, or if grown in modules they can be planted directly into a well-prepared site in the garden after a period of hardening off, when there is no threat of frost.

Bergenia *Saxifragaceae*

A genus of hardy evergreen perennials. For the best colour, plant in a poor, well-drained soil in full sun.

Bergenia purpurascens AGM
Small seeds: 3,500 per gram
Hardy evergreen perennial
Height 45cm (18in)
Rich red racemes of open, cup-shaped flowers
Flowers in spring
Can take up to 3 years to reach full flowering potential
Oval, flat, dark green leaves that turn red in late autumn

Sow fresh seed in early spring into pots or modules using standard soil-less seed compost (substrate), either a peat free proprietary brand or composted fine propagating bark. Cover with perlite or vermiculite and place under protection at 20°C (68°F). Germination takes 2–4 weeks.

Buphthalmum *Asteraceae*

A genus of hardy summer-flowering perennials. Plant in any except rich soil, in a sunny situation.

Buphthalmum salicifolium (Yellow ox-eye)
Medium seeds: 1,000 per gram
Hardy perennial
Height 60cm (2ft)
Deep yellow, daisy-like flowers
Flowers throughout the summer
Oval, pointed, mid-green leaves

Sow seed in spring into pots or modules using standard soil-less seed compost (substrate), either a peat free proprietary brand or composted fine propagating bark. Cover with perlite or vermiculite and place under protection at 20°C (68°F). Germination takes 4–8 days. Flowers in first year, but offers a better show in second year.

Calamintha *Lamiaceae*

A genus of hardy perennials. Plant in a well-drained to dry soil in a sunny situation.

Calamintha nepeta (Lesser calamint)
Small seeds: 3,300 per gram
Hardy perennial
Height 37cm (15in)
Loose clusters of small, tubular, pale lilac-pink to white flowers
Flowers in summer
Oval, toothed, green-grey, mint-scented leaves

Sow seed in autumn into pots or modules using standard loam-based seed compost (substrate) mixed with coarse horticultural sand. Mix to a ratio of 1 part compost + 1 part sand. Cover lightly with coarse horticultural sand and place in a cold frame. Germination takes 5–6 months.

These seeds can be tricky – the most successful method to date is the one mentioned above, although full stratification (see page 233) may work better for those in warmer climates.

Campanula *Campanulaceae*

A genus of half-hardy to hardy annuals, biennials and perennials. Plant in a moist but well-drained soil in partial shade

Campanula glomerata 'Superba' AGM (Clustered bellflower)
Small seeds: 9,000 per gram
Hardy perennial
Height 75cm (30in)
Clusters of dark violet flowers
Flowers in summer
Oval, green leaves in basal rosettes

Sow seed in spring into pots or modules, using standard soil-less seed compost (substrate), either a peat free proprietary brand or composted fine propagating bark. Place in a cold frame. DO NOT cover. Germination takes 2–3 weeks. Divide and replant established plants regularly.

Canna *Cannaceae*

A genus of half-hardy rhizomatous perennials. Plant in a humus-rich moist soil in a sunny sheltered position. Often used in garden displays and lifted for the winter in cool damp climates.

Canna's are commonly propagated by division, however seed is not difficult and it is very rewarding,

Canna x generalis (Canna lily)
Large seeds: 5 per gram
Half-hardy perennial
Height 90cm (36in)
Spikes of stunning, orchid-like flowers. Colours vary from crimson to orange and yellow
Flowers in summer
Broad, bronze/green, lance-shaped leaves

In early spring soak fresh seeds in hot, not boiling, water for 12 hours prior to sowing. Remove and discard any floating seeds and sow remainder in pots. Use standard soil-less seed compost (substrate), either a peat free proprietary brand or composted fine propagating bark. Cover with perlite or vermiculite and place under protection at 21°C (70°F). Germination takes 3–4 weeks. Will flower in its first year.

***Recipe for sowing, planting and growing* Canna x generalis**

This is structurally a stunning plant, the foliage looks striking and the flowers display a wonderful range of colours. Well worth growing as a container plant if you live in cooler climates – make sure the container has a good base so the plant will not topple over in high winds.

Ingredients
2 seeds per pot
Small china bowl
Hot water
1 x 8cm (4in) pot
Standard soil-less seed compost (substrate), either a peat free proprietary brand or composted fine propagating bark
Fine-grade perlite (wetted) or vermiculite
White plastic plant label

Method In spring fill a china bowl with hot, not boiling, water. Add the seeds to the liquid and soak for 12 hours. Fill the pots with compost, smooth over, tap down and water in well. Place 2 seeds equally spaced on the surface of the compost in each pot. Cover the seeds with fine-grade perlite (wetted) or vermiculite and label with the plant's name and the date. Place the pot in a warm, light place out of direct sunlight at an optimum temperature of 21°C (70°F). Keep watering to a minimum until germination has taken place, which takes 3–4 weeks. Pot up as soon as the seedlings are large enough to handle, keep the young plants under protection until large enough to stand outside or incorporate in a summer bedding scheme. As tender perennials, these plants will suffer if planted out before all threat of frost has passed.

Catananche *Asteraceae*

A genus of hardy, daisy-like, summer-flowering perennials. Plant in a light, well-drained soil in a sunny position.

Catananche caerulea (Blue cupidone, Cupid's dart)
Medium seeds: 300 per gram
Hardy perennial
Height 60cm (24in)
Attractive, daisy like, blue-mauve flowers
Flowers all summer
Grass-like mid-green leaves
Flowers dry well for winter displays

Sow seed in spring into pots or modules using standard soil-less seed compost (substrate), either a peat free proprietary brand or composted fine propagating bark. Cover with vermiculite or perlite and place under protection at 20°C (68°F). Germination takes 4–10 days. Will flower in its first year although there is a better show in the second year.

Centaurea *Asteraceae*

A genus of hardy annuals and perennials which all have attractive flowers. Plant in a well-drained soil and a sunny position.

Centaurea macrocephala
Medium seeds: 60 per gram
Hardy perennial
Height 1m (3ft)

Catananche caerulea

Yellow flowers enclosed in papery, silvery-brown bracts
Flowers in summer
Light green oval or lance-shaped, deeply cut, rough leaves

Centaurea montana (Perennial cornflower, Mountain bluet)
Medium seeds: 80 per gram
Hardy perennial
Height 60cm (24in)
Lovely, large, blue flowers with thistle-like centres which are encircled by star-shaped ray petals
Flowers in summer
Lance-shaped, mid-green hairy leaves

Sow seed in spring into pots or modules, using standard soil-less seed compost (substrate), either a peat free proprietary brand or composted fine propagating bark. Cover with perlite or vermiculite and place under protection at 20°C (68°F). Germination takes 7–14 days. Will flower in its first year, although there is a better show in the second year.

Centranthus *Valerianaceae*

A genus of hardy summer-flowering perennials. Plant in poor soil, with a bias to alkaline, in a sunny situation.

Centranthus ruber (Valerian red)
Medium seeds: 700 per gram
Hardy perennial
Height up to 1m ($3^1/_2$ft)
Small, red/pink or white lightly fragrant flowers in loose clusters
Flowers all summer
Oval, pointed, smooth, fleshy, pale green leaves
Happily self seeds and is often seen growing out of stone walls

Sow seed in autumn into pots or modules, using standard loam-based seed compost (substrate) mixed with coarse horticultural sand. Mix to a ratio of 1 part compost + 1 part sand. Cover lightly with coarse horticultural sand and place in a cold frame. Germination takes 5–6 months.

Cephalaria *Dipsacaceae*

A genus of hardy summer-flowering perennials. Plant in a well-drained soil in a sunny situation.

Cephalaria gigantea (Giant scabious, Yellow scabious)
Medium seeds: 60 per gram
Hardy perennial
Height up to 2m (6ft)
Primrose-yellow scabious-like flowers on wiry stems
Flowers all summer
Dark green, lance-shaped, deeply cut leaves

Sow seed in spring into pots or modules using standard soil-less seed compost (substrate), either a peat free proprietary brand or composted fine propagating bark. Cover lightly with perlite or vermiculite and place in a cold frame. Germination takes 5–6 weeks. Flowers in its second year.

Chelidonium *Papaveraceae*

A one-species genus, fully hardy perennial. Suits all soil types, with the exception of the very wet. Plant in sun or partial shade.

Chelidonium majus (Greater celandine)
UK native wildflower
Small seeds: 1,500 per gram
Hardy perennial
Height 60cm (24in)
Cup-shaped, sunny yellow flowers
Flowers from late spring until early summer
Mid-green, divided leaves

Sow seed in autumn into pots or modules using standard loam-based seed compost (substrate) mixed with coarse horticultural sand. Mix to a ratio of 1 part compost + 1 part sand. Cover lightly with coarse horticultural sand and place in a cold frame. Germination takes 5–6 months.

Chelone *Scrophulariaceae*

A genus of hardy summer- and autumn-flowering perennials. Plant in a moist soil in semi-shade.

Chelone obilqua (Turtle head)
Small seeds: 1,150 per gram
Hardy perennial
Height 1m (3ft)
Terminal spikes of lilac/pink hooded flowers
Flowers from late summer to early autumn
Dark green lance-shaped leaves

Sow seed in spring into pots or modules using standard loam-based seed compost (substrate) mixed with coarse horticultural sand. Mix to a ratio of 1 part compost + 1 part sand. Cover with perlite or vermiculite and place in a cold frame. Germination takes 2–6 weeks.

Chrysanthemum *Asteraceae*

There have been many botanical name changes to this plant family. To give you one example *Chrysanthemum parthenium* 'Snow Lady' is now *Tanacetum parthenium* 'Snow Lady'. So, if you cannot find your favourite, try looking under *Argyanthemum, Leucanthemum, Rhodanthemum, Tanacetum* or *Xanthophthalmum*. For those outdoor species that have not been reclassified, plant in well-drained soil in a sunny position.

Chrysanthemum 'Autumn Glory'
Small seeds: 2,000 per gram
Hardy perennial
Height 30cm (12in)
Flowers of all shades from white to orange, yellow and dusky pink
Flowers in late summer until first frosts
Mid-green, cut, lobed leaves

Sow seed in spring in pots or modules using standard soil-less seed compost (substrate), either a peat free proprietary brand or composted fine propagating bark. Cover with perlite or vermiculite and place under protection at 16°C (60°F). Germination takes 7–14 days.

Cirsium *Asteraceae*

A genus of hardy annuals, biennials and perennials. Plant in any soil, with the exception of wet sites, in sun or partial shade. A word of warning, some species of this genera are not cultivated, in fact they are deterred because they are pernicious weeds. However, there are some very attractive garden varieties now available.

Cirsium japonicum 'Pink Beauty' (Japanese thistle, Azami)
Medium seeds: 600 per gram
Hardy perennial, often grown as an annual
Height 75cm (30in)
Thistle, or pincushion-like, pink flowers
Flowers all summer
Lance-shaped, deeply cut, mid-green/grey leaves
More often grown as cut flower plant than a perennial border plant

Sow seed in spring in pots or modules using standard soil-less seed compost (substrate), either a peat free proprietary brand or composted fine propagating bark. Cover with perlite or vermiculite. Place under protection at 18°C (65°F). Germination takes 7–14 days.

Coreopsis *Asteraceae*

A genus of hardy annuals and perennials grown for their daisy-like flowers. Plant in a well-drained soil in a sunny position.

Coreopsis grandiflora
Medium seeds: 400 per gram
Hardy perennial
Height 90cm (36in)
Large, golden-yellow, daisy-like flowers
Flowers all summer
Lance-shaped, divided, mid-green leaves

Coreopsis tinctoria (Tickseed)
Small seeds: 2,300 per gram
Hardy annual
Height 90cm (36in)
Large, daisy-like, bright yellow flowers with rust-red centres
Flowers all summer.
Lance-shaped, mid-green leaves

Sow seed in spring in pots or modules, using standard soil-less seed compost (substrate), either a peat free proprietary brand or composted fine propagating bark. Cover with vermiculite or perlite. Place under protection at 18°C (65°F). Germination takes 10–14 days.

Crocosmia *Iridaceae*

A genus of frost-hardy perennials, usually grown from corms, which should, in very cold areas, be lifted for the winter. Plant in a well-drained soil and a sunny situation.

Crocosmia x *crocosmiiflora*
Medium seeds: 200 per gram
Hardy perennial
Height 60cm (24in)
Tall stems of tubular, orange-red flowers with spreading petals, which are very good for cutting
Flowers in summer during second season
Dense clumps of sword-shaped leaves

Sow fresh seed in autumn into pots or modules, using standard loam-based seed compost (substrate) mixed with coarse horticultural sand to a ratio of 1 part compost + 1 part sand. Cover lightly with coarse horticultural sand and place outside to expose to all the weathers. (See Breaking Seed Dormancy, page 233, for more information.) Germination takes place the following spring.

***Recipe for sowing, planting and growing* Crocosmia hybrida**
This popular border perennial, with its dense spikes of tubular flowers, is excellent for floral displays.

Ingredients
5 seeds per module or 8 seeds per pot
1 module tray
OR
1 x 8cm (4in) pot
Standard loam-based seed compost (substrate) mixed with coarse horticultural sand. Mix to a ratio of 1 part compost + 1 part sand
Extra coarse horticultural sand to cover the pot
White plastic plant label

Method In autumn fill the tray or pot with compost, smooth over, tap down and water in well. Sow the seeds thinly on to the surface of the compost. Press gently into the compost with the flat of the hand. Cover the seed with coarse horticultural sand. Label with the plant name and date. Place the tray or pot outside, on a level surface, so it is exposed to all the weathers, including frosts. Do not worry if you live in a snowy area and the containers get immersed in snow, as melting snow will aid germination. If you do not live in an area which will get a winter frost, it is a good idea to put the seed plus a handful of damp sand into a plastic bag. Seal and label the bag. Place in a refrigerator for 3 weeks. Remove and sow as described above, then place outside. Whichever method you use, germination is a bit erratic, taking anything from 1–12 months. Do not give up and discard your compost, it might just germinate next week.

Prick out when the seedlings are large enough to handle. If you are using modules, you can plant directly into the garden as soon as the soil is warm enough to dig over, prior to planting out.

Cuphea *Lythraceae*

A genus of half-hardy to tender annuals and perennials, some of which are evergreen. Plant in a fertile, well-drained soil in a sunny situation. If grown as a container plant, cut watering down in winter.

Cuphea ignea AGM (Platycentra, Mexican cigar plant)
Medium seeds: 700 per gram
Half-hardy evergreen perennial
Bright scarlet, narrow, tubular flowers with a dark band and a white ring at the tip
Flowers from summer to autumn
Dark green, oval leaves with a point

Sow seed in early spring in pots or modules using standard soil-less seed compost (substrate), either a peat free proprietary brand or composted fine propagating bark. Cover with perlite or vermiculite and place under protection at 18°C (65 °F). Germination takes 2–3 weeks.

Dahlia *Asteraceae*

A genus of half-hardy summer- and autumn-flowering tuberous perennials. There are many varieties of hybrid now available, which can be grown from seed. The flowers come in stunning colours and all shapes and sizes. Plant in a well-drained soil in a sunny position.

Dahlia 'Figaro Red'
Medium seeds: 100 per gram
Half-hardy perennial often grown as an annual
Height 40cm (16in)
Very attractive crimson flowers
Flowers all summer
Divided, mid-green, oval leaves

Sow seed in early spring in pots or modules using standard soil-less seed compost (substrate), either a peat free proprietary brand or composted fine propagating bark. Cover with perlite or vermiculite, place under protection at 18°C (65°F). Germination takes 7–14 days.

Delphinium *Ranunculaceae*

A genus of fully- to half-hardy perennials and annuals grown for their beautiful flowers. Plant in a rich, fertile well-drained soil in a sunny position.

Delphinium elatum
Medium seeds: 350 per gram
Hardy perennial
Height 1.35m to 2.2m ($4^1/_2$ft–7ft)
Spikes of semi-double flowers, regularly spaced, colours from white through to sky blue, to purple, with contrasting centres
Flowers all summer
Large palmate, divided leaves

Delphinium nudicaule
Medium seeds: 850 per gram
Hardy, short-lived perennial
Height 20cm (8in)
Spikes of hooded red or occasionally yellow flowers
Flowers in summer
Mid-green, basal, deeply-divided leaves
Will flower in first year

Sow fresh seed individually into pots or modules in autumn using standard soil-less compost (substrate), either a peat free proprietary brand or composted fine propagating bark, mixed with extra silver or fine sand for extra aeration. Mix to a ratio of 3 parts compost + 1 part sand. Cover with perlite or vermiculite, place in a cold frame. Germination takes 10–14 days. Overwinter young plants in a cold frame. Do not worry when the plant dies back, it is meant to, they will reappear in spring with lots of new, lush growth. However, beware of slugs.

Dicentra *Papaveraceae*

A genus of hardy perennials grown for their elegant flowers. Plant in a moist but well-drained soil in semi- shade.

Dicentra spectabilis AGM **(Bleeding heart, Dutchman's trousers)**
Medium seeds: 220 per gram
Hardy perennial
Height 75cm (30in)
Beautiful stalks with pendulous heart-shaped pinkish-red and white flowers
Flowers from late spring to mid-summer
Fern-like, deeply cut mid-green leaves

Sow fresh seeds in autumn into pots, using standard loam-based seed compost (substrate) mixed with coarse horticultural sand. Mix to a ratio of 1 part compost + 1 part sand. Cover lightly with coarse horticultural sand and place outside, exposed to all the weathers (see 'Breaking Seed Dormancy', page 233, for more information). Germination takes place the following spring. Flowers in its second season.

Dodecatheon *Primulaceae*

A genus of hardy perennials; plant in a moist but well-drained soil in sun or partial shade.

Dodecatheon meadia AGM
Small seeds: 1,800 per gram
Hardy perennial
Height 30cm (12in)
Large umbels of rose/purple flowers, with reflex petals and yellow anthers. The nickname of this flower is 'shooting stars' because once the flowers are pollinated they turn their faces to the sky.
Flowers from late spring
Rosettes of broad, light green, lance-shaped leaves

Sow fresh seeds in autumn into pots or modules using standard soil-less seed compost (substrate), either a peat free proprietary brand or composted fine propagating bark mixed with silver or fine sand for extra aeration. Mix to a ratio of 3 parts compost + 1 part sand. Cover with fine sand and place in a cold frame. Germination takes 1–6 months, but can be erratic. This plant prefers to be planted in partial shade.

Doronicum *Asteraceae*

A genus of hardy perennials grown for their attractive daisy-shaped flowers. Plant in a well-drained soil in sun or light shade.

Doronicum orientale 'Magnificum' **(Leopards bane)**
Medium seeds: 1,000 per gram
Hardy perennial
Height 51cm (20in)
Large, cheerful, daisy-shaped, yellow flowers
Flowers from early spring
Bright green, heart-shaped leaves

Dodecatheon meadia

Sow seed in spring into pots or modules, using standard loam-based seed compost (substrate) mixed with coarse horticultural sand. Mix to a ratio of 1 part compost + 1 part sand. Cover with coarse horticultural sand and place in a cold frame. Germination takes 3–4 weeks. This plant does not like high humidity, which can make it wilt. However, it will return the following spring.

Dracocephalum *Lamiaceae*

A genus of hardy annuals and perennials which flower from early spring and through the summer. Plant in a fertile well draining soil in a sunny situation.

Dracocephalum botryoides **(Dragon's head)**
Small seeds: 1,400 per gram
Hardy evergreen perennial
Height 15cm (6in)
Clusters of small-lipped pink flowers
Flowers in late spring and early summer
Grey-green, pinnate, soft green leaves

Sow fresh seeds in autumn into pots or modules using standard loam-based seed compost (substrate) mixed with coarse horticultural sand. Mix to a ratio of 1 part compost + 1 part sand. Cover with coarse horticultural sand and place in a cold frame. Germination takes 7–8 months, but can be erratic.

Echinops *Asteraceae*

A genus of hardy summer-flowering perennials. Plant in any poor soil with the exception of clay, in a sunny position.

Echinops ritro L. AGM **(Blue globe thistle)**
Medium seeds: 90 per gram
Hardy perennial
Height 1.2m (4ft)
Lovely, steel-blue, globular flower heads, which dry well
Flowers in summer
Sharply divided, green leaves with a pale, downy underside

Sow seed in spring into pots using standard soil-less seed compost (substrate), either a peat free proprietary brand or composted fine propagating bark. This plant is not suitable for growing in modules. Cover with perlite or vermiculite, and place in a cold frame. Germination takes 2–3 weeks.

Epilobium *Onagraceae*

A genus of hardy annuals, biennials and perennials. Plant in a moist but well-drained soil in sun or partial shade.

Epilobium dodonaei **(Alpine willowherb)**
Small seeds: 2,700 per gram
Hardy perennial
Height 30cm (12in)
Clusters of deep-rose-coloured flowers
Flowers in summer
Narrow, glossy, green leaves

Sow fresh seeds in autumn into pots or modules, using standard loam-based seed compost (substrate) mixed with coarse horticultural sand. Mix to a ratio of 1 part compost + 1 part sand. Cover with coarse horticultural sand and place outside, exposed to all the weathers (see 'Breaking Seed Dormancy', page 233, for more information). Germination takes 1–6 months and can be erratic.

Eranthis *Ranunculaceae*

A genus of hardy tuberous perennials. Plant in a well-drained soil that does not totally dry out in summer, in partial shade.

Eranthis hyemalis AGM **(Winter aconite)**
Medium seeds: 240 per gram
Hardy perennial
Height 5–10cm (2–4in)
Glossy, bright yellow, buttercup-shaped flowers
Flowers in early spring
Deeply cut, mid-green leaves which form a ruff beneath each bloom

Sow fresh seeds in autumn into pots using standard loam-based seed compost (substrate) mixed with coarse horticultural sand. Mix to a ratio of 1 part compost + 1 part sand. Cover with coarse horticultural sand and place outside, exposed to all the weathers. It is essential that this plant has a period of true cold, -4–0°C (25–32°F), for at least one month (see 'Breaking Seed Dormancy', page 233, for more information). Germination takes 5–6 months and can be erratic.

Eremurus *Asphodelaceae*

A genus of hardy perennials. Plant in a well-drained soil in a warm sunny position. This plant has the habit of growing fast in early spring, and this growth is easily damaged by frost, so cover with straw or horticultural fleece to protect young shoots.

Eremurus x *isabellinus* Shelford hybrids **(Foxtail lily)**
Medium seeds: 140 per gram
Hardy perennial
Height 1.5m (5ft)
Long racemes of star-shaped flowers which vary from orange to pink, with the occasional white
Flowers in summer
Star-shaped leaves which form a rosette around the base of the plant

Sow seeds in autumn into pots using standard loam-based seed compost (substrate) mixed with coarse horticultural sand. Mix to a ratio of 1 part compost + 1 part sand. Cover with coarse horticultural sand and place under cover at 25°C (77°F) for a month, then move the container to a cold frame and cover with black plastic. The temperature needs to be a minimum of 2°C (36°F) for 8–10 weeks, then remove the black plastic and leave container in the cold frame. Germination takes 4–6 months in total.

***Recipe for sowing, planting and growing* Eremurus x isabellinus**
These stately perennials, with their noble spikes of flowers, look great in a border or against a dark fence.

Ingredients
4 seeds per module or 8 seeds per pot
1 module tray
OR
1 x 8cm (4in) diameter pot
Standard loam-based seed compost (substrate) mixed with coarse horticultural sand. Mix to a ratio of 1 part compost + 1 part sand
Extra coarse sand for covering the seeds
Black plastic large enough to cover module tray or pot
White plastic plant label

Method In autumn fill the tray or pot with compost, smooth over, tap down and water in well. Sow thinly into the container, spacing the seeds well. Press gently into the compost with the flat of the hand. Cover thinly with the coarse sand. Label the container with the plant name and date. Place the tray or pot in a warm light place, out of direct sunlight, at an optimum temperature of 25°C (77°F). After one month move container to a cold frame and cover with black plastic. Keep the temperature to a minimum of 2°C (36°F). After 8 weeks lift the black plastic and check whether the seeds are starting to chit (break their shells). If not, return the cover and check weekly, chitting should have started within 10 weeks of being covered with the plastic. Once it has started, remove the plastic, leaving the container in the cold frame until spring. Keep watering to a minimum until spring. Pot up or prick out when all threat of frost has passed. Harden off and plant out into a prepared site in the garden in late spring, early summer. In the following autumn, mulch the plants with straw or bark to protect new growth from frost damage.

Erigeron *Asterace*

A genus of hardy annuals, biennials and perennials which all have daisy-like flowers. Plant in a well-drained soil in a sunny position.

Erigeron aurantiacus 'Spanish Lady'
Small seeds: 3,000 per gram
Hardy perennial
Height 35cm (14in)
Bright orange, daisy-like flowers
Flowers all summer
Oval, grey-green leaves

Erigeron 'Azurfee' (Azure Fairy)
Small seeds: 3,500 per gram
Height 60cm (24in)
Daisy-like, semi-double, lavender-blue flowers
Flowers all summer
Oval, greenish-grey leaves

Sow fresh seeds in spring into pots or modules using standard soil-less seed compost (substrate), either a peat free proprietary brand or composted fine propagating bark. Cover with perlite or vermiculite and place in a cold frame. Germination takes 2–3 weeks.

Eryngium *Apiaceae*

A genus of half-hardy to hardy biennials and perennials and some evergreens. Plant in a fertile, well-drained soil in a sunny situation.

Eryngium maritimum (Sea holly)
Medium seeds: 100 per gram
Hardy perennial
Height 45cm (18in)
Umbels of thistle-like, powder blue flowers surrounded by spiny, leaf-like bracts
Flowers in summer
Leathery blue-green, spiked holly-like leaves

Eryngium planum
Medium seeds: 900 per gram
Hardy perennial
Height 1.2m (4ft)
Blue, globular, thistle-like flower heads
Flowers in late summer
Heart-shaped, dark green leaves

Sow seeds in autumn into pots or modules using standard loam-based seed compost (substrate) mixed with coarse horticultural sand. Mix to a ratio of 1 part compost + 1 part sand. Cover with coarse horticultural sand and place in a cold frame. Germination takes 2–3 months, but can be erratic.

Fatsia *Araliaceae*

A genus of one species. In temperate climates can be planted in a fertile well-drained soil in sun or partial shade. Protect from strong winds. If grown as pot plant keep watering to the minimum in winter.

Fatsia japonica AGM (syn. *Aralia sieboldii*) (Japanese fatsia)
Medium seeds: 175 per gram
Half-hardy evergreen perennial, grown as a pot plant for conservatory, house or greenhouse
Height, in native conditions, up to 3m (10ft)
Dense clusters of tiny white flowers followed by round black fruits
Flowers in early autumn
Rich glossy deep green deeply lobed leaves

Sow in spring or late autumn in pots or modules using standard soil-less seed compost (substrate), either a peat free proprietary brand or composted fine propagating bark. Cover with perlite or vermiculite and place under protection at 21°C (70°F). Germination takes 4–6 weeks. If sowing in autumn keep young plants frost free.

Freesia *Iridaceae*

A genus of half-hardy perennials, which are usually grown from corms. The flowers have a lovely fragrance. Grown as a pot plant in cooler climates.

Freesia hybrids
Medium seeds: 100–280 per gram
Half-hardy perennial
Height 30cm (12in)

Loose spikes of very fragrant white, mauve or yellow flowers
Flowers all summer from second season
Narrow lance-shaped mid-green leaves

In spring soak the seeds in hot, not boiling, water overnight. Remove and discard any floating seeds and sow the remainder in pots or modules using standard soil-less seed compost (substrate), either a peat free proprietary brand or composted fine propagating bark. Cover lightly with perlite or vermiculite and place under protection at 21°C (70°F). Germination takes 3–4 weeks.

Gaillardia *Asteraceae*

A genus of hardy annuals and short-lived perennials. Plant in a well-drained soil in a sunny situation.

Gaillardia x grandiflora 'Dazzler' AGM **(Blanket flower)**
Medium seeds: 250 per gram
Hardy perennial
Height 60cm (24in)
Large, daisy-like, red flowers which have yellow tips to the petals
Does need staking
Flowers from summer until early autumn
Divided, soft, mid-green leaves

Sow seeds in spring into pots or modules using standard soil-less seed compost (substrate), either a peat free proprietary brand or composted fine propagating bark. Cover with perlite or vermiculite, place in a cold frame. Germination takes 2–3 weeks.

Galega *Papilionaceae*

A genus of hardy summer-flowering perennials. Plant in well-drained soil in a sunny position.

Galega officinalis **(Goat's rue)**
Medium seeds: 120 per gram
Hardy perennial
Height 90cm (36in)
Spikes of small, pea-like, mauve flowers
Flowers in summer of second season
Oblong, lance-shaped leaves with oval leaflets

Sow fresh seeds in autumn into pots or modules using standard soil-less seed compost (substrate), either a peat free proprietary brand or composted fine propagating bark. Cover with perlite or vermiculite and place in a cold frame. Germination takes 2–3 weeks. Overwinter young plants in a cold frame.

Galium *Rubiaceae*

A genus of hardy perennials. Plant in any well-drained soil, in partial shade – ideal for deciduous woodland.

Galium verum **(Lady's bedstraw, Cheese rennet)**
Native wildflower of the UK
Small seeds: 1,500 per gram
Hardy perennial
Height 15–90cm (6–36in)
Panicles of sweetly-scented, tiny, yellow flowers
Flowers in summer of second season
Whorls of small, linear leaves

Sow fresh seeds in late summer into pots or modules using standard loam-based seed compost (substrate) mixed with coarse horticultural sand. Mix to a ratio of 1 part compost + 1 part sand. Cover with coarse horticultural sand and place in a cold frame. Germination takes 2–3 months and can be erratic.

Gaura *Onagraceae*

A genus of hardy biennials and perennials. Plant in a light, well-drained soil in a sunny situation.

Gaura lindheimeri AGM
Medium seeds: 60 per gram
Hardy perennial
Height 1.2m (4ft)
Racemes of tubular, white flowers which have a pink hue
Flowers in summer of second season
Lance-shaped mid-green leaves

Sow seeds in spring into pots or modules using standard soil-less seed compost (substrate), either a peat free proprietary brand or composted fine propagating bark. Cover with perlite or vermiculite and place in a cold frame. Germination takes 2–3 months. Overwinter young plants in a cold frame.

Gazania *Asteraceae*

A genus of half-hardy perennials which are often grown as annuals. In warm climates plant in a well-draining sandy soil in a sunny situation. Otherwise grow as pot plants, keep watering to the minimum in winter.

Gazania 'Daybreak Red Stripe' Daybreak Series **(Treasure flower)**
Medium seeds: 400 per gram
Half-hardy perennial, often grown as an annual
Height 20cm (8in)
Large daisy-like flowers in a mixture of colours from bronze, yellow, orange, pink, and white
Flowers in summer
Lance-shaped mid-green leaves

Sow seeds in spring into pots or modules using standard soil-less seed compost (substrate), either a peat free proprietary brand or composted fine propagating bark. Cover with perlite or vermiculite and place under protection at 21°C (70°F) or 15°C (60°F). Germination takes 10–14 days or 14–21 days at the cooler temperature. Will flower in its first season.

Geranium *Geraniaceae*

A genus of hardy perennials, some of which are semi-evergreen. Plant in most soils, with the exception of waterlogged sites. Likes a sunny situation, although some species prefer a bit of shade.

Geranium pratense **(Splish-splash, Meadow cranesbill)**
Medium seeds: 130 per gram
Hardy perennial
Height 50cm (20in)
Saucer-shaped, 5-petalled blue/mauve/white speckled flowers
Flowers all summer from the second season
Rounded, lobed, deeply divided, mid-green leaves

Galega officinalis

Sow seeds in summer into pots or modules using standard soil-less seed compost (substrate), either a peat free proprietary brand or composted fine propagating bark. Cover with perlite or vermiculite and place under protection at 15°C (60°F). Germination takes 10–14 days. Overwinter young plants in a cold frame.

Grevillea *Proteaceae*

A genus of half-hardy evergreen shrubs and trees. In warm climates, plant in a well-drained acid soil in a sunny situation. In cooler climates grow as a pot plant and keep watering to a minimum in winter.

Grevillea robusta AGM **(Silky oak)**
Medium seeds: 85 per gram
Half-hardy evergreen perennial
Height in natural habitat 30m (100ft)
Mature plants have bell-shaped, yellow or orange flowers which grow on one-sided spikes
Flowers all summer
Fern-like, long leaves

Sow seeds in early spring into pots or modules using standard soil-less seed compost (substrate), either a peat free proprietary brand or composted fine propagating bark. Cover with perlite or vermiculite and place under protection at 18°C (65°F). Germination takes 3–4 weeks.

If growing on as a container plant in cool climates, use a peat free proprietary brand or composted fine propagating bark (substrate) as a compost.

Helenium *Asteraceae*

A genus of hardy perennials grown for their daisy-like flowers. Plant in a well-drained soil in a sunny situation.

Helenium autumnale
Small seeds: 4,000 per gram
Hardy perennial
Height 90cm (36in)
Large red and gold daisy-shaped flowers
Flowers in summer and early autumn
Lance-shaped, mid-green leaves

Sow seeds in spring into pots or modules using standard soil-less seed compost (substrate), either a peat free proprietary brand or composted fine propagating bark. Cover with perlite or vermiculite. Place in a cold frame. Germination takes 3–4 months. Overwinter young plants in a cold frame. Flowers in its second season.

Heliopsis *Asteraceae*

A genus of hardy perennials. Plant in any free-draining soil in a sunny situation.

Heliopsis helianthoides var. *scabra* 'Sommersonne'
Medium seeds: 240 per gram
Hardy perennial
Height 1.2m (4ft)
Large, golden-yellow flowers
Flowers from late summer to early autumn
Narrow, oval, coarsely toothed, mid-green leaves

Sow seeds in spring into pots or modules using standard soil-less seed compost (substrate), either a peat free proprietary brand or composted fine propagating bark. Cover with perlite or vermiculite and place in a cold frame. Germination takes 3–4 weeks.

Helleborus *Ranunculaceae*

A genus of hardy to half-hardy perennials, some of which are evergreen. Plant in a moisture-retentive, well-drained soil in semi-shade.

Helleborus argutifolius (corsicus) AGM
Medium seeds: 125 per gram
Hardy perennial
Height 60cm (24in)
Large panicles of yellowish-green, cup-shaped flowers
Flowers in early spring
Thick, leathery, spiny, three-lobed leaves

Helleborus niger AGM **(Christmas rose)**
Medium seeds: 125 per gram
Hardy evergreen perennial
Height 30cm (12in)
Cup-shaped, white flowers with golden stamens
Flowers from winter to early spring
Mid-green, divided, oval leaves

Sow fresh seeds in early autumn into pots using standard loam-based seed compost (substrate) mixed with coarse horticultural sand. Mix to a ratio of 1 part compost + 1 part sand. Cover with coarse horticultural sand and place under protection at 21°C (70°F) for 6–7 weeks. Then place outside, exposed to all the weathers (see 'Breaking Seed Dormancy', page 233, for more information). Germination takes 5–12 months, so do not give up. If there is no germination in the first year, start the process again in the following autumn, with warmth for the first 6–7 weeks. Then place the container outside.

Recipe for sowing, planting and growing **Helleborus niger**
This beautiful winter flowering plant is a must for any garden, it shows one that spring is not far away.

Ingredients
5 seeds per module or 8 seeds per pot
1 module tray
OR
1 x 8cm (4in) pot
Standard loam-based seed compost (substrate) mixed with coarse horticultural sand to a ratio of 1 part compost + 1 part sand
Extra coarse horticultural sand to cover the pot
White plastic plant label

Method In autumn fill the tray or pot with compost, smooth over, tap down and water in well. Sow the fresh seeds thinly on to the surface of the compost. Press gently into the compost with the flat of the hand. Cover the seed with coarse horticultural sand. Label with the plant name and date. Place the tray or pot in a warm light place, out of direct sunlight, at an optimum temperature of 21°C (70°F).

After 6–7 weeks place the tray or pot outside, on a level surface, so it is exposed to all the weathers, including frosts. Do not worry if

Helleborus niger

you live in a snowy area and the containers get immersed in snow, as melting snow will aid germination. If you do not live in an area which will get a winter frost, it is a good idea to put the container, after its period of heat, into a plastic bag, seal it and place into a refrigerator for 3 weeks. Remove the container from the refrigerator, then remove the plastic bag and place it outside.

Whichever method you use, germination is a bit erratic taking anything from 5–12 months. Do not give up and discard your compost, it might just germinate next week. If there is no germination in the first year, start the process again in the following autumn, with initial warmth for 6–7 weeks, followed by a period outside.

Prick out when the seedlings are large enough to handle. If you are using modules, you can plant directly into the garden as soon as the soil is warm enough to dig over, prior to planting out.

Hemerocallis *Hemerocallidaceae*

A genus of hardy perennials. Plant in a fertile, well-drained soil in a sunny situation. When growing day lilies from seed it is worth noting that cultivars will not come true to type, but will still give an interesting display. Also species will only come true if grown in isolation from other day lilies to prevent cross pollination.

Hemerocallis (Day lily)
Medium seeds: 35 per gram
Hardy perennial
Height 45cm (18in)
The trumpet-shaped flowers come in a mixture of colours from pale orange, yellow and white to deep red and lavender pink
Flowers in summer from its second year
Mid-green, arching, strap-shaped leaves

Iris foetidissima seeds

Sow seeds in early to mid-spring into pots or modules using standard soil-less seed compost (substrate), either a peat free proprietary brand or composted fine propagating bark. Cover with perlite or vermiculite and place in a cold frame. Germination takes 3–4 weeks. A word of warning, protect young shoots from slugs.

Hosta *Hostaceae*

A genus of hardy perennials, grown for their attractive foliage. Plant in a rich, moist, well-drained, neutral soil in partial to full shade.

Hosta sieboldiana
Medium seeds: 290 per gram
Hardy perennial
Height 90cm (36in)
Racemes of trumpet-shaped, white flowers with a hint of lilac
Flowers in early summer
Large, heart-shaped, ribbed, puckered, bluish-grey leaves

Sow seeds in early to mid-spring into pots or modules using standard soil-less seed compost (substrate), either a peat free proprietary brand or composted fine propagating bark. Cover with perlite or vermiculite and place in a cold frame. Germination takes 1–3 months.

Incarvillea *Bignoniaceae*

A genus of hardy perennials. Plant in a well-drained soil in a sunny situation. It is worth protecting the crowns of this plant in winter with compost, leaf mould, straw or bracken.

Incarvillea delavayi
Medium seeds: 200 per gram
Hardy perennial
Height up to 90cm (36in)
Clusters of beautiful, bright rose-red, trumpet-shaped flowers which are followed by attractive seed pods
Flowers from late spring until early summer
Deeply divided, mid-green leaves

Sow seeds in spring into pots or modules using standard soil-less seed compost (substrate), either a peat free proprietary brand or composted fine propagating bark. Cover with perlite or vermiculite and place in a cold frame. Germination takes 3–4 weeks.

Iris *Iridaceae*

This very large genus is made up of rhizomatous or bulbous perennials some of which are evergreen, most of which are hardy. There are irises suitable for the rock garden, woodland, waterside, alpine house, in fact most areas of the garden. For the ideal growing conditions check with each species.

Iris foetidissima AGM (Galdwin, Roast-beef plant, Stinking iris)
Medium seeds: 20 per gram
Hardy evergreen
Height 1m (3½ft)
Each branched stem can carry up to 9 yellow-tinged, dull purple and occasionally pure yellow flowers, which are followed by cylindrical seed pods with orange fruits
Flowers in summer
Spear-shaped, mid-green leaves.
Plant in a bog or water garden

Iris setosa AGM (Bristle pointed iris)
Medium seeds: 120 per gram
Hardy evergreen
Height up to 1m (3ft)
Each branched stem can carry anything from 2–13 deep blue or purple-blue flowers
Flowers in late spring to early summer
Spear-shaped, mid-green leaves

Scarify the fresh seed (see page 233) before sowing in early autumn into pots. Use standard loam-based seed compost (substrate) mixed with coarse horticultural sand. Mix to a ratio of 1 part compost + 1 part sand. Cover with coarse horticultural sand and place under protection at 20°C (68°F) for one month. Place outside, exposed to all the weathers (see 'Breaking Seed Dormancy', page 233, for more information). Germination takes 5–12 months, so do not give up. Young plants can winter happily outside. Flowers in the following season.

***Recipe for sowing, planting and growing* Iris setosa**
Ingredients
3 seeds per module or 5 seeds per pot (sow 3 seeds per pot for *Iris foetidissima*)
1 sheet of fine sandpaper cut in half
1 module tray
OR
1 x 8cm (4in) pot
Standard loam-based seed compost (substrate) mixed with coarse horticultural sand to a ratio of 1 part compost + 1 part sand
Extra sand for covering seeds
White plastic plant label

Method In autumn fill the tray or pot with compost, smooth over, tap down and water in well. Select a small amount of seed, place it on half a sheet of fine sandpaper. With the other half of the sandpaper, either make a sandwich holding it between both hands and sliding back and forth to gently scratch the surface of the seed, or simply put the other half of the sandpaper on top of the seed and gently push the paper up and down which will have the same effect. Sow this scarified seed thinly on to the surface of the compost. Press in gently with the flat of the hand and cover with coarse horticultural sand. Label with the plant name and date. Place the tray or pot outside, on a level surface, so it is exposed to all the weathers, including frosts. Do not worry if you live in a snowy area and the containers get immersed in snow, for melting snow will aid germination. If you do not live in an area which will get a winter frost, it is a good idea to put the scarified seed mixed with a handful of damp sand into a clearly marked plastic bag. Seal the bag and place it in a refrigerator for 3 weeks. Remove and sow as described, then place outside. Germination will occur in the following spring and flowering the year after that.

Prick out when the seedlings are large enough to handle. If you are using modules, you can plant directly into the garden as soon as the soil is warm enough to dig over, prior to planting out.

Jasione *Campanulaceae*

A genus of hardy annuals, biennials and perennials. Plant in a well-drained sandy soil in a sunny situation.

Jasione laevis (perennis) (Sheep's bit)
Tiny seeds: 18,000 per gram
Hardy perennial
Height 5–30cm (2–12in)
Spherical, spiky, blue flower heads
Flowers in summer
Narrow oblong grey-green leaves

Sow fresh seeds in autumn into pots using standard soil-less seed compost (substrate), either a peat free proprietary brand or composted fine propagating bark mixed with extra silver or fine sand for extra aeration. Mix to a ratio of 3 parts compost + 1 part sand. As these are very fine seeds, mix with the finest sand or talcum powder for an even sowing. Do not cover. Water from the bottom or with a fine spray. Place in a cold frame. Germination takes 1–6 months. Overwinter young plants in cold frame. Flowers in its second year.
OR
Sow seeds in spring into pots or modules using standard soil-less seed compost (substrate), either a peat free proprietary brand or composted fine propagating bark. As these are very fine seeds, mix with the finest sand or talcum powder for an even sowing. Do not cover. Water from the bottom or with a fine spray and place in a cold frame. Place under protection at 20°C (68°F). Germination takes 10–14 days.

Knautia *Dipsacaceae*

A genus of hardy annuals and perennials. Plant in a well-drained soil in a sunny situation.

Knautia arvensis (Field scabious)
Medium seeds: 150 per gram
Hardy perennial
Height up to 1.2m (4ft)
Blue-lilac, pincushion-shaped flowers surrounded by petals
Flowers in summer
Deeply divided, mid-green leaves

Sow seeds in autumn into pots or modules using standard loam-based seed compost (substrate) mixed with coarse horticultural sand. Mix to a ratio of 1 part compost + 1 part sand. Cover with coarse horticultural sand. Then place outside, exposed to all the weathers (see 'Breaking Seed Dormancy', page 233, for more information). Germination takes 4–6 months, but it can be erratic. Be patient and do not discard the compost.

Kniphofia *Asphodelaceae*

A genus of hardy to half-hardy perennials, some of which are evergreen. Plant in a well-drained soil in a sunny position.

Kniphofia uvaria (Red hot poker)
Medium seeds: 350 per gram
Hardy perennial
Height 1.2m (4ft)
Tubular, bright red flowers in dense terminal racemes
Flowers from summer into autumn
Strap-shaped dark green leaves

Sow seeds in spring into pots or modules using standard soil-less seed compost (substrate), either a peat free proprietary brand or composted fine propagating bark. Cover with perlite or vermiculite and place in a cold frame. Germination takes 2–3 weeks.
OR
Sow seeds in early spring into pots or modules using standard soil-less seed compost (substrate), either a peat free proprietary brand or composted fine propagating bark. Cover with perlite or vermiculite and place under protection at 18°C (65°F). Germination takes 14–21 days. Flowers in its first season.

Lantana *Verbenaceae*

A genus of tender evergreen perennials which needs a minimum temperature of 10°C (50°F). In warm climates, plant in light fertile well-drained soil in sun or partial shade. In cooler climates grow in containers and water sparingly in winter.

Lantana hybrida
Medium seeds: 50 per gram
Half-hardy evergreen perennial
Height 1m (3½ft)
Tiny, tubular flowers which grow in dense clusters making a rounded head, in a range of pastel colours from cream through to pink, changing colour as they mature
Flowers in summer
Wrinkled, dark green leaves
This is a good butterfly plant

Sow seeds in early spring into pots or modules using standard soil-less seed compost (substrate), either a peat free proprietary brand or composted fine propagating bark. Cover with perlite or vermiculite and place under protection at 20°C (68°F). Germination takes 4–6 weeks. If growing on as a container plant, use a peat free proprietary brand or composted fine propagating bark as a compost.

Leontodon *Asteraceae*

A genus of hardy annuals, biennials and perennials. Plant in any soil, with the exception of waterlogged sites, in sun or partial shade.

Leontodon rigens (Microseris)
Small seeds: 1,200 per gram
Hardy perennial
Height 50cm (20in)
Clusters of small, yellow, dandelion-like flowers
Flowers all summer
Rosettes of toothed, serrated, shiny green leaves

Sow seeds in spring into pots or modules using standard soil-less seed compost (substrate), either a peat free proprietary brand or composted fine propagating bark. Cover with perlite or vermiculite, place in a cold frame or under protection at 70°C (68°F). Germination takes 2–4 weeks cold or 5–8 days with heat. Plants will flower in their first year.

Liatris *Asteraceae*

A genus of hardy summer-flowering perennials. Plant in a well-drained soil in a sunny position.

Liatris spicata (Gay feathers, Kansas gay feather, Blazing star)
Medium seeds: 300 per gram
Hardy perennial
Height 60cm (24in)
Spikes of purple-rose flower heads on stiff stems
Flowers in summer
Grass-like, mid-green leaves

Sow seeds in spring into pots or modules using standard soil-less seed compost (substrate), either a peat free proprietary brand or composted fine propagating bark. Cover with perlite or vermiculite and place in a cold frame or under protection at 18°C (65°F). Germination takes 3–4 weeks cold or 2–3 weeks with heat.

Lilium *Liliaceae*

A genus of, in the majority, hardy flowering bulbs. Plant in any well-drained soil in a sunny situation.

Lilium longiflorum AGM (Bermuda lily, Easter lily)
Medium seeds
Hardy perennial
Height 30cm–1m (1–3ft)
1–6 fragrant, funnel-shaped, white flowers
Flowers from mid summer until autumn in second year
Lance-shaped leaves

Lilium regale AGM (Regal Lily)
Medium seeds: 450 per gram
Hardy perennial
Height 50cm –2m (20in–6ft)
Can produce up to 25 fragrant funnel-shaped flowers, white on the inside, pinkish on the outside
Flowers in second summer
Lance-shaped leaves

Lilium regale

Growing plants from seed produced from a bulb-producing plant is a slow process, but with patience you can produce plants in 2 years and flowers in 2–3 years. The major advantage of growing lilies this way is that they will be virus free.

Sow fresh (this is most important) seeds in autumn into pots using standard loam-based seed compost (substrate) mixed with coarse horticultural sand to a ratio of 1 part compost + 1 part sand. Cover with coarse horticultural sand. Place outside, exposed to all weathers (see 'Breaking Seed Dormancy', page 233, for more information). Germination takes 4–6 months.

Leave undisturbed in the pots for the first season, allow the green growth to die back and stop watering. In the second year when the bulbs are dormant, repot them into fresh compost, the same mix as above, again winter them outside. In the following autumn repeat the process, but this time the bulbs can be planted in the garden.

Lotus *Papilionaceae*

A genus of hardy to half-hardy perennials, some of which are evergreen. Plant in a well-drained soil in a sunny situation.

Lotus maritimus **(Tetragonolobus)**
Medium seeds: 200 per gram
Hardy perennial
Height 25cm (10in)
Light yellow flowers, like a small sweet pea, which grow in profusion
Flowers in summer
Blue-green foliage

Sow seeds in spring into pots or modules using standard soil-less seed compost (substrate), either a peat free proprietary brand or composted fine propagating bark. Cover with perlite or vermiculite and place in a cold frame. Germination takes 3–4 weeks, but can be a bit erratic, occurring spasmodically over a long period.

Lupinus *Papilionaceae*

A genus of hardy annuals, perennials and semi-evergreen shrubs. Plant in a well-drained, preferably alkaline, soil in a sunny position. Lupins are known for self seeding and cross pollinating.

Lupinus arboreus AGM **(Tree lupin)**
Medium seeds: 45 per gram
Hardy semi-evergreen shrub
Height 1.2–2m (4–6ft)
Short spikes of fragrant yellow flowers
Flowers in early summer of second or third season
Pale green leaves which are divided into leaflets

Sow fresh seeds in autumn into pots or modules using standard soil-less seed compost (substrate), either a peat free proprietary brand or composted fine propagating bark. Cover with perlite or vermiculite and place in a cold frame. Germination takes 2–3 weeks. Overwinter young plants in a cold frame.

Lupinus 'The Governor'
Medium seeds: 45 per gram
Hardy perennial
Height 1m (3ft)
Large blue with white flower spikes
Flowers in summer of second season
Palmate, mid-green leaves

In autumn soak fresh seeds in hot (not boiling) water for 12 hours prior to sowing. Remove and discard any floating seeds and sow the remainder in pots, using standard soil-less seed compost (substrate), either a peat free proprietary brand or composted fine propagating bark mixed with 3mm (1/8in) grit. Mix to a ratio of 3 parts compost + 1 part fine grit. Cover lightly with perlite or vermiculite, place in a cold frame. Germination takes 2–5 weeks. Overwinter young plants in a cold frame. Do not worry when they die back, they will return in the spring. Protect young shoots from slugs. I exhibit alongside the Woodfields Brothers at the Chelsea Flower Show, where they put on stunning displays of lupins, showing them to perfection. I am grateful to them for giving me these growing instructions.

Lysimachia *Primulaceae*

A genus of hardy to half-hardy annuals and perennials. Plant in a moist but well-drained soil in sun or partial shade.

Lysimachia punctata **(Garden loosestrife)**
Small seeds: 3,000 per gram
Hardy perennial
Height 75cm (30in)
Spikes of bright yellow, cup-shaped flowers
Flowers throughout the summer
Broad, mid-green leaves

Sow seeds in spring into pots or modules using standard soil-less seed compost (substrate), either a peat free proprietary brand or composted fine propagating bark. Cover with perlite or vermiculite and place in a cold frame. Germination takes 2–4 weeks.

Lythrum *Lythraceae*

A genus of hardy perennials. Plant in a moist or wet soil, in sun or partial shade – lovely around ponds.

Lythrum salicaria **(Purple loosestrife)**
Native wildflower of the UK
Tiny seeds: 13,000 per gram
Hardy perennial
Height 60–120cm (2–4ft)
Whorled spikes of bright pink/purple flowers
Flowers from summer through to autumn
Willow-like leaves

Sow fresh seeds in autumn into pots using standard soil-less seed compost (substrate), either a peat free proprietary brand or composted fine propagating bark mixed with extra silver or fine sand for extra aeration to a ratio of 3 parts compost + 1 part sand. Mix these very fine seeds with the finest sand or talcum powder for an even sowing. Do not cover. Water from the bottom or with a fine spray, place in a cold frame. Germination takes 5–7 months but can be erratic.

Recipe for sowing, planting and growing Lythrum salicaria
This handsome and graceful native plant looks lovely growing alongside a stream or at the edge of a pond.

Ingredients
10 seeds per module or 15 seeds per pot (or as near as you can manage)
Talcum powder or fine plain white flour
1 piece white card 14 x 8.5cm ($5^{1}/_{2}$ x $3^{1}/_{2}$in) folded in half
1 module tray
OR
1 x 8cm (4in) pot
Standard soil-less seed compost (substrate), either a peat free proprietary brand or composted fine propagating bark mixed with silver or fine sand for extra aeration. Mix to a ratio of 3 parts compost + 1 part sand
White plastic plant label

Method In autumn, fill the tray or pot with compost, smooth over, tap down and water in well. As the seeds are very fine, it is a good idea to mix them with talcum powder or extra fine white flour, which will make the seeds show up. Put a very small amount of this seed mix into the crease of the folded card, gently tap the card to sow the seed thinly on to the surface of the compost. Do not cover, label with the plant name and date. Place the tray or pot outside, on a level surface, so it is exposed to all the weathers, including frosts. Do not worry if you live in a snowy area and the containers get immersed in snow, for melting snow will aid germination. If you do not live in an area which will get a winter frost, it is a good idea to put the seed and flour mix plus a handful of damp sand into a plastic bag. Seal and label the bag and place it in a refrigerator for 3 weeks. Remove and sow as above, then place outside. Germination will occur in the following spring and flowering the year after that. Prick out the seedlings when they are large enough to handle, harden them off before planting out. If you are using modules, you can plant directly into the garden when there is no further threat of frost.

Malva *Malvaceae*

A genus of hardy annuals, biennials and short-lived perennials. Plant in a fertile, well-drained soil in a sunny position.

Malva sylvestris (Zebrina)
Medium seeds: 220 per gram
Hardy perennial
Height 1.2m (4ft)
Striking, bi-coloured flowers – pale pink/lilac boldly marked with deep purple stripes
Flowers in summer
Divided, mid-green leaves

Sow in spring or late summer in pots or modules using standard soil-less seed compost (substrate), either a peat free proprietary brand or composted fine propagating bark. Cover with perlite or vermiculite and place under protection at 20°C (68°F). Germination takes 6–10 days. Germination can be irregular.

Meconopsis *Papaveraceae*

A genus of hardy perennials some of which are monocarpic (meaning that they die after flowering). Plant in a humus-rich, free-draining, neutral to acid soil in partial to fully shady areas.

Meconopsis betonicifolia (syn. *baileyi*) AGM **Blue Himalayan poppy**
Small seeds: 3,000 per gram
Hardy perennial
Height 1–1.2m (3–4ft)
Beautiful, sky-blue, saucer-shaped flowers with yellow stamens
Flowers in summer
Rosettes of oblong, mid-green leaves at the base of the plant

Sow seeds in autumn into pots or modules using standard loam-based seed compost (substrate) mixed with coarse horticultural sand. Mix to a ratio of 1 part compost + 1 part sand. Cover with coarse horticultural sand. Place outside, exposed to all the weathers (see 'Breaking Seed Dormancy', page 233, for more information). Germination takes 3–4 weeks. Overwinter young plants in a cold frame.

Penstemon *Scrophulariaceae*

A genus of hardy to half-hardy annuals, perennials and shrubs, most of which are evergreen or semi-evergreen. Plant in a fertile, well-drained soil in a sunny position.

Penstemon barbatus 'Jingle Bells'
Medium seeds: 900 per gram
Hardy perennial
Height 1.3m (5ft)
Spikes of tubular, 2-lipped red flowers
Flowers in summer to early autumn
Rosettes of oblong, mid-green leaves

Sow seeds in spring into pots or modules using standard soil-less seed compost (substrate), either a peat free proprietary brand or composted fine propagating bark. Cover with perlite or vermiculite and place in a cold frame. Germination takes 2–3 weeks. If no germination occurs, put under cover for one month at 21°C (70°F), then return to the cold frame.

Persicaria *Polygonaceae*

A genus of hardy to half-hardy annuals and perennials some of which are evergreen. Plant in a damp but well-drained soil in sun or partial shade.

Persicaria bistorta (Bistort, Snake Root)
Native wildflower in the UK
Medium seeds: 140 per gram
Hardy perennial
Height 75cm (30in)
Small spikes of soft pink flowers
Flowers in summer
Oval, mid-green leaves
This plant can be invasive

Sow seeds in autumn into pots or modules using standard loam-based seed compost (substrate) mixed with coarse horticultural sand to a ratio of 1 part compost + 1 part sand. Cover with coarse horticultural sand and place outside to expose to all the weathers (see 'Breaking Seed Dormancy', page 233, for more information). Germination takes 4–6 months, but can be erratic, so be patient and do not discard container.

Phormium *Phormiaceae*

A genus of hardy to half-hardy evergreen perennials. Plant in a moist but well-drained soil in a sunny position.

Phormium tenax AGM
Medium seeds: 125 per gram
Half-hardy evergreen perennial
Height up to 3m (10ft)
Panicles of tubular, red flowers
Flowers in summer
Long, leathery, narrow, stiff, dark green leaves

Sow seeds in early spring into pots or modules using standard soil-less seed compost (substrate), either a peat free proprietary brand or composted fine propagating bark. Cover with perlite or vermiculite and place under protection at 18°C (65°F). Germination takes 1–6 months. If growing on as a container plant, use a peat free proprietary brand or composted fine propagating bark as a compost.

Physalis *Solanaceae*

A genus of hardy to half-hardy annuals and perennials. Plant in a well-drained soil in sun or partial shade.

Physalis alkekengi var. *franchetii* (Lantern plant, Chinese lantern, Winter cherry)
Medium seeds: 650 per gram
Hardy perennial, sometimes grown as an annual
Height 45cm (18in)
Small star-shaped white flower, followed by round bright orange/red fruits surrounded by inflated orange calyces
Flowers from summer until early autumn
Oval mid-green leaves

Sow seeds in spring into pots or modules using standard soil-less seed compost (substrate), either a peat free proprietary brand or composted fine propagating bark. Cover with perlite or vermiculite. Place in a cold frame or with protection at 18°C (65°F). Germination takes 3–6 weeks cold or 7–14 days with warmth.

Physostegia *Lamiaceae*

A genus of hardy perennials. Plant in a fertile, moist but well-drained soil in a sunny position.

Physostegia virginiana (Obedient plant, False dragonhead)
Medium seeds: 500 per gram
Hardy perennial
Height 1m (3ft)
Spikes of hooded, 2-lipped rich pink flowers
Flowers in late summer
Toothed, lance-shaped, mid-green leaves

Sow seeds in spring into pots or modules using standard soil-less seed compost (substrate), either a peat free proprietary brand or composted fine propagating bark. Cover with perlite or vermiculite and place in a cold frame or with protection at 18°C (65°F). Germination takes 2–3 weeks cold or 7–14 days with warmth.

Platycodon *Campanulaceae*

A genus of one hardy perennial species. Plant in a light sandy soil in a sunny situation.

Platycodon grandiflorus 'Mariesii' AGM (Balloon flower, Chinese bellflower)
Medium seeds: 850 per gram
Hardy perennial
Height 45cm (18in)
Single, balloon-like flower buds open to bell-shaped, bluish flowers
Flowers in summer
Toothed, oval, bluish-green leaves

Sow seeds in spring into pots or modules using standard soil-less seed compost (substrate), either a peat free proprietary brand or composted fine propagating bark. Cover with perlite or vermiculite, place in a cold frame or with protection at 20°C (68°F). Germination takes 3–4 weeks cold or 7–14 days with warmth.

Recipe for sowing, planting and growing* Platycodon grandiflorus *'Mariesii'

This is an indispensable plant for the summer herbaceous border. Whichever way you sow the seeds, you will reap the rewards.

Ingredients
5 seeds per module or 10 seeds per pot
1 module tray
OR
1 x 8cm (4in) pot
Standard soil-less seed compost (substrate), either a peat free proprietary brand or composted fine propagating bark
Fine-grade perlite (wetted) or vermiculite
White plastic plant label

Method In spring fill the tray or pot with compost, smooth over, tap down and water in well. Sow the seed spaced out on to the surface of the compost. Press gently into the compost with the flat of the hand. Cover with the wetted fine-grade perlite or vermiculite. Label with the plant name and date. Place the tray or pot in a cold frame. Restrict watering to an absolute minimum until germination has taken place. Germination will take 3–4 weeks.
OR
Sow the seeds following the instructions as above, but this time place the container in a warm, light place out of direct sunlight, at an optimum temperature of 20°C (68°F). Keep watering to a minimum until germination has taken place. Germination takes 7–14 days with warmth.

Prick out when the seedlings are large enough to handle, or if you are using modules, plant directly into a container or the garden after a period of hardening off, when there is no threat of frost. Whichever way you choose, flowering will take place in the following season

Polemonium *Polemoniaceae*

A genus of hardy annuals and perennials. Plant in fertile well-drained soil.

Polemonium caeruleum **(Jacob's ladder)**
Medium seeds: 700 per gram
Hardy perennial
Height 45cm (18in)
Clusters of cup-shaped, lavender-blue flowers with yellow stamens
Flowers in summer
Finely divided, mid-green leaves

Sow fresh seeds in autumn into pots or modules using standard soil-less seed compost (substrate), either a peat free proprietary brand or composted fine propagating bark. Cover with perlite or vermiculite, place in a cold frame. Germination takes 4–8 weeks. Overwinter young plants in a cold frame. Flowers in its second season.
OR
Sow in spring or late summer in pots or modules using standard soil-less seed compost (substrate), either a peat free proprietary brand or composted fine propagating bark. Cover with perlite or vermiculite, place under protection at 20°C (68°F). Germination takes 6–10 days but can be irregular.

Polygonatum *Convallariaceae*

A genus of hardy to half-hardy rhizomatous perennials. Plant in a fertile, well-drained soil in a cool shady position.

Polygonatum multiflorum L. **(Solomon's seal)**
Medium seeds: 40 per gram
Hardy perennial
Height 1m (3ft)
Cluster of pendent, tubular, white flowers which have green tips on arching stems followed by round black fruits
Flowers in spring to early summer
Oval, lance-shaped, mid-green leaves

Sow seeds in autumn into pots or modules using standard loam-based seed compost (substrate) mixed with coarse horticultural sand. Mix to a ratio of 1 part compost + 1 part sand. Cover with coarse horticultural sand. Place outside, exposed to all the weathers (see 'Breaking Seed Dormancy', page 233, for more information). Germination takes 12–18 months, but can be erratic, so be patient and do not discard the container.

Potentilla *Rosaceae*

A genus of hardy perennials and deciduous shrubs. Plant in a well-drained soil in sun or partial shade.

Potentilla nepalensis 'Miss Willmott' AGM
Small seeds: 3,000 per gram
Hardy perennial
Height 50cm (20in)
Pink flowers with cherry-red centres
Flowers throughout the summer
Palmate, strawberry-like, bright green leaves

Potentilla recta
Small seeds: 2,500 per gram
Hardy perennial
Height 50cm (20in)
Clusters of sulphur-yellow flowers
Flowers all summer from second season
Palmate strawberry-like dark green leaves

Sow fresh seeds in autumn into pots or modules using standard soil-less seed compost (substrate), either a peat free proprietary brand or composted fine propagating bark. Cover with perlite or vermiculite. Place in a cold frame. Germination takes 1–6 months. Overwinter young plants in the cold frame.
OR
Sow in spring or late summer in pots or modules using standard soil-less seed compost (substrate), either a peat free proprietary brand or composted fine propagating bark. Cover with perlite or vermiculite and place under protection at 20°C (68°F). Germination takes 6 –10 days. Germination can be irregular.

Rehmannia *Scrophulariaceae*

A genus of half-hardy perennials. Plant in a light, well-drained soil in a sunny position.

Rehmannia elata (syn. *angulata*) AGM **(Chinese foxglove)**
Tiny seeds: 14,000 per gram
Half-hardy perennial
Height 75cm (30in)
Racemes of funnel-shaped purplish flowers with orange markings
Flowers from spring until mid summer
Oblong, hairy, mid-green leaves

Sow fresh seeds in autumn into pots or modules using standard soil-less seed compost (substrate), either a peat free proprietary brand or composted fine propagating bark. As these are very fine seeds, mix with the finest sand or talcum powder for an even sowing. Do not cover. Water from the bottom or with a fine spray and place in a cold frame. Germination takes 1–6 months. Overwinter young plants in cold frame. Flowers in its second season.
OR
Sow in spring or late summer in pots or modules using standard soil-less seed compost (substrate), either a peat free proprietary brand or composted fine propagating bark. As these are very fine seeds, mix with the finest sand or talcum powder for an even sowing. Do not cover. Water from the bottom or with a fine spray and place under protection at 20°C (68°F). Germination takes 10–14 days, but can be irregular.

Rheum *Polygonaceae*

A genus of hardy perennials. Plant in a rich, deep, well-drained soil in sun or partial shade. Some of these species do grow very large, so allow them plenty of space.

Rheum palmatum 'Bowles Crimson' **(Bowles Rhubarb)**
Medium seeds: 55 per gram
Hardy perennial
Height 2m (6ft)
Large panicles of small, pinkish-red flowers
Flowers in early summer
Rounded, long, large, 5-lobed green/red leaves

Sow seeds in spring into pots or modules using standard soil-less seed compost (substrate), either a peat free proprietary brand or composted fine propagating bark. Cover with perlite or vermiculite and place in a cold frame. Germination takes 1–2 weeks. Makes a very striking plant.

Scabiosa *Dipsacaceae*

A genus of hardy annuals and perennials, some of which are evergreen. Plant in a well-drained alkaline soil in a sunny situation.

Scabiosa caucasica **(Pincushion flower)**
Medium seeds: 70 per gram
Hardy perennial
Height 60cm (24in)
Pretty, frilled, blue/violet/lilac flowers with pincushion-like centres
Flowers all summer
Lance-shaped light green leaves around the base of the plant

Sow seeds in spring into pots or modules using standard soil-less seed compost (substrate), either a peat free proprietary brand or composted fine propagating bark. Cover with perlite or vermiculite and place in a cold frame or with protection at 20°C (68°F). Germination takes 3–4 weeks cold or 10–18 days with warmth.

Sidalcea *Malvaceae*

A genus of hardy perennials. Plant in any well-drained soil in a sunny position.

Sidalcea x hybrida 'Party Girl'
Medium seeds: 350 per gram
Hardy perennial
Height 90cm (3ft)
Spikes of pretty, mallow-like, rosy red flowers
Flowers in summer
Divided, mid-green leaves

Sow seeds in spring into pots or modules using standard soil-less seed compost (substrate), either a peat free proprietary brand or composted fine propagating bark. Cover with perlite or vermiculite and place in a cold frame. Germination takes 2–3 weeks.

Silene *Caryophyllaceae*

A genus of hardy to half-hardy annuals and perennials, some of which are evergreen. Plant in a fertile, well-drained soil, in a sunny position.

Silene dioica **(Red campion)**
Native wildflower in the UK
Medium seeds: 1,000 per gram
Hardy short-lived perennial
Height 60cm (24in)
Flowers which can vary in colour from red through to white
Flowers in summer
Oval, tipped, mid-green leaves
These plants grow naturally in woods and at the edges of woods

Sow seeds in autumn into pots or modules using standard loam-based seed compost (substrate) mixed with coarse horticultural sand to a ratio of 1 part compost + 1 part sand. Cover with coarse horticultural sand, then place outside, exposed to all the weathers (see 'Breaking Seed Dormancy', page 233, for more information). Germination takes 4–6 months.

Sinningia *Gesneriaceae*

A genus of half-hardy tuberous perennials, growing at a minimum temperature of 10°C (50°F). In warm climates can be planted out in a rich, well-drained soil in partial shade. In cool climates grow as a pot plant, which should be kept on the dry side in winter.

Sinningia speciosa
Tiny seeds: 20,000 per gram
Tender perennial
Height 30cm (12in)
Funnel, pouch-shaped flowers in various colours from violet and red to white
Flowers in mid- to late summer
Large, oval, velvety green leaves

Sow seeds in early spring into pots or modules using standard soil-less seed compost (substrate), either a peat free proprietary brand or composted fine propagating bark. As these are very fine seeds, mix with the finest sand or talcum powder for an even sowing. Do not cover. Water from the bottom or with a fine spray and place under protection at 21°C (70°F). Germination takes 2–3 weeks. Will flower in its first season.

***Recipe for sowing, planting and growing* Sinningia speciosa**
These tender perennials originate in Japan and make a lovely container display.

Ingredients
10 seeds per module or 15 seeds per pot (or as near as possible)
Talcum powder, or fine plain white flour
1 piece white card 14 x 8.5cm (5½ x 3½in) folded in half
1 module tray
OR
1 x 8cm (4in) pot
Standard soil-less seed compost (substrate), either a peat free proprietary brand or composted fine propagating bark
White plastic plant label

Method In early spring fill the tray or pot with compost, smooth over, tap down and water in well. As the seeds are very fine it is a good idea to mix them with talcum powder or extra-fine white flour. Put a very small amount of this seed mix into the crease of the folded card. Gently tap the card and sow thinly on to the surface of the compost.

Do not cover, label with the plant's name and the date. Place the tray or pot in a warm light place out of direct sunlight, at an optimum temperature of 21°C (70°F). Keep watering to a minimum until germination has taken place and then only water from the bottom or with a fine spray so as not to disturb the seeds. Germination takes 2–3 weeks with warmth. Shortly after germination has taken place, and when the seedlings are fully emerged, put the containers in a cooler environment 15°C (59°F). Prick out when the seedlings are large enough to handle and grow on under protection, only placing containers outside when there is absolutely no threat of frost.

Solenostemon *Lamiaceae*

A genus of half-hardy annuals, perennials and evergreen shrubs. In warm climates plant in a fertile well-drained soil in a sunny position, or grow as a container plant.

Solenostemon 'Wizard Series' (*Coleus* 'Wizard Series')
Small seeds: 3,700 per gram
Half-hardy perennial
Height 30cm (12in)
Spikes of insignificant flowers
Flowers in summer
Broad, heart-shaped, serrated leaves which are very varied in colour

Solenostemon 'Black Dragon' (*Coleus* 'Black Dragon')
Small seeds: 3,700 per gram
Half-hardy perennial
Height 30cm (12in)
Spikes of insignificant flowers
Flowers in summer
Broad, oval, lobed leaves with red-black edges and with pink centres

Sow seeds in early spring into pots or modules using standard soil-less seed compost (substrate), either a peat free proprietary brand or composted fine propagating bark. Cover with perlite or vermiculite and place under protection at 20°C (68°F). Germination takes 1–3 weeks. If growing on as a container plant, use a peat free proprietary brand or composted fine propagating bark as a potting compost.

Solidago *Asteraceae*

A genus of hardy perennials. Plant in any well-drained soil in sun or partial shade.

Solidago canadensis 'Golden Baby' (Golden rod)
Small seeds: 1,200 per gram
Hardy perennial
Height 60cm (24in)
Large plumes of tiny, golden-yellow flowers
Flowers from mid-summer
Lance-shaped, mid-green leaves

Sow seeds in early spring into pots or modules using standard soil-less seed compost (substrate), either a peat free proprietary brand or composted fine propagating bark. Cover with perlite or vermiculite and place in a cold frame or under protection at 20°C (68°F). Germination takes 2–3 weeks cold or 5–8 days with warmth.

Stachys *Lamiaceae*

A genus of hardy to half-hardy perennials and shrubs, some of which are evergreen. Plant in any free-draining soil in sun or partial shade.

Stachys byzantina (Stachys lanata) Lamb's ear
Medium seeds: 500 per gram
Hardy evergreen perennial
Height 30cm (12in)
Woolly spikes with small purple flowers
Flowers in summer
Dense, thick, soft, woolly, silver-white leaves

Sow in spring into pots or modules using standard soil-less seed compost (substrate), either a peat free proprietary brand or composted fine propagating bark mixed with 3mm (1/8in) grit. Mix to a ratio of 3 parts compost + 1 part fine grit. Cover with perlite or vermiculite and place in a cold frame or with protection at 21°C (70°F). Germination takes 3–4 weeks cold or 1–2 days with heat.

Stachys officinalis (*Betonica officinalis*) Betony, Bishopswort
Native wildflower in the UK
Medium seeds: 700 per gram
Hardy perennial
Height up to 60cm (24in)
Spikes of bright magenta, pink or white tubular flowers
Flowers in summer
Oblong, dark green, toothed leaves

Sow fresh seeds in autumn into pots or modules using standard soil-less seed compost (substrate), either a peat free proprietary brand or composted fine propagating bark. Cover with perlite or vermiculite, place in a cold frame. Germination takes anything from 3 weeks to 6 months. Overwinter young plants in a cold frame. Flowers in second season.

Stellaria *Caryophyllaceae*

A genus of hardy annuals and perennials, not many of which are good garden plants. Plant in any moist but well-drained soil in sun or partial shade.

Stellaria holostea (Greater stitchwort, Moon flower)
Native wildflower in the UK
Medium seeds: 550 per gram
Hardy perennial
Height 15–60cm (6–24in)
Clusters of delicate, star-shaped, pure white flowers
Flowers in late spring
Small, lance-shaped leaves

Sow seeds in autumn into pots or modules using standard loam-based seed compost (substrate) mixed with coarse horticultural sand. Mix to a ratio of 1 part compost + 1 part sand. Cover with coarse horticultural sand, then place outside, exposed to all the weathers (see 'Breaking Seed Dormancy', page 233, for more information). Germination takes 4–6 months, but can be erratic, so be patient and do not discard container.

Streptocarpus *Gesneriaceae*

A genus of tender perennials, some of which are evergreen, grown at a minimum temperature of 10°C (50 °F). Grow as a house plant in cool climates.

Steptocarpus Mixed Hybrids (Cape primrose)
Minute seeds: 50,000 per gram
Tender perennial
Height 30cm (12in)
Clusters of trumpet-shaped flowers in many different shades of purple, blue, white and rose
Flowers throughout the summer
Rosettes of strap-shaped, wrinkled, green leaves
Ideal for the greenhouse, conservatory or a windowsill

Sow seeds in early spring into pots or modules using standard soil-less seed compost (substrate), either a peat free proprietary brand or composted fine propagating bark. As these are very fine seeds, mix with the finest sand or talcum powder for an even sowing. Do not cover. Water from the bottom or with a fine spray and place under protection at 20°C (68°F). Germination takes 3–4 weeks. When growing on as a container plant use a peat free proprietary brand or composted fine propagating bark as a potting compost.

Succisa *Dipsacaceae*

A genus of hardy annuals and perennials, some of which are evergreen. Plant in a well-drained, alkaline soil in a sunny situation.

Succisa pratensis **(Devil's-bit scabious)**
Medium seeds: 700 per gram
Hardy perennial
Height 60cm (24in)
Small, attractive, blue-purple, pincushion flowers
Flowers in summer
Lance-shaped, slightly toothed, mid green leaves

Sow fresh seeds in autumn into pots or modules using standard soil-less seed compost (substrate), either a peat free proprietary brand or composted fine propagating bark, mixed with additional silver or fine sand for extra aeration. Mix to a ratio of 3 parts compost + 1 part sand. Cover with fine sand and place in a cold frame. Germination takes 1–6 months, but can be erratic.

Thalictrum *Ranunculaceae*

A genus of hardy perennials. Plant in a light, well-drained soil, in sun or partial shade.

Thalictrum delavayi AGM
Medium seeds: 400 per gram
Hardy perennial
Height 75cm (30in)
Panicles of rose/lilac flowers with prominent, yellow anthers
Flowers in mid summer
Very divided, mid-green leaves

Sow seeds in late spring into pots or modules using standard soil-less seed compost (substrate), either a peat free proprietary brand or composted fine propagating bark. Cover with perlite or vermiculite and place in a cold frame. Germination takes 3–4 weeks.

Thermopsis *Papilionaceae*

A genus of hardy perennials. Plant in a rich, light soil in a sunny position.

Thermopsis lanceolata
Medium seeds: 110 per gram
Hardy perennial
Height up to 1m (3ft)
Lupin-like spikes of clear yellow flowers
Flowers in summer
Divided, mid-green leaves

Sow seeds in early spring into pots or modules using standard soil-less seed compost (substrate), either a peat free proprietary brand or composted fine propagating bark. Cover with perlite or vermiculite. Place in a cold frame. Germination takes 3–4 weeks.

Trachelium *Campanulaceae*

A genus of hardy to half-hardy perennials. Plant in fertile, very well-drained soil in a sunny position.

Trachelium caeruleum AGM **(Throatwort)**
Dust-like seeds: 90,000 per gram
Half-hardy perennial, often grown as an annual
Height 60cm (24in)
Wonderful clusters of small, tubular, lilac-blue flowers
Flowers in summer
Oval, mid-green, serrated leaves

Sow seeds in early spring into pots or modules using standard soil-less seed compost (substrate), either a peat free proprietary brand or composted fine propagating bark. As these are very fine seeds, mix with the finest sand or talcum powder for an even sowing. Do not cover. Place in a cold frame. Water from below or with a fine spray. Germination takes 3–4 weeks. This plant dislikes wet winters.

Tradescantia *Commelinaceae*

A genus of hardy to tender perennials, some of which are evergreen. Plant in a moist but free-draining soil in sun or partial shade.

Tradescantia virginiana
Medium seeds: 280 per gram
Hardy perennials
Height 60cm (24in)
Clusters of deep blue flowers
Flowers all summer
Dark green, pointed leaves

Sow seeds in spring into pots or modules using standard soil-less seed compost (substrate), either a peat free proprietary brand or composted fine propagating bark. Cover with perlite or vermiculite and place in a cold frame. Germination takes 3–4 weeks.

Trollius *Ranunculaceae*

A genus of hardy perennials. Plant in a moist soil in sun or partial shade. Lovely around a pond.

Trollius chinensis **(Globe flower)**
Medium seeds: 800 per gram
Hardy perennial
Height 75cm (30in)
Deep, golden-yellow, globular flowers
Flowers in summer
Deeply divided, mid-green leaves

Sow fresh seeds in autumn into pots or modules using standard soil-less seed compost (substrate), either a peat free proprietary brand or composted fine propagating bark mixed with silver or fine sand for extra aeration. Mix to a ratio of 3 parts compost + 1 part sand. Cover with fine sand and place in a cold frame. Germination takes 1–6 months and can be erratic.

Verbascum *Scrophulariaceae*

A genus of hardy biennials, perennials and shrubs, some of which are evergreen. Plant in any well-drained soil in sun or partial shade.

Verbascum bombyciferum
Small seeds: 7,000 per gram
Hardy perennial, sometimes biennial
Height 2m (6ft)
Long spikes densely covered with sulphur yellow flowers
Flowers in summer
Oval leaves covered with silky, silver hairs

Verbascum phoeniceum (Purple mullein)
Small seeds: 7,000 per gram
Hardy perennial
Height 1m (3ft)
Long spikes of vivid purple flowers
Flowers in early summer
Oval, mid-green leaves

Sow fresh seeds in autumn into pots using standard soil-less seed compost (substrate), either a peat free proprietary brand or composted fine propagating bark mixed with extra silver or fine sand for extra aeration. Mix to a ratio of 3 parts compost + 1 part sand. As these are very fine seeds, mix with the finest sand or talcum powder for an even sowing. Do not cover. Water from the bottom or with a fine spray. Place in a cold frame. Germination takes 1–7 months but can be erratic. Flowers in its second year.

OR

Sow seeds in early spring into pots or modules using standard soil-less seed compost (substrate), either a peat free proprietary brand or composted fine propagating bark. Cover with perlite or vermiculite and place under protection at 20°C (68°F). Germination takes 4–7 days but can be spasmodic.

Trollius chinensis

shrubs

Growing shrubs from seed is very satisfying. As there are very few commercial suppliers of seed, collecting your own is doubly worthwhile. It is great fun to collect the seed from a shrub that you admire in a friend's garden. Two years later you will be watching it flourish in your own garden.

Remember that most shrubs need to be grown on in containers for two years before planting out into their growing positions.

Shrub seed is very seldom sold by number, so in this chapter I have only provided an indication of the size. For more information on seed size see page 242.

Cytisus scoparius, see page 178

Abutilon *Malvaceae*

A genus of hardy and half-hardy annuals, perennials, evergreen and semi-evergreen or deciduous shrubs. Plant in a fertile well-drained soil in sun or partial shade.

Abutilon megapotamicum AGM (Flowering maple, Indian mallow)
Medium seeds
Evergreen half-hardy shrub
Height 3m (10ft)
Pendent bell-shaped yellow and red flowers
Flowers in late spring to summer
Dark green, oval, slightly lobed leaves

Sow seeds in early spring into pots or modules using standard soil-less compost (substrate), either a peat free proprietary brand or composted fine propagating bark. Cover with perlite or vermiculite, place under protection at 18°C (65°F). Germination takes 3–4 weeks. Flowers in two years.

Arctostaphylos *Ericaceae*

A genus of hardy to half-hardy evergreen trees and shrubs. Plant in a well-drained acid soil in a sunny situation.

Arctostaphylos uva-ursi (Bearberry)
Medium seeds
Evergreen hardy shrub
Height 15cm (6in)
Pink urn-shaped flowers followed by brilliant red berries
Flowers in spring
Small oval, shiny, green leaves

In autumn, rub the berries in a rough cloth or use your thumb nail to remove the flesh from the seeds. Soak the seeds in hot water for 24 hours prior to sowing. Sow immediately, so that the seeds do not have a chance to dry out. Sow singly into pots or modules using standard ericaceous seed compost (substrate), either a peat free proprietary brand or composted fine propagating bark, mixed with horticultural sand. Mix to a ratio of 1 part compost + 1 part sand. Cover with coarse horticultural sand. Place outside exposed to all the weathers (see 'Breaking Seed Dormancy', page 233, for more information). Germination takes 4-6 months, or even as long as 18, so be patient.

Aucuba *Aucubaceae*

A genus of hardy evergreen shrubs. Plant in any soil, with the exception of waterlogged sites, in sun or partial shade.

Aucuba japonica
Large seeds
Evergreen hardy shrub
Height 2.5m (8ft)
Small purple/pink flowers followed by bright red berries on female plants
Flowers in mid-spring
Lance-shaped dark green glossy leaves

In autumn rub the berries in a rough cloth or use your thumb nail to remove the flesh from the seeds. Sow the seed immediately so they do not dry out. Sow individually into pots or modules, using standard loam-based seed compost (substrate) mixed with coarse horticultural sand. Mix to a ratio of 1 part compost + 1 part sand. Cover with coarse horticultural sand. Place outside, exposed to all the weathers (see 'Breaking Seed Dormancy', page 233, for more information). Germination takes 4–6 months, or even as long as 18, so be patient.

Berberis *Berberidaceae*

A genus of hardy, deciduous and evergreen, spiny shrubs. Plant in any soil, except for waterlogged sites, in sun or partial shade.

Berberis julianae AGM
Medium seeds
Evergreen hardy shrub
Height up to 3m (10ft)
Clusters of lightly scented yellow flowers followed by blue black berries in autumn
Flowers from late spring to early summer
Spine-toothed leaves that are copper tinted when young

Chill the seed within the ripe fruit before sowing. Do this by mixing the fruit with sharp sand and then spreading this mixture into a seed tray. Leave outside for the winter to allow the fruit to decompose naturally. Alternatively, mix the fruit and sand, put the mixture into a plastic bag and place in the refrigerator for the winter.

Sow the clean seed in spring into pots or modules using standard loam-based seed compost (substrate). Cover with perlite or vermiculite and place in a cold frame. Germination takes 3–4 months.

***Recipe for sowing, planting and growing* Berberis julianae**
This berberis with its fine, dense, spiky habit makes a very good hedge.

Ingredients
Seeds in berries
1 seed tray
Sharp sand
White plastic plant label
Waterproof pen
OR
Seeds in berries
1 plastic bag
Damp sand
Waterproof pen
1 plastic tie
1 sieve
5 seeds per pot
1 x 8cm (4in) pot
Standard loam-based seed compost (substrate)
Coarse grit
White plastic plant label

Method In autumn collect the ripe fruit, remove it from the stems, mix with sharp sand and spread the mixture on to a seed tray. Label, and place the tray outside on a level surface, so it is exposed to all weathers, including frosts. Do not worry if you live in a snowy area and the containers get immersed in snow, for melting snow will aid germination. If you live in a warm climate you will need to put the sand and fruit mix into a plastic bag, label and seal it and put it into a refrigerator for the whole winter.

In spring, place the sand mixture, either from the seed tray or from the refrigerator, into a sieve and wash away the sand and the pulp, leaving only the clean seeds.

Fill some pots with standard loam-based seed compost to just below the ridge at the top of the pot. Sow the seeds on to the surface of the compost, then cover with coarse grit to just below the rim. Label each pot.

Place the container in a cold frame. Germination should take a further 3–4 months, in good seasons it can be quicker. When the seedlings are large enough to handle, divide and repot singly into 8cm (4in) pots and grow on in a cold frame. Plant out in the garden the following season.

Buddleja *Buddlejaceae*

A genus of hardy to half-hardy deciduous and evergreen shrubs and trees.

Buddleja davidii (Butterfly bush, Summer lilac)
Minute seeds
Deciduous hardy shrub
Height up to 3m (10ft)
Dense clusters of lilac/purple flowers
Flowers in summer
Lance-shaped, grey-green leaves

Sow fresh seeds in autumn into pots or modules using standard soil-less compost (substrate), either a peat free proprietary brand or composted fine propagating bark. As these are very fine seeds, mix with the finest sand or talcum powder for an even sowing. Do not cover. Water from the bottom or with a fine spray. Place under protection at 20 °C (68°F). Germination takes 10–20 days. Overwinter young plants under protection in a cold frame or unheated glass house. Can flower in its first year.

Callicarpa *Verbenaceae*

A genus of hardy deciduous shrubs. Plant in a fertile, well-drained soil in a sunny position.

Callicarpa bodinieri
Small seeds
Deciduous hardy shrub
Height up to 3m (10ft)
Clusters of numerous star-shaped lilac flowers, followed by masses of small berries in shades of lilac, violet and rich purple
Flowers in mid-summer
Narrow leaves that turn deep rose-purple in autumn

Chill the seed within the ripe fruit before sowing. Do this by mixing the fruit with sharp sand then spreading this mixture into a seed tray. Leave outside for the winter to allow the fruit to decompose naturally. Sow the clean seed in spring into pots or modules, using standard loam-based seed compost (substrate). Cover with perlite or vermiculite and place in a cold frame. Germination takes 3–4 months.

Camellia *Theaceae*

A genus of hardy to tender evergreen shrubs and trees. Plant in a well-drained neutral to acid soil in semi-shade and preferably sheltered from strong winds.

Camellia japonica (Common camellia)
Small seeds
Evergreen hardy shrub
Height up to 10m (30ft)
Double flowers in shades of white, pink and red
Flowers in spring to early summer
Lance-shaped dark green leaves

Sow the fresh seed as soon as the fruits split revealing the seed. Sow in autumn into pots or modules using standard ericaceous seed compost (substrate). Cover with perlite or vermiculite, place in a cold frame. Germination takes 2–6 months. Keep young plants in a cold frame for their first year.

Carissa *Apocynaceae*

A genus of tender, evergreen shrubs. In warm climates plant out in a well-drained soil in partial shade. In cool climates grow as a container plant.

Carissa macrocarpa (grandiflora) (Natal plum)
Medium seeds
Evergreen tender shrub (minimum temperature 10°C / 50°F)
Fragrant white jasmine-like flowers followed by edible plum-like fruits
Flowers in summer
Dark green glossy leaves and thorny stems

Sow fresh seed in autumn into pots or modules using standard soil-less compost (substrate), either a peat free proprietary brand or composted fine propagating bark. Cover with perlite or vermiculite, place under protection at 18°C (65°F). Germination takes 14–21 days. Overwinter young plants in a frost-free environment above the minimum temperature.

Caryopteris *Verbenaceae*

A genus of hardy deciduous shrubs. Plant in a light well-drained soil in a sunny situation.

Caryopteris incana
Small seeds
Deciduous hardy shrub
Pretty scented tubular blue/violet flowers
Flowers in summer
Lance-shaped, grey-green leaves

Sow fresh seed in spring into pots or modules, using standard soil-less compost (substrate), either a peat free proprietary brand or composted fine propagating bark. Cover with perlite or vermiculite. Place under protection at 18°C (65°F). Germination takes 14–21 days. Flowers in 2–3 years from germination.

Catharanthus *Apocynaceae*

A genus of tender evergreen shrubs. In warm climates plant outside in a light, well-drained soil in a sunny position. In cool climates grow as a container plant or as a summer bedding plant.

Catharanthus roseus AGM **Rose periwinkle**
Medium seeds
Evergreen half-hardy shrub (minimum temperature 5°C/40°F)
Height up to 30cm (12in)
Flowers white to shades of pink
Flowers from spring until early autumn in cool regions, and well into winter in warm regions
Oval green leaves

Sow fresh seed in spring into pots or modules using standard soil-less compost (substrate), either a peat free proprietary brand or composted fine propagating bark. Cover with perlite or vermiculite, and cover with black plastic cut to the size of the container. Place under protection at 18°C (65°F). Germination takes 14–21 days. After 10 days check regularly to see if the seeds have germinated. As soon as they do, remove the black plastic, maintain warmth for a further 3 days, then place in a light but cooler area. Be very careful with the watering, these young plants are very sensitive to overwatering.

Chaenomeles *Rosaceae*

A genus of hardy deciduous shrubs. Plant in a well-drained soil in a sunny position.

Chaenomeles speciosa (Japonica, Japanese quince)
Medium seeds
Deciduous hardy shrub
Height up to 1m (3½ft)
Red, orange/red cup-shaped flowers followed by yellow fruits
Flowers in early spring
Oval mid-green leaves

Catharanthus roseus

Sow fresh seeds in autumn into pots or modules, using standard loam-based seed compost (substrate) mixed with coarse horticultural sand to a ratio of 1 part compost + 1 part sand. Cover with coarse horticultural sand. Place outside, exposed to all the weathers (see 'Breaking Seed Dormancy', page 233). Germination takes 4–6 months.

Cistus *Cistaceae*

A genus of hardy to half-hardy evergreen shrubs. Plant in a light, well-drained soil in a sunny position.

Cistus ladanifer L. AGM (Rock rose, Gum cistus)
Small seeds
Evergreen half-hardy shrub
Height up to 1m (3½ft)
Large, pretty, white flowers with red/purple triangular markings around the centre
Flowers in early summer
Lance-shaped sticky, narrow, dark green leaves

Sow fresh seed in spring into pots or modules using standard soil-less compost (substrate), either a peat free proprietary brand or composted fine propagating bark. Cover with perlite or vermiculite. Place under protection at 18°C (65°F). Germination takes 14–21 days.
OR
Sow in late spring into prepared open ground, when the air temperature does not go below 7°C (45 °F) at night. Germination takes 3–4 weeks.

Cotoneaster *Rosaceae*

A genus of hardy deciduous, evergreen shrubs and trees. Can be planted in all but waterlogged soils in sun or partial shade.

Cotoneaster bullatus AGM
Medium seeds
Deciduous hardy shrub
Clusters of small pink flowers followed by small bright red fruits
Flowers in late spring
Large, oval, dark green leaves which turn to red in autumn

Chaenomeles speciosa

Collect berries in late winter and extract the seeds (average 2 per berry).

Sow seed into pots or modules using standard, loam-based seed compost (substrate) mixed with coarse horticultural sand to a ratio of 1 part compost + 1 part sand. Cover with coarse sand and place under protection at 18ºC (65ºF) for 4 weeks. Then place outside to expose to all weathers. (See 'Breaking Seed Dormancy', page 233, for more information.) Germination can occur from spring until the following spring. Do not give up.

Cytisus *Papilionaceae*

A genus of hardy to half-hardy deciduous and evergreen shrubs. Plant in a light, fertile, well-drained soil in a sunny position.

Cytisus scoparius **(Broom, Common broom)**
Medium seeds
Deciduous hardy shrub
Profusions of bright, yellow, pea-like flowers
Flowers all summer
Small, narrow, dark green, divided leaves

In autumn soak the seeds in hot, not boiling, water overnight. Remove and discard any floating seeds and sow the remainder in pots or modules, using standard loam-based seed compost (substrate) mixed with coarse horticultural sand to a ratio of 1 part compost + 1 part sand. Cover with coarse horticultural sand and then place outside exposed to all the weathers. (See 'Breaking Seed Dormancy' for more information.) Germination takes 4–6 months.

Daphne *Thymelaeaceae*

A genus of hardy evergreen and deciduous shrubs. Plant in a well-drained fertile soil in sun or partial shade.

Daphne mezereum
Large seeds
Deciduous hardy shrub
Height up to 1.2m (4ft)
Clusters of scented, purple/pink blooms followed by red fruits
Flowers from late winter until early spring, fruits appearing in spring
Small, oval, grey-green leaves

Sow fresh seed in spring, having removed the pulp with a rough cloth or thumb nail, into pots or modules, using standard loam-based seed compost (substrate) mixed with coarse horticultural sand. Mix to a ratio of 1 part compost + 1 part sand. (Do not allow the seeds to dry out.) Cover with coarse horticultural sand. Place in a cold frame. Germination takes 4–6 months. Overwinter young plants in a cold frame.

Elaeagnus *Elaeagnaceae*

A genus of hardy deciduous and evergreen shrubs or trees. Plant in fertile, well-drained soil in sun or partial shade.

Elaeagnus pungens
Medium seeds
Evergreen hardy shrub
Height up to 3m (10ft)
Clusters of fragrant cream-white flowers followed by red edible fruit
Flowers in mid- to late autumn
Lance-shaped, dark green glossy leaves

Sow fresh seed in spring, having removed the pulp with a rough cloth or thumb nail. Sow into pots or modules using standard loam-based seed compost (substrate) mixed with coarse horticultural sand to a ratio of 1 part compost + 1 part sand. Cover with coarse horticultural sand. Place in a cold frame. Germination takes 1–2 months but can take longer, so if necessary leave in container for a further season. Overwinter young plants in a cold frame.

Fatsia *Araliaceae*

A genus of one species, see below. Plant in a fertile, well-drained soil in sun or partial shade. In cold areas protect from strong winds.

Fatsia japonica AGM
Small seeds
Evergreen hardy shrub
Height up to 3m (10ft)
Dense clusters of small, white flowers followed by black berries in winter
Flowers in mid-autumn
Large, lobed, glossy, dark green leaves

Sow fresh seed extracted from the ripe black fruit in early winter into pots or modules, using standard soil-less compost (substrate), either a peat free proprietary brand or composted fine propagating bark. Cover with perlite or vermiculite. Place under protection at 18°C (65°F). Germination takes 10–21 days. Grow seedlings on under protection and protect young plants from frost for two winters.

Forsythia *Oleaceae*

A genus of hardy deciduous shrubs which usually have masses of yellow flowers which open before the leaves appear. Plant in a fertile, well- drained soil in a sunny position.

Forsythia suspensa
Small seeds
Deciduous hardy shrub
Height up to 2m (6ft)
Small trumpet-shaped bright yellow flowers before leaves appear
Flowers in early spring
Small mid-green leaves

Collect seeds in late summer. Sow fresh seed in early spring into pots or modules using standard loam-based seed compost (substrate) mixed with coarse horticultural sand. Mix to a ratio of 1 part compost + 1 part sand. Cover with coarse horticultural sand. Place in a cold frame. Germination takes 1–2 months.

Fremontodendron *Steruliaceae*

A genus of hardy evergreen or semi-evergreen shrubs grown for their attractive flowers. Plant in a well-drained, light soil in a sunny position. In cold areas plant against a warm wall.

Daphne mezereum

Fremontodendron californicum (Flannel bush)
Medium seeds
Evergreen hardy shrub
Height up to 6m (20ft)
Large saucer-shaped bright yellow flowers
Flowers from late spring to mid-autumn
Lobed dark green leaves.

Sow fresh seed in spring into pots or modules using standard soil-less compost (substrate), either a peat free proprietary brand or composted fine propagating bark. Cover with perlite or vermiculite and place under protection at 18°C (65°F). Germination takes 4–5 weeks. Do not overwater young seedlings as they are prone to 'damping off'.

Fuchsia *Onagraceae*

A genus of hardy to tender deciduous, evergreen shrubs and trees. Plant in fertile moist, but not over-wet, soil in partial shade. This is a large family so there are exceptions to the general rules. It is always worth talking to a fuchsia specialist about individual varieties. In cool climates, tender plants should be grown as container plants.

Fuchsia magellanica (Lady's ear drops)
Small seeds
Deciduous hardy shrub
Height up to 3m (10ft)
Small flowers with red tubes and long red sepals and purple petals followed by black fruits
Flowers in summer
Mid-green oval pointed leaves.

Fuchsia procumbens
Small seeds
Deciduous hardy shrub
Height up to 10cm (4in)
Masses of tiny upright, yellow tubed flowers with purple sepals and bright blue pollen, followed by red berries
Flowers in summer
Dark green oval pointed leaves

Collect the seeds from the fleshy fruit in late winter, store in a sealed plastic bag placed in the refrigerator. Sow chilled seed in spring into pots or modules using standard soil-less compost (substrate), either a peat free proprietary brand or composted fine propagating bark. Cover with perlite or vermiculite and place under protection at 20°C (68°F). Germination takes 3–4 weeks. Can flower in its first year and will certainly flower in its second.

Gardenia *Rubiaceae*

A genus of tender evergreen shrubs and trees with lovely flowers. Plant in a humus-rich neutral to acid soil in partial shade. In cool climates grow as a container plant in ericaceous compost.

Gardenia jasminoides (*G. florida*) AGM
Small seeds
Evergreen tender shrub (minimum temperature 15°C/60 °F)
Height up to 1.5m (5ft)
Strongly scented pure white flowers
Flowers from summer until winter
Oval dark green glossy leaves

Collect seeds in winter and sow in the spring into pots or modules, using standard ericaceous seed compost (substrate), either a peat free proprietary brand or composted fine propagating bark. Cover with perlite or vermiculite and place under protection at 20°C (68°F). Germination takes 1–3 weeks. Grow on with protection at all times. The plants will take up to 7 years to flower.

Hamamelis *Hamamelidaceae*

A genus of hardy deciduous shrubs. Plant in a well-drained, fertile, peaty, acid soil in sun or semi-shade.

Hamamelis virginiana (Witch hazel, Virginian witch hazel)
Small seeds
Deciduous hardy shrub
Height up to 4m (12ft)
Small fragrant yellow flowers
Flowers from mid-winter until spring
Oval mid-green leaves

In cool climates collect seed capsules just as they turn brown in autumn. Put them in a paper bag, seal the bag, and put it in a warm place. When ripe and dry, the seed capsules will explode.

Sow fresh seed in spring into pots or modules, using standard soil-less compost (substrate), either a peat free proprietary brand or composted fine propagating bark, mixed with coarse horticultural sand to a ratio of 1 part compost + 1 part sand. Cover with coarse horticultural sand. Place outside exposed to all the weathers (see 'Breaking Seed Dormancy', page 233, for more information). Germination will occur the following spring. Overwinter young plants in a cold frame the following year.

Hibiscus *Malvaceae*

A genus of hardy to tender perennials, annuals, shrubs and trees, either evergreen or deciduous. Plant in a humus-rich, well-drained soil in a sunny position.

Hibiscus mutabilis (Cotton rose, Confederate rose)
Medium seeds
Evergreen tender shrub/tree (minimum temperature 5°C/40 °F)
Height up to 5m (15ft)
Funnel-shaped white or pink flowers that darken with age and can occasionally be double
Flowers from summer until early autumn
Rounded lobed leaves

Collect seed from large, dry capsules in autumn.

Sow fresh seed in spring into pots or modules using standard soil-less compost (substrate), either a peat free proprietary brand or composted fine propagating bark. Cover with perlite or vermiculite place under protection at 20°C (68°F). Germination takes 1–3 weeks. Grow on under protection.

Hydrangea quercifolia

Hydrangea *Hydrangeaceae*

A genus of hardy, deciduous shrubs and climbers which can also be evergreen

Hydrangea quercifolia AGM **(Oak-leaved hydrangea)**
Small seeds
Deciduous hardy shrub
Height up to 1.5m (5ft)
Clusters of small white flowers
Flowers in summer until autumn
Deeply lobed, green leaves which, in autumn, turn red and purple

Collect seed from dried capsules in late autumn, early winter. Sow fresh seed in spring into pots or modules using standard soil-less seed compost (substrate), either a peat free proprietary brand or composted fine propagating bark. Cover with perlite or vermiculite and place under protection at 10°C (50°F). Germination takes 1–3 weeks.

Ligustrum *Oleaceae*

A genus of hardy deciduous, semi-evergreen and evergreen shrubs and trees. Plant in any well-drained soil in sun or partial shade.

Ligustrum ovalifolium **(Oval-leaved privet)**
Medium seeds
Hardy evergreen shrub
Height up to 3m (10ft)
Clusters of small dull white flowers which are followed by round shiny black berries
Flowers in summer
Oval smooth darkish-green leaves

Collect seeds from ripe berries in autumn (1–4 seeds per berry). Mix the seeds with a small amount of damp vermiculite, put the mixture into a plastic bag. Seal, label and put into a refrigerator for 3 weeks.

Nerium subsp. *oleander*

Sow the chilled seeds in winter into pots or modules using standard loam-based seed compost (substrate) mixed with coarse horticultural sand. Mix to a ratio of 1 part compost + 1 part sand. Cover with coarse horticultural sand, then place outside exposed to all weathers (see 'Breaking Seed Dormancy', page 233, for more information). Germination takes 4–6 months. Grow on in a cold frame for the next season.

Mahonia *Berberidaceae*

A genus of hardy to half-hardy evergreen shrubs, grown for their flowers. Plant in a fertile well-drained soil that does not dry out in summer in partial shade or even full shade.

Mahonia acanthifolia
Medium seeds
Hardy evergreen shrub
Height up to 4m (12ft)
Long chains of rich yellow flowers followed by blue/black berries
Flowers from late autumn to early winter
Dark green holly-like spiny leaflets

Collect the ripe fruits in early summer, remove the seeds and wash thoroughly in running water. Sow into pots or modules using standard loam-based seed compost (substrate) mixed with coarse horticultural sand. Mix to a ratio of 1 part compost + 1 part sand. Cover with coarse horticultural sand. Place in a cold frame. Germination takes 1–2 months but can take longer, so leave in container for a further season. Overwinter young plants in a cold frame.

Mimosa *Mimosaceae*

A genus of tender shrubs (minimum temperature 10°C/50°F) grown for their flowers. Plant in a well-drained soil in a sunny situation. In cool climates grow as a container plant.

Mimosa pudica **(Humble plant, Sensitive plant)**
Medium seeds
Tender evergreen shrub (minimum temperature 10°C/50°F)
Height 30cm (12in)
Pretty pink fluffy flowers which close when touched
Flowers from summer to autumn
Small pinnate foliage, which curls when touched

Collect the hard-coated seeds in late summer when ripe.

In spring, soak the seeds in hot, not boiling, water for 12 hours prior to sowing into pots or modules, using standard loam-based seed compost (substrate) mixed with coarse horticultural grit. Mix to a ratio of 1 part compost + 1 part 5mm (1/4in) grit. Cover with sharp grit. Place the container under protection at a temperature of 18°C (65°F). Germination takes 3–4 weeks. Flowers during second season. Overwinter the young plants under protection, minimum temperature 10°C (50°F).

Myrtus *Myrtaceae*

A genus of hardy to half-hardy evergreen shrubs, grown for their attractive flowers and aromatic foliage. Plant in a well-drained soil in a sunny position.

Myrtus communis AGM **(Myrtle)**
Medium seeds
Hardy evergreen shrub
Small, white flowers followed by edible, black, oval berries
Flowers in summer
Small oval aromatic dark green leaves

Sow fresh seed in spring, having removed the pulp with a rough cloth or thumbnail. Sow into pots or modules using standard loam-based seed compost (substrate) mixed with coarse horticultural sand. Mix to a ratio of 1 part compost + 1 part sand. Cover with coarse horticultural sand and place under protection at 15°C (60°F). Germination takes 1–2 months, but can take longer.

Nerium *Apocynaceae*

A genus of tender shrubs (minimum temperature 10°C/50°F) grown for their flowers. Plant in a well-drained soil in a sunny situation. In cool climates grow as a container plant.

Nerium subsp. *oleander*
Medium seeds
Tender evergreen shrub (minimum temperature 10°C/50°F)
Height up to 4m (12ft)
Clusters of pink, white, red, apricot flowers
Flowers from spring until autumn
Lance-shaped leathery green leaves

Collect seeds from bean-like pods in autumn.

Sow in spring or late summer in pots or modules, using standard soil-less compost (substrate), either a peat free proprietary brand or composted fine propagating bark. Cover with perlite or vermiculite, place under protection at 18°C (65°F). Germination takes 2–3 weeks. Grow on under protection at 10°C (50°F).

Paeonia *Paeoniaceae*

A genus of hardy perennials and deciduous shrubs grown for their showy flowers and foliage. Plant in fertile, well-drained soil in a sunny position. Can tolerate partial shade.

Paeonia delavayi AGM **(Tree peony)**
Large seeds
Hardy deciduous shrub
Height up to 2m (6ft)
Bowl-shaped, single, deep red flowers
Flowers from spring to early summer
The mid-green leaves are divided into pointed oval leaflets

This seed has a double dormancy, producing roots in its first year and leaves in its second. It needs two cold periods, with warmth in between.

Collect ripe, fresh seeds in early autumn.

Sow individually into pots, using standard soil-less seed compost (substrate), either a peat free proprietary brand or composted fine propagating bark mixed with coarse horticultural sand. Mix to a ratio of 1 part compost + 1 part sand. Cover with coarse grit, then place outside exposed to all the weathers (see 'Breaking Seed Dormancy', page 233, for more information). Visible germination occurs during the second spring. Grow on in a cold frame for 2 years before planting out.

Philadelphus *Hydrangeaceae*

A genus of hardy deciduous shrubs grown for their fragrant flowers. Plant in a fertile well-drained soil in a sunny position.

Philadelphus coronarius (Mock orange)
Medium seeds
Height up to 3m (10ft)
Hardy deciduous shrub
Clusters of very fragrant creamy white flowers
Flowers in late spring and early summer
Oval green leaves

In early autumn, collect the ripe seeds, mix with a handful of damp vermiculite, then place in a plastic bag, seal and place in a refrigerator for 8 weeks. In winter, sow the chilled seed into pots or modules using standard, loam-based seed compost (substrate) mixed with coarse horticultural sand to a ratio of 1 part compost + 1 part sand. Cover with coarse horticultural sand. Place in a cold frame. Germination takes 2–3 months but can take longer. Grow on in a cold frame for 2 years before planting out.

Phlomis *Lamiaceae*

A genus of hardy evergreen shrubs and perennials grown for their interesting flowers. Plant in a well-drained soil in a sunny position.

Phlomis fruticosa AGM (Jerusalem sage)
Medium seeds
Hardy evergreen shrub
Height 1m ($3^1/_2$ft)
Tight clusters of golden flowers
Flowers in summer
Coarse grey-green felt-like leaves

Sow seeds in early spring into pots or modules using standard, soil-less seed compost (substrate), either a peat free proprietary brand or composted fine propagating bark. Cover with perlite or vermiculite. Place under protection at 18°C (65°F). Germination takes 2–3 weeks. Grow on in a cold frame for 2 years before planting out.

Pieris *Ericaceae*

A genus of hardy evergreen shrubs grown for their foliage. Plant in a moist, peaty acid soil in semi- to full shade.

Pieris japonica
Small seeds
Hardy evergreen shrub
Height up to 3m (9ft)
Lovely drooping racemes of white, lily-of-the-valley-like flowers
Flowers in spring
Dark green leaves that are bronze when young

Sow seeds in early spring into pots or modules using standard ericaceous seed compost (substrate). Do not cover, place under protection at 18°C (65°F). Germination takes 3–4 weeks.

Pittosporum *Pittosporaceae*

A genus of hardy to half-hardy evergreen trees and shrubs. Plant in a well-drained soil in sun or partial shade. In cooler climates grow plants against a south- or west-facing wall.

Pittosporum undulatum (Victorian box)
Medium seeds
Half-hardy shrub
Scented, star-shaped, white flowers followed by round orange fruits
Flowers from spring until early summer
Narrow, long, oval, pointed, dark green leaves with a wavy edge

Sow seeds in early spring into pots or modules using standard soil-less seed compost (substrate), either a peat free proprietary brand or composted fine propagating bark. Cover with perlite or vermiculite and place under protection at 20°C (68°F). Germination takes 6–8 weeks. This plant can be grown as a container plant. Use a soil-based potting compost for potting on.

Potentilla *Rosaceae*

A genus of hardy perennials and deciduous shrubs grown for their attractive flowers. Plant in a well-drained soil in a sunny situation.

Potentilla fruticosa 'Elizabeth'
Small seeds
Hardy, deciduous shrub
Height 1m ($3^1/_2$ft)
Saucer-shaped, golden-yellow flowers
Flowers all summer
Divided, grey-green leaves

Sow seeds in early spring into pots or modules using standard soil-less seed compost (substrate), either a peat free proprietary brand or composted fine propagating bark. Cover with perlite or vermiculite, place under protection at 18°C (65°F). Germination takes 2–3 weeks. This plant flowers two years after germination.

Pyracantha *Rosaceae*

A genus of hardy evergreen shrubs grown for their flowers and fruits. Plant in a fertile free-draining soil, in sun or partial shade that is sheltered from the cold winds.

Pyracantha angustifolia (Fire thorn)
Small seeds
Hardy evergreen shrub
Height up to 3m (10ft)
Clusters of small, white flowers followed by orange-red berries
Flowers in early summer
Dark green, narrow oblong leaves with grey underneath

Collect the ripe berries in autumn, remove the seeds and wash with running water. Store the seeds in damp vermiculite in the refrigerator or sow immediately. These seeds need a long period of cold to germinate.

Sow fresh seed in autumn into pots or modules, using standard soil-less seed compost (substrate), either a peat free proprietary brand or composted fine propagating bark mixed with coarse horticultural sand. Mix to a ratio of 1 part compost + 1 part sand. Cover with coarse grit then place outside exposed to all the weathers (see 'Breaking Seed Dormancy', page 233, for more information). Germination takes place the following spring.

OR

Sow chilled seed in spring following the directions above placing the container in a cold frame. Germination takes 1–2 months. Grow on in a container for a further season before planting out.

Rhododendron *Ericaceae*

A genus of hardy to tender evergreen, semi-evergreen or deciduous shrubs, grown for their lovely flowers. Plant in a humus-rich, well-drained neutral to acid soil in partial shade.

Rhododendron auriculatum
Tiny seeds
Hardy evergreen shrub
Height up to 6m (20ft)
Scented funnel-shaped white flowers
Flowers in late spring or early summer
Large oblong mid-green leaves
Ideally suited to growing in a light wood

Collect dry pods before they split open in early autumn.

Sow seeds in spring into pots or modules using standard ericaceous seed compost (substrate), either a peat free proprietary brand or composted fine propagating bark. Cover the seeds with a sheet of glass or cling film and place under protection at 15°C (60°F). Germination takes 14 –28 days. Prick out and pot up when large enough to handle. Overwinter young plants in a cold frame. Plant out in the following spring.

Rosa *Rosaceae*

A genus of hardy, deciduous, or semi-evergreen shrubs and climbers grown for their lovely, often scented, flowers. Plant in a fertile, free-draining soil that does not dry out in summer, in a sunny situation.

It is worth mentioning that only old shrub roses and species roses can be grown successfully from seed.

Rosa gallica

Rosa canina (Dog rose)
Medium seeds
Hardy deciduous shrub
Height up to 3m (10ft)
Lovely scented pale pink/white small open flowers in clusters of 1–4 flowers followed by oval hips
Flowers from early to mid-summer
Divided small green leaves and very prickly stems

Rosa gallica (Apothecary's rose, Red rose of Lancaster)
Medium seeds
Hardy deciduous shrub
Height up to 2m (6ft)
Lovely flat double pink/red fragrant flowers followed by brick red hips in autumn
Flowers in summer
Divided oval mid-green leaves and prickly stems

Collect the seeds in autumn from ripe hips. Mix the seed with propagating coir and put the mixture into a plastic bag. Seal and label the bag and put it in a warm place at 20°C (68°F) for 2 months. Place the plastic bag into the refrigerator for a further month. Finally sow the seeds into pots or modules using standard loam-based seed compost (substrate) mixed with coarse horticultural sand. Mix to a ratio of 1 part compost + 1 part sand. Cover with coarse horticultural sand and place in a cold frame. Germination takes 2–3 months but can take longer. When the seedlings are strong enough, pot up singly into 8cm (4in) pots using a loam-based potting compost. Grow on in the cold frame for a further season before planting out.

Sambucus *Caprifoliaceae*

A genus of hardy perennials, deciduous shrubs and trees grown for their flowers and fruits. Plant in a fertile, moist soil in a sunny situation.

Sambucus nigra (Common elder)
Small seeds
Hardy deciduous shrub
Height up to 6m (20ft)
Attractive flat heads of lightly scented creamy-white star-shaped flowers, which are followed by masses of small round black fruits
Flowers in early summer
Large leaves are made up of green saw-edged leaflets

In late summer collect the fruit, wash off the pulp and sow immediately into pots or modules using standard loam-based seed compost (substrate) mixed with coarse horticultural sand. Mix to a ratio of 1 part compost + 1 part sand. Cover with coarse horticultural sand, then place outside exposed to all the weathers (see 'Breaking Seed Dormancy', page 233, for more information). Germination takes 4–6 months or may not be until the following spring, so do not give up. Pot up, placing the young plants in a cold frame for the first winter, then plant out the following spring.

***Recipe for sowing, planting and growing* Sambucus nigra**

The berries of *Sambucus nigra* (common elder) make a great wine and the flowers make a delicious cordial This may not look like a Rolls-Royce of a plant in the garden, but it is certainly very useful.

Ingredients
Rubber gloves
1 sieve
5 seeds per module or 8 seeds per pot
1 x 8cm (4in) pot
Standard loam-based seed compost (substrate) mixed with coarse horticultural sand. Mix to a ratio of 1 part compost + 1 part sand
Coarse horticultural sand
White plastic plant label

Method In late summer, collect the ripe fruit and remove them from the stems. Place the fruit in a sieve. Put the sieve with the berries under running water and gently crush the fruit through the sieve. The seed is small, approximately 3 seeds per small berry, so make sure that the sieve is not too coarse or you will lose them. Having cleaned the seed, fill the tray or pot with compost, smooth over, tap down and water in well.

Sow the seeds thinly on the top of the compost, press gently in with a flat hand, cover with coarse horticultural sand, label with the name and date. Place the container outside on a level surface, so that it is exposed to all weathers, including frosts. Do not worry if you live in a cold area and the containers get immersed in snow, as melting snow will aid germination. Germination can take 4–6 months or may not occur until the following spring, so do not give up.

Divide the seedlings when they are large enough to handle and pot up into 8cm (4in) pots. Place the young plants in a cold frame for the first winter, then plant out the following spring.

Santolina *Asteraceae*

A genus of hardy evergreen shrubs grown for their attractive aromatic foliage. Plant in a well-drained soil in a sunny situation.

Santolina chamaecyparissus AGM (Cotton lavender)
Small seeds
Hardy evergreen shrub
Height up to 75cm (30in)
Yellow button flowers
Flowers in summer
Silver coral-like serrated foliage

Sow fresh seeds in autumn in pots or modules using standard loam-based seed compost (substrate) mixed with coarse horticultural sand. Mix to a ratio of 1 part compost + 1 part sand. Cover with coarse horticultural sand, then place in a cold frame. Germination takes 4–6 months. Grow on in a cold frame for 2 years before planting out.

Sophora *Papilionaceae*

A genus of hardy deciduous or semi-evergreen trees and shrubs grown for the foliage. Plant in fertile free-draining soil in a sunny, warm situation. Ideal for a south wall.

Sophora davidii
Medium seeds
Hardy deciduous shrub
Height up to 2m (6ft)
Short clusters of small pea-like flowers in shades of mauve and white
Flowers in summer
Leaves are mid-green and divided into many leaflets

In spring before sowing the seed, soak for 24 hours in hot, not boiling, water.

Sow in pots or modules using standard loam-based seed compost (substrate) mixed with coarse horticultural sand. Mix to a ratio of 1 part compost + 1 part sand. Cover with coarse horticultural sand, then place in a cold frame. Germination takes 1–2 months, but can be temperamental. Grow on in a cold frame for 2 years before planting out.

Staphylea *Staphyleaceae*

A genus of hardy deciduous shrubs and trees grown for their flowers and fruits. Plant in a fertile moist, not waterlogged, soil in sun or partial shade.

Staphylea colchica (Bladder nut)
Medium seeds
Hardy deciduous shrub
Height up to 4m (12ft)
Upright clusters of bell-shaped fragrant white flowers followed by large pale green fruits which are in the shape of a bladder!
Flowers in late spring
Mid-green leaves which are composed of up to 5 oval leaflets

Sow fresh seeds in early autumn into pots using standard, loam-based seed compost (substrate) mixed with coarse horticultural sand to a ratio of 1 part compost + 1 part sand. Cover with coarse horticultural sand and place under protection at 21°C (70°F) for 6–7 weeks. Then place outside exposed to all the weathers. (see 'Breaking Seed Dormancy', page 233, for more information). Germination takes 5–12 months, do not give up. If there is no germination in the first year, start the process again in the following autumn with the warmth for 6–7 weeks followed by placing the container outside.

Syringa *Oleaceae*

A genus of hardy deciduous shrubs and trees grown for their fragrant flowers. Plant in a fertile well-drained alkaline soil in a sunny situation.

Syringa reticulata (Lilac)
Small seeds
Hardy deciduous shrub/tree
Height up to 10m (30ft)
Large clusters of fragrant tubular creamy-white flowers
Flowers in summer
Oval green leaves

Sow fresh seed in autumn into pots or modules using standard soil-less compost (substrate), either a peat free proprietary brand or composted fine propagating bark mixed with coarse horticultural sand. Mix to a ratio of 1 part compost + 1 part sand. Cover with coarse horticultural sand, then place outside exposed to all the weathers (see 'Breaking Seed Dormancy', page 233, for more information). In early spring place the containers under protection at 20°C (68°F). Germination takes 4–8 weeks after heat has been applied. Overwinter young plants in a cold frame for the first winter.

Tamarix *Tamaricaceae*

A genus of hardy deciduous or evergreen shrubs and trees, grown for their profusion of small flowers. Plant in a fertile, well-drained soil in a sunny position.

Tamarix gallica (Common tamarisk)
Medium seeds
Hardy deciduous shrub/tree
Height up to 4m (12ft)
Masses of tiny star-shaped pink flowers in thin chains – when in full flower it looks like plumes of feathers
Flowers all summer
Scale-like blue-green leaves

In autumn collect the seeds, mix with damp vermiculite and store in a refrigerator for the winter. In spring sow these chilled seeds into pots or modules using standard loam-based seed compost (substrate) mixed with coarse horticultural sand. Mix to a ratio of 1 part compost + 1 part sand. Cover with coarse horticultural sand, then place in a cold frame. Germination takes 1–2 months. Overwinter young plants in a cold frame, plant out in the following spring.

Ulex *Papilionaceae*

A genus of hardy evergreen shrubs grown for the flowers. Plant in any poor, well-drained acid soil in a sunny position.

Ulex europaeus (Gorse, Furze, Whin)
Medium seeds
Hardy evergreen shrub
Height up to 2m (6ft)
Clusters of small yellow pea-shaped flowers
Flowers in spring until early summer
Almost leafless, the green stems are covered with masses of sharp spines

In autumn soak fresh seeds in hot water for 24 hours prior to sowing. Sow into pots or modules using standard ericaceous seed compost (substrate) mixed with coarse horticultural sand. Mix to a ratio of 1 part compost + 1 part sand. Cover with sharp sand and place in a cold frame. Germination takes 1–6 months. Prick out and pot up when large enough to handle. Beware of the sharp spines as the plant grows.

Vaccinium *Ericaceae*

A genus of hardy evergreen shrubs and trees grown for their autumn colour, flowers and fruits. Plant in a moist, not waterlogged, peaty, sandy acid soil in sun or partial shade.

Vaccinium myrtillus (Bilberry, Whortleberry)
Medium seeds
Hardy deciduous shrub
Height 15cm (6in) prostrate habit
Small pale pink bell-shaped flowers followed by round blue-black edible fruits in early autumn
Flowers in summer
Heart-shaped dark green leaves that turn red and purple in autumn
This plant prefers dappled shade

Sow seeds in autumn into pots or modules using standard ericaceous seed compost (substrate), either a peat free proprietary brand or composted fine propagating bark mixed with coarse horticultural sand. Mix to a ratio of 1 part compost + 1 part sand. Cover with coarse horticultural sand, then place outside exposed to all the weathers (see 'Breaking Seed Dormancy', page 233, for more information). Germination takes 4–6 months, but can be erratic, be patient, and do not discard container.

Viburnum *Caprifoliaceae*

A genus of hardy deciduous semi-evergreen or evergreen shrubs and trees, which are grown for their foliage, flowers and fruits. Plant in a deep fertile soil that does not dry out in summer in sun or partial shade.

Viscum album

Viburnum betulifolium
Medium seeds
Hardy deciduous shrub
Height up to 3m (10ft)
Clusters of small white flowers are followed by a profusion of small bright red fruits in autumn
Flowers in summer
Bright green lance-shaped leaves

Collect the ripe berries in autumn, crush the berries and sow seed and pulp on to the surface of pots using standard loam-based seed compost (substrate) mixed with coarse horticultural sand. Mix to a ratio of 1 part compost + 1 part sand. Cover with coarse horticultural grit, then place outside exposed to all the weathers (see 'Breaking Seed Dormancy', page 233, for more information). Germination takes 6–18 months, but it can be erratic, be patient and do not discard compost. Grow on as a container plant for 2 years before planting out.

***Recipe for sowing, planting and growing* Viburnum betulifolium**
Viburnum offers year-round interest. It is easy to grow and the autumn-berry varieties look attractive and are a great source of food for the birds.

Ingredients
Rubber gloves
1 sheet polythene or flexible plastic
8 seeds per pot
1 x 8cm (4in) pot
Standard loam-based seed compost (substrate) mixed with coarse horticultural sand to a ratio of 1 part compost + 1 part sand
Coarse horticultural grit
White plastic plant label

Method In late autumn collect the ripe fruit, remove them from the stems. Fill the tray or pot with compost, smooth over, tap down and water in well. On a piece of polythene or a sheet of flexible plastic, spread the fruit out and gently crush it. Sow the crushed fruit thinly on the top of the compost, press gently in with a flat hand, cover with coarse horticultural grit and label with plant name and date. Place the container outside on a level surface, so it is exposed to all weathers, including frosts. Do not worry if you live in a snowy area and the containers get immersed in snow, the melting snow will aid germination. Germination can take 6–18 months, so do not give up. Divide the seedlings when they are large enough to handle and pot up into 8cm (4in) pots, placing the young plants in a cold frame for the first winter, then plant out the following autumn.

Viscum *Viscaceae*

A genus of hardy to tender parasitic shrubs. On my farm there is a cider apple tree where we now have masses of mistletoe growing very successfully.

Viscum album (Mistletoe)
Medium seeds
Hardy parasitic evergreen shrub
Small pale green flowers followed by white round fruit which contain one seed
Flowers in early spring
Green, oblong leaves which grow in pairs

In spring find a healthy vigorous host tree, either apple, hawthorn, lime, cedar, poplar, oak or ash. On the underside of a branch, make a slit and raise a piece of bark, then with blunt knife push some seeds into the wound. If you can find some damp clay, cover the wound with the soil, if not wrap a piece of moss over the wound and tie it on. This will protect the seeds both from drying out and from birds who may want a quick snack. Germination occurs the following spring. The growth will be slow for the first few years.

Weigela *Caprifoliaceae*

A genus of hardy deciduous shrubs grown for their flowers. Plant in a fertile soil in a sunny position.

Weigela florida
Small seeds
Hardy deciduous shrub
Height up to 2.5m (8ft)
Lovely deep pink tubular flowers, paler on the inside
Flowers in spring until mid-summer
Mid-green oval toothed leaves

Sow seeds in early spring into pots or modules using standard soil-less compost (substrate), either a peat free proprietary brand or composted fine propagating bark. Cover with perlite or vermiculite, place under protection at 18°C (65°F). Germination takes 2–3 weeks. Overwinter young plants in a cold frame for the first winter.

Yucca *Agavaceae*

A genus of hardy to tender evergreen shrubs and trees grown for their architectural structure. Plant in a well-drained soil. Can grow happily as a container plant.

Yucca filamentosa AGM
Medium seeds
Hardy evergreen shrub
Height up to 2m (6ft) in flower
Clusters of small tulip-shaped creamy white flowers grow on stalks 1–2m (3–6ft) high
Flowers in summer
Long sword-shaped deep green leaves with twisted white threads along the edges

In spring soak the seeds for 24 hours in hot, not boiling, water then sow into pots or modules using standard soil-less compost (substrate), either a peat free proprietary brand or composted fine propagating bark. Cover with perlite or vermiculite, place under protection at 18°C (65°F). Germination takes 2–3 weeks. Overwinter young plants in a cold frame for the first winter.

Outside my children's primary school there is a horse-chestnut tree, *Aesculus hippocastanum*, which was planted by one of my neighbour's sons, now a grown up. Recently, he returned to the village with his family and took his own children to see the tree that he had planted at their age. It now towers over the school fence, providing shade in summer, a good supply of conkers in autumn, and giving endless pleasure to the children playing in the school grounds. To me, the most amazing feat of the seed is to produce a tree that can grow for over 30m (100ft) and live for more than a century, giving pleasure to many generations.

Being so large, trees are slower growers than flower seeds and need a little more care while growing on, before planting out into their permanent position. There are very few tree seeds commercially available, however they are not difficult to collect, and are all best sown fresh. If you have a refrigerator large enough, it is worth storing the seeds in damp vermiculite and sowing later in winter, so protecting your harvest from predators, such as mice and squirrels.

trees

Corylus avellana, see page 196

Acacia *Mimosaceae*

A genus of hardy to tender evergreen or semi-evergreen deciduous trees and shrubs. Grown for their attractive flowers. Plant in a well-drained soil in a sunny situation.

Acacia longifolia (Sidney golden wattle)
Medium seeds
Evergreen hardy tree
Height up to 6m (20ft)
Pendent clusters of golden yellow flowers
Flowers in spring
Oblong, narrow dark green phyllodes

Before sowing, gently rub the hard-coated seeds with sandpaper then soak for 24 hours in hot, not boiling, water. Sow the seeds in early spring into pots or modules using standard loam-based seed compost (substrate). Cover with vermiculite or compost and place under protection at 15°C (60°F). Germination takes 3-4 weeks. Grow on as a container plant in soil-based compost for 2 years, then plant out in the garden. This plant will flower when it is 3-4 years old. It is best grown in large pots and overwintered with protection.

Acer *Aceraceae*

A genus of hardy evergreen or deciduous trees and shrubs which are renowned for their autumn colours. Plant in a fertile, well-drained soil in sun or partial shade.

Acer platanoides AGM (Norway maple)
Medium-sized winged seeds
Deciduous hardy tree
Height up to 25m (80ft)
Clusters of small yellow flowers before the leaves appear
Flowers in spring
Broad, lobed green leaves that turn yellow and orange in autumn

Acer pseudoplatanus (Sycamore)
Medium-sized winged seeds
Deciduous hardy tree
Height up to 35m (115ft)
Clusters of small, pendulous green/yellow flowers
Flowers appear with the leaves in spring
Broad 5-lobed green leaves

It is important that this seed does not dry out, either sow fresh in autumn or the following spring. If sowing seeds in spring, soak them in hot, not boiling, water for 48 hours.

Sow the seeds into pots or modules using standard loam-based seed compost (substrate). Cover with compost then a thin layer of coarse grit and place in a cold frame. Germination occurs when the temperature reaches a constant 10°C (50°F). It is worth noting that in some years the seed will not germinate until the second spring.

Pot up when seedlings are large enough to handle. Plant into its growing position 2 years after germination.

Aesculus *Hippocastanaceae*

A genus of hardy deciduous trees and shrubs, grown for their bold flowers and fruits. Plant in a fertile well-drained soil in sun or partial shade.

Aesculus hippocastanum AGM (Horse-chestnut, Buckeye)
Large seeds
Deciduous hardy tree
Height up to 35m (115ft)
Spikes of white flowers followed by spiny fruits which contain one or more shiny conkers
Flowers in early summer
Leaves have 5 to 7 large, thick, stalkless leaflets

Sow fresh conkers in autumn in individual pots using standard loam-based seed compost (substrate). Cover with compost, followed by a layer of coarse grit.

Put outside exposed to all weathers (see 'Breaking Seed Dormancy', page 233 for more information). Germination will occur the following spring, when the temperature reaches a constant 10°C (50°F).

Alternatively, if you cannot sow immediately on day of collection, remove the husks from the conker and place in a plastic bag filled with damp vermiculite, seal and store at 3°C (37°F). Sow, following directions above, in winter. Plant into growing position 18 months after germination.

***Recipe for sowing, planting and growing* Aesculus hippocastanum**

The horse-chestnut tree is very easy to raise from seed and will convince anyone that growing plants from seed is a wonderful thing.

Ingredients
1 seed per pot
1 x 8cm (4in) diameter pot
Standard loam-based seed compost (substrate)
Coarse grit
White plastic plant label
OR
1 seed
1 plastic bag
Damp sand
Waterproof pen
1 wire tie

Method Collect the conkers in autumn, remove the outer green husk. Half fill the pot with compost, place the conker, shiny side up, on the surface of the compost, cover with the remaining compost to below the ridge of the pot. Cover the surface of the compost with grit up to just below the rim of the pot. Water in well. Label the pot with the date and name. Place the pot outside on a level surface, exposed to all weathers, including frosts. Do not worry if you live in a snowy area and the containers get immersed in snow, melting snow will aid germination. If you do not live in an area which will get a winter frost, it is a good idea to put the seed plus a handful of damp sand into a plastic bag which is clearly marked. Seal the bag. Place in a refrigerator for 3 weeks. Remove and sow as instructed above, then place outside. Make sure the pot does not dry out, and guard against raids by small rodents. Germination should occur the following spring. Allow the seedling to become fully rooted in the container before planting out 18 months later.

Aesculus hippocastanum

Ailanthus *Simaroubaceae*

A genus of hardy deciduous trees. Plant in a deep, fertile, well-drained soil in sun or partial shade.

Ailanthus altissima (Tree of heaven)
Medium-sized winged seeds
Deciduous hardy tree
Height up to 25m (80ft)
Clusters of small green flowers which are followed by winged seeds. Male and female flowers usually grow on separate trees
Flowers in mid-summer
Large, dark green leaves, divided into 13 to 25 oval leaflets per stalk

Sow fresh seed into pots in late summer or early autumn, using standard loam-based seed compost (substrate). Cover with compost followed by a layer of coarse grit and place in a cold frame. Germination takes 4-12 weeks. Overwinter young seedlings in the cold frame. Plant out 2 years after germination.

Alnus *Betulaceae*

A genus of hardy deciduous trees and shrubs. Plant in any moist to waterlogged soil in a sunny situation.

Alnus incana (Alder, Grey alder)
Small seeds
Deciduous hardy tree
Height up to 24m (80ft)
Male and female catkins are borne on the same tree in early spring
Oval, dark green leaves

Collect the seeds in late autumn. Put them in a plastic bag with a small amount of damp vermiculite. Label and place in refrigerator for a month.

Sow the chilled seed in winter into pots using standard loam-based seed compost (substrate). Cover with a layer of coarse grit and place under protection at 10°C (50°F). Germination takes 4-12 weeks. Overwinter young seedlings in the cold frame. Plant out 2 years after germination.

Arbutus *Ericaceae*

A genus of hardy evergreen trees and shrubs, grown for their attractive bark and fruits. Plant in a fertile well-drained soil. Provide extra protection from strong, cold winds.

Arbutus andrachne **(Strawberry tree, Grecian strawberry tree)**
Medium seeds
Evergreen hardy tree
Height up to 6m (20ft)
Clusters of urn-shaped cream/white flowers, followed by small, round, orange to red fruits
Flowers in late spring
Attractive peeling reddish bark. Oval glossy dark green leaves which have a yellow-green underside

Collect the fruit in autumn when they are red. Soak them for a minimum of 48 hours in hot, not boiling, water, this will soften the pulp from around the seed. Remove the pulp and sow immediately into pots using standard loam-based seed compost (substrate). Cover with a layer of coarse grit and place under protection at 15°C (60°F). Germination takes 4 to 12 weeks. If no germination occurs, place the container outside exposed to all weathers, or place in the refrigerator for 8 weeks, then return to a warm area. Overwinter young plants in a frost-free environment for 2 years then plant out.

Alternatively, store the cleaned seed in damp sand in the refrigerator and sow as above in the spring.

Betula *Betulaceae*

A genus of hardy deciduous trees and shrubs grown for their autumn colours and attractive bark.

Betula pendula AGM **(Silver birch)**
Medium seeds
Hardy deciduous tree
Height up to 15m (50ft)
Purple/brown male catkins, pale green female catkins which stay on the tree until winter
Catkins appear in spring
Straight silver/white trunk, with pendulous branches
Triangular mid-green leaves with toothed edges

Collect the seeds in late autumn. Put them in a plastic bag with a small amount of damp vermiculite. Label and place in refrigerator for a month. Sow the chilled seed in winter into pots using standard loam-based seed compost (substrate). Cover with a layer of coarse grit and place under protection at 10°C (50°F). Germination takes 4–12 weeks. Overwinter young seedlings in the cold frame. Plant out 2 years after germination.

Carica *Caricaceae*

A genus of tender evergreen trees and shrubs, minimum temperature 13 °C (55°F). Plant in rich, loamy soil in sun or partial shade. In cool climates grow as a container plant.

Carica papaya **(Common pawpaw, Papaya)**
Medium seeds
Evergreen tender tree
Height up to 6m (20ft)
Green-white flowers followed by large, pear-shaped fruit with yellow-green skin, apricot pulp and round, black seeds in a central cavity
Flowers in summer
Large, palmate, lobed green leaves
Both male and female trees are needed for fruiting

Sow fresh seeds very thinly in early spring into pots, using standard loam-based seed compost (substrate) mixed with coarse horticultural sand. Mix to a ratio of 1 part compost + 1 part sand. Cover with perlite or vermiculite and place under protection at 24°C (75°F). Germination takes 3–4 weeks. Plant into growing position 2 years after germination.

If growing on as a container plant, use a standard loam-based potting compost mixed with coarse horticultural sand. Mix to a ratio of 1 part compost + 1 part sand.

Carpinus *Corylaceae*

A genus of hardy deciduous trees grown for their autumn colour. Plant in a fertile well-drained soil in sun or partial shade.

Carpinus betulus **(Hornbeam)**
Medium seeds
Hardy deciduous tree
Height up to 24m (80ft)
Male flowers form in drooping catkins. Female flowers have crimson styles and green bracts grouped in shorter catkins. The fruit develops into triangular nutlets with three long-lobed bracts.
The mid-green leaves are oval and pointed

Sow fresh seed in autumn into pots or modules using standard loam-based seed compost (substrate). Cover with coarse grit, then place outside exposed to all weathers (see 'Breaking Seed Dormancy', page 233, for more information). Germination occurs when the temperature reaches a constant 10°C (50°F). Grow on for 2 seasons before planting out.

Cedrus *Pinaceae*

A genus of hardy evergreen conifer. Plant in any soil, with the exception of waterlogged sites, in a sunny situation.

Cedrus deodara AGM
Medium seeds
Evergreen hardy tree
Height up to 25m (80ft)
The male flowers are erect, releasing yellow pollen in autumn. Female flowers are green. The cones are barrel-shaped and turn brown when ripe, which takes 2 years
Needle-like grey-green leaves

Collect the seeds in autumn from ripe, 2-year-old cones. Break the wings off the seeds before putting them in a plastic bag with a small amount of damp vermiculite. Label and place in a refrigerator for 3 to 4 weeks. Sow the chilled seed in winter into pots using standard loam-based seed compost (substrate). Cover with a layer of coarse grit and place under protection at 15°C (60°F). Germination takes 4–12 weeks. Overwinter young seedlings in the cold frame. Plant out 2 years after germination.

Cedrus deodara

Cercis *Caesalpiniaceae*

A genus of hardy deciduous shrubs and trees with attractive pea-like flowers. Plant in a deep, fertile, well-drained soil in a sunny position.

Cercis siliquastrum AGM (Judas tree)
Medium seeds
Hardy deciduous tree
Height up to 10m (30ft)
Clusters of bright pink flowers, which appear before the leaves, followed by long maroon/purple pods
Flowers in mid spring
Heart-shaped, green leaves

Before sowing, gently rub the hard coated seeds with sandpaper then soak for 24 hours in hot, not boiling, water. Sow seeds in autumn into pots or modules using standard loam-based seed compost (substrate). Cover with vermiculite or compost and place under protection at 15°C (60°F). Germination takes 3-4 weeks. Overwinter the young plants in a frost-free environment. Plant into growing position 2 years after germination.

Chamaecyparis *Cupressaceae*

A genus of hardy evergreen conifer. Plant in any soil, with the exception of waterlogged sites, in sun or partial shade.

Chamaecyparis lawsoniana (Lawson cypress)
Medium seeds
Evergreen hardy tree
Height up to 25m (80ft)
Female flowers grow on the ends of small branchlets. Male flowers grow on the ends of branches and have black scales edged with white, becoming red when ripe. The cones are small and brown
Leaves are aromatic, dark green on top and lighter green below

Collect the seeds from ripe, 1-year-old cones in autumn. Put them in a plastic bag with a small amount of damp vermiculite. Place this bag, labelled, into a refrigerator for 3–4 weeks. Sow the chilled seed in winter into pots using standard loam-based seed compost (substrate). Cover with a layer of coarse grit and place under protection at 15°C (60°F). Germination takes 4–12 weeks. Overwinter young seedlings in the cold frame. Plant into growing position 3 years after germination.

Citrus *Rutaceae*

A genus of half-hardy evergreen trees and shrubs grown for their fruit. Plant in a fertile, well-drained soil in a sunny situation. In cool climates grow as a container plant and protect from frosts.

Citrus limon **(Lemon)**
Medium seeds
Evergreen tender tree, minimum temperature 7°C (45°F)
Height up to 7m (22ft)
Red-budded flowers with white petals followed by oval yellow fruits
Flowers in spring and summer
Light green oval leaves

Sow fresh seeds in summer into pots or modules using standard soil-less seed compost (substrate), either a peat free proprietary brand or composted fine propagating bark. Cover with perlite or vermiculite and place under protection at 18°C (65°F). Germination takes 3–4 weeks. For the first 2 years, grow on as a container plant using a standard loam-based potting compost mixed with coarse horticultural sand to a ratio of 1 part compost + 1 part sand. Flowers 7 years after germination.

Cornus *Cornaceae*

A genus of half-hardy to hardy evergreen and deciduous trees and shrubs grown for their flowers and winter colour. Plant in a well-drained fertile soil in sun or partial shade.

Cornus florida **(Flowering dogwood)**
Medium seeds
Hardy deciduous tree
Height up to 6m (20ft)
The small flowers are surrounded by white, pinkish/white bracts
The flowers are followed by small red fruits
Flowers in late spring to early summer
Oval dark green leaves that turn to reds and purples in autumn
This plant prefers full sun

Collect the fruits in autumn when they are red. Soak them for a minimum of 48 hours in hot, not boiling, water. This will soften the pulp from around the single seed. Remove the pulp and sow immediately, or store in damp sand in the refrigerator.

Sow fresh, cleaned seeds in autumn into pots, using standard loam-based seed compost (substrate). Cover with a layer of coarse grit and place under protection at 15°C (60°F). Germination takes 4–12 weeks. If no germination occurs, place the container outside exposed to all weathers, or place in the refrigerator for 8 weeks, then return to a warm area. Overwinter young plants in a cold frame. Plant into growing position 2 years after germination. Alternatively, sow the stored seed in winter following the above instructions.

Corylus *Corylaceae*

A genus of hardy deciduous trees and shrubs grown for their catkins and nuts. Plant in a fertile well-drained soil in sun or semi-shade.

Corylus avellana **(Hazel, Cobnut)**
Large seed
Hardy deciduous tree
Height up to 9m (30ft)
Male flowers hang in catkins, often called lamb's tails. Female flowers are tiny buds with red tassels which develop into nuts
Flowers in spring
Oval leaves with saw-tooth edges.

Collect the nuts as soon as they fall in early autumn. Either sow immediately or store in damp sand in a refrigerator.

Sow fresh seed in autumn into pots or modules, using standard loam-based seed compost (substrate) mixed with coarse horticultural sand. Mix to a ratio of 1 part compost + 1 part sand. As the shells of these seeds are hard, it is a good idea to scarify them, using fine sandpaper, before sowing, (see 'Scarification' page 233). Cover with sharp grit and place outside exposed to all weathers (see 'Breaking Seed Dormancy', page 233, for more information). Germination takes 1–4 months. Overwinter young plants in a cold frame. Plant into growing position 2 years after germination. Alternatively, sow the stored seed in winter following the above instructions.

Crataegus *Rosaceae*

A genus of hardy deciduous, semi- evergreen trees and shrubs, grown for their flowers and fruits. Plant in all soils with the exception of waterlogged sites, in a sunny situation.

Crataegus monogyna **(Common hawthorn)**
Medium seeds
Hardy deciduous tree
Height up to 10m (30ft)
Clusters of fragrant white flowers which are followed by red fruits
Flowers in late spring to early summer
Lobed oval dark green glossy leaves

Collect the fruit in summer while they are green, before they turn red in autumn. Soak the seed in warm water for 48 hours. Remove the pulp from the single seed and sow immediately, or store in damp sand in the refrigerator.

Sow either fresh seed in summer or stored seeds in early spring into pots or modules, using standard loam-based seed compost (substrate). Cover with compost then a thin layer of coarse grit and place in a cold frame. Germination occurs when the temperature reaches a constant 10°C (50°F). It is worth noting that in some years the seed will not germinate until the second spring.

Cupressus *Cupressaceae*

A genus of hardy evergreen conifer. Plant in a well-drained soil in a sunny situation. Will grow happily in dry sandy soil.

Cupressus sempervirens **(Mediterranean cypress, Italian cypress)**
Medium seeds
Evergreen hardy tree
Height up to 15m (50ft)
Small yellow egg-shaped male flowers
Flowers in summer
Glossy grey-brown oval cones
Aromatic grey-green foliage

Collect the seeds from ripe 2-year-old cones (choose the largest cones) in autumn. Put them in a plastic bag with a small amount of damp vermiculite. Place this bag, labelled, into a refrigerator for 3–4 weeks.

Sow the chilled seed in winter into pots using standard loam-based seed compost (substrate). Cover with a layer of coarse grit and place under protection at 15°C (60°F). Germination takes 4–12 weeks. Overwinter young seedlings in a cold frame. Plant into growing position 3 years after germination.

Davidia *Cornaceae*

A genus of hardy deciduous trees grown for their showy white bracts. Plant in a fertile, well-drained soil that does not dry out in summer and is not waterlogged in winter, in sun or partial shade.

Davidia involucrata AGM **(Pocket handkerchief tree, Dove tree, Ghost tree)**
Medium seeds
Hardy deciduous tree
Height up to 10m (30ft)
Small purple/mauve flowers surrounded by a pair of white bracts (the bracts only appear on mature trees). The flower is followed by green fruit which turn purple when ripe
Flowers in late spring and early summer
Heart-shaped green leaves which are felted underneath

The seeds of this tree have a double dormancy. Collect the ripe fruits in late autumn and clean the flesh off the seed.

Sow fresh seeds, once cleaned, into individual pots, using standard loam-based seed compost (substrate). Cover with a layer of coarse grit and place under protection at 21°C (70°F) for 3 months. Place the container outside exposed to all weathers throughout 2 full seasons. Germination will occur after 2 seasons. Plant into growing position 2 years after germination.

Eucalyptus *Myrtaceae*

A genus of tender to hardy evergreen trees and shrubs grown for their aromatic foliage, flowers and bark. Plant in a fertile well-drained soil in a sunny sheltered position.

Eucalyptus gunnii AGM **(Cider gum)**
Small seeds
Half-hardy evergreen tree, minimum temperature 1°C (34°F), but will reshoot from the base if frost damaged
Height up to 30m (100ft)
Small clusters of pale yellow flowers
Flowers in spring to mid-summer
The leaves of young trees are round and stalkless. They develop into lance-shaped blue-grey leaves

Collect the seeds from ripe seed capsules in spring. Put them in a plastic bag with a small amount of damp vermiculite. Place this bag, labelled, into a refrigerator for 3–4 weeks.

Sow the chilled seed immediately into pots using standard loam-based seed compost (substrate). Cover with a layer of coarse grit and place under protection at 15°C (60°F). Germination takes 4–12 weeks. Overwinter young seedlings in the cold frame. Plant out in the following spring.

Euonymus *Celastraceae*

A genus of hardy evergreen and deciduous shrubs and trees grown for their autumn colour. Plant in a well-drained soil in sun or partial shade.

Euonymus europaeus **(Spindle tree)**
Medium seeds
Hardy deciduous tree
Height up to 6m (20ft)
Small green-yellow flowers followed by amazing pink seed capsules with orange seeds
Flowers in early summer
Lance-shaped green leaves

Sow fresh seed in autumn into pots or modules using standard loam-based seed compost (substrate) mixed with coarse horticultural sand. Mix to a ratio of 1 part compost + 1 part sand. Cover with coarse grit and place outside exposed to all weathers (see 'Breaking Seed Dormancy', page 233, for more information). Germination takes place the following spring. Plant into growing position 2 years after germination.

Fagus *Fagaceae*

A genus of hardy deciduous trees grown for their foliage and autumn colour. Plant in any soil, except in waterlogged sites, in a sunny situation.

Fagus sylvatica AGM **(Beech)**
Medium seeds
Hardy deciduous tree
Height up to 36m (120ft)
Long-stalked yellow male flowers, greenish-white female flowers followed by small husks which contain 2 triangular nutlets
Flowers in spring
Oval green leaves that turn orangey-brown in autumn

Because these seeds are a delicacy for mice and squirrels, it is worth collecting them in autumn, storing them in damp sand in a plastic bag in the refrigerator and sowing when the mice have gone into hibernation.

Sow fresh seed in autumn or stored seed in winter into pots or modules, using standard loam-based seed compost (substrate). Cover with coarse grit. Place outside exposed to all weathers (see 'Breaking Seed Dormancy', page 233, for more information). Germination occurs when the temperature reaches a constant 10°C (50°F). Grow on for 2 seasons before planting out.

Fraxinus excelsior

Fraxinus *Oleaceae*

A genus of hardy deciduous trees and shrubs grown for their foliage. Plant in a fertile, well-drained soil, which does not dry out too much in summer, in a sunny situation.

Fraxinus excelsior **(Common ash)**
Medium seeds
Hardy deciduous tree
Height up to 30m (100ft)
Male and female flowers often occur on the same tree on separate twigs, giving the tree a purple hue before the leaves come out in spring. Flowers are followed by bunches of single long-winged seed (often called keys)
Green leaves are divided into 9–13 leaflets

The seeds have a double dormancy. Collect them in autumn, and place in a plastic bag with a small amount of damp sand. Label and put in the refrigerator for 8 weeks. In winter, sow the chilled seed into pots, using standard loam-based seed compost (substrate). Cover with coarse grit. Place outside exposed to all weathers (see 'Breaking seed Dormancy'. page 233, for more information). Germination occurs after 2 winters outside. Plant into growing position 2 years after germination.

Genista *Papilionaceae*

A genus of fully to half-hardy deciduous shrubs and trees with pea-like flowers. Plant in fertile well-drained soil in a sunny situation.

Genista aetnensis AGM **(Mount Etna broom)**
Medium seeds
Hardy deciduous tree
Height up to 8m (25ft)
Masses of fragrant golden yellow pea-like flowers
Flowers in mid-summer
Bright green branches which are almost leafless

Before sowing in spring, scarify the fresh seeds using fine sandpaper (see page 233) then soak them in hot, not boiling, water. Discard any floating seeds and sow the remainder in pots, using standard soil-less seed compost (substrate), either a peat free proprietary brand or composted fine propagating bark mixed with 3mm (1/8in) fine grit. Mix to a ratio of 3 parts compost + 1 part fine grit. Cover lightly with perlite or vermiculite and place in a cold frame. Germination takes 2–5 weeks. Overwinter young plants in a cold frame. Plant into growing position 2 years after germination.

Ginkgo *Ginkoaceae*

A genus of hardy evergreen trees. Plant in a rich, fertile well-drained soil in a sunny position.

Ginkgo biloba AGM
Large seeds
Hardy deciduous tree
Male and female flowers grow on separate trees. Males appear as small green catkins, females are small, stalked, round and knob-like followed by oval fruit that look like small green plums
Fan-shaped, 2-lobed, mid-green leaves

Fertilisation of the seeds is by free-swimming male sperm which reach the ovules through a film of water, this is a method found in ferns, but in no other tree living today. In autumn remove the pith from around the seed and then wash the seed in a mild detergent to remove any germination inhibitors.

Sow immediately into individual pots or modules, using standard loam-based seed compost (substrate) mixed with coarse horticultural sand. Mix to a ratio of 1 part compost + I part sand. Cover with coarse grit and place in a cold frame. Germination takes 4–6 months, however it can take longer, so do not discard the container until the following spring. Plant into growing position 5 years after germination.

Ilex *Aquifoliaceae*

A genus of hardy to half-hardy evergreen and deciduous trees and shrubs grown for their berries and foliage. Plant in a well-drained soil in sun or partial shade.

Ilex aquifolium AGM **(Common holly)**
Medium seeds (TOXIC SEED)
Hardy evergreen tree or shrub
Height up to 20m (70ft)
Small scented male and female flowers on separate trees. Round red berries on the female trees only
Flowers appear in late spring
Dark glossy spined, lobed leaves

In autumn collect the fruit, clean the pith from the seeds (average 4 per fruit). Please note that although the seed is toxic, the fruit is not.

Sow immediately into pots or modules using standard loam-based seed compost (substrate) mixed with coarse horticultural sand. Mix to a ratio of 1 part compost + 1 part sand. Cover with coarse grit, water very well and place in a cold frame. Germination takes 4–6 months, however it can take longer, so do not discard container until the following spring. Plant into growing position 2 years after germination.

Jacaranda *Bignoniaceae*

A genus of half-hardy deciduous or evergreen trees, minimum temperature 7°C (45°F). In warm climates plant in fertile, well-drained soil in a sunny situation. In cool climates grow as a container plant.

Jacaranda mimosifolia
Medium seeds
Half-hardy perennial
Height up to 9m (30ft)
Trusses of vivid purple-blue flowers
Flowers in spring and early summer
Fast-growing, deciduous, rounded tree, with fern-like leaves

Sow seeds in early spring into pots or modules using standard soil-less seed compost (substrate) either a peat free proprietary brand or composted fine propagating bark. Cover with perlite or vermiculite. Place under protection at 20°C (68°F). Germination takes 4–6 weeks. It can be grown as a container plant for the conservatory although it grows fast and will need clipping. Use a loam-based compost with good drainage in the bottom of the pot.

Juglans *Juglandaceae*

A genus of hardy deciduous trees with aromatic leaves. Plant in a deep, fertile, well-drained soil in a sunny position.

Juglans regia AGM (Walnut)
Large seeds
Hardy deciduous tree
Height up to 30m (100ft)
Green-yellow male flowers borne in catkins. Female flowers of the same colour stand upright in twos or threes
Catkins appear in early spring and summer
Rounded green fruit containing a crinkled nut with an edible kernel
The mid-green leaf is usually divided into seven leaflets

In autumn clean off the green husk and sow the nuts immediately into pots using standard loam-based seed compost (substrate). Cover with coarse grit and place outside exposed to all weathers (see 'Breaking seed Dormancy', page 233, for more information). Germination occurs when the temperature reaches a constant 10°C (50°F). Grow on for 2 seasons before planting out.

Juniperus *Cupressaceae*

A genus of hardy evergreen conifers. Plant in a well-draining soil in a sunny position.

Juniperus communis (Juniper)
Medium seeds
Hardy evergreen tree
Height 6m (20ft)
Small male (yellow) and female (green) flowers grow on separate trees. Berries form on the female tree, green in the first year ripening to dark purple in the second and third year
The leaves are spikey blue-green needles

This is not the easiest tree to grow from seed. Firstly you need to have a male and female tree to have viable seed, and secondly germination can take 2–5 years.

In autumn collect the mature, ripe fruit. Remove the seed and sow thinly into pots, using standard loam-based seed compost (substrate). Cover with coarse grit. Then place outside exposed to all weathers (see 'Breaking Seed Dormancy', page 233, for more information). Germination can take 2–5 years. Do not allow the container to dry out in summer. Plant into growing position 2 years after germination.

Laburnum *Papilionaceae*

A genus of hardy deciduous trees with a profusion of pendent flowers. Plant in a sunny position, avoiding waterlogged soil.

Laburnum anagyroides (Common laburnum, Golden chain)
Medium seeds (TOXIC SEEDS)
Hardy deciduous tree
Clusters of yellow, sweet-scented, pea-like, poisonous flowers hanging in long chains, followed in autumn by long brown pods which contain poisonous black seeds
Flowers in late spring
The leaves have three oval leaflets

Before sowing, gently rub the hard-coated seeds with sandpaper, then soak for 48 hours in hot, not boiling, water. Sow seeds in late autumn or early spring into pots, using standard loam-based seed compost (substrate). Cover with vermiculite or compost and place under protection at 15°C (60°F). Germination takes 12–15 weeks. Grow on for 2 seasons before planting out.

***Recipe for sowing, planting and growing* Laburnum anagyroides**

If you have ever walked through a laburnum walk, surrounded by the cascades of yellow, sweet-smelling flowers, you will understand why this recipe is included.

Ingredients
3 seeds per pot
Sandpaper
Small china bowl or kitchen paper
Warm water
1 x 13cm (5in) pot
Standard soil-less seed compost (substrate), either a peat free proprietary brand or composted fine propagating bark
Fine-grade perlite (wetted) or vermiculite
White plastic label

Method Before sowing the seeds in autumn or early spring, scarify them by rubbing gently on sandpaper, thereby allowing the water to penetrate more easily. Then soak the seeds for 2 days in hot water prior to sowing. Fill the pots with compost, smooth over, tap down and water in well. Put 3 pre-soaked and scarified seeds equally spaced on the surface of the compost in each pot. Gently press the seeds into the compost. Cover the seeds with fine-grade perlite (wetted) or vermiculite and label with the plant name and date. Place the pot in a cool light place out of direct sunlight at an optimum temperature of 15°C (60°F). Germination takes 12–15 weeks. Once the seed has germinated place the containers in a cold frame or unheated glasshouse. When the seedlings are large enough, divide them to 1 seedling per pot using a soil-based potting compost. Grow on in a cold frame for a further 18 months before planting out in their permanent growing position.

Larix *Pinaceae*

A genus of hardy deciduous conifer. Plant in a well-drained soil in a sunny situation.

Larix decidua AGM (Larch, European larch)
Medium seeds
Hardy deciduous tree
Height 38m (125ft)
Male flowers are yellow and globe-shaped. Female flowers are loganberry-red with green stripes. Cones are small and oval
Flowers in spring
Light green needle-like aromatic leaves

Collect seed in autumn from mature cones, mix the seed with damp vermiculite, place in a refrigerator for 3 weeks, then sow into pots or modules using standard loam-based seed compost (substrate). Cover with vermiculite or compost and place under protection at 15°C (60°F). Germination takes 4–12 weeks. Overwinter young plants under protection for first year then plant out. Young plants are prone to frost damage.

Magnolia *Magnoliaceae*

A genus of hardy deciduous, semi-evergreen or evergreen trees and shrubs grown for their showy flowers. Plant in a fertile well-drained soil in a sheltered sunny or semi-shaded site.

Magnolia campbellii subsp. *mollicomata*
Medium seeds
Hardy deciduous tree
Height up to 18m (54ft)
Lovely deep pink buds which develop into lilac-pink slightly scented flowers
Flowers from late winter until late spring on a tree of 10 years or older
Fruit is cone-like on stubby stalks and appears in early autumn
Pointed, oval mid-green leaves develop after the flower

Pick a fresh cone in late autumn, dry in a light airy place until the fleshy fruit falls away, soak the fruits in some warm liquid detergent for 2 days. Remove all the flesh and dry the seeds. Mix the seed with some damp vermiculite, place in a plastic bag and refrigerate for 2 months. In early spring sow the chilled, clean seed into pots or modules using standard loam-based seed compost (substrate). Cover with vermiculite or compost and place under protection at 20°C (68°F). Germination takes 5–7 weeks. Overwinter young plants under protection for 2–3 years prior to planting out. Young plants are prone to frost damage. These plants will not flower for 10–15 years.

Malus *Rosaceae*

A genus of hardy deciduous trees grown for their flowers, foliage and fruits. Plant in all but waterlogged soil in sun or partial shade.

Larix decidua

Malus sylvestris **(Crab apple, Wild crab apple)**
Medium seeds
Hardy deciduous tree
Height up to 9m (30ft)
Pretty cup-shaped pale pink flowers followed by small bitter hard fruit, which makes good jelly, jam and wine
Flowers in spring
Pointed oval leaves with smooth undersides
This wild crab apple is the ancestor of modern cultivated apples

In autumn collect the seed from the centre of the fruit, either sow immediately or store the seeds mixed with some damp vermiculite in the fridge for sowing in late winter.

Sow the fresh seed in autumn, or chilled seed in late winter, thinly into pots, using standard loam-based seed compost (substrate). Cover with coarse grit. Put outside exposed to all weathers (see 'Breaking Seed Dormancy', page 233, for more information). Germination takes 3–6 months. Grow on as a container plant for 2 years before planting out.

Persea *Lauraceae*

A genus of tropical evergreen shrubs and trees. Plant in a humus-rich soil in a sunny situation. In cool climates grow as a container plant.

Persea americana **(Avocado pear)**
Very large seeds
Tender evergreen tree
Height up to 18m (60ft)
Small, green flowers develop into pear-shaped, skinned fruit, ripening from green to brown. Rarely fruits when grown as a container plant
Flowers in spring
Large leathery dark green oval leaves

You can use the fruit from avocados purchased from the supermarket in summer. Soak healthy, undamaged seed in hot water, not boiling, for one hour. Insert 3 cocktail sticks into the seed. Fill a glass with water and suspend the seed on its sticks over the water, point-end up, making sure that the flat end is just touching the water not submerged. Place the seed and container in a warm light place. Top up water as necessary. Germination takes approximately 4 weeks. When there are 2 small roots, pot up into a soil-based compost (substrate). Place the container in a warm light environment to grow on at 15°C (60°F).

Picea *Pinaceae*

A genus of hardy evergreen conifers. Plant in a sunny situation, avoiding waterlogged soil.

Picea abies **(Common spruce, Norway spruce, Christmas tree)**
Medium seeds
Hardy evergreen tree
Height up to 40m (130ft)
Yellow male flowers grow in clusters at the end of the shoots and open in late spring. Female flowers are pink, the cones ripening in autumn
The leaves are light green prickly needles

Collect seed in autumn from mature cones, mix the seed with damp vermiculite, place in a refrigerator. In spring sow seed into pots or modules, using standard loam-based seed compost (substrate) mixed with coarse horticultural sand. Mix to a ratio of 1 part compost + 1 part sand. Cover with coarse grit and place in a cold frame. Germination takes 1–4 months, however it can take longer. Transplant seedlings, which are very slow growing, in their second season. Plant into growing position 3 years after germination.

Pinus *Pinaceae*

A genus of hardy evergreen conifers. Plant in a sunny situation, avoiding waterlogged sites.

Pinus sylvestris AGM **(Scots pine)**
Medium seeds
Hardy evergreen perennial
Yellow male flowers grow at the base of the shoot in clusters.
Crimson female flowers are carried in pairs at the end of the current year's shoot
Small oval cones start green and ripen to dark brown
Long aromatic green needles

Collect seed in autumn from 2-year-old cones. Mix the seed with damp vermiculite and place in a refrigerator for 3 weeks. Sow into pots or modules using standard loam-based seed compost (substrate) mixed with coarse horticultural sand. Mix to a ratio of 1 part compost + 1 part sand. Cover with vermiculite or compost and place under protection at 15°C (60°F). Germination takes 4–12 weeks. Overwinter young plants in a cold frame. Plant into growing position 3 years after germination.

***Recipe for sowing, planting and growing* Pinus sylvestris**
Conifers differ from other trees because they produce seeds exposed or uncovered on the scales of fruits. The fir cone, which houses the seeds, takes time to develop. Young cones are nearer the tip of the branch; more mature ones develop further in. If you look carefully, it is quite easy to age them using this method, they also change from green to brown in most cases.

Ingredients
1 plastic bag
Seeds
Damp vermiculite
1 waterproof pen
1 tie
5 seeds per module or 8 seeds per pot
1 module tray
OR
1 x 8cm (4 in) pot
Standard loam-based seed compost (substrate) mixed with coarse horticultural sand to a ratio of 1 part compost + 1 part sand
Pre-wetted vermiculite
White plastic label

Method **In autumn collect the seeds from ripe (2-year-old) cones. Mix the seed with a handful of damp vermiculite and place this mixture into a plastic bag. Seal the bag and label using the waterproof pen. Place the bag into a refrigerator for 3 weeks. In late autumn or**

early winter, fill the tray or pot with compost, smooth over, tap down and water in well. Sow the chilled seeds mixed with the vermiculite (you do not need to clean the old vermiculite off) thinly. Sow on to the surface of the compost. Press gently into the compost with the flat of the hand. Cover the seed with more vermiculite. Label with the plant name and date. Place the container in a warm light place out of direct sunlight at an optimum temperature of 15°C (60°F). Germination takes 4–12 weeks. Winter the young seedlings in a cold frame. When the seedlings are strong enough (they are very slow growing) divide them and repot individually using the same size pot. Grow on outside for a further 2 years before planting out into their final growing position.

Populus *Salicaceae*

A genus of hardy deciduous trees, popular for their rapid growth rate. The western balsam poplar, for example, can grow up to 1.8m (6ft) in a year. Plant in a fertile, moist soil (not waterlogged and not dry in summer) in a sunny position.

Populus trichocarpa (Western balsam poplar, Black cottonwood)
Small seeds
Hardy deciduous tree
Height up to 33m (110ft)
The male flowers appear in dull crimson catkins. On a separate tree, the female catkins are long and pale green and develop fluffy seeds that are dispersed in late spring
Male flowers in early spring
Leaves are triangular, green and greyish-white underneath. They grow from sticky buds which have a strong sweet smell

Collect the fluffy seeds in late spring early summer, there is no need to clean them. Sow into pots using standard loam-based seed compost (substrate). Cover with sharp grit and place under protection at 10°C (50°F). Germination takes 4–7 days. Overwinter young plants in a cold frame. Plant out 18 months after germination.

Prunus *Rosaceae*

A genus of hardy evergreen and deciduous trees and shrubs, grown for their flowers, fruit, bark and autumn colours. Plant in any but waterlogged soil in a sunny situation.

Prunus avium AGM (Wild cherry)
Medium seeds
Hardy deciduous tree
Height up to 12m (40ft)
Lovely white flowers appear before the leaves. They are followed by bright red cherries in mid-summer
Flowers in spring
Long, oval, pointed leaves turn orange and crimson in autumn

In summer collect the cherries and remove the flesh. Mix the seed with damp vermiculite, place in a plastic bag and put in the refrigerator for a minimum of 4 weeks. Sow the chilled seeds individually into modules or well spaced in pots, using standard loam-based seed compost (substrate). Cover with sharp grit and place in a cold frame. Germination takes 2–4 months. Grow on in the cold frame. Plant into growing position 2 years after germination.

Prunus dulcis (Almond)
Medium-large seeds
Hardy deciduous tree
Height up to 9m (30ft)
Lovely pink flowers appear before the leaves and are followed by green fruit in late summer. Almonds are stone fruits, not nuts
Flowers in spring
Lance-shaped, mid-green leaves

In autumn, collect the almonds when they fall. Remove the soft husks and mix the seed with damp vermiculite. Place in a plastic bag and put in the refrigerator for a minimum of 4 weeks. If you have the space, the seeds can stay there until the spring. Sow the chilled seeds individually into large modules or well spaced in pots, using standard loam-based seed compost (substrate). Cover with sharp grit and place in a cold frame. Germination takes 2–4 months. Grow on in the cold frame. Plant into growing position 2 years after germination.

Pyrus *Rosaceae*

A genus of hardy deciduous trees, grown for their flowers and edible fruit. Plant in a well-drained fertile soil in a sunny position.

Pyrus communis (Common pear)
Medium seeds
Hardy deciduous tree
Height up to 15m (50ft)
White flowers followed by fruits which ripen from yellow/green to brown in early autumn
Flowers in spring
The oval leaves are dark glossy green

In autumn collect the seed from the centre of the fruit, either sow immediately or store the seeds mixed with some damp vermiculite in the fridge. Sow the fresh seed in autumn or chilled seed in late winter and sow thinly into pots, using standard loam-based seed compost (substrate). Cover with coarse grit, then place outside exposed to all weathers (see 'Breaking Seed Dormancy', page 233, for more information). Germination takes 3–6 months. Grow on as a container plant for 2 years before planting out.

Quercus *Fagaceae*

A genus of hardy evergreen or deciduous trees and shrubs. Plant in a deep, well-drained soil in sun or partial shade.

Quercus robur AGM (Common oak)
Large seeds
Hardy deciduous tree
Height up to 35m (115ft)
Male greeny-yellow flowers hang in slim catkins; the females are small pale green flowers that occur at the tips of the shoot. These develop into the acorns, which start green and ripen to pale brown
Catkins in spring
The mid-green leaves are stalkless and lobed

Quercus robur

Collect the fresh acorns in early autumn as they fall. Check that they have no holes. Sow directly into deep, 3cm (1in) pots, using standard loam-based seed compost (substrate). Place the pots outside, exposed to all weathers (see 'Breaking Seed Dormancy', page 233, for more information). Germination takes 3–6 months. Grow on as a container plant for 2 years before planting out. Protect containers from being raided by rodents.

Robinia *Papilionaceae*

A genus of hardy deciduous trees and shrubs, grown for their attractive pea-like flowers. Plant in any free-draining soil in a sunny position.

Robinia pseudoacacia **(Locust tree or False acacia)**
Medium seeds
Hardy deciduous tree
Height up to 25m (83ft)
Scented clusters of pea-like white/mauve flowers followed by brown seed pods with black kidney-shaped seeds
Flowers from late spring to early summer
Oval leaves divided into leaflets

Before sowing, gently rub the hard-coated seeds with sandpaper, then soak for 48 hours in hot, not boiling, water. Sow seeds in late autumn or early spring into pots or modules using standard loam-based seed compost (substrate). Cover with vermiculite or compost and place under protection at 15°C (60°F). Germination takes 12–15 weeks. Grow on for 2 seasons before planting out.

Salix *Salicaceae*

A genus of hardy deciduous trees and shrubs grown for their foliage and catkins. Plant in all but very dry soils in a sunny situation.

Salix caprea (Pussy willow, Goat willow)
Small seeds
Hardy deciduous tree/shrub
Height up to 15m (50ft)
Male catkins are silky-grey, turning yellow when ripe with pollen
Female catkins, born on a separate tree, are pale green turning silver as the woolly seed develops
Catkins in spring
Leaves are oval, mid-green, slightly woolly on the underside

Collect the fluffy seeds in late spring early summer, there is no need to clean them. Sow into pots using standard loam-based seed compost (substrate). Cover with sharp grit and place under protection at 10°C (50°F). Germination takes 4–7 days. Overwinter young plants in a cold frame. Plant out 18 months after germination.

***Recipe for sowing, planting and growing* Salix caprea**
Pussy willow, with its silver, silky catkins, is a lovely herald of spring. This tree looks most graceful growing in a hedgerow.

Ingredients
6 seeds per module or 10 seeds per pot
1 module tray
OR
1 x 8cm (4in) pot
Standard loam-based seed compost (substrate)
Sharp grit
White plastic plant label
Waterproof pen

Method Collect the fluffy seeds in early summer, gently separate them, there is no need to clean them. Fill the modules or pot with compost, smooth over, tap down and water in well. Sow the seeds thinly on to the surface of the compost. Press gently into the compost with the flat of the hand. Cover lightly with sharp grit and label with the plant name and date. Place the pot in a warm light place out of direct sunlight at an optimum temperature of 10°C (50°F). Keep watering to a minimum until germination has taken place, which takes 4–7 days in warmth. Overwinter the seedlings in a cold frame. In the following spring divide the seedlings and repot individually into 8cm (4in) pots. Grow on in these pots and plant out in the following spring.

Sorbus *Rosaceae*

A genus of hardy deciduous trees and shrubs grown for their attractive fruits. Plant in any sunny or partially- shaded site, as long as the soil does not dry out in summer and is not waterlogged.

Sorbus aucuparia (Mountain ash, Rowan tree)
Medium seeds
Hardy deciduous tree
Height up to 20m (65ft)
Attractive clusters of creamy-white flowers followed by lovely clusters of red berries in autumn
Flowers in late spring
The mid-green leaves are oval and divided into lots of pairs of leaflets

Collect the seeds from the berries (2–8 seeds per berry) in late summer while the berries are still green. Mix the cleaned seed with damp vermiculite, place in a plastic bag, put in the refrigerator for 8 weeks then sow immediately into pots or modules using standard loam-based seed compost (substrate). Cover with vermiculite or perlite, then place under protection at 15°C (60°F). Germination takes 1–4 weeks. Overwinter young plants under protection. Transplant individually in the spring, plant out in the following autumn.

Tilia *Tiliaceae*

A genus of hardy, deciduous trees grown for their fragrant small flowers. Plant in a well-drained fertile soil in sun or partial shade.

Tilia x europaea (Common lime, Linden)
Medium seeds
Hardy deciduous tree
Height up to 40m (130ft)
Small clusters of greenish-yellow, sweet-smelling flowers, followed by small hanging fruits which ripen to pale brown
Flowers in summer
Heart-shaped mid-green leaves

Collect the seeds in early autumn while they are still green, and sow immediately into pots or modules, using standard loam-based seed compost (substrate) mixed with coarse horticultural sand to a ratio of 1 part compost + 1 part sand. Cover with coarse grit and place in a cold frame. Germination takes up to 3 months. If germination has not occurred during this period it is worth moving the container outside, exposed to all weathers. Plant into growing position 2 years after germination.

Ulmus *Ulmaceae*

A genus of hardy deciduous trees, grown for their foliage. Plant in a fertile well-drained soil in a sunny situation.

Ulmus glabra (Wych elm)
Medium seeds
Hardy deciduous tree
Height up to 30m (100ft)
The small clusters of purplish flowers appear before the leaves, then turn into clusters of winged fruits which fall in summer
Flowers in early spring
The green leaves are oval and pointed

Sow in early autumn into pots or modules using standard loam-based seed compost. Cover with coarse grit and then place outside exposed to all weathers (see Breaking Seed Dormancy, page 233, for more information). Germination takes 3–6 months. Grow on as a container plant for 2 years before planting out.

vegetables, fruit & salads

There is nothing to beat home-grown vegetables. The information contained in this section has been either tried and tested on my herb farm, gleaned from fellow enthusiasts or from experts like Jim of D.T. Browns. Vegetable seed-counts in this chapter are only approximate, because exact counts depend on variety.

The most important element of a successful vegetable garden is the soil, and it must be correctly fed. In the majority of cases vegetables need a soil that is free draining, rather than waterlogged, but does not dry out in summer. Where relevant, I have given an optimum growing temperature to act as a general guide. With this information to hand, your crops are sure to be successful.

Rheum rhaponticum, *see page 224*

Abelmoschus *Malvaceae*

Plant in a rich, open soil. In any but a hot climate, okra must be grown under glass or polythene to maintain a high humidity. It should be grown directly in the ground as the roots do not like being confined to a pot.

Abelmoschus esculentus (Hibiscus esculentus) 'Clemson Spineless'
(Okra, Ladies fingers, Gumbo)
Medium seeds: 18 per gram
Half-hardy annual
Height up to 1.2m (4ft)
Yellow flowers with crimson centres
Heart-shaped, lobed, toothed leaves
Optimum growing temperature 15–24°C (60–75°F)

Soak seed for 24 hours prior to sowing in early spring, discarding any floating seeds. Sow into pots or modules using standard soil-less seed compost (substrate), either a peat free proprietary brand or composted fine propagating bark. Cover with perlite or vermiculite, and place under protection at 20°C (68°F). Germination takes 5–10 days. When the seedlings are large enough to handle, plant out into a greenhouse bed 20cm (8in) apart.
OR
Sow seeds under cover in late spring into prepared open ground, when the air temperature does not go below 15°C (60°F) at night. Germination takes 2–3 weeks. Thin seedlings to 20cm (8in) apart. Harvest at 8–11 weeks.

Allium *Alliaceae*

Plant in a rich soil that has been well fed with well-rotted manure the previous autumn. It is worth letting a few plants of each species run to flower so that you can collect the seed in early autumn.

Allium cepa **(Onion)**
Medium seeds: 300 per gram
Hardy annual
Height approx 60cm (24in)
Optimum growing temperature 15–24°C (60–75°F)

Allium porrum **(Leek)**
Medium seeds: 280 per gram
Hardy biennial
Height approx 80cm (32in)
Optimum growing temperature 10–15°C (50–60°F)

Sow seeds from late winter to early spring into pots or modules, using standard soil-less seed compost (substrate), either a peat free proprietary brand or composted fine propagating bark. Cover with perlite or vermiculite, place under protection at 20°C (68°F). Germination takes 5–10 days.
OR
Sow seeds in late spring into prepared open ground, when the air temperature does not go below 13°C (55°F) at night. Germination takes 2–3 weeks. Thin seedlings to 5cm–10cm apart, depending on size of allium bulb.

Amaranthus *Amaranthaceae*

This is a vast group of plants which are largely native to warm climates and need protecting from frost in cooler climates. The leaves of all the amaranths are edible and the seeds can be harvested for grain, but some are better suited to one of these purposes. All prefer to be planted in well-drained soil in sun or partial shade.

Amaranthus giganticus **(Edible amaranth, Leafy amaranth)**
Small seeds: 1,300 per gram
Half-hardy annual
Height 30–60cm (12–24in)
Oval to heart-shaped, mid-green leaves

Sow seeds in early spring into pots or modules, using standard soil-less seed compost (substrate), either a peat free proprietary brand or composted fine propagating bark. Cover with perlite or vermiculite, place under protection at 20°C (68°F). Germination takes 5–10 days. Plant out 20cm (8in) apart when all threat of frost has passed.

Apium *Apiaceae*

Plant in a deep rich moist soil that has been mulched with well-rotted manure the previous autumn. Do not be tempted to use celery seed that has been bought for culinary use as it will not germinate.

Apium graveolens **(Celery)**
Small seeds: 2,400 per gram
Hardy biennial
Height 60–90cm (2–3ft)
Optimum growing temperature 15–21°C (60–70°F)

Sow seeds in early spring into pots or modules using standard soil-less seed compost (substrate), either a peat free proprietary brand or composted fine propagating bark. Cover with perlite or vermiculite, place under protection at 15°C (60°F). Germination takes 2–3 weeks. Plant out 38cm (15in) apart after all threat of frost has passed.
OR
Sow seeds in late spring into prepared open ground, when the air temperature does not go below 13°C (55°F) at night, as seedlings may bolt if temperature falls below 10°C (50°F). Germination takes 3–5 weeks. Thin out seedlings to 38cm (15cm) apart.

Grow self-blanching varieties in blocks 23cm (9in) square to encourage the stems to blanch naturally.

Apium graveolens var. *rapaceum* **(Celeriac, Turnip-rooted celery)**
Small seeds: 2,500 per gram
Hardy biennial
Height 30cm (1ft)
Optimum growing temperature 10–21°C (50–70°F)

Sow seeds in early spring into pots or modules using standard soil-less seed compost (substrate), either a peat free proprietary brand or composted fine propagating bark. Cover with perlite or vermiculite, place under protection at 18°C (65°F). Germination takes 3–4 weeks. Plant out 30cm (12in) apart in early summer, when all threat of frost has passed and the seedlings have been hardened off. Make sure that the little bulbous swellings at the bases of the plants stay at soil level. They must not be buried. Harvest in the autumn.

Allium porrum

Asparagus *Asparagaceae*

Plant in raised beds made up of free-draining soil and well fed with plenty of organic manure, in sun or partial shade.

Asparagus officinalis **(Asparagus)**
Medium seeds: 50 per gram
Hardy perennial with separate male and female plants
Height 1.5m (5ft)
Optimum growing temperature 15–21°C (60–70°F)

Sow the seeds in early spring into pots or modules using standard soil-less seed compost (substrate), either a peat free proprietary brand or composted fine propagating bark. Before sowing the seed soak them for 24 hours in warm water. Cover with perlite or vermiculite and place under protection at 15°C (60°F). Germination takes 2–4 weeks. Pot up seedlings in 8cm (3in) pots and place outside for the growing season. Move to the cold frame for the winter. In the following spring, plant the seedlings into their permanent beds 30cm (12in) apart. Harvest after 2 years.

OR

Sow the seeds in late spring into prepared open ground, 2. 5cm (1in) deep, 8cm (3in) apart, when the air temperature does not go below 13°C (55°F) at night. Before sowing the seeds, soak them for 24 hours in warm water. Germination takes 3–5 weeks

The following spring, lift the plants and replant into their final growing positions 30cm (12in) apart. Harvest after 2 years.

Asparagus officinalis

***Recipe for sowing, planting and growing* Asparagus officinalis**

Asparagus is a wonderful vegetable if you have the space to set aside a permanent area, patience during the first three years, then enough will power to curb your greed so that you do not eat the asparagus bed to death. When the plants are 5 years old, a couple of flourishing plants should provide one person with one helping each week for six weeks of cutting.

Ingredients

2 seeds per pot
Small china bowl
Warm water
1 module tray
OR
1 x 8cm (4in) pot
Standard soil-less seed compost (substrate), either a peat free proprietary brand or composted fine propagating bark
Perlite fine-grade (wetted) or vermiculite
White plastic plant label
OR
Prepared site in the garden
2 white plastic plant labels

Method In spring, fill a china bowl with warm water, add the seeds and soak for 24 hours. Fill the modules or pots with compost, smooth over, tap down and water in well. Place 1 seed in each module or 2 seeds in each pot, equally spaced on the surface of the compost. Cover with fine-grade perlite (wetted) or vermiculite and label with the plant's name and the date. Place the pot in a warm, light place out of direct sunlight at an optimum temperature of 15°C (60°F). Keep watering to a minimum until germination has taken place, which takes 2–4 weeks. If grown in modules, pot up into 8cm (4in) pots as soon as the seedlings are big enough to handle. Keep the young plants under protection until well rooted and then place outside in pots for the growing season. In late autumn move the pots to a cold frame for the winter. The following spring, when you can see the new buds appearing, plant out into a well-prepared bed which has been fed in the previous autumn with well-rotted manure or compost. Plant 30cm (12in) apart.

OR

Sow directly into a prepared site in the garden when the night-time temperature does not fall below 13°C (55°F). Space the seeds 8cm (3in) apart in a drill 2. 5cm (1in) deep. Cover lightly with soil and water in well. Label either end of the seed row. Germination takes 3–5 weeks.

In the autumn prepare the area with well-rotted manure or compost. After the last frosts of spring, when the young buds are just developing, lift the plants from the growing area, being careful not to damage the roots too much, and replant in the permanent bed 30cm (12in) apart. Mulch after replanting to retain moisture and cover the bud tips with 5cm (2in) of loose soil to stop them drying out.

Atriplex *Chenopodiaceae*

This decorative vegetable has tiny, reddish flowers in summer and red or purple triangular leaves. Plant in a rich, moisture-retentive soil in sun or partial shade.

Atriplex hortensis var. *rubra* **(Red orach, Mountain spinach)**
Medium seeds: 400 per gram
Hardy annual
Height 1.2m (4ft)
Optimum growing temperature 15–18°C (60–65°F)

If the seed is missing its outer, papery bract it will be infertile, so discard. Sow in late spring into prepared, open ground when the air temperature does not go below 13°C (55°F) at night. Germination takes 1–3 weeks. Thin the seedlings to 20–30cm (8–12in) apart. This plant is prone to bolting in hot weather, and it can be invasive if allowed to self seed.

Beta *Chenopodiaceae*

Plant in a deep, rich, moist soil that has been mulched with well-rotted manure the previous autumn.

Beta vulgaris subsp. *rubra* **(Beetroot)**
Medium seeds: 60 per gram
Hardy biennial grown as an annual
Height 27–38cm (11–15in)
Optimum growing temperature 15–18°C (60–65°F)

Sow seeds in early spring into pots or modules using standard soil-less seed compost (substrate), either a peat free proprietary brand or composted fine propagating bark. Before sowing, place the seeds in a sieve and rinse thoroughly under cold running water. This removes the chemicals that inhibit germination, so sow immediately and afterwards cover with perlite or vermiculite. Place under protection at 15°C (60°F). Germination takes 7–10 days.

OR

Sow rinsed seed in late spring into prepared ground, when the soil temperature is above 7°C (45°F) Sow seeds 20cm (8in) apart in drills that are 30cm (12in) apart. Germination takes 2–3 weeks. Once growing in the ground, it should be ready to harvest in about 6–12 weeks.

Beta vulgaris subsp. *cicla* **(Chard)**
Medium seeds: 60 per gram
Hardy biennial
Height 45cm (18in)
Optimum growing temperature 15–18°C (60–65°F)

To get the best crop from this vegetable, it is worth sowing directly into a prepared site after mid-spring, and then keeping it well watered. Early autumn sowings tend to go to seed by late spring, and even earlier if it gets too warm too quickly.

Sow seeds in late spring into prepared open ground, when the soil temperature is above 7°C (45°F). Sow 3 seeds together, 1cm (1/2in) deep, every 38cm (15in), in drills 45cm (18in) apart. Thin the seedlings when large enough. Germination takes 2–3 weeks. A repeat sowing can be made in summer. Given protection in winter, summer-sown seeds will crop in the early spring. If you live in a cold climate you can start the seeds under protection to get a head start on the season. Sow seeds in early spring into pots of modules using standard soil-less seed compost (substrate), either a peat free proprietary brand or composted fine propagating bark. Cover with perlite or vermiculite and place under protection at 15°C (60°F). Germination takes 4–8 days. Plant out when threat of frost has passed.

Brassica *Brassicaceae*

All brassicas like to feed well, although Brussels sprouts need more feeding than cabbages and cauliflowers are positively greedy. However, do not become too enthusiastic and give them too much nitrogen, because this will promote soft growth and make the plants unable to survive the winter. Try to prepare your permanent beds the autumn before planting out, giving the site a good feed of well-rotted manure and compost. Traditionally, brassicas were all started off in outdoor seedbeds and then transplanted into permanent beds for growing on. However, if you live in a small garden and space is a luxury, you can sow into large modules outside and then transplant these into the garden.

Brassica oleracea Botrytis Group **(Cauliflower)**
Medium seeds: 325 per gram
Hardy biennial
Height winter cauliflower 60cm (24in), summer cauliflower 45cm (18in)
Optimum growing temperature 7–21°C (45–70°F)

Cauliflower can be sown throughout the growing season, it is vital to choose the correct cultivar for the required cropping season. Consult current seed catalogues for the optimum sowing time for each variety.

In general, sow in late winter to early spring in pots or modules using standard soil-less seed compost (substrate), either a peat free proprietary brand or composted fine propagating bark. Cover with perlite or vermiculite and place under protection at 20°C (68°F). Germination takes 6–10 days. Transplant in mid-spring or early summer to a permanent growing area. The distance between plants depends on the variety. Harvest approximately 16–35 weeks later.
OR
Sow in late spring to early summer in pots or modules using standard soil-less seed compost (substrate), either a peat free proprietary brand or composted fine propagating bark, or into a seedbed. Cover with perlite or vermiculite. Place containers outside on a hard standing. Germination takes 6–10 days. Transplant in midsummer to a permanent growing area at a distance of 60cm (2ft) apart. Harvest approximately 40 weeks later
OR
Sow seeds in late spring to early summer into prepared open ground, when the air temperature does not go below 10°C (50°F) at night. Germination takes 2–3 weeks. Thin seedlings to 60cm (2ft) apart.

Brassica oleracea var. *capitata* **(Cabbage)**
Medium seeds: 325 per gram
Hardy biennial grown as an annual
Height spring cabbage 25–30cm (10–12in), summer cabbage 30–40cm (12–16in), winter cabbage 40cm (16in)
Optimum growing temperature 15–18°C (60–65°F)

Cabbage can be sown throughout the growing season; it is vital to choose the correct cultivar for the required cropping season. Consult current seed catalogues for the optimum sowing time for each variety.

Sow in late winter to early spring in pots or modules using standard soil-less seed compost (substrate), either a peat free proprietary brand or composted fine propagating bark. Cover with perlite or vermiculite and place under protection at 20°C (68°F). Germination takes 6–10 days. Plant out after a period of hardening off 38cm (15in) apart.
OR
Sow in late spring to early summer in pots or modules using standard soil-less seed compost (substrate), either a peat free proprietary brand or composted fine propagating bark. Cover with perlite or vermiculite and place outside on a hard surface. Germination takes 6–10 days. Plant out at a distance of 38cm (15in) apart.
OR
Sow seeds in late spring to early summer into prepared, open ground, when the air temperature does not go below 10°C (50°F) at night. Germination takes 2–3 weeks. Thin seedlings to 38cm (15in) apart. Do not allow seedlings to dry out during hot spells.

Brassica oleracea Gemmifera Group **(Brussels sprouts)**
Medium seeds: 325 per gram
Hardy biennial grown as an annual
Height 1m (3½ft)
Optimum growing temperature 7–21°C (45–70°F)

Brussels sprouts must have a fertile soil, however it is better if the soil has been well manured for a previous crop because they need a firm soil in which to anchor themselves. Dig the site as early as possible to allow the soil to settle.

Sow in early to late spring in pots or modules using standard soil-less seed compost (substrate), either a peat free proprietary brand or composted fine propagating bark. Cover with perlite or vermiculite and place under protection at 20°C (68°F). Germination takes 6–10 days. Plant out after a period of hardening off 45–60 (18–24in) apart, depending on variety.
OR
Sow seeds in late spring to early summer into prepared open ground, when the air temperature does not go below 10°C (50°F) at night. Germination takes 2–3 weeks. Thin seedlings to a distance of 45–60 (18–24in) apart, depending on variety.

***Recipe for sowing, planting and growing* Brassica oleracea Gemmifera Group**
Brussels sprouts are one of the great vegetables of autumn and winter if picked at the right moment, when they are small and firm. For the best flavour, do not over cook.
Ingredients
3 seeds per module or 7 seeds per pot
1 module tray
OR
1 x 8cm (4in) pot
Standard soil-less seed compost (substrate), either a peat free proprietary brand or composted fine propagating bark
Fine-grade perlite (wetted) or vermiculite
White plastic plant label
OR
A prepared site in the garden

Method **Fill the modules or pots with compost, smooth over, tap down and water in well. Place 3 seed per module or 5 seeds per pot equally spaced on the surface of the compost. Press gently into the compost with the flat of the hand. Cover the seeds with fine-grade perlite (wetted) or vermiculite and label with the plant name and date. Place the pot in a warm light place out of direct sunlight at an optimum temperature of 20°C (68°F). Restrict watering to a minimum until**

germination has taken place, after 6–10 days. The seedlings will be ready to plant out or pot up approximately 2–3 weeks after germination. Plant out after a period of hardening off 45–60cm (18–24in) apart, depending on variety, into their permanent growing position. Firm the young plants in well and protect from birds as they love sprouts.
OR
Sow directly into a prepared site in the garden when the night-time temperature does not fall below 10°C (50°F). Sow the seeds thinly approximately 8cm (3in) apart in a drill 2.5cm (1in) deep. Lightly cover with soil and water in well. Label either end of the seed row. Germination takes 2–3 weeks. Thin seedlings to a distance of 45–60cm (18–24in) apart depending on variety. Protect young plants from bird damage. In summer replant the seedlings into a well-firmed bed 60–90cm (24–36in) apart, depending on the variety, and thin for a second time. Firm the soil around each plant. Firming the plants helps produce tight, firm sprouts.

Brassica oleracea Gonglodes Group **(Kohlrabi)**
Medium seeds: 320 per gram
Hardy biennial grown as an annual
Height 30cm (12in)

Kohlrabi is a cabbage with a swollen stem. It looks like the root of a turnip growing out of the ground. It can be grown in counties where the summers are hot and dry as it is drought tolerant, which is totally unlike its cousin the turnip. Plant in a light soil that has been well fed with rotted manure or compost before sowing.

Sow seeds in early spring into pots or modules using standard soil-less seed compost (substrate), either a peat free proprietary brand or composted fine propagating bark. Cover with perlite or vermiculite and place either under protection at 10°C (50°F) or outside if the night-time temperature does not fall below 7°C (45°F). Germination takes 1–2 weeks. Protect seedlings from frost. Plant out after a period of hardening off 25cm (10in) apart.
OR
Sow seeds in late spring into prepared open ground, when the air temperature does not go below 10°C (50°F) at night, in rows 30cm (12in) apart. Germination takes 2–3 weeks. Thin seedlings to a distance of 25cm (10in) apart.

Brassica oleracea Italica Group **(Broccoli, Calabrese)**
Medium seeds: 325 per gram
Hardy biennial grown as an annual
Height 60cm (24in)

Broccoli can be sown throughout the growing season; it is vital to choose the correct cultivar for the required cropping season.

Calabrese hate being transplanted. For an early crop sow 2–3 seeds in early spring into pots or modules, using standard soil-less seed compost (substrate), either a peat free proprietary brand or composted fine propagating bark. Cover with perlite or vermiculite. Place either under protection at 10°C (50°F), or outside if the night-time temperature does not fall below 7°C (45°F). Germination takes 1–2 weeks. Protect seedlings from frost. From late spring, after a period of hardening off, plant out 30–45cm (12–18in) apart.

OR
For later crops, sow seeds in late spring or early summer into prepared, open ground in rows 30cm (12in) apart, when the air temperature does not go below 10°C (50°F) at night. Germination takes 2–3 weeks. Thin seedlings to 30–45cm (12–18in) apart, depending on variety.

Brassica oleracea Italica Group **(Sprouting broccoli)**
Medium seeds: 250 per gram
Hardy short-lived perennial
Height 1m ($3^{1}/_{2}$ft)

Sow seeds in early spring into pots or modules using standard soil-less seed compost (substrate), either a peat free proprietary brand or composted fine propagating bark. Cover with perlite or vermiculite. Place either under protection at 10°C (50°F) or outside if the night-time temperature does not fall below 7°C (45°F). Germination takes 1–2 weeks. Protect seedlings from frost. Plant out after hardening off 60cm (24in) apart.
OR
Sow seeds in late spring into prepared open ground in rows 30cm (12in) apart, when the air temperature does not go below 10°C (50°F) at night. Germination takes 2–3 weeks. Thin seedlings to 60cm (24in) apart. Harvest from January to May. Make sure you cut off all flowering shoots to conserve the plants' vigour.

Brassica rapa var. *crispifolia* **(Mizuna greens, Japanese greens)**
Medium seeds: 350 per gram
Hardy annual
Height 23cm (9in)
Small, yellow flowers
Serrated, green leaves

Sow seeds in early spring or early autumn into pots or modules using standard soil-less seed compost (substrate), either a peat free proprietary brand or composted fine propagating bark. Do not sow in the hot weather of mid-summer, as the plants will quickly run to flower. Cover with perlite or vermiculite and place under protection at 15°C (60°F). Germination takes 5–10 days. Plant out in a fertile, moisture-retentive soil at a distance of 20cm (8in) after hardening off.
OR
Sow seeds in late spring or early autumn into prepared open ground, when the air temperature does not go below 7°C (45°F) at night. Germination takes 2–3 weeks. Thin seedlings to 20cm (8in) apart.

Brassica rapa var. *purpurea* **(Purple choy sum, Purple-flowered pak choi)**
Medium seeds: 350 per gram
Hardy annual
Height 80cm ($2^{1}/_{2}$ft)

Plant purple choy sum in a fertile, moisture-retentive soil; do not sow in the hot weather of summer as the plants will quickly run to flower.

Sow seeds in early spring or early autumn into pots or modules using standard soil-less seed compost (substrate), either a peat free proprietary brand or composted fine propagating bark. Cover with perlite or vermiculite. Place under protection at 15°C (60°F). Germination takes 5–10 days. Plant out after hardening off at a distance of 30cm (12in).

OR
Sow seeds in late spring or early autumn into prepared open ground, when the air temperature does not go below 7°C (45°F) at night. Germination takes 2–3 weeks. Thin seedlings to 30cm (12in).

Brassica napus Napobrassica Group **(Swede)**
Medium seeds: 375 per gram
Hardy biennial grown as an annual
Oval, lobed, toothed mid-green leaves.
Rounded root crop – larger and sweeter than turnips.

Plant swedes in a fertile moisture-retentive soil.

Sow seeds from late spring until early summer into prepared, open ground, in rows 38cm (15in) apart, when the air temperature does not go below 10°C (50°F) at night. Germination takes 2–3 weeks. Thin seedlings to 23cm (9in) apart. Harvest 26 weeks from sowing.

Brassica rapa Rapifera Group **(Turnip)**
Medium seeds: 500 per gram
Hardy biennial grown as an annual
Oval, lobed, toothed, mid-green leaves
Small, rounded root crop
Plant in moisture-holding soil which has been manured the year before.

Sow in late winter for harvest in early spring in pots or modules using standard soil-less seed compost (substrate), either a peat free proprietary brand or composted fine propagating bark. Cover with perlite or vermiculite and place under protection at 18°C (65°F). Germination takes 6–10 days. Plant out 10cm (4in) apart in late spring.
OR
Sow in late summer for harvest in early autumn, into prepared open ground in rows 38cm (15in) apart. Germination takes 2–3 weeks. Thin seedlings to 15cm (6in) apart.

Capiscum *Solanaceae*

In cool climates sweet peppers and chilli peppers must be grown under protection in a glasshouse or conservatory. Being tropical or subtropical species, they require a minimum growing temperature of 17°C (62°F) and a temperature of 21°C (70°F) for fruit to set.

Capsicum annuum Longum Group

Capsicum annuum Grossum Group **(Sweet peppers, Bell peppers)**
Medium seeds: 140 per gram
Half-hardy annual
Optimum growing temperature 21–28°C (70–83°F)

Capsicum annuum Longum Group **(Chilli peppers)**
Medium seeds: 120 per gram
Half-hardy annual
Optimum growing temperature 21–30°C (70–86°F)

Sow seeds in spring into pots or modules using standard soil-less seed compost (substrate), either a peat free proprietary brand or composted fine propagating bark. Cover with perlite or vermiculite. Place under protection at 22°C (72°F). Germination takes 6–10 days. Plant out in a greenhouse bed 45cm (18in) apart.
OR
Grow on as a pot plant using a peat free proprietary brand or composted fine propagating bark potting compost or grow bags. Pots should have a minimum diameter of 20cm (8in). Harvest in mid-summer.

Cichorium *Asteraceae*

Plant in a well-drained fertile soil that is low in nitrogen.

Cichorium intybus **(Chicory)**
Medium seeds: 500 per gram
Hardy and half-hardy perennial, grown as an annual
Height 10–120cm (4in–4ft) depending on variety and flower
Flowers in its second season
It is worth leaving a few plants to go to seed as the flowers are very pretty – pink, white or blue
Leaves vary in colour and shape from oblong to round and from red/purple to mid-green

Sowing techniques vary on variety. In general, sow seeds of tall and hardy varieties in late spring into pots or modules, using standard soil-less seed compost (substrate), either a peat free proprietary brand or composted fine propagating bark. Cover with perlite or vermiculite and place under protection at 15°C (60°F). Germination takes 5–10 days. Plant out 10–30cm (4–12in) apart depending on variety.
OR
Sow seeds in late summer into prepared open ground. Germination takes 2–3 weeks. Thin seedlings to 10–30cm (4–12in) apart, depending on variety.

Cichorium endivia **(Endive)**
Medium seeds: 500 per gram
Hardy and half-hardy perennial, grown as an annual
Height 10–45cm (4–18in) depending on variety
Leaves vary in colour and shape depending on variety.

Endive can be sown throughout the growing season, it is vital to choose the correct cultivar for the cropping season, so consult current seed catalogues for the optimum sowing time for each variety. However, if sown too early and at temperatures below 5°C (41°F) the plants are liable to bolt.

Sow seeds of hardy varieties in late spring into pots or modules using standard soil-less seed compost (substrate), either a peat free proprietary brand or composted fine propagating bark. Cover with perlite or vermiculite and place under protection at 15°C (60°F). Germination takes 5–10 days. Plant out 10cm (4in) apart.
OR
Sow seeds in late summer into prepared open ground. Germination takes 2–3 weeks. Thin seedlings to 10cm (4in) apart.

Citrullus *Cucurbitaceae*

Water-melons originate in the tropics; they require a minimum temperature of 25°C (77°F). In hot climates plant out in a fertile sandy loam which has been fed with well-rotted manure prior to sowing. Otherwise grow under protection planted out in a greenhouse bed or as a container plant.

Citrullus lanatus **(Water-melon)**
Medium seeds: 10 per gram
Half-hardy annual
Optimum growing temperature 21–30°C (70–86°F)

Sow seeds in early spring into pots using standard loam-based seed compost (substrate). Cover with perlite or vermiculite and place under protection at 21°F (70°C). Spray with water regularly to create moist, humid conditions. Germination takes 4–8 days. Plant out in a greenhouse bed at 90cm (3ft) apart.
OR
Grow on as a container plant. Use a standard loam-based potting compost in a 20–30cm (8–12in) pot.

Claytonia *Portulacaceae*

This is an excellent cold-weather salad plant. Plant in any fertile soil, with the exception of a waterlogged one. Claytonia is prone to self seeding in light, well-drained soils. Will disappear in hot summers, reappearing in autumn or spring.

Claytonia perfoliata **(Winter purslane, Miners lettuce)**
Small seeds: 1,750 per gram
Hardy annual
Height 10–15cm (4–6in)
Small, white flowers from summer until early autumn
Mid-green leaves

Sow in early spring in pots or modules using standard soil-less seed compost (substrate), either a peat free proprietary brand or composted fine propagating bark. Cover with perlite or vermiculite and place under protection at 18°C (65°F). Germination takes 6–10 days. Plant out after a period of hardening off, as soon as there is no serious threat of frost, at a distance of 15cm (6in).
OR
Sow in mid-summer into prepared open ground. Germination takes 6–10 days. Thin seedlings to 15cm (6in) apart.

Cryptotaenia *Apiaceae*

Plant in a fertile, well-draining soil, in a sunny position.

Cryptotaenia japonica **(Japanese parsley, Mitsuba)**
Medium seeds: 420 per gram
Hardy perennial
Height 30cm (12in)
Tiny, white flowers in summer
Interesting, heart-shaped, mid-green leaves

Sow seeds in early spring into pots using standard soil-less seed compost (substrate), either a peat free proprietary brand or composted fine propagating bark. Cover with perlite or vermiculite and place under protection at 15°C (60°F). Germination takes 8–14 days. Plant out 25cm (10in) apart, after a period of hardening off.
OR
Sow seeds in late spring into prepared open ground, when the air temperature does not go below 7°C (45°F) at night. Germination takes 2–3 weeks. Thin seedlings to 25cm (10in) apart.

Cucumis *Cucurbitaceae*

Both melons and cucumbers are climbers, so will need to be trained up canes or wires. In hot climates plant in a rich soil that is both moisture retentive and free draining. Both crops need to be regularly watered and both will damage if grown below 10°C (50°F). If growing under protection, use a rich soil that is moisture retentive and free draining and large containers or organic-based grow bags for the final stages of growing-on.

Cucumis melo (Sweet melon)
Medium seeds: 45 per gram
Half-hardy annual
Climber
Optimum growing temperature 20–30°C (68–86°F)

Sow seeds singly in early spring into pots or modules, using standard soil-less seed compost (substrate), either a peat free proprietary brand or composted fine propagating bark. Cover with perlite or vermiculite. Place under protection at 21°C (70°F) day and night. Germination takes 7–10 days. Plant out in a greenhouse bed or grow bag 90cm (3ft) apart.
OR
Grow on as a container plant, using a standard loam-based potting compost in a pot 30–45cm (12–18in) in diameter.

Cucumis sativus (Cucumber)
Medium seeds: 35 per gram
Half-hardy annual
Climber
Optimum growing temperature 18–30°C (64–86°F)

As cucumbers hate being transplanted, sowing thinly will keep plant stress to the minimum.

Sow the seeds in early spring (or later if you live in a cold climate). Use standard soil-less seed compost (substrate), either a peat free proprietary brand or composted fine propagating bark. Plant the seeds on edge into the compost, not flat on the surface. Plant two seeds per pot or a single seed in modules. Cover with perlite or vermiculite. Place under protection at 21°C (70°F) day and night. Germination takes 2–7 days. Plant out in a greenhouse bed or grow bag 45cm (18in) apart for climbers, 75cm (30in) for bushy varieties.
OR
Grow on as a container plant. Use a standard loam-based potting compost in a 30–45cm (12–18in) pot.

***Recipe for sowing, planting and growing* Cucumis sativus**
Cucumbers have been grown for thousands of years. They are much maligned, but there is nothing better than a cucumber picked and eaten the same day, before it loses its succulence, either in a salad or as a vegetable in its own right.

Ingredients
1 seed per module or 2 seeds per pot
1 module tray
OR
1 x 8cm (4in) pot
Standard soil-less seed compost (substrate), either a peat free proprietary brand or composted fine propagating bark
White plastic plant label

Method Fill the modules or pots with compost, smooth over, tap down and water in well. Sow 1 seed per module or 2 seeds per pot. Gently push the seed edge-ways into the compost 2cm (3/4in) deep. Do not firm. Place the pots or modules in a warm, light place out of direct sunlight, and at an optimum temperature of 21°C (70°F). Germination takes 2–7 days. When the seedlings show through, make sure they have plenty of light, but not direct sunlight, and keep them moist. Remove from the direct heat; temperatures should be about 18°C (65°F) by day and no less than 16°C (60°F) by night. The seedlings will be ready to plant out or pot up when the third or fourth true leaves have appeared. Plant out in a greenhouse bed at 45cm (18in) apart for climbers, 75cm (30in) for bushy varieties or grow on as a container plant using a standard loam-based potting compost in a pot 30–45cm (12–18 in) diameter. For cucumbers to do their best, they like a warm, humid atmosphere.

Cucurbita *Cucurbitaceae*

Plant in a rich soil that is moisture retentive and free draining. All crops need to be regularly watered. All cucurbita hate having their roots disturbed so, if you are starting your crop early under protection, sow seeds singly into small pots or large modules.

Cucurbita pepo (Marrow)
Large seeds: 5 per gram (approx.)
Half-hardy annual
Optimum growing temperature 18–27°C (65–80°F)

Sow seeds in early spring into pots using standard soil-less seed compost (substrate), either a peat free proprietary brand or composted fine propagating bark. Cover with perlite or vermiculite. Place under protection at 21°C (70°F). Germination takes 5–10 days. After hardening off, plant out at a distance of 90cm–2m (3–6ft) depending on variety. For trailing varieties, increase the distance to 1.2–2m (4–6ft).
OR
Sow seeds in late spring into prepared, open ground at a distance of 90cm (3ft) apart, when the air temperature does not go below 10°C (50°F) at night. Germination takes 10–18 days. Plant out after a period of hardening off at a distance of 90cm–2m (3–6ft) depending on variety. For trailing varieties increase the distance to 1. 2–2m (4–6ft).

Cucurbita pepomaxima (Squashes)
Large seeds: 10 per gram
Half-hardy annual
Optimum growing temperature 18–30°C (65–85°F)

The squash requires a richer soil than the marrow. It is a good idea to add extra mulch after sowing or planting out, to help retain moisture.

Sow seeds in early spring into pots, using standard soil-less seed compost (substrate), either a peat free proprietary brand or composted fine propagating bark. Cover with perlite or vermiculite and place under protection at 15°C (60°F). Germination takes 5–10 days. Plant out, after a period of hardening off, at a distance of 90cm–2m (3–6ft) depending on variety.
OR
Sow seeds in late spring into prepared, open ground, at a distance of 90cm–2m (3–6ft) depending on variety, when the air temperature does not go below 10°C (50°F) at night. Germination takes 10–18 days.

Cucurbita pepo **(Courgettes)**
Large seeds: 5 per gram (approx.)
Half-hardy annual
Optimum growing temperature 18–27°C (65–80°F)

Sow seeds in early spring into pots using standard soil-less seed compost (substrate), either a peat free proprietary brand or composted fine propagating bark. Cover with perlite or vermiculite and place under protection at 21°C (70°F). Germination takes 5–10 days. Plant out, after a period of hardening off, at a distance of 90cm–2m (3–6ft) depending on variety. For trailing varieties, increase the distance to 1. 2–2m (4–6ft).
OR
Sow seeds in late spring into prepared open ground, at a distance of 90cm (3ft) apart, when the air temperature does not go below 10°C (50°F) at night. Germination takes 10–18 days. Plant out after a period of hardening off at a distance of 90cm–2m (3–6ft) depending on variety. For trailing varieties, increase the distance to 1. 2–2m (4–6ft).

Cucurbita maxima **(Pumpkin)**
Large seeds: 7 per gram
Half-hardy annual
Optimum growing temperature 18–30°C (65–85°F)

Cucurbita maxima

Pumpkins require a richer soil than marrows, so it is a good idea to add extra mulch after sowing or planting out to help retain moisture. Soak seeds overnight before sowing in early spring into pots, using standard soil-less seed compost (substrate), either a peat free proprietary brand or composted fine propagating bark. Cover with perlite or vermiculite and place under protection at 20°C (68°F). Germination takes 5–10 days. Plant out, after a period of hardening off, at a distance of 2–3m (6–10ft) depending on variety.
OR
Soak seeds overnight before sowing in late spring into prepared open ground, 90cm–2m (3–6ft) depending on variety, when the air temperature does not go below 10°C (50°F) at night. Germination takes 10–18 days.

Cynara *Asteraceae*

Plant in a fertile, moist soil, which has been fed with plenty of well-rotted manure or compost in the previous autumn.

Cynara scolymus **(Globe artichoke)**
Medium seeds: 25 per gram
Hardy perennial
Height 1–1.5m (3–5ft)
Optimum growing temperature 13–18°C (55–64°F)
Attractive, beautifully shaped edible flower buds which develop into a blue thistle flower
Large, serrated, silvery, grey-green stiff leaves

Sow seeds in early spring into pots using standard soil-less seed compost (substrate), either a peat free proprietary brand or composted fine propagating bark. Cover with perlite or vermiculite and place under protection at 15°C (60°F). Germination takes 5–10 days. Plant young plants out after all threat of frost has passed, at a distance of 1m (3ft).
OR
Sow seeds in late spring into prepared open ground, 38cm (15in) apart, when the air temperature does not go below 7°C (45°F) at night. Germination takes 2–3 weeks. Thin seedlings to 1m (3ft) apart. Pick the heads before they flower. Harvest starts in the second year and the plant remains productive for up to 4 years.

Daucus *Apiaceae*

Plant in a light, fertile well-drained soil in a sunny position.

Daucus carota **(Carrots)**
Medium seeds: 620 per gram
Hardy biennial grown as an annual
Height 23-30cm (9-12in)

Sow seeds from early spring-late spring into prepared open ground. If temperatures fall below 7°C (45°F) protect with a cloche or agricultural fleece. Germination takes 2–3 weeks or longer depending on the time of year. Thin the seedlings to 4–8cm (1½–3in) apart. To protect the crop from being attacked by carrot root fly, I recommend that you do this in the evening and then cover the crop with horticultural fleece which will act as a barrier against the fly. Harvest 9–12 weeks later, depending on cultivar and season.

***Recipe for sowing, planting and growing* Daucus carota**
Carrots have been grown for over 2,000 years. There are some wonderful varieties available, all of them slightly different shapes, colours and flavours. Their feathery top growth looks great as an edging to a formal vegetable garden.

Ingredients
Seed
Prepared site in the garden
Silver sand
A cloche or agricultural fleece
2 white plastic plant labels

Method Sow directly into a prepared site in the garden, the ideal soil is deep, sandy loam which allows the root to develop. On heavier soils, choose a short variety. Dig heavy soils the winter before, so that the frost can break it up. Do not manure the soil because this will encourage the roots to fork. Sow in early to late spring, depending on the variety, and when the night-time temperature does not fall below 7°C (45°F). In lower temperatures protect the crop with a cloche or agricultural fleece. Before sowing the seeds, line the 2.5cm (1in) drill with silver sand so that you can see the small seed. Sow thinly, lightly cover with soil and water in well. Label either end of the seed row. Germination takes 2–3 weeks. When it is time to thin the seedlings, water them well, then in the evening thin them to 4–8cm (1½–3in) apart depending on variety. Protect the remaining seedlings from carrot root fly by covering with agricultural fleece for one week. After a week remove the fleece and allow to grow on as normal. Harvest at 9–12 weeks, depending on cultivar and season.

Fragaria *Rosaceae*

Plant in a fertile, moisture-retentive and free-draining soil in sun or partial shade.

Fragaria vesca **(Wild strawberry)**
Small seeds: 3,000 per gram
Hardy perennial
Height 15–30cm (6–12in)
Small white flowers with yellow centres followed by small red fruit
Flowers in spring
Three bright green leaflets with toothed edges

Sow seeds in spring into pots or modules, using standard soil-less seed compost (substrate), either a peat free proprietary brand or composted fine propagating bark. Cover with perlite or vermiculite and place under protection at 18°C (65°F). Germination takes 3–4 weeks. Plant out, after a period of hardening off, when all threat of frost has passed, at a distance of 20cm (8in).

Ipomoea *Convulvulaceae*

Sweet potato is native to the tropics. In warm humid climates plant in a very fertile, light sandy soil that has been well fed prior to planting. In cool climates grow under cover in high humidity. There are some varieties that have been bred for cooler climates. A word of warning, this plant spreads up to 3m (10ft) and more if not kept in check by removing the growing tips.

Ipomoea batatas (Sweet potato)
Medium seeds
Half-hardy perennial grown as an annual
Height 45cm (18in)
Pretty white flowers with dark purple/maroon centres
Mid-green large leaves

Sow seeds in spring into pots or modules using standard soil-less seed compost (substrate), either a peat free proprietary brand or composted fine propagating bark. Cover with perlite or vermiculite and place under protection at 24°C (75°F). Germination takes 10–20 days. Plant out after all threat of frost has passed at a distance of 30cm (12in) apart.
OR
Plant out in a greenhouse bed at 30cm (12in) apart.
OR
Grow on as a container plant. Use a standard loam-based potting compost in a 20–30cm (8–12in) pot. Harvest 12–20 weeks after planting out.

Lactuca *Asteraceae*

Lettuce is a cool-climate plant, growing best at temperatures below 21°C (70°F). It is a fast-growing vegetable, so plant in a very fertile soil that has been well fed in the previous autumn and which retains moisture throughout the growing season. If grown in too high a temperature, it will bolt and taste bitter, and in cold damp weather it is prone to disease and slugs.

Lactuca sativa (Lettuce)
Medium seeds: 520 per gram
Height 7–30cm (3–12in) depending on variety
Optimum growing temperature 10–20°C (50–68°F)

There are many types of lettuce, varying in colour from green to rust, with leaves of all shapes and sizes from round to serrated. Lettuce can be sown throughout the growing season. It is vital to choose the correct cultivar for the cropping season, so consult current seed catalogues for the optimum sowing time for each variety.

Sow seeds in late spring into prepared open ground in drills, when the night-time temperature does not go below 10°C (50°F). Germination takes 10–14 days. Thin seedlings to 15–30cm (6–12in) depending on variety.
OR
Sow seeds in spring and autumn into pots or modules using standard soil-less seed compost (substrate), either a peat free proprietary brand or composted fine propagating bark. Cover with perlite or vermiculite and place in a cold frame. Do not allow the young plants to get too hot, ventilation is important. Germination takes 8–14 days. Plant out after a period of hardening off at a distance of 15–30cm (6–12in) depending on variety.

Lepidium *Brassicaceae*

Cress prefers growing in cool, moist conditions, so plant in a fertile, moist soil. If grown in conditions that are too hot, it will bolt and go to seed very quickly.

Lepidium sativum (Cress, Garden cress, Pepper cress)
Medium seeds: 400 per gram
Half-hardy annual
Height 7.5–15cm (3–6in)
Deeply curled, deep green leaves with a spicy flavour.

Sow seeds in late spring into prepared open ground, when the air temperature does not go below 10°C (50°F) at night. Germination takes 2–4 days. Thin seedlings to 2cm (3/4in) apart so they are not overcrowded.

Lycopersicon *Solanaceae*

Tomatoes are native to the tropics where they are perennials. In cool climates they are grown as annuals. Plant in a rich, moist soil in a sunny position.

Lycopersicon esculentum (Tomato)
Half-hardy perennial grown as an annual
Medium seeds: 350 per gram
Height 90cm–1.2m (3–4ft) for bush varieties, up to 2.1m (7ft) for cane or wire varieties
Optimum growing temperature 21–24°C (70–75°F)
Small yellow flowers in summer followed by red fruit
Mid-green leaves. Some cultivars have serrated leaves, some lobed

Tomatoes can be sown throughout the spring and early summer, it is vital to choose the correct cultivar for required sowing time. Consult current seed catalogues for the optimum sowing time for each variety.

Sow seeds in spring into pots or modules using standard soil-less seed compost (substrate), either a peat free proprietary brand or composted fine propagating bark. Cover with perlite or vermiculite and place under protection at 21°C (70°F). Germination takes 5–10 days. Plant out, after a period of hardening off and when all threat of frost has passed, at a distance of 30–60cm (12–24in) depending on variety.
OR
Sow seeds in late spring into prepared open ground, when the air temperature does not go below 7°C (45°F) at night. Germination takes 10–14 days. Thin seedlings to a distance of 30–60cm (12–24in) depending on variety.

Pastinaca *Apiaceae*

Parsnip is a cool-season crop. Plant in a deep fertile, light, free draining soil in sun or partial shade.

Pastinaca sativa (Parsnip)
Medium seeds: 240 per gram
Hardy biennial grown as an annual
Height 38cm (15in)
Small yellow-green flowers in second season followed by golden-yellow seed heads
Mid-green, lobed leaves

For good germination it is most important that the seed is fresh.

Sow the seeds thinly in spring for autumn and early winter crops into prepared open ground, 2cm (3/4in) deep, when the soil temperature is above 10°C (50°F). Germination should take 10–14 days. In lower temperatures it is very slow. Be careful when thinning the plants out to 10cm (4in) apart not to attract the carrot root fly. The best prevention is to water the site well, thin the plants in the early evening and cover with agricultural fleece for a few days.

Lycopersicon esculentum

OR

Sow the seeds in early autumn for early spring crops. Sow into prepared open ground 2cm (3/4in) deep and 10cm (4in) apart. Germination takes 10–14 days. This is a good option if you live in a warm climate but not recommended in very cold climates.

Phaseolus *Papilionaceae*

Prepare the ground thoroughly for beans, with plenty of well-rotted compost. The soil should be fertile, moisture retentive and free draining, and the best situation is sunny and sheltered from strong winds to encourage pollination by bees.

Phaseolus coccineus **(Runner beans)**
Very large seeds: 1 per gram (very approx.)
Half-hardy perennial grown in cool climates as an annual
Height 3m (10ft) or more

Seeds do not germinate below 12°C (54°F), so if you want an early crop start sowing seeds singly in early spring into pots or modules using standard soil-less seed compost (substrate), either a peat free proprietary brand or composted fine propagating bark. Cover with perlite or vermiculite and place under protection at 18°C (65°F). Germination takes 7–10 days. Plant out after a period of hardening off at a distance of 15cm (6in).

OR

Sow seeds in late spring into prepared, open ground at a depth of 5cm (2in), 15cm (6in) apart, when the air temperature does not go below 7°C (45°F) at night. Germination takes 2–3 weeks.

Phaseolus vulgaris **(French beans)**
Large seeds: 3–11 per gram
Half-hardy annual
Height up to 45cm (18in) for bush forms, climbers up to 3m (10ft)
French beans prefer a lighter soil than runner beans

Sow seeds singly in early spring into pots or modules, using standard soil-less seed compost (substrate), either a peat free proprietary brand or composted fine propagating bark. Cover with perlite or vermiculite and place under protection at 18°C (65°F). Germination takes 5–10 days. After hardening off, plant out at a distance of 6–23cm (2 1/2–9in)

Phaseolus coccineus

depending on variety. Harvest from mid-summer onwards.
OR
Sow seeds in late spring, at a depth of 5cm (2in) and 6–23cm (2½–9in) apart, depending on variety. Sow into prepared, open ground, when the air temperature does not go below 7°C (45°F) at night. Germination takes 2–3 weeks. Harvest from early autumn onwards.

Pisum *Papilionaceae*

Peas are quite fussy, they like a moisture-retentive, free-draining soil which should be fed with well-rotted compost in autumn. They suffer in both cold, wet soil and drought conditions.

Pisum sativum (Garden peas)
Large seeds: 3–6 per gram
Annual
Height 45cm–1.8m (18in–6ft) depending on variety
Optimum growing temperature 13–18°C (55–64°F)
Small white, pink or purple flowers
Small oval leaves

The seeds will not germinate in a soil below 7°C (45°F) or in hot conditions.

Sow in spring as soon as the soil temperature reaches 10°C (50°F). Prior to sowing, soak the seeds overnight in warm water. Sow at a depth of 5cm (2in) and 5cm (2in) apart into a prepared site or a length of plastic guttering (see recipe below). Germination takes 7–14 days.
OR
If you live in a cold area and want to start your crop off as soon as possible, sow seeds singly in early spring into pots or modules using standard soil-less seed compost (substrate), either a peat free proprietary brand or composted fine propagating bark.

Place under protection at 18°C (65°F). Germination takes 5–10 days. Plant out when all threat of frost has passed at a distance of 5cm (2in).

Pisum sativum var. *saccharatum* (Mangetout, Sugar peas)
Large seeds: 3–6 per gram
Annual
Optimum growing temperature 13–18°C (55–65°F)
Small, white or red flowers
Oval, pointed, green leaves

The seeds will not germinate in a soil below 7°C (45°F), nor in hot conditions. Therefore, sow in spring as soon as the soil temperature reaches 10°C (50°F). Prior to sowing, soak the seeds overnight in warm water. Sow at a depth of 5cm (2in) and 5–8cm (2–3in) apart into prepared, open ground. Germination takes 7–14 days.
OR
If you live in a cold area and want to start your crop off as soon as possible, sow the seeds in early spring into pots or modules, using standard soil-less seed compost (substrate), either a peat free proprietary brand or composted fine propagating bark. Cover with perlite or vermiculite and place under protection at 18°C (65°F).

Germination takes 5–10 days. Plant out when all threat of frost has passed at a distance of 5–8cm (2–3in).

***Recipe for sowing, planting and growing* Pisum sativum**

Peas have been found on an archaeological dig dating back to 9750 BC. They did not become fashionable until the seventeenth century in the UK. They are an immensely versatile vegetable; both the pod and the peas are edible and great as a vegetable or as a soup.

Ingredients
1 seed per pot or module
Small china bowl
Warm water
1 module tray
OR
1 x 8cm (4in) pot
Standard soil-less seed compost (substrate), either a peat free proprietary brand or composted fine propagating bark
White plastic plant label
OR
Length of plastic guttering 90cm–2m (3–6ft) long
Standard soil-less seed compost (substrate), either a peat free proprietary brand or composted fine propagating bark
2 white plastic plant labels

Method In spring fill a china bowl with warm water, add the seeds to the water and soak for 12 hours. Fill the modules or pots with compost, smooth over, tap down and water in well. Put 1 seed in each module or pot. Gently press the seed into the compost until it is totally buried, water lightly again, then label with the plant name and date. Place the pot or modules in a warm, light place out of direct sunlight at an optimum temperature of 18°C (65°F). Keep watering to a minimum until germination has taken place, which takes 5–10 days. Once germinated, move the seedlings into a cooler environment, then slowly harden the young plants off before planting out into a prepared site when all threat of frost has passed. Plant out at a distance of 5cm (2in).

OR
When the night-time temperature is about 10°C (50°F) fill a length of plastic guttering with compost, 1cm (½in) from the rim. Sow the pre-soaked pea seeds in double rows about 5cm (2in) apart. Water them to settle the compost and cover the seeds with more compost, filling the gutter up to the rim. Give a further, light watering and label. Place the guttering on a sunny windowsill or in a sheltered place to germinate. When the seedlings are 8–10cm (3–4in) tall they can be planted in the garden. Dig a shallow trench the same length and depth as the gutter. Gently ease the well rooted seedlings, just as they are, into the trench, firm in well, water and label. If you are having difficulties, you can divide the pea seedlings into 30cm (12in) lengths then plant them out in the trench a section at a time.

Raphanus *Brassicaceae*

Grown slowly, radishes have a strong flavour and can be chewy. Grown in a rich, moisture-retentive soil they will be sweet and crisp.

Raphanus sativus (Radish)
Medium seed: 80–180 per gram
Hardy and half-hardy biennial grown as an annual
Height 10–45cm (4–18in), depending on variety
Small, pink-white flowers in summer, depending on variety
Mid-green leaves

Radishes can be sown throughout the spring and early summer, it is vital to choose the correct cultivar for required sowing time. So consult current seed catalogues for the optimum sowing time for each variety. There are many to choose from, small round, small long, large and all the oriental ones which are known as mooli.

Sow seeds thinly in late spring into prepared open ground, when the air temperature does not go below 7°C (45°F) at night. Germination takes 5–10 days. Thin seedlings to 5–15cm (2–6in) apart, depending on variety.

Rheum *Polygonacaeae*

Rhubarb should be grown in a moisture-retentive soil which has been fed with well-rotted manure or compost in the autumn in sun or light shade. Once established it needs winter cold to bring it out of dormancy. For this reason, it does not do well in warm climates.

Rheum rhaponticum **(Rhubarb)**
Medium seeds: 100 per gram
Hardy perennial
Height 1m (3ft)
Frothy, small, cream flowers in early summer which should be cut off to stop the plant becoming weak
Large green leaves.

Sow seeds in early spring into pots or modules using standard soil-less seed compost (substrate), either a peat free proprietary brand or composted fine propagating bark. Cover with perlite or vermiculite and place under protection at 18°C (65°F). Germination takes 4–14 days. Plant out, when all threat of frost has passed, at a distance of 90cm (3ft) apart.
OR
Sow seeds thinly in late spring into prepared open ground, when the air temperature does not go below 10°C (50°F) at night. Germination takes 10–20 days. Thin seedlings in two sessions, first to 30cm (12in) apart, then to 90cm (3ft) apart.

Seed-grown rhubarb can be harvested gently from the second year's growth.

Rorippa *Brassicaceae*

Plant in a very moist soil at the waters edge, in a shady position. If you do not have a pond, line a container with polythene before filling with potting compost, this will help keep the compost moist. Place the container in a shady position.

Rorippa nasturtium aquaticum (*Nasturtium officinale*) **(Watercress)**
Small seeds: 6,000 per gram
Hardy perennial
Height 10–60cm (4–24in)
Clusters of tiny white flowers in summer, followed by seed pods.
Dark green, lobed, strong tasting leaves.

Sow seeds in early spring into pots using standard soil-less seed compost (substrate), either a peat free proprietary brand or composted fine propagating bark. Cover with perlite or vermiculite and place under protection at 18°C (65°F). Germination takes 5–10 days. Keep well watered during germination. Once germinated, continue to water frequently, plant out as soon as all threat of frost has passed. Plant either into a calm part of an unpolluted stream or into a container, as described in the introduction to this entry, at a distance of 15cm (6in) apart.

Rumex *Polygonaceae*

Sorrel will tolerate any soil, but thrives in a damp fertile soil in sun or partial shade. Both varieties mentioned below are known as French sorrel which is confusing.

Rumex acetosa **(Broad-leaved sorrel, French sorrel)**
Small seeds: 1,000 per gram
Hardy perennial
Height up to 1.2m (4ft) when in flower
Boring rust-coloured flowers in summer
Long, oval, mid-green leaves.

Rumex scutatus **(Buckler leaf sorrel, French sorrel)**
Small seeds: 1,000 per gram
Hardy perennial
Height 50cm (20in)
Small, green-red flowers in summer
Shield-shaped, mid-green leaves.

Sow seeds in early spring into pots or modules using standard soil-less seed compost (substrate), either a peat free proprietary brand or composted fine propagating bark. Cover with perlite or vermiculite and place under protection at 15°C (60°F). Germination takes 5–10 days. Plant out after a period of hardening off at a distance of 30cm (12in).
OR
Sow seeds thinly in late spring into prepared open ground, when the air temperature does not go below 7°C (45°F) at night. Germination takes 2–3 weeks. Thin seedlings to 30cm (12in) apart.

Sium *Apiaceae*

Skirret prefers a sunny site and a soil that has not been recently manured. It is quite happy to follow a crop which was fed and survive on what is left, as long as the soil is light and free draining.

Sium sisarum **(Skirret)**
Medium seeds: 800–1,000 per gram
Hardy perennial usually grown as an annual
Height up to 1m (3ft) when in flower
Umbels of white flowers in late summer on second year's growth
Sharply-toothed oval leaves

Sow seeds thinly into prepared open ground, from early spring for autumn harvest or autumn for late spring harvest, in drills 2cm (1in) deep. Germination takes 2–3 weeks or longer depending on the time of year. Thin seedlings to 2.5cm (10in) apart. Roots take about 4 months to mature.

Solanum *Solanaceae*

Aubergines and potatoes should be planted in a fertile, deep, free-draining soil in a sunny position.

Rumex acetosa

Solanum melongena **(Aubergine)**
Medium seeds: 200 per gram
Half-hardy perennial grown as an annual in cool climates
Height 30–75cm (12–30in)
Optimum growing temperature 25–30°C (77–86°F) plus high humidity
Small, mauve flowers followed by fruit in various shapes and colours
Large, oval, soft green leaves

Before sowing the seeds soak them for 12 hours then sow in early spring into pots or modules using standard soil-less seed compost (substrate), either a peat free proprietary brand or composted fine propagating bark. Cover with perlite or vermiculite and place under protection at 21°C (70°F). Germination takes 7–14 days. Plant out after a period of hardening off, when all threat of frost has passed, at a distance of 60cm (24in).
OR
Plant out in a greenhouse bed at 60cm (24in) apart.
OR
Grow on as a container plant, use a standard, loam-based potting compost in a 20–30cm (8–12in) pot.

***Recipe for sowing, planting and growing* Solanum melongena**
Ingredients
3 seeds per module or 5 seeds per pot
Small china bowl
Warm water
1 module tray
OR
1 x 8cm (4in) pot
Standard soil-less seed compost (substrate), either a peat free proprietary brand or composted fine propagating bark
Fine-grade perlite (wetted) or vermiculite
White plastic plant label

Method Before sowing the seeds soak them for 12 hours, then fill the modules or pots with compost, smooth over, tap down and water in well. Sow 3 seeds per module or 5 seeds per pot. Cover with fine-grade perlite (wetted) or vermiculite. Label with the plant name and date. Place the pot into a warm light place out of direct sunlight at an optimum temperature of 21°C (70°F). Germination takes 7–14 days. When the seedlings show, move them to a cooler environment, 18°C (65°F) by day and no less than 16°C (60°F) by night. Make sure they have plenty of light but avoid direct sunlight. Keep the seedlings moist. They will be ready to plant out or pot up when they are 8–10cm (3–4in) in height. Plant out in a greenhouse bed at 60cm (24in) or grow on as a container plant using a standard loam-based potting compost in a 20–30cm (8–12in) pot. They will grow on best in 75 per cent humidity, so make sure you do not grow them with tomatoes. However they combine well with cucumbers.

Solanum tuberosum **(Potato)**
Small seeds: 1,750 per gram
Half-hardy perennial grown as an annual
Height up to 75cm (30in) and taller for some varieties
Optimum growing temperature 15–18°C (60–64°F)
Flowers can vary in colour from mauve, purple, pink to cream.
Mid-green leaves.

Potatoes can be grown from seed, the tubers that are produced are smaller and their skin is thin so they make a very good summer crop. However, in cool climates with a short growing season, seed potatoes are often chitted under cover, to give the plant a good start.

Sow seeds in early spring into pots or modules using standard soil-less seed compost (substrate), either a peat free proprietary brand or composted fine propagating bark. Cover with perlite or vermiculite and place under protection at 15°C (60°F). Germination takes 7–14 days. Plant out when all threat of frost has passed, at a distance of 30cm (12in).

Spinacia *Chenopodiaceae*

Plant in a fertile moisture-retentive soil in partial shade. Spinach is notoriously prone to bolt if grown in hot, dry conditions.

Spinacia oleracea **(Spinach)**
Medium seeds: 90 per gram
Hardy annual
Height up to 30cm (12in)
Long, oval, pointed leaves

Sow seeds in early spring into pots or modules using standard soil-less seed compost (substrate), either a peat free proprietary brand or composted fine propagating bark. Cover with perlite or vermiculite and place under protection at 18°C (64°F). Germination takes 5–10 days. Plant out after a period of hardening off at a distance of 15cm (6in) apart.
OR
Sow seeds thinly in late spring or early autumn for hardy varieties into prepared, open ground at a depth of 2cm (3/4in), when the air temperature does not go below 7°C (45°F) at night. Germination takes 2–3 weeks. When the seedlings are large enough, thin to 15cm (6in) apart.

Tragopogon *Asteraceae*

Plant in a light, free-draining, fertile soil and a sunny position.

Tragopogon porrifolius **(Salsify)**
Medium seeds: 300 per gram
Hardy biennial grown as an annual
Height up to 1.2m (4ft) in flower
Pretty mauve flowers in summer of second year (the flower buds are edible)
Grass-like leaves

Always use fresh seed. Sow seeds in early spring into pots or modules using standard soil-less seed compost (substrate), either a peat free proprietary brand or composted fine propagating bark. Cover with perlite or vermiculite and place under protection at 15°C (60°F). Germination takes 7–14 days. Plant out when all threat of frost has passed at a distance of 10cm (4in).
OR
Sow seeds thinly in late spring into prepared, open ground at a depth of 2cm (3/4in), when the air temperature does not go below 7°C (45°F) at night. Germination takes 2–3 weeks. When seedlings are large enough, thin to 10cm (4in) apart.

Valerianella *Valerianaceae*

Plant in any site, with the exception of waterlogged soil, in sun or light shade. Will not grow well in hot climates.

Valerianella locusta **(Corn salad, Lamb's lettuce)**
Small seeds: 1,150 per gram
Hardy annual
Height 10cm (4in)
Spoon-shaped leaves, colour and size dependent on cultivar, mid-green to dark green.

Sow seeds in late spring into pots or modules using standard soil-less seed compost (substrate), either a peat free proprietary brand or composted fine propagating bark. Cover with perlite or vermiculite and place under protection at 15°C (58°F). Germination takes 4–5 days. Plant out after a period of hardening off, when there is no threat of frost, at 10cm (4in) apart.
OR
Sow seeds thinly in mid-summer into prepared, open ground. Germination takes 7–10 days. Thin seedlings to 10cm (4in) apart. Do not allow late sowings to dry out. Water well.

Vicia *Papilionaceae*

Broad beans prefer a free-draining, well-manured soil in a sunny position.

Vicia faba **(Broad beans or fava beans)**
Very large seeds: 1 per gram (very approx.)
Half-hardy and very hardy annual
Height 30cm–1.2m (1–4ft) depending on variety
White flowers in summer
Grey-green oval leaflets

Broad beans can be sown throughout the growing season. It is vital to choose the correct cultivar for the cropping season, so consult current seed catalogues for the optimum sowing time for each variety.

Sow seeds in autumn or early spring into pots or modules using standard soil-less seed compost (substrate), either a peat free proprietary brand or composted fine propagating bark. Cover with perlite or vermiculite and place either under protection at 10°C (50°F) or outside if the night temperature does not fall below 7°C (45°F). Germination takes 1–2 weeks. Protect seedlings from frost. Plant out after a period of hardening off at a distance of 25–30cm (10–12in) depending on variety.
OR
Sow seeds in late spring into prepared open ground 5cm (2in) deep, 10cm (4in) apart, when the air temperature does not go below 5°C (40°F) at night. Germination takes 2–3 weeks.

The main harvest time for broad beans is from early summer until early autumn. If you have old plants left, dig them into the garden as they make a very good green manure, fixing nitrogen into the soil. They also give bulk to compost.

Xanthophthalmum *Asteraceae*

Plant in a fertile well-draining soil in sun or partial shade.

Xanthophthalmum coronarium **(Chopsuey green, Chrysanthemum greens)**
Medium seeds: 420 per gram
Hardy annual
Height 15cm (6in) in the green, 1m (3ft) in flower
Yellow, white and yellow, daisy-like flowers in summer
Serrated, spoon-shaped leaves.

If you want to grow this plant as a crop, pick regularly to delay the plant running to seed and becoming tough.

Sow seeds in early spring into pots or modules using standard soil-less seed compost (substrate), either a peat free proprietary brand or composted fine propagating bark. Cover with perlite or vermiculite and place under protection at 15°C (60°F). Germination takes 7–10 days.
OR
Sow seeds in late spring into prepared open ground, when the soil temperature is 7°C (45°F) at a distance of 20cm (8in) in drills 30cm (12in) apart. Germination takes 2–3 weeks.

Zea *Poaceae*

Plant in full sun in a free-draining site fed with well-rotted manure. Once the cobs start to form, water regularly.

Zea mays var. *saccharata* **(Sweet corn)**
Large seeds: 5 per gram
Half-hardy annual
Height 1.2–2.75m (4–9ft) depending on variety
The male flowers grow in spikes, the soft silks come in shades of silver, gold, bronze and red.
Long, lance-shaped, green leaves

Sweet corn hates being transplanted, so it is best to grow it in its final growing position. Sow the seeds in pairs (thin the weaker seedling later) in late spring, in prepared, open ground, when the soil temperature is 10°C (50°F). Sow at a distance of 40cm (16in) apart in drills 60cm (24in) apart. Germination takes 2–3 weeks but can be faster in warmer weather.
OR
If you live in a cold climate, sow single seeds in early spring into modules using standard soil-less seed compost (substrate), either a peat free proprietary brand or composted fine propagating bark. Cover with perlite or vermiculite and place under protection at 15°C (60°F). Germination takes 7–10 days.

Transplant to its growing position as soon as there is no threat of frost, at a distance of 40cm (16in) apart.

practical information

Viburnum opulus berries ready for seed extraction, see page 236

how plants reproduce

Before growing from seed, it is helpful to understand how plants work. Understanding the process as it occurs naturally helps the gardener to reproduce the correct growing conditions in the garden.

Plant structure

In its simplest form, every plant is made up of four essential parts:

The roots anchor the plant firmly in the growing medium (usually soil) and prevent it from being blown over by the wind. Roots absorb water, nutrients and mineral salts from the soil and pass them into the stem. They frequently act as a food store.

The stem is the super-highway of the plant. It supports the shoots, spaces out the leaves so that they receive adequate air and sunlight, conducts water from the soil to the leaves and food from the leaves to other parts of the plant. In some cases, it also holds the flowers above ground, thus assisting in pollination. Photosynthesis may also occur in some green stems.

The leaves are, in most plants, the primary organs of photosynthesis, the process by which the chlorophyll in a plant captures light energy and converts it into chemical energy. The plant needs a good supply of water and carbon dioxide from the air in order to achieve this.

The flower produces seed, ensuring that there will be new plants in the future. Some plants have bisexual flowers. These contain both stigmas and stamens. Others have separate male and female flowers. Dioecious plants have flowers of only one sex borne on each plant.

The female part of the flower, called the pistil, is made up of the stigma, the style and the ovary. The stigma is at the tip of the style, a tube that connects it to the ovary. Pollen is deposited on to the surface of the stigma during pollination. The ovary, which is usually hollow, varies in shape, size and colour. Ovules are attached to the walls of the ovary. It is these ovules that develop into the seeds once they have been fertilised by pollen from the male parts of a flower.

The ovary, style and stigma form the carpel. There may be several carpels per flower, or only one. The carpel is always positioned in the centre or apex of the flower, giving the maximum chance of pollination.

The male part of the flower consists of the stamens. Each stamen is composed of a stalk or filament and an anther, which contains and dispenses the pollen. It is the pollen that fertilises the female parts and turns the ovules into viable seed.

Pollination

Before a plant can produce seed, the flower of the plant must first be pollinated.

Animals, birds, bees and the wind are all used as vehicles for transporting the pollen from one plant on to the stigma of another. This begins the process of fertilisation. Cross-fertilisation often produces healthier and more viable seed than self-fertilisation. The majority of plants, especially wild species, have systems to prevent self-pollination. However, in nature there are always exceptions to the rule and self-fertilisation does sometimes occur.

Fertilisation

Once the pollen is deposited on the stigma, it absorbs the sugar from the syrupy liquid which is on the surface of the stigma.

The pollen swells and eventually grows a pollen tube which is hollow but contains the three essential nuclei necessary for fertilisation. The tube grows into the style and all the way along it to reach the ovary. Once it reaches the ovary, one of the nuclei, the vegetative one, disappears and the remaining two travel on and reach the ovum. Here one of the nuclei fuses with the ovum nucleus. At this stage fertilisation is accomplished and the ovum becomes a live embryo inside the ovule, which now develops into a viable seed. The petals of the flower begins to fade and fall and the ovary begins to swell.

Seed dispersal

Once seeds have matured they must be dispersed.

If all the seeds fell in one place they would have to compete for water, light and nutrients. Many seeds are surrounded by flesh, which may be soft or hard and dry. These seed cases may provide food for insects, animals or humans. In this way, the seeds are carried great distances before being excreted. The digestive processes of certain animals boost germination. Some seeds actually rely on this process to break their dormancy. Other plants have seeds encased in burrs or attached to thorns or hooks which are carried by animals who brush past the parent plant. Other seeds are winged and are carried by the wind. These plants produce very light seeds with plumes or feather-like parachutes, making them easily dispersed by the wind over long distances. Some plants which grow by water produce seeds or fruits that are waterproof and buoyant.

Hybridisation

At its simplest, a hybrid is a cross between two different plants.

Commercial growers spend a lot of time and money creating new, stable hybrids which can be relied upon not to revert to the form and colour of one or other of the parent plants. With patience, the amateur gardener can produce some very attractive hybrids. There are a number of plants that hybridise naturally in the garden, such as *Aquilegia* and *Iris*. Natural hybrids are rarely stable so plants grown from their seed are usually different from the parent plant.

To create a hybrid select two stable parent plants. Choose one to be the female (seed producer) and one the male (pollen producer). Remove the stamens from the female plant to make quite sure it will not self-pollinate. With the pollen from the male plant, hand pollinate the stigma on the female plant, then cover the female flower with a muslin bag to protect it from contamination by insects or wind until the seeds are developed.

The first generation of plants are called F1 hybrids. If they in turn are crossed with themselves, the second generation are called F2 hybrids. It is worth remembering that seeds from F1 hybrids are rarely worth saving. If sown, they will almost invariably produce plants inferior to the parent plants.

Buddleja davidii, see page 177

seed germination

There are several factors that affect the germination of viable seed. Water, light, oxygen, temperature and soil conditions can all act as triggers to germination. When sowing seed, it is important to consider the plant's native habitat. For example, if a plant originates in a mountainous region, it will usually require a cold temperature to trigger germination, a sunny position and very free-draining soil. On the other hand, if the plant originated in a temperate climate and is an annual, it will need warm temperatures, sun and a moist soil to trigger germination.

Water

Water is essential in the first phase of germination.

Water penetrates the seed coat and causes the endosperm to swell. The swelling endosperm splits. The water dissolves nutrients in the endosperm, making them available to the embryo, and growth begins. The growing medium must be kept constantly moist, but not wet. A dry period can cause the death of the sprouting embryo.

Oxygen

Oxygen is required by the embryo to begin growing.

The seed must respire to break down the food stored in the seed. This is one reason for using a light, well-aerated growing medium for starting seeds.

Light

Light can stimulate or inhibit a seed's germination.

This determines whether the seed should be sown on the surface of the growing medium or below the surface. Some seeds must be germinated under a covering of glass or black polythene. In the majority of cases, the larger the seed the deeper it needs to be sown. Very small seeds need to be sown on the surface of the soil.

If you live in an area which has long, dark winters you can use artificial lights to extend the daylight hours. This can help to trigger germination, especially when it is combined with warmth. Flower, vegetable and herb seeds treated in this way will be ready for planting out as soon as the soil is sufficiently warm.

Temperature

Every seed has an optimum temperature for germination.

In spring, germination is triggered in many types of seed by the temperature change. Spring-germinated seedlings have time to become established before the winter. Many seeds will germinate within a fairly wide temperature range. Some are limited, however, so it is worth checking before you start sowing. Using artificial heat can be of benefit when germinating seed under cover. However, do not be tempted to sow seed above the recommended temperature for germination because this could send the seed into a secondary dormancy, or produce weak, etiolated seedlings.

Soil

The soil is the engine which supports the seed to full maturity.

Again, it is important to know where your plant originated. An ericaceous plant, for example, will require an acid soil, and a Mediterranean one will need a free-draining soil. If you are using a compost, you must make a mix that will suit your plant (see 'Composts' (substrate) for more details).

The structure of a seed.

Iris seeds in pods

The seed is made up of 3 parts:

1 The testa, an outer protective coat which surrounds the food supply. The testa is very important. It prevents the plant sprouting until the growing conditions are ideal and it protects the embryo from fungi, bacteria, insects and, in some cases, animals. It also protects the seed from excessive drought, flooding and extreme temperatures, either cold or hot.

2 The endosperm is the food supply under the testa. It surrounds the embryo. This gives the young seed a good start in life before it becomes established and able to source food for itself.

3 The embryo of a young plant, which consists of the embryonic shoot (plumule), the embryonic root (radicle) and the leaves (cotyledons).

breaking seed dormancy

In order to enjoy a wide range of plants in the garden, we must sometimes fool nature. For example, seed must occasionally be helped to germinate, by artificially breaking its dormancy. In the wild, the Alps for example, the deep cold breaks down the tough testa or protective coat of the seed. At the opposite extreme, the Australian wattle only begins to germinate after being scorched by fire. When you sow seed away from its natural environment, the gardener must mimic nature in order to trigger germination.

The germination instructions in this book are many variations on a theme.

Some seed types, like echinacea for example, are erratic germinators. They can sometimes be induced to do better if they are given a shock. If they still show no signs of germination 2–3 weeks after being sown in spring at 18°C (65°F), give them 3–4 weeks of cold before putting them back to 18°C (65°F). They will usually germinate within another two weeks. This shock treatment helps trigger germination in seeds that are locked into dormancy.

The process described above is 'stratification'. It is particularly useful for hard-coated seeds and fruits with thick or pithy coverings, such as alpine plants, hardy trees and shrubs which originate in temperate climates.

There are two forms of stratification, cold temperatures followed by warm, to mimic winter followed by spring, or warm temperatures followed by cold, which in most cases is followed by a second period of warmth, to mimic summer followed by winter, followed by spring. The temperature changes help to break down the hard casing of the seed, allowing water to penetrate and start the germination process. Some very hard-coated seeds may need extra help to make the casing penetrable to water. This is known as scarifying and it is explained later on in this chapter.

Natural stratification

If you live in an area where the temperature in winter drops below 0°C (32°F) for at least 3 weeks over the 3 months of winter, natural stratification is possible.

In autumn, fill a module tray or pot with a standard soil-based seed compost, smooth over, tap down and water in well. Sow the seeds thinly on to the surface of the compost. Press them gently into the compost with the flat of the hand. Cover the seed with coarse horticultural sand or coarse grit. Label with the plant's name and the date.

Place the tray or pot outside on a level surface, so that it is exposed to all weathers, including frosts. The fluctuating temperatures will help to break down the outer, protective coat of the seed, allowing water to permeate the endosperm and starting the germination process. Do not worry if you live in a cold area and the containers get immersed in snow, the melting snow will aid germination by helping the endosperm to swell.

These are general guidelines. For more specific instructions see details within the plant sections.

Artificial Stratification

If you live in an area which benefits from warm winters, you may need to apply artificial stratification.

This is simply done by placing the seed in the refrigerator for a period of time. The length of time is dependent on the degree of dormancy the seed needs to experience in order to germinate, and this, in general, depends on its size and its original habitat. On average seed should be kept at 0–5°C (32–41°F) for 3–4 weeks for shallow dormancy, 4–8 weeks for intermediate dormancy or 8–20 weeks for deep dormancy. It is worth mixing small seed with damp vermiculite, sand or coir. (Do not over-damp the sand as this will rot the seed.) This treatment increases the continuous contact between the surface area of the seed and a cold damp substance. It also makes the seed a lot easier to sow after germination occurs. Put the seed mixture in a plastic bag, label it clearly and place it in the refrigerator. Turn the bag from time to time to allow the air to circulate.

Larger seeds, such as the seeds of trees, should be soaked in cold water for 48 hours, drained and placed in a plastic bag, sealed, labelled and refrigerated for an average of 12 weeks.

When about 30 per cent of the seeds have started chitting (producing embryo roots) they can then be sown in the normal way. Start checking your seeds regularly after three weeks to see if this is happening.

If you are planning to sow a lot of seed you may need a separate refrigerator. In my house we sometimes have more seeds than food in the refrigerator, which can cause a family rebellion!

Scarification

In some cases stratification on its own is not enough to penetrate very hard-coated seed – a bit of muscle has to be applied in the form of scarification.

While in natural conditions the seed's hard coat would eventually be broken down, the impatient gardener can use a knife or file to make a shallow cut, or sandpaper to weaken the skin of the coat. For example, the seed of Acacias and Robinias respond to being rubbed with sandpaper. Another option is to prick the seed coat with a sharp pin or to rub the seeds between your hands with a handful of fine sand. The objective is to allow moisture to penetrate and trigger germination. Be careful not to damage the 'eye', or hilum, which is a little depression or mark where the seed is attached to the ovary.

Soaking

Some seeds benefit from a period of soaking in hot water.

Baptisia and *Laburnum* are both examples of this seed type. Place seeds in a bowl and pour over 4–5 times their volume of very hot, not boiling, water. Soak for 24 hours or until they swell, discarding any floating seeds as unviable. As soon as the seed swells it must be sown before it dries out. If seeds do not swell, scarify them by either pricking the seed all over (avoiding the hilum) or rubbing them with sandpaper. A good way to do this is to line a jam jar with fine sandpaper, put the drained seeds into the jar and shake from side to side so they are gently abraded by the sandpaper, then soak them again. If soaking for longer than 24 hours, change the water every day.

Seeds which contain natural inhibitors to induce dormancy also benefit from soaking as this will leach out the inhibitor. In some cases, the seed will also need washing with a mild detergent to remove the inhibitor. This technique is helpful when germinating *Gingko* seed.

Another method of soaking seed, particularly suitable for sweet peas, is to soak two or three layers of kitchen paper on a plate, space the seeds evenly on the paper and cover with two or three further layers of pre-soaked kitchen paper. Keep moist and check daily by lifting the corner of the paper. As soon as the seeds begin to sprout they can be transplanted.

Fire and smoke

In nature, some seeds germinate only after a bush fire.

Many of the seeds requiring this treatment originate in South Africa and Australia. Trying to replicate these conditions in the domestic environment can get a bit too exciting! However, you can buy kits containing smoke water and sheets of paper that have been smoke treated. Seeds are sown directly on to the smoke-treated paper and allowed to germinate in the usual way. If you are feeling brave, you can make your own tent-like contraption over the trays or pots, light a fire of damp bracken and green sticks, guide the smoke into the tent and leave the seeds in the smoke for 3–24 hours. Alternatively, you can cover a seed tray containing the seeds with dry bracken, set it alight and then water in the ashes.

For more detailed instructions, please refer to specific plants in the book. Here you will find instructions regarding extra heat, the need to mix different temperatures and the types of compost to use.

Seed

Whether you choose to use home-harvested seed or bought seed, you will derive great pleasure from growing your own plants. Organic gardeners should avoid chemically-treated seed.

Untreated or Natural Seeds Used by organic gardeners, these seeds have been harvested, dried and cleaned. They will have received no other treatment.

Primed or Sprinter Seeds These seeds have been treated so that they germinate quickly. Follow the instructions on the seed packet.

Chitted seeds Chitted or pre-germinated seeds get the gardener off to an early start. They are usually sold in plastic containers and should be sown immediately, following the instructions on the container.

Pelleted seeds These seeds are encased in a coating or pellet that makes them easier to handle. They are also easier to sow evenly. It is crucial to water the seeds in very well after sowing, in order to dissolve the pellets.

Coated and Dusted Seeds Be careful with these seeds. They have been treated with a chemical fungicide, so it is important to wear gloves when sowing.

Water-soluble Seed Tapes The seeds have been stuck on to water-soluble tapes. You simply lay the tape out in the garden, cover lightly with soil and water in very well. This is an expensive way to buy seeds, but is very suitable for those who have difficulty in handling tiny seeds or in bending down to sow them.

Left: using sand to scarify seed. Above left: scarifying using sandpaper. Above right: soaking sweet pea seeds.

harvesting and storing seed

One of the joys of having my own nursery is collecting seed from my own plants. The disadvantage is that visitors to the nursery in autumn think that it is full of half dead plants. This is not the case, of course! I am simply allowing them to go to seed so that I can collect them for next year's crop.

Although I find collecting seed immensely rewarding, it can also be time consuming and frustrating.

Some plants demand endless patience and determination. Cleaning the seed and sorting it from the chaff can be even more time consuming. For home use, however, you do not need to be too pedantic about this stage, and you won't need a great deal of seed. I was delighted when I discovered that some seeds need their chaff! It helps them hold their viability and increases the germination rate.

It is vital to collect seed at the correct time. You will notice that I have stipulated the collection of unripe berries in many cases, to be sown in the green before the inhibitor locks in. In the case of Borage (*Borago officinalis*) on the other hand, the seeds ripen from the bottom, while the top is still flowering. You must either collect a few ripe seeds each day or decide when to cut the plant down, whichever will give the largest yield. Some seeds are very attractive to insects or worms and will have had large bites taken out of them. These are best abandoned. Try to be quicker so that you get to the plant before its predators.

Cleaning seeds

Seed left in its capsules or with its chaff often remains viable for longer than cleaned seed.

However, if you wish to clean the seed you can use the following methods:

Small seeds can be placed in a container and the dust and chaff gently blown off.

Larger seeds can be cleaned using an assortment of sieves with different sizes meshes. Use one sieve to collect coarse chaff, a finer sieve to catch the seeds and finally a tray to collect dust.

Seeds encased in berries In the majority of cases, seeds encased in berries should be collected as soon as they are ripe. To clean them, either put the berries in a sieve, hold under running water and rub off the pulp. Alternatively, place the berries in a piece of muslin and slowly squeeze the cloth under running water. After a time, you will be left with nothing but the seed. Seed collected from berries should be sown immediately or stored in damp (not wet) vermiculite in a refrigerator.

To remove seeds from berries such as those of Phytolacca americana, *wrap the seed head in a clean cloth. Rinse under a cold tap, squeezing to separate the seeds from the flesh. Open the cloth from time to time to check your progress.*

Storing Seed

It is difficult to give general rules about seed storage to maintain optimal viability.

In general, a cool dark place is the preferred choice. Some seeds, however, need to be stored in a refrigerator, and others need to maintain their moisture content in order to remain viable. To avoid disappointment try and sow seeds when they are as fresh as possible. In this way you will avoid the problems associated with storage entirely.

After cleaning, keep the seeds in small, dark bottles or jars. Film canisters are perfect, and paper bags or envelopes are also suitable.

Always label clearly with the common and botanical names, date and place of collection.

Store the seeds in a dark, dry place. Protect from rats and mice if necessary.

Before storing, remove any damaged or shrivelled seeds.

When storing seeds in a refrigerator, make sure that they are thoroughly dry, otherwise they can rot or develop diseases.

Make sure that *Magnolia* seeds do not dry out. Store them in a plastic bag mixed with damp (not wet) vermiculite or sand.

Seeds kept in completely anaerobic conditions, such as vacuum packed foil sachets, may be so dry and starved of oxygen that they die in the sachet if stored over a long period.

Tips for successful seed harvesting

1 Choose vigorous, healthy plants and harvest when most of the seed appears to be ripe.

2 Only cut seed heads on a sunny day, when they are really dry.

3 After cutting the seed heads, allow them to dry out naturally in a warm dry place with good air circulation, a sunny window-sill is ideal. The kitchen is the worst place.

4 Always label your seeds.

5 While the seed heads are drying out thoroughly, let them lie loosely in open cardboard boxes or in open paper bags. Do not use plastic because the plants and seeds will sweat and the seed will rot. If the capsules tend to explode when they are dry (violets and geraniums are prone to this) loosely tie a paper bag over the capsules so that you do not lose the seeds.

If you are using commercial seed, always close the packet and seal with a paper clip or elastic band. Keep the name on the packet, and write the date you bought it and the first date you opened it. Put it back in a dry, dark, cool, box or cupboard. Do not leave it in the greenhouse, conservatory or garden shed.

When most of the flesh has been removed from the seeds and rinsed away, squeeze the cloth firmly to get rid of the water. You are left with just seed. It is a good idea to wear rubber gloves to avoid staining your hands.

CONGLETON

composts (substrates)

Please be fussy about your seed compost. Do not use soil taken directly from the garden, or a poor quality compost. Garden soil is not sterile, so your lovingly collected seeds will have to compete with weed seed, which will certainly win. Old compost may contain pests and diseases which will attack and damage your seeds.

You can make your own compost or buy it ready made. There are now some good organic mixes available from garden centres or via the internet.

A good seed compost (substrate) is made up of loam, a peat free proprietary brand or composted fine propagating bark, mixed with sand, grit and a small amount of fertiliser. You can now buy certified organic fertiliser. This is the most convenient choice if you are mixing a small amount of compost as you will get the ratio correct. If you are making a big batch of compost, you can mix your own fertiliser made up of 14g (1/2oz) of ammonium nitrate, 28g (1oz) of potassium nitrate, 56g (2oz) super phosphate, 85g (3oz) chalk, 85g (3oz) magnesium limestone and 14g (1/2oz) of prepared horticultural trace elements. For an ericaceous mix, omit the chalk. This amount of fertiliser should be mixed with 36 litres (8 gallons) of compost. I have taken these measurements from the RHS book on propagation. When I was first taught to make this mix, by a wonderful gardener called Mr. Bell, it was measured in handfuls. One of his handfuls equalled two of mine! However, nowadays we need to be more exact.

Store your compost mixture in a dedicated dustbin which has a close-fitting cover, it will last up to 6 months. Remember, wherever you mix up your compost, make sure it is clean before you start, so you do not mix in old compost, weeds etc. If you have a seed and you are unsure which compost to use, always err on the side of more drainage rather than less. Seeds hate being over wet.

Ingredients

The common ingredients used in compost (substrate) are:

Loam High quality sterilised garden soil. This is very good for seed that has to overwinter outside. When using garden soil in your compost you must sterilise it first. You can do this by baking it in the oven at 200°C (400°F) for 30–40 minutes, or putting it in a plastic bag and placing it in a microwave. In this case, seal and pierce the bag with a few holes. This will stop it popping and plastering your microwave with soil. Cook on high, full power, for 10 minutes.

Coir Derived from the waste fibre of coconut, coir makes a very good base for soil-less composts (substrate). The seedlings will need feeding within three weeks of germination.

Bark This is a good compost which comes in many grades. You will need the fine- or propagating-grade bark for seed sowing. Bark is particularly useful when making a mix for acid-loving plants.

Leaf Mould You can use well-rotted, sieved leaf mould as a peat substitute. It is fine for potting on, but it can harbour pests and diseases, so I do not recommend it for seed sowing.

Clockwise from top left: trays of bark, grit, coir and perlite

Grit Grit comes in many shapes and sizes and can be added to compost for extra drainage and aeration. It can also be used as a covering for seeds instead of compost.

Sand There are many horticultural sands available, from fine silver sand to very coarse sand. Do not use it directly from the seaside as it will be too salty. It can either be added to compost for extra drainage and aeration, or used as a covering over the seeds instead of compost.

Perlite Perlite is made of sterile, light, expanded volcanic granules and it comes in fine, medium or coarse grades. It can either be added to composts (substrate), for extra drainage and aeration, or used as a covering over the seeds instead of compost.

Vermiculite This is expanded mica, similar to perlite but it holds more water and less air. It comes in various grades, from fine to coarse, and can be added to compost (substrate) for extra drainage and aeration, or used as a covering over the seeds instead of compost.

The following mixes are ones I have used in the book

Standard soil-less mix
Standard soil-less seed compost (substrate), either a peat free proprietary brand or composted fine propagating bark

Standard soil-less mix plus extra sand
Standard soil-less seed compost (substrate), either a peat free proprietary brand or composted fine propagating bark mixed with silver or fine sand for extra aeration, mixed to a ratio of 3 parts compost + 1 part sand

Standard soil-less mix plus extra grit
Standard soil-less seed compost (substrate), either a peat free proprietary brand or composted fine propagating bark, mixed with fine (2–3mm / 1/8 – 1/4in) grit mixed to a ratio of 3 parts substrate + 1 part fine grit

Standard loam mix
Standard loam-based seed compost (substrate)

Standard loam mix plus extra sand
Standard loam-based seed compost (substrate) mixed with coarse horticultural sand to a ratio of 2 parts compost + 1 part sand

Standard loam mix plus equal parts sand
Standard loam-based seed compost (substrate) mixed with coarse horticultural sand to a ratio of 1 part compost + 1 part sand

Standard loam mix plus extra grit
Standard loam-based seed compost (substrate) mixed with (5mm / 1/4in) sharp grit to a ratio of 1 part compost + 1 part grit

Standard ericaceous (acid mix)
Standard ericaceous seed compost (substrate)

Standard ericaceous plus extra bark (acid mix)
Standard ericaceous seed compost (substrate) mixed with fine-grade composted bark, to a ratio of 2 parts compost + 1 part bark.

equipment

There is a plethora of equipment available for the enthusiastic gardener, however, you do not need to spend a fortune to get started. A few simple and easily obtainable tools are the starting point.

Sieves

If you are collecting your own seed, you will need to clean it.

Sieves of various mesh sizes are useful for removing the chaff. Be gentle, do not rub the seeds through the mesh as you could damage their outer coating. Shaking out the chaff is much better.

Have dedicated sieves for seed harvesting, do not use them in the kitchen as some seeds are toxic.

Seed-sowers

The most important implements for sowing seeds are the lines in your hand.

I remember watching Geoff Hamilton demonstrating seed sowing many years ago. He said that the lines in our hands evolved so that we could sow seed successfully. How true, you can control the flow of seeds very easily with a bit of practice. For those of you with hot hands, a small piece of stiff white cardboard folded in half makes an ideal sowing implement. You can see the seed and control the flow by pinching the card. Otherwise, there are numerous seed-sowers on the market. Choose something simple, you do not want to spend hours setting it up.

Seed trays

The seed tray should be 5cm (2in) deep and have adequate drainage holes in the bottom.

They should be sturdy enough not to lose their shape when full of wet compost, or to bend when you pick them up or move them. They should be big enough not to dry out too quickly, but not so large that they are awkward to move or lift. I prefer seed trays of 24 x 37cm (9½ x 14½in). There are now modular trays available in units of 6 to 200. They are very useful if you only have a small amount of seed to sow. If the seedlings do not like being transplanted, you can pop the entire module directly into a pot or the flower-bed without disturbing the root ball. The disadvantage of modules is that they dry out much more quickly than seed trays, so they need to be checked more regularly.

Seed and module trays can be made of plastic, reconstituted peat or polystyrene. They all have their advantages and disadvantages. You can also buy filled trays, however I do not recommend these as they can be difficult to 'wet up' prior to sowing.

Pots and containers

There are a wide range of pots and containers available, plastic pots are light, easy to clean and retain moisture, clay pots look good, give better aeration and drainage but are heavy and difficult to clean.

You can also get plastic sleeves that you fill with compost, however they are awkward to pick up. There are pots made of reconstituted peat or cardboard. These are fine, but they can disintegrate very easily and are no use for wintering outside.

There is a new pot on the market which looks very exciting. It is made from elephant grass (*Miscanthus* x *giganteus*) bound with natural tree resin. These pots are firm enough for overwintering spring plantings, but they eventually decompose when planted into the garden.

Labels

The label is essential for identifying what you have sown.

You can have copper labels that last forever, however once they are engraved, they are difficult to reuse. There are also black plastic scratch labels which look smart, are permanent but also become brittle with age and are not reusable. White plastic labels are cheap, although they too become brittle with age. You can write on them in pencil, which fades, but does make them reusable.

Waterproof pen

This is very useful for writing on labels or on plastic bags for storing seeds in the refrigerator.

Plastic bags

I seem to get through endless supplies of plastic bags, but luckily they are reusable.

I use them for storing seeds in the refrigerator, for collecting cuttings and also for making a tent or small greenhouse over containers. Once used, wash out carefully, turn inside out and dry on the washing line.

Watering can and spray

As watering plays such a vital part in the greenhouse and garden, it is worth investing in a good plastic or galvanised watering can with a fine brass rose which should be turned upwards when watering to create a light spray.

When sowing very fine seeds, you may find a spray easier to use. There are two kinds available, the small hand spray which is very useful but does not hold a large amount of water, or a large pump spray which can be a bit heavy when full but does mean you do not have to fill up continuously when you are sowing a lot of seed.

Top left: equipment for chaffing; top right: seed trays and flowerpots; bottom right: two different seed sowers, labels, marker pen, folded card; bottom left: watering can, label

Propagator

Using a propagator to start the seeds germinating allows you to adjust the humidity, temperature, air flow and light to suit specific seeds, giving the seeds the best chance of germination.

There are lots of domestic propagators available. Small ones hold four pots and can be placed on a window-sill to use the natural light. Propagators with a heating element provide the seedlings with bottom heat. They are all useful, and your choice will depend on your needs and your purse. When you buy a propagator, heated or unheated, do make sure that the lid has a vent which allows the excess humidity to be controlled. Otherwise, you can find that some seeds will rot if the humidity gets too high.

For the garden

When sowing directly into the soil in the garden, you will need some basic equipment:

Garden line This can be very basic. I have two stout sticks and a length of twine. You can of course buy purpose-built garden lines, which also have a depth gauge marked on them. Their use is to give a good, straight line when establishing the drill prior to sowing.

Measuring dibber A dibber is used for making holes in the soil. It is always useful for sowing large seeds, allowing you to sow each one at the same depth.

Cloches You can buy a wide variety of cloches, ranging from lovely, Victorian, bell-shaped replicas to the expandable cloches which can cover a whole drill. Alternatively, you can cut the bottom off a plastic bottle and pop that over a seed or young plant. Protection is essential if you want to start your seeds off in the garden early in the season.

Agricultural fleece I have found this a wonderful invention, light and reusable. It protects crops from light frosts and acts as a barrier against pests, including carrot root fly and flea beetle.

general instructions on how to sow seeds

Fill your clean seed tray, pots or modules with the mixed compost (substrate), smooth over, tap down and water in well.

Sowing seeds in trays or pots

Before you start sowing your seed, it is a good idea to prepare everything that you need first, just as you would when you cook a meal from a recipe.

large seeds (1–10 seeds per gram) Space large seeds, which are easy to handle, evenly on the surface of compost, or sow them individually. Then gently press them into the compost to a depth equal to that of the seed.

medium-sized seed (10–1,000 seeds per gram) is also easy to handle. Space the seeds out evenly on the surface of the compost, then gently press them in until you can no longer see them, just below the surface of the compost.

Before you start...

Have your seed trays, pots or modules clean and ready.

Have the area where you will be putting your seed trays clean.

Have the labels to hand, and a waterproof pen.

Have the compost (substrate) mix prepared.

Have the seed prepared for sowing.

Have a rubber band or paper clip ready to re-seal the seed packet if you are using bought seed for the first time.

small seeds (1,000–10,000 seeds per gram) should be tipped in small quantities into the palm of your hand. Allow the seeds to settle in the crease of your palm and then let a small amount trickle on to the surface of the compost.

tiny seed (10,000–20,000 seeds per gram) If the seed is very small, use a label to gently control the flow of the seed.

minute seed (20,000–50,000 seeds per gram) A very small amount of fine seed should be put into the crease of a folded white card. To sow the seed, gently tap the card. This will allow you to see what you are sowing and will also enable you to sow thinly on to the surface of the compost.

extremely fine seed (appears as dust) (over 50,000 seeds per gram) Mix extremely fine seeds with talcum powder or extra-fine white flour as this will make them easier to see. Put a very small amount of the seed mix into the crease of the folded card. Gently tap the card to sow the seed thinly on to the surface of the compost.

Whichever method you use, cover the seeds, following the instructions specific to the plant, using either perlite, vermiculite, horticultural sand or coarse grit. Label with the plant's name and date. Place the tray or pot under protection, in a cold frame or on a hard standing. Watch your watering! Keep it to the absolute minimum until germination has taken place, but do not allow the compost to dry out.

Germination

The average germination time is 10–14 days. However, some seeds take over a year.

The most important thing is to watch your watering. For very fine seed, use a spray, not a watering can. If you are growing seeds using bottom heat, remove the container from the heat, when 70 per cent of the seedlings have emerged and place in a warm, light, airy place to grow on. Seedlings left on the heat for too long grow soft and leggy and become prone to disease. If you have sown too thickly and all the seedlings emerge, gently remove a few using tweezers. This will allow more room for the other seedlings to develop and encourage air movement, preventing mildew or other root or stem problems associated with overcrowding.

Once the seedlings are large enough to handle, either plant them out into a prepared site or pot them on.

Pest control under protection

The major pests of plants grown under protection are aphids, whitefly and sciarid fly, all of them potentially fatal to young seedlings. To control these pests organically, I suggest the following:

Sticky yellow traps hung in the greenhouse will help you identify which pest you have.

Spray with pesticides containing fatty acids or plant oils to control aphids, red spider mite and whitefly.

Use predators in the form of nematodes to control sciarid fly larvae.

Use the parasitic *Encarsia formosa*, a minute wasp, if you have an infestation of whitefly.

Use *Phytoseiulus persimilis* to control red spider mite.

The above predators can only be used when the night temperature does not fall below 8°C (45°F). Do not use a predator and pesticides simultaneously.

'Damping-off' is a disease caused by fungi in non-sterile soil, water or dirty containers. There is no organic remedy, so make sure everything is clean and your soil is sterile before you start.

Powdery mildew is a common air-borne fungal disease which can occur when the plants are overcrowded. It may be prevented by watering well during dry spells, following the recommended planting distances and clearing away any fallen leaves.

Sowing seeds in a seed bed

To save space in the main garden, seed can be sown fairly closely in a separate seedbed, from which the young plants will later be lifted and transplanted into their permanent positions.

What went wrong?

If you have sown your seeds according to the instructions and there is no sign of germination:

1 **Check how old your seeds are.** Most vegetable seeds are best sown fresh or kept for no more than a few years. For example, chervil, angelica and lovage are only viable for one year.

2 **You may have sown too deeply,** so that the seed takes longer to emerge.

3 **Check that your seed has not rotted in over-wet compost.**

4 **As a final resort,** try and find a seed in the compost. If it is very small, get a magnifying glass and give it a thorough inspection! You can quickly tell if all is well. The seed should have swelled to at least double its original size, and it should be splitting it's casing. If nothing at all has changed, then I suggest you put the seed outside in a secured polythene bag on to a flat surface (so it doesn't roll away) and be patient. Nature is marvellous. The seed may germinate a few weeks later or next year.

If your seedlings die unexpectedly:

1 **You may have overwatered them.**

2 **You may have used old compost, non-sterile water or a dirty container,** causing the plants to 'damp off'.

3 **Because of a dirty container or non-sterile compost,** you have attracted the sciarid fly. You will see these if you move the container and there are some minute flies buzzing around.

4 **You are using water from an old water butt and have developed pythium,** a water-borne pathogen which causes root rot

Half the tray has germinated and the other half has not, what should you do?

If the existing seedlings are large enough to handle, prick them out carefully and pot up.

If you have used a seed tray or pot, fill the gap created by the removal of the seedlings with fresh compost so the container is full again. If you have used a module tray, leave the modules empty so that you know which is which. Make a new label. Write the original date of the sowing on it and add the date of the first potting.

Place the container in a cold frame and restart the whole sequence the following season.

Coriandrum sativum seedlings

This is quite a common method for growing vegetables, perennials, shrubs and trees. The advantage is that you have one area to protect from the weather and from pests, instead of different patches throughout the garden. The negative aspect is that the roots can and do get damaged when they are lifted. This will check the growth of the young plant. This is not so important for perennials, shrubs and trees, but it can be a disadvantage when growing vegetables other than brassicas and leeks. I recommend a raised- or deep-bed system for growing vegetables so that the seedlings can remain undisturbed.

Sowing seeds in the open ground

Before sowing seeds in the open ground prepare the site thoroughly.

The time of year for digging will depend on the crop. I prefer to use a raised- or deep-bed system, with beds 1m (3ft) wide. The maximum size for beds in my garden is 1.5m (5ft) so that I can reach both sides without treading on the soil. Once it is thoroughly dug, feed the soil with well-rotted manure or compost. This can be either your own, home-made, well-rotted compost or farmyard manure. In the very early spring, weather permitting, dig the site over again to make a very fine tilth. As soon as the temperature starts to rise you can prepare to sow. If the weather has been very dry, water the site well before sowing.

Using the garden line, make a straight drill with the edge of a hoe to the required depth. The drill should be twice the depth of the seed, unless instructed otherwise. Stand on a plank so you do not compact the soil, sow the seeds thinly and evenly along the drill, then gently cover with the soil, being careful not to dislodge the seed. 'Water in' using the fine rose of the watering can. Label the row at both ends with the name of the plant and the date. When the seedlings emerge, thin to the recommended spacing. Do not let the seedlings dry out and protect if necessary from pests and unseasonable weather, using fine netting, horticultural fleece or cloches.

If you want to 'scatter sow' a flower-bed with a splash of colourful annuals, prepare the site well by digging over to remove any weeds, then rake to create a fine, free-draining tilth. Sow the seed thinly to the depth of the seed, cover with soil, water in well and label. When the seedlings emerge, thin to the required spacing. Do not let the seedlings dry out and protect if necessary from pests and unseasonable weather, using horticultural fleece or cloches.

Pest control for seeds grown outside

Young seedlings are a 'bonne bouche' for all passing slugs, snails, caterpillars, cutworms, earwigs and wood lice, so do not thin too enthusiastically.

If, for example, the final spacing is to be 5cm (2in) between each plant, only thin initially to 2.5cm (1in). As the plants mature, thin down to 5cm (2in). The best control for slugs and snails is a night patrol with a torch, rubber gloves and a bucket of hot water. Or try scattering charcoal, grit or crushed eggshell around your plants, or erect a ring of dry holly leaves.

There is now a form of biological control which can be used on slugs. It is a microscopic nematode that infects the slugs with a bacterium to stop them feeding within a week and kill them within two. This is an expensive method, but worth it in cases of serious infestation.

The maggots of carrot fly tunnel into the roots of plants during early summer, especially those of the Apiaceae family which have a long tap root. Feeding the plants with liquid seaweed after transplanting is one deterrent. Another is to make a vertical polythene barrier 75cm (30in) around the crop during mid-spring, or cover the young plants with horticultural fleece. By sowing seeds after mid-summer you will avoid an attack by the first generation of carrot flies.

Flea beetles make little holes in plants leaves, especially those belonging to the Brassicaceae family. The major attacks happen in late spring. Cover young plants with horticultural fleece as a physical barrier.

Lunar sowing

Sowing seeds to a lunar calendar is not as mad as it sounds. There is no reliable scientific data to support sowing in relation to the phases of the moon, but it works for me and my publisher.

If you stop to consider the power that the moon exerts on the ocean tides and ground water, then it is logical to consider this when sowing seed. The time to plant or transplant annuals, perennials, trees and leafy vegetables, cucumbers, parsley, peppers and grain crops is from the appearance of the new moon, and the period during which it is growing or waxing. Once the third quarter is reached, when the moon is on the wane, it is the time to plant root crops. It is said that when the moon is in the last quarter, one should not plant anything at all. This is thought to be the best time to weed or cultivate, ready for the first quarter to come again. If you want more information on this growing method, there are a number of specialised books available (see 'Further Reading').

Remember ...

Remember to label and date not only when you collect and packet the seeds, but also when you have sown them.
Do not overwater, seedlings watered too much can rot. Even if they do survive, they will become very weak and transplant badly.
If you have used bottom heat to germinate your seeds, remove the container from the heat as soon as 70 per cent has germinated.
If you leave young seedlings on the heat for too long, they will become weak and stretched and you will have difficulty transplanting them.
Remember to put your remaining seeds away into a dark, cool dry place after sowing.
Do not sow the complete seed packet in one go, sow half at a time as an insurance against crop failure or for sequential cropping of vegetables.
Do not sow too many varieties of seed at once as they will all have to be potted up or planted out at the same time.
Do not harvest too much seed as you may not have the space to dry it.
Remember to sow thinly. Overcrowding causes 'damping off'.

further reading

Royal Horticultural Society Propagating Plants, Dorling Kindersley, 1999

RHS Plant Finder, Dorling Kindersley, revised every year

Flowerdew, Bob *The Complete Fruit Book*, paperback edition, Kyle Cathie Limited, 2000

Kollerstrom, Nick *Planting by the Moon 2001: A Gardener's Calendar*, Prospect Books, 2000

Larkcom, Joy *Creative Vegetable Gardening* Mitchell Beazley, 1997

Mabey, Richard *Flora Britannica*, Sinclair Stevenson, 1996

Hillier, J *The Hillier Manual of Trees and Shrubs*, David & Charles, 2001

Huxley, Anthony, Griffiths, Mark and Levy, Margot *The New Royal Horticultural Society Dictionary of Gardening*, Macmillan Reference Books, 1999

Stevens, John *Wild Flower Gardening* Dorling Kindersley

stockists

CHASE ORGANICS Ltd
Riverdene Business Park
Molesey Road
Hersham
Surrey
KT12 4RG

CHILTERN SEEDS
Botree Stile
Ulverston
Cumbria
LA12 7PB
Tel 01229 581137
www.chilternseeds.co.uk

D.T. BROWN
Station Road
Poulton-le-Fylde
Lancs
FY6 7HX
Tel 01253 882371
www.users.globalnet.co.uk/dtbrown

JEKKA'S HERB FARM
Rose Cottage
Shellards Lane
Alveston
Bristol
BS35 3SY
Tel 01454 418878
www.jekkasherbfarm.com

JELITTO STAUDENSAMEN GmbH
Am Toggraben 3
D-29690 Schwarmstedt
Germany
Tel 00 49 50 71 98 29 0
www.jelitto.com

S.E. MARSHALLS & Co Ltd
Wisbech
Cambs
PE13 2RF
Tel 01945 583 407
www.marshalls-seeds.co.uk

MR. FOTHERGILL'S SEEDS Ltd
Gazeley Road
Kentford
Newmarket
Suffolk
CB8 7QB
Tel 01638 751161
www.mr.fothergills.co.uk

W.ROBINSONS & Sons Ltd.
Sunny Bank
Forton
Nr. Preston
Lancashire
PR 3 0BN
Tel 01524 791210
www.mamothonions.co.uk

PALM SEEDS
Paul Boyson
73 Spa Crescent
Little Hulton
Manchester
M38 9SF

PLANT WORLD SEEDS
St Mary Church Road
Newton Abbot
Devon
TQ12 4SE

RICHTERS
Goodwood
Ontario L0C 1A0
Canada
Tel 1.905.640.6677
www.richters.com

SANDEMAN SEEDS
7 route de Burosse
64350 Lalongue
France
Tel 0559682886
Fax 0559692882
www.sandemanseeds.com

SARAH RAVEN'S CUTTING GARDEN Ltd.
Perch Hill Farm
Brightling
East Sussex
TN32 5HP

SUFFOLK HERBS
Monks Farm
Coggeshall Road
Kelvedon
Essex
CO5 9PG
Tel 01376 572456
www.suffolkherbs.com

SUTTONS CONSUMER PRODUCTS Ltd.
Woodview Road
Paignton
Devon
TQ4 7NG
Tel 01803 696300
www.sutton.co.uk

THOMPSON AND MORGAN
Poplar Lane
Ipswich
Suffolk
IP8 3BU
Tel 01473 688821
www.thompson-morgan.com

UNWINS SEEDS LTD.
Mail Order Dept.
Histon
Cambridge
CB4 4ZZ
Tel 01945 588522
www.unwins-seeds.co.uk

index

A

B

acknowledgements

I am very grateful to my fellow exhibitors on the RHS Flower Show circuit. My special thanks goes to Dave Clarke for his knowledge on grasses, Brian Goodey for his knowledge on cacti, Brian Hiley for his knowledge on tender perennials. A very big thank you to Jim Juby from DT Browns for his immense patience and infinite knowledge of vegetables.

I thank Marianne Majerus for her beautiful photographs, Vanessa Courtier for designing the book, Helena Attlee for wading through my script and Helen Woodhall for keeping everything together. A special thank you goes to Kyle for producing another beautiful book and to Anthea for being a tame rottweiler. And finally this would not have been possible without the support of my family Mac, Hannah, Alistair and my animals, William, Blackie and Catmint.